QUEER NEWARK

QUEER NEWARK

STORIES OF RESISTANCE, LOVE, AND COMMUNITY

EDITED BY WHITNEY STRUB

RUTGERS UNIVERSITY PRESS

New Brunswick, Camden, and Newark, New Jersey

London and Oxford

Rutgers University Press is a department of Rutgers, The State University of New Jersey, one of the leading public research universities in the nation. By publishing worldwide, it furthers the University's mission of dedication to excellence in teaching, scholarship, research, and clinical care.

Library of Congress Cataloging-in-Publication Data
Names: Strub, Whitney, editor.
Title: Queer Newark: stories of resistance, love, and community / edited by Whitney Strub.
Description: New Brunswick: Rutgers University Press, [2024] | Includes bibliographical references and index.
Identifiers: LCCN 2023019432 | ISBN 9781978829213 (paperback) | ISBN 9781978829220 (cloth) | ISBN 9781978829237 (epub) | ISBN 9781978829244 (pdf)
Subjects: LCSH: Sexual minority community—New Jersey—Newark—Social conditions. | Sexual minority community—New Jersey—Newark—Economic conditions. | Newark (N.J.)—Race relations | Newark (N.J.)—Economic conditions. | Newark (N.J.)—Social conditions. | Working class—New Jersey—Newark—Social conditions. | Working class—New Jersey—Newark—Economic conditions.
Classification: LCC HQ73.3.U62 N4978 2024 | DDC 306.7609749/32—dc23/eng/20230526
LC record available at https://lccn.loc.gov/2023019432

A British Cataloging-in-Publication record for this book is available from the British Library.

rutgersuniversitypress.org

I am not dead yet
I am not perfect but I am at ease
Disable and trying to get back stabled
Only to be knocked back down
Poverty not a choice I would make
But poor I am hard to survive in this land
New policies day to day
Set backs draw backs but here I am still
Stepped on played on and just forgot about
I still survive I am not dead yet as you
Continue to kill me quietly day to day
I am not dead yet

—Aaron Frazier, from *Tears of a Poet* (2018)

CONTENTS

QUEER NEWARK

FIGURE I.1. Queer Newark history in the built environment as one drives into downtown: Tatyana Fazlalizadeh's *Sakia, Sakia, Sakia, Sakia* mural and the New Jersey Transit/PATH tracks. Photo by Mary Rizzo.

Introduction

Hidden in Plain Sight: Finding and Remembering LGBTQ Newark History

WHITNEY STRUB

DRIVE NORTH INTO downtown Newark on McCarter Highway, the main road in, and as you approach the city, you'll see a mural on your right along the train tracks to Newark's Penn Station. At 1.4 miles, it's the longest mural on the East Coast, part of the Newark Downtown District's effort to "beautify each of the city's entryways via public art and landscape improvements."[1] Completed in 2016, component parts by eighteen artists offer a rich historical tapestry of Newark's Black and Latinx heritage.

As you reach South Street and pass a set of colorful abstract designs intended to evoke the secret messages that were passed along the Underground Railroad on quilt patterns (according to legend), you encounter six repeated images of a young Black face set against a red backdrop. With close-cropped hair and a purple and black shirt over a white tee, the subject's gender reads as somewhat ambiguous, but there's no mistaking the facial expression: a buoyant smile. If you don't recognize the face, you might reasonably interpret the mural segment as a general testament to the resilience and joy of young Black Newarkers.

If you *do* know the young person pictured, artist Tatyana Fazlalizadeh's work takes on a different meaning. On May 11, 2003, Sakia Gunn was murdered at the age of fifteen in the heart of downtown Newark while attempting to fend off a street harasser after telling him she was a lesbian. Two days later, Gunn's friends and relatives gathered at the corner of Broad and Market Streets to honor her passing with votive candles, flowers, and a basketball that many of her friends had autographed. By the end of the week, an estimated 2,500 people had attended her funeral and a new movement was born. The sorrow and anger over her needless death animate many of the stories told in this book. Fazlalizadeh's mural honors her life, and its title, *Sakia, Sakia, Sakia, Sakia,* asks you to say and repeat her name—but that only works if you know the title and the story. For many North Jersey drivers, the mural is thus a powerful queer artistic intervention hidden in plain sight—and as such, the perfect entry point to the history of queer Newark.[2]

Today nothing marks the spot at Broad and Market, Newark's busiest intersection, twenty-odd blocks north of the six smiling Sakias, where she was killed. Nor do any historical markers grace the site a few blocks away where Murphy's Tavern once sat, a bar that anchored LGBTQ Newark for decades and helped win a landmark 1967 state supreme court case for gay rights. City Hall raises a rainbow flag each June to commemorate the 1969 Stonewall rebellion in New York City, a tradition begun by Mayor Cory Booker in 2007, but there is little commemoration of Newark's own queer past. Begin looking, though, and it is everywhere, if not always evident to pedestrians and commuters: the very next mural after *Sakia* is Khari Johnson-Ricks's *BootyBounce to Dis,* whose three scenes of kinetic motion evoke dance and karate—and draw on the queer vogueing traditions of Newark's ballroom scene to consider the nature of movement.[3]

The chapters in *Queer Newark* make Newark's LGBTQ history more visible than it's ever been before. When the Queer Newark Oral History Project (QNOHP) began in 2011, founded by Beryl Satter, Darnell Moore, and Christina Strasburger, our sense was that Newark's LGBTQ history had gone unwritten. In fact, that wasn't quite accurate (as discussed below), but the traces of that history were scattered in diffuse directions. LGBTQ written, public, and oral history have always held an intimate relationship, with lived memories filling crucial gaps where other forms of documentary evidence have been lost, suppressed, and destroyed over the years. In launching QNOHP, we held listening sessions with community elders, youth, and those in between. The goal was to relocate both history and the power of narrating it away from the Ivory Tower and into the community as much as possible. As Moore put it at the time, "the making of history is not a project that is relegated only to those in the academy, those who do the work of observing our lives and attending to our voices from a distance. History is made through the living and the telling of our lives."[4]

As such, public programming and events driven by community needs and interest have been as central to QNOHP's mission as scholarship.

When it did come to the scholarly, we looked to pioneering work on working-class lesbian culture in mid-twentieth-century Buffalo, New York, as well as more recent work by the Twin Cities GLBT Oral History Project and Pittsburgh Queer History Project, among so many other aligned efforts, as models for our work. Of special interest was work in Black queer oral history, such as Rochella Thorpe's recovery of Black lesbian nightlife in Detroit, and E. Patrick Johnson's deep dives into the queer South.[5]

The chapters in this book make extensive use of QNOHP materials, as well as plenty of archival research and other scholarly investigation, but more than anything they draw on the survival work of the community itself—or rather *communities,* as queer Newark has never been monolithic. For decades, queer Newarkers have struggled against poverty, religious intolerance, racism, various forms of violence, the AIDS epidemic, hostile policing, immigration enforcement, gentrification, and other forms of oppression. Sustained LGBTQ rights organizing developed later in Newark than in many other cities, spurred on by outrage not just over Sakia Gunn's death but also a lackluster response by city officials. When the movement emerged, it looked different than queer activism in most places in that it was led by working-class Black women. This makes *Queer Newark* not just a book of local interest but an important departure from the dominant story of LGBTQ history, which tends to center places like New York City, Philadelphia, Chicago, San Francisco, and Los Angeles—large metropolitan areas with plenty of diversity and inequality, but also enough wealth to fund LGBTQ organizations historically led by middle-class white professionals with connections to resources. The romantic allure of those cities, combined with the historical whiteness and tourist economies of their gay districts—Greenwich Village, the Gayborhood, Boystown, the Castro, and West Hollywood—have reinforced widespread perceptual links between queer urban space and whiteness.

As a city, Newark's counterparts are Gary, Flint, Cleveland, Baltimore, Milwaukee, and Detroit: postindustrial Black cities, less often identified as queer spaces but no less queer for their lack of recognition. These cities are rarely thought of as sexual or erotic spaces at all; indeed, postindustrial Blackness seems to foreclose the sort of urban erotics bestowed on other cities. Look at the ways historians frame other urban histories: eighteenth-century Philadelphia begins with *Sex among the Rabble* and grows into the postwar *City of Sisterly and Brotherly Loves*; New York gets both *Licentious Gotham* and *Prurient Interests*; San Francisco is simply *Erotic City*. Even Kansas gets *Sex in the Heartland*; Minnesota, *Land of 10,000 Loves*; and Arkansas, the enticingly queer *Un-Natural State*. Yet when it comes to Newark and its peers, urban history seems to flatten into a familiar but desexualized arc of immigration, redevelopment, riots, Black Power, and urban decay. *No Cause for Indictment* is the ultimate Newark book title, a self-declared "autopsy" of the city. Even Kevin Mumford, a leading scholar in the history of sexuality, who wrote a book on Newark in between his pioneering history of interracial sex districts and his field-defining Black gay history monograph *Not Straight, Not White*, framed Newark's story as one of "race, rights, and riots."[6]

Queer Newark reclaims Newark as a place of desire, love, eroticism, community, and resistance. It highlights the intersectional ties between not only queerness and race and gender, but also queerness and class, for, like straightness in Newark, queerness here is markedly poor and working-class. Queer politics are always *classed* politics here. "You wouldn't know that Greenwich Village is 10 miles away," longtime activist James Credle told the *New York Times* in 2007, "people here feel like we don't deserve to be alive. For us, it's about survival." At the time, a great deal of national LGBTQ activism focused on marriage equality and the right to be openly gay in the military. But "all this talk of gay marriage," Credle continued, "is just a luxury." Queer Newarkers needed housing, health care, jobs, food, and physical safety—things that in more middle-class LGBTQ circles don't necessarily register as queer issues, because often they don't register as needs at all.[7]

This book uncovers Queer Newark's distinctive history, marked by Black women's leadership, by a nationally renowned ballroom scene, by the resilience of young lesbians finding joy and freedom in spaces the media defines through death and criminality, by queer Brazilian immigrants embracing the hustle of entrepreneurial values, and more. But to understand all of this, we need to begin with a quick survey of Newark's overarching history.

Three Centuries of Newark

In their broadest strokes, Newark's last three centuries each have a defining arc. The nineteenth century saw industrialization, urbanization, and white ethnic immigration. In the twentieth century, the story is marked by the Great Migration of African Americans from the South; the departure of white residents and white-owned businesses; and the rise of Black Power in the face of a devastating economic decline and state and federal neglect of the city's Black residents. The twenty-first century has witnessed uneven gentrification in the city as well as Latinization, as immigration patterns shifted from Southern and Eastern Europe to Central and South America.

Like most of the contemporary United States, Newark was founded on the dispossession of Indigenous people, in this case the Lenni-Lenape. The roots of the modern city date to 1666, when Puritans from Connecticut ventured south, and the town remained small and agricultural into the nineteenth century. Then, with the Industrial Revolution, it exploded: a radical transformation between 1820 and 1860 elevated Newark to the eleventh-largest city in the United States and the "leading industrial city in the nation," with 74 percent of its workforce employed in manufacturing. This made Newark a laboratory for class formation as a distinct working class took form.[8]

In this era, less than 6 percent of the city's population was Black, but capitalism in Newark was always racialized. Local industries such as leather-, shoe-, and saddle-making were tied to the southern slave states for supplies and markets, and white Newarkers and New Jerseyans were arguably more committed to white supremacy than many Northerners in other states. Newark's first riot, in 1834, was a white attack on an abolitionist lecture. The city's economic ties to the South fostered sympathy for the Confederacy, and indeed, not only did Abraham Lincoln fail to carry New Jersey in the presidential election of 1860, it was the only northern state to go against him during his second run in 1864. He didn't win in Newark, either (though it was closely split, with a three-hundred-vote difference). The last northern state to abolish slavery, New Jersey also initially rejected the Thirteenth Amendment, shoring up the racial values that dominated Newark.[9]

Like other northern port cities, Newark was transformed in the late nineteenth and early twentieth centuries by the arrival of waves of immigrants—Irish, German, Italian, Eastern European, Catholic, and Jewish. As historian Clement Price notes, between 1890 and 1920 the population grew by 128 percent but housing construction lagged—nearly a fifth of city land was uninhabitable marshland, and Newark was hemmed in by New Jersey's tendency to overmunicipalize (Newark's last successful annexation effort occurred in 1905, with the Vailsburg neighborhood). Despite intergroup competition for housing and jobs, Price concludes that "the period had a superficial racial tolerance"—mostly because the small Black population "seemed of little threat to the whites." Still, as southern Blacks began to arrive they were routed into the "distinct ghetto" of the Third Ward, a district whose character as the city's hub for vice, including gambling and sex work, was memorably captured in local writer Curtis Lucas's 1946 pulp novel *Third Ward, Newark*.[10]

By the 1920s, Newark's economy had begun shifting away from manufacturing toward banking and insurance, and as the skyline grew the elite began a suburban exodus that would continue for decades. For those who remained, the ensuing Depression years of the 1930s proved politically volatile, marked by both the far right of Nazi sympathizers and the far left of communist organizers. While police repressed the communists, it was left to working-class Jews to combat Nazis, which they often did using street-fighting tactics in conjunction with Jewish underworld kingpin Abner "Longy" Zwillman. For Black Newarkers, the Depression eviscerated their modest advances of the early twentieth century.[11]

In the interwar years, a new and often militant Black freedom struggle challenged segregation in Newark's stores, pools, blood banks, and restaurants. Despite small, hard-won victories, the city's white power structure was largely intransigent. Around 1965, Newark became a Black-majority city—but with almost no Black political representation or authority positions in the police or other civic institutions. With one of the most aggressive urban renewal strategies in the nation, Newark bulldozed buildings with impunity in the name of "slum clearance," affecting many communities, but particularly Black ones. The early promise of public housing soured into decaying high-rise buildings by the 1960s, and exploitative landlords dominated the private renters' market. Educational and career opportunities for Black Newarkers were severely constrained, and police violence went unchecked.[12]

These conditions set the stage for the explosive events of July 1967, called the Newark riots in the press but recalled locally as the Newark rebellion, when the city erupted after the police beat and arrested Black taxi driver John Smith and word on the street had it that he was dead. He wasn't, but by the week's end twenty-six others were, almost all Black Newarkers killed by city police or state troopers. Tanks rolled through the streets and buildings burned. The rebellion was broadcast nationally, setting an enduring national image of Newark as urban dystopia.[13]

The fallout of 1967 accelerated Newark's economic decline, as white flight and disinvestment destroyed its tax base but also paved the way for Black Power politics, marked by the election of Kenneth Gibson as the first Black mayor of a major East Coast city in 1970. The bittersweet irony of this long-in-the-making victory is that, occurring just as President Richard Nixon gutted federal funding for cities, the election left Gibson—like so many other first Black mayors in the urban North—holding a fairly empty bag. The corruption that seeped into Gibson's and his successor Sharpe James's administrations was no surprise; municipal ties to the mafia ran deep. Hugh Addonizio, Newark's last white mayor, had campaigned against Gibson while on trial for conspiracy and extortion; he was convicted of sixty-four counts and sentenced to ten years in federal prison. Fiscal options for the Black mayors were extremely limited. Gibson assiduously courted federal agencies, but it was clear that Newark desperately needed private investment and didn't have a particularly inviting portfolio to display: losing a third of its population between 1960 and 1990, Newark also lost control of its school district to the state in 1995 after too much graft and scandal, and Macy's, the last downtown department store, closed in 1992.[14]

Gibson and James were relentless Newark boosters, willing to try anything while confronting an era of crushing recessions and continuing disinvestment. An attempt to generate energy by incinerating garbage in the city's marshland failed, and James turned to downtown development as the solution, declaring a Newark renaissance that took some time to materialize, though the 1997 opening of the $180 million New Jersey Performing Arts Center gave some substance to his plan to woo back middle-class suburbanites, wealthy philanthropists, and corporate leaders.[15]

The real steward of Newark's third phase, however, was mayor Cory Booker, who ushered Newark into a period of neoliberalism and gentrification. Though raised in the North Jersey suburbs, Booker moved to Newark in 1996 while attending Yale Law School. He worked in a tenants' law clinic. Entering local politics, he won a spot on the city council within a few years and ran for mayor against incumbent Sharpe James in 2002. The glaring gulf between Booker and James was generational, racial, and political. While James proudly wore the mantle of hard-won Black Power, Booker positioned himself in a lineage of "deracialized" Black politicians such as New York mayor David Dinkins and Virginia governor Douglas Wilder. James slammed him for this, calling him a carpetbagger, questioning his Blackness by labeling him a "faggot white boy," and playing on anti-Semitism by falsely claiming Booker was Jewish. It worked—James won handily, though Booker won the white and Latinx vote.[16]

Booker won in 2006, though—this time Mayor James was on his way to indictment for corruption, which eventually landed him in federal prison for eighteen months. From the start, Booker had what Robert Curvin, a cofounder of the Newark-Essex Congress of Racial Equality, dryly called "a tenuous relationship with the black community." His close ties to venture capitalists, investment firms, and charter school proponents swerved away from James's more familiar patronage politics rooted in local public-sector employment, and his fabricated stories of local gang members such as "T-Bone" seemed geared to white audiences who held Hollywood images of "the ghetto."[17] Booker's frequent media appearances made him seem opportunistic to many locals; his wooing of such corporations as Audible and Panasonic seemed disconnected from the material needs of poor Newarkers beyond the downtown core, and on his watch a $100 million educational donation from Facebook CEO Mark Zuckerberg evaporated into a nexus of high-priced consultants, with disappointingly little benefit to Newark youth. Booker did, however, adopt a strikingly pro-LGBTQ tone and delivered ceremonial recognition of LGBTQ Newarkers, like a Pride flag raising at city hall, a departure from the practices of James. More broadly, he helped change the public narrative of Newark, replacing the shadows of 1967 with new "next Brooklyn" aspirations of a hip, up-and-coming city, signified by the ultimate early twenty-first-century marker of gentrification, a Whole Foods that opened in 2017 (by which point Booker had jumped to the U.S. Senate). For many Newarkers, Booker seemed to be inviting in white, middle-class, and corporate residents and seemed less interested in the plight of those already here and struggling.[18]

The other major trend in twenty-first-century Newark is the demographic rise of Latinx communities. Latinx Newark is extremely diverse, counting Ecuadorians, Salvadorans, Dominicans, and many others among its population. Puerto Ricans are the oldest group, predominant in the North Broadway area since the 1950s, and Brazilians are the largest group in the Ironbound neighborhood. The population defined by the census as Hispanic nearly doubled between 1980 and 2010 from 18.6 to 32.6 percent, and racial/ethnic tensions in Newark have rarely been defined by a Black/white binary since the 1960s, when efforts at Black/Puerto Rican solidarity faltered. By 1974, Puerto Rican frustration with Black machine politics had grown explosive, culminating in a little-remembered riot that summer after aggressive policing during annual *fiestas patronales* (patron saint festivals) in Branch Brook Park. Since then, Latino Newark has assiduously built its own civic, political, and cultural organizations, much the way Italian and Black Newark did in earlier generations.[19]

But where in this three-century history is queer Newark?

Locating LGBTQ Newark

Newark is not a place many people associate with queerness; indeed, in many ways it's easier to see its *antigay* history. That history is evident in the tragic killing of Sakia Gunn and the gay-baiting jeers of Sharpe James, but it long predates Black political empowerment. In 1967, white Newark police chief Dominic Spina deplored "the antics and behavior of these unfortunate people," referring to gays and lesbians; a few years later, the local *Italian Tribune News* called effeminacy in boys a "great concern" and offered parents tips on "preventing homosexuality."[20] Such attitudes rang through the pews of a great many Newark churches, and Sakia Gunn was far from the only victim of anti-LGBTQ violence. Seven years after her death, an Essex County Sheriff's officer shot and killed DeFarra Gaymon in Newark's Branch Brook Park, a popular cruising site. Whether or not Gaymon was seeking sex in the park's brambles, it was aggressive policing of consensual gay encounters that brought this fatal armed surveillance to bear.

Beyond these and other manifestations of antigay violence and oppression, there is a historical layer of obfuscation and forgetting. When Anthony Heilbut was writing his landmark study of Black gospel music, *The Gospel Sound*, in 1971, he came to Newark to interview the nationally influential singer Alex Bradford, the choir director at Newark's Greater Abyssinian Baptist Church. In barely coded language, he wrote, "in his flamboyant robes, Bradford is gospel's Little Richard, letting it all hang out," and also compared him to Detroit's Prophet Jones (who "has been overtaken by scandals," he noted without elaboration). But he stopped short of acknowledging that the queerness of Bradford and his social world was an open secret, something Heilbut well knew but only wrote about four decades later in a subsequent 2012 book. Without that second book and the memoir of singer Carl Bean, performer of the gay anthem "I Was Born This Way," Bradford's sexuality might be lost to history—as a great deal of queer Newark's past is. Bean spent time with Bradford in Newark before later serving as archbishop of the gay-friendly Unity Fellowship Church. Indeed, the fact that

Bradford's work with Prophet Jones and Bean are rarely cited shows that Newark's key role in the genealogy of Black queer culture is sadly overlooked and easily missed.[21]

These are some of the challenges of writing LGBTQ Newark history—challenges that the essays in this book meet and overcome, thankfully. It turns out that once you begin digging, Newark's queer history is everywhere: in vice reports of the 1910s; in state liquor board surveillance records of 1940s gay bars; in the lived memories and personal memorabilia of people from the 1950s onward; and in the bold, vibrant art and activism on ample display in the twenty-first century. Newark itself has been the site of a great deal of queer knowledge production, ranging, as discussed below, from William J. Fielding's pioneering booklet *Homo-Sexual Life* (1925) to Hilda Hidalgo's foundational studies of Puerto Rican lesbians in the 1970s.

Scholarship about queer Newark emerged in the 1990s. Gary Jardim's two-volume *Blue: Newark Culture* offered a rich and vivid recounting of 1970s nightlife that remains definitive, though under-read because it was published by a small press.[22] At Drew University, anthropologist Karen McCarthy Brown headed the Newark Project (1994–2006), a massive Ford Foundation–funded research project on local religion, including LGBTQ religious expression, particularly in the context of the AIDS epidemic.

From the Newark Project came a proliferation of research and writing. Brown's own landmark essay on the ballroom scene, discussed throughout this book, drew heavily on her student Peter Savastano's extensive insider knowledge and oral history work. Savastano himself published studies of gay Italian American Catholic men in Newark and their devotion to St. Gerard Maiella, whose gentleness and perseverance in the face of violence are easily adopted as inspiring emotional and spiritual reference points by the men who relate to him. Aryana Bates's 2001 dissertation examined Black lesbian religion and activism at Newark's Liberation in Truth Church, founded by Reverend Jacquelyn Holland in 1995 as a branch of the national Unity Fellowship Church Movement that former Newarker Carl Bean founded in Los Angeles. The next year, Eugenia Lee Hancock's dissertation looked at religion and the AIDS epidemic in Newark. This cluster of work from the Newark Project forms the foundation of queer Newark studies.[23]

Joining these were crucial works by Zenzele Isoke, Ana Ramos-Zayas, and Arlene Stein. Ramos-Zayas dedicated a chapter of her book *Street Therapists* to the ways even queer and lesbian Latinas built their racialized identities against their perception of Blackness. Stein looked at the politics of same-sex marriage in Newark and its suburb Maplewood, affectionately known as "Gayplewood" for its large gay and lesbian population. Before the legalization of gay marriage, when same-sex spouses were relegated to civil unions, Maplewood had eight times as many of them as Newark, despite Newark having twelve times the suburb's population. This suggested other, more pressing, material priorities for queer Newarkers, Stein showed, and indicated "the limits of queer liberalism."[24]

Meanwhile, Isoke's book *Urban Black Women and the Politics of Resistance* attends to various forms of often unrecognized organizing and activism among Black women, and in particular meticulously charts the emergence of an LGBTQ movement in Newark after the death of Sakia Gunn, largely led by working-class Black women, often with connections to the Liberation in Truth Unity Fellowship Church—a movement that extends the legacy of the 1950s homophile Mattachine Society of Los Angeles and Daughters of Bilitis in San Francisco, the New York City radicalism of gay liberation in the 1970s and ACT-UP in the 1980s, and the many other familiar groups of modern American LGBTQ history, but with a distinctly Newark spin.[25]

All of these precedents are rich and remarkable works necessary to a full understanding of queer Newark. For the most part, though, they were written by sociologists and anthropologists, with an eye toward ethnography rather than building a historical archive. This is where the Queer Newark Oral History Project intervened; beginning with long-form oral history interviews of dozens of Newarkers, it also found and built an archive. As it turned out, pockets of queer history *had* already been preserved, such as Hilda Hidalgo's papers at the Newark Public Library's Puerto Rican Community Archives and Derek Winans's at the New Jersey Historical Society. Interview subjects donated materials, including Pucci Revlon's photos from the 1980s ballroom scene and even the duffel bag of sex toys, condoms, and lubricant that James Credle had dutifully lugged to one safer-sex display after another in the 1990s. In oral history interviews, Louie Crew Clay told of the struggle for gay-affirmative religious practice, June Dowell-Burton about the emergence of LGBTQ activism, Ruby Rims about 1970s drag performances in Newark bathhouses and gay bars, Aaron Frazier about living for decades with HIV (also a poet, his short declaration of survival and resilience graces the opening of this book), Yvonne Hernandez about life as a Puerto Rican lesbian artist, and Pucci Revlon about where she scored hormones as a young trans woman in the 1970s. The chapters in this book draw on all of this work, and they are interspersed with history excerpts to vary the reading and keep the research rooted in community voices.

Organization of the Book

Newark geography is a central motif of the chapters here. In various selections, you will encounter the bustling downtown nightlife scene of the mid-twentieth century, and later stroll down gay-friendly Halsey Street from the 1970s to the early 2000s. You'll visit the "G Corner" at Broad and Market Streets, where young lesbians congregated—and also where Sakia Gunn was murdered. Then there's Ferry Street, which traverses queer life in the Latinx Ironbound neighborhood on Newark's east side. In the final chapter, a contemporary walking tour highlights the challenges of queer absence and erasure in the built (and frequently rebuilt) environment.

The book unfurls chronologically, and in the first chapter, Peter Savastano and Timothy Stewart-Winter outline the structural conditions for the emergence of LGBTQ life in Newark, examining how urbanization and proximity to New York City allowed sexual cultures to flourish—though this era can mostly be seen only in glimpses, with limited archival materials documenting it. Savastano's and Stewart-Winter's collaboration is an unusual one that deserves comment: this chapter began as a paper Savastano wrote as a graduate student in the 1990s, when he was almost certainly the first scholar to conduct archival research on LGBTQ Newark history. It then went unpublished as he moved into his academic field of training, anthropology, only to be revived, revised, and expanded by Stewart-Winter over two decades later when he brought his own historical expertise in LGBTQ history to bear in locating material that was unearthed in the intervening years. As such, it offers both a rich history and a delightful model of scholarly collaboration across time.

Queer Newark life begins to come into clearer view in the 1940s—and was often preserved by the very forces that sought to destroy it. Anna Lvovsky uncovers a rich, bustling nexus of gay and lesbian bars from the 1940s to 1960s. Building on her book *Vice Patrol*, Lvovsky explores the complicated fact that most of what we can know about this world comes from the records of the very state agency that oppressed it, the New Jersey Division of Alcoholic Beverage Control (ABC), headquartered in Newark.[26] By keeping queer bars under intense surveillance, the ABC inadvertently built New Jersey's first LGBTQ archive, and Lvovsky mines it to reconstruct a world that no one has written about since those antigay spies filed their reports. The only records we have of people like Birdie, who openly expressed queer desire by making arrangements with three men to "take them out for a perverted sexual act" in 1950, or Francie, whom ABC agents called "a 'male' known as the Belle of Mulberry Street" and who approached undercover agents and "with the use of vile language, solicited them to engage in two different acts of sexual perversion," come from the ABC. When another undercover agent accosted Francie about this solicitation in 1962, Francie defiantly cried, "they are taking me out, what is wrong with that?"[27] As Lvovsky shows, the ABC's archives of oppression cannot but contain proof of bold queer resistance that, in the end, always outpaced state repression.

Not all queer life was contained in bars, of course. Newark has a rich radical history of labor organizers, socialists, communists, Jewish antifascism, Black Power politics, Puerto Rican mobilization, and environmental justice work. But while leftists challenged bosses, capitalists, and political repression on many fronts, they did not always confront sexual hegemony. My own chapter looks at the ways queer Newark leftists navigated spaces where radical politics did not always make room for their identities, focusing primarily on the 1960s through the 1980s, the era of the New Left and Black Power. It also discusses Amiri Baraka, one of Newark's most famous literary and political figures. Often noted for his antigay vitriol during the Black Power era of the 1960s and 1970s, Baraka left a complicated legacy: before that period, he wrote avant-garde plays, poetry, and novels that were saturated with queer imagery, and frequently Newark-specific; later, after the murder of his lesbian daughter Shani Baraka and her partner Rayshon Holmes in 2003, he embraced LGBTQ rights. Baraka thus occupies a complex place in the story of the queer Newark left.

By the 1970s, what Zenzele Isoke calls "Black heteropatriarchy" had set in as the dominant mode of Newark politics. It could never suffocate queer creativity and desire, though, and in the aftermath of *One Eleven Wines & Liquors, Inc. v. Division of Alcoholic Beverage Control*, the 1967 state supreme court decision curtailing antigay state liquor regulators, in which the owner of longtime Newark gay bar Murphy's was a plaintiff, a resurgent queer nightlife emerged, particularly along Halsey Street in downtown Newark. As Kristyn Scorsone notes in their chapter, these years are frequently described as Newark's nadir; "post-1967" generally invokes the period after the Newark rebellion/riots, when accelerated white flight and disinvestment sent the city into an economic downward spiral. But it's specifically after 1967 that queer Newark flourished. This blossoming of queer community thus challenges the pervasive narrative of Newark's decline; while the city's finances certainly deteriorated, the 1970s look very different from a queer perspective.

One of the major factors that destroyed the vibrant queer life on Halsey Street and elsewhere was the HIV/AIDS epidemic, which hit Newark with devastating ferocity. The narratives built around the epidemic here differ from some of the more familiar national ones. Probably the most infamous version of the national AIDS narrative is that of conservative political leaders castigating gay men, weaponizing the pre-existing homophobia of the right (latent too in 1980s liberalism) to blame victims of the epidemic for their own suffering and turning a medical crisis into a moral one. Newark had no lack of homophobia, but with its LGBTQ communities less visible than those of New York, Chicago, or San Francisco, the local story of HIV/AIDS focused almost exclusively on women (presumed to be heterosexual) and children. To a great degree, this reflected the epidemiology of AIDS in Newark, where pediatric cases and transmission through IV drug use were more heavily represented. But as Jason Chernesky shows in his chapter, a confluence of factors colluded to make the gay side of the epidemic nearly invisible. To commentators at the local, state, and national levels, *gay* often implied white, while *Newark* represented a Blackness read as heterosexual. Thus, the plight of Black gay men struggling with HIV/AIDS drew little attention. Chernesky carefully traces the various factors that facilitated this erasure, then examines how Black gay men in Newark fought back with the innovative Project Fire, which was inspired by queer Harlem Renaissance radicalism and involved meeting queer people of color where they lived and played and bringing educational, explicit, and affirmative safer-sex materials to house parties and ballroom shows.

Project Fire participated in Newark's nationally renowned ballroom scene—one of queer Newark's signature cultural offerings. Because ballroom culture is so well represented in QNOHP interviews, chapter 6 consists primarily of oral history excerpts, allowing participants to narrate their own experiences of the Newark ballroom runway.

If it was mostly—though certainly not entirely—Black men who pioneered safer-sex HIV/AIDS educational work in Newark, it was Black women who mostly led LGBTQ activism after the murder of Sakia Gunn. LeiLani Dowell's chapter confronts the demeaning dominant tropes of Newark as "the ghetto," a dangerous, crime-ridden place of extinction, and counters that image by drawing attention to the creativity and resilience of the queer Black women who defiantly plot life in these same spaces. Employing an archive of Black queer and feminist theory, Dowell shows how the "G Corner" at Broad and Market Streets, downtown Newark's major intersection, where young Black lesbians hung out in public—and where Gunn was killed—also resisted the gentrifying impulses of racial capitalism as it remade (and still remakes) Newark. As both a radical critique and a historical argument for taking very seriously the layered nuances of queer urban Black women's voices, Dowell's chapter also urges us to think more rigorously about the nature and meaning of violence.

One thing largely missing from these various lenses on queer Newark history is actual sex. While desire, love, community, solidarity, and other forms of intimacy and togetherness are central to LGBTQ history, so too is the more openly carnal element. As Dominique Rocker shows in her chapter, there are gendered and racialized factors at play in how the sexual archive of queer Newark history takes shape. Gay men, for whom sex has often been theorized as political since the gay liberation movement in the early 1970s, have been the most open narrators of their sex lives for the Queer Newark Oral History Project. But the ongoing shaming and stigmatization of women's sexualities, and in particular the historical baggage that Black women carry, burdened by racist imagery of mammys and Jezebels, work as disincentives that foster strategic silences as they narrate their queer lives. Rocker unpacks these dynamics with sensitivity and examines one striking counterexample, the Newark-based magazine *La'Raine*, the city's first transgender-run publication and, in the hands of founder and editor Angela Raine, a site for frank sexual discussion from a Black trans perspective. At a time when LGBTQ sexual visibility is under attack everywhere, from school libraries to drag queen story hours, Rocker makes a political case for including sex in queer (and other) histories.

Meanwhile, the dominant racial narrative of Newark remains an oversimplified Black/white binary, when in fact Newark has long been a truly multiracial city, with such places as its forgotten early twentieth century Chinatown receiving only belated attention.[28] In the twenty-first century, the major demographic story of Newark is Latinx. But even as Newark is poised to reach a Latinx majority in the coming decades, queer Latinx Newarkers have drawn little scholarly attention. One major exception is the work of Yamil Avivi, who has studied queer

Brazilian immigrant men and the ways they have acclimated themselves to the Ironbound neighborhood, often by buying into neoliberal American ideas about individual self-worth defined through consumer and market frameworks.[29] For his chapter in this book, Avivi builds on his previous work, returning to interview subjects a decade later to see what changed during the 2010s. As he relates, gay visibility increased in the Ironbound, but dominant values remain difficult to resist internalizing, and LGBTQ Latinx organizing has proven difficult in a heavily immigrant neighborhood where both survival needs and an understandable fear of visibility under conditions of extreme state hostility to immigrants (under presidents Barack Obama, Donald Trump, and Joseph Biden) can prevent outspoken activism.

Policing is a recurring theme in this book, and in their chapter, Danielle M. Shields and Carse Ramos provide unprecedented detail on the experiences of LGBTQ Newarkers with the Newark Police Department. Unsurprisingly, those experiences are overwhelmingly negative. Newark holds a claim to being the foundational site for the birth of broken windows theory, which was introduced in 1982 by Rutgers-Newark professor George Kelling and his Harvard-based coauthor James Q. Wilson. Broken windows policing calls for strong assertions of public order, targeting graffiti artists, public drunkenness, and vagrancy to prevent worse crimes. While broken windows theory has generated an enormous body of scholarly literature refuting its basic assumptions and showing in painful detail how it leads to the over-policing of communities of color, its fundamentally antiqueer foundation is less often acknowledged. Kelling and Wilson's basic social unit was "the family," understood as heterosexual, and sexual deviations from that norm were central concerns for them. Prostitution and "pornographic displays," they wrote, "can destroy a community more quickly than any team of professional burglars."[30] Indeed, so deeply entrenched are the ideas of the broken windows framework that even ostensibly radical mayor Ras Baraka, willing to confront the Newark Police Department by backing a powerful civilian review board, endorsed "quality of life" sweeps of gentrifying downtown Newark that benefited developers but funneled others into the carceral system—including sex workers, among whom queer and transgender Newarkers are disproportionately represented.[31]

The gentrification that undergirds Newark's "quality of life" policing, so deeply tied to the long history of urban renewal targeting poor and sexually nonconforming communities to clear the way for development, also has another effect on queer memory: it erases the physical traces of queer history. Murphy's Tavern, Club Zanzibar, Le Joc, and nearly all the other important physical sites of queer Newark nightlife have been demolished. As mentioned, the intersection of Broad and Market Streets, where Sakia Gunn was killed, bears no memorial marker to remember the tragedy (though as this book goes to press, a nearby downtown street has been renamed Sakia Gunn Way). This is the conundrum Mary Rizzo and Christina Strasburger contemplate in the final chapter. The Queer Newark Oral History Project has been offering downtown walking tours since 2017. But where do you walk when there's nothing to see? And how do you narrate a past so heavily marked by loss, oppression, and violence without reinscribing fatalistic narratives of Newark and its LGBTQ life? Strasburger and Rizzo consider both the ethical and the pragmatic challenges of the Queer Newark walking tour, while also emphasizing that in contemporary Newark, gentrification is a queer issue.

Lastly, in an epilogue both poetic and righteously polemical, Zenzele Isoke returns to the memory of Sakia Gunn twenty years after her death, to pay tribute; to imagine lost futures; to consider the current national moment of backlash against Black, queer, and trans lives; and to dream of liberation.

Queer Newark describes a great deal of hardship, suffering, violence, and oppression. But that is not what this book is about. This book is openly and unapologetically a celebration of the courage, resilience, creativity, love, and genius of LGBTQ Newarkers. Every painful incident mentioned in this book is something the community survived—though not every member, and the chapters in *Queer Newark* are also a tribute to those who did not make it, because the weight of oppression was unbearable at times. Some of the chapters challenge you to grapple with academic theory, but they do so because queer Newark deserves not platitudes but rigorous analysis; every one of these chapters *wants* to be read. This is, ultimately, an academic history book, but also a labor of love. All of the contributors write from ethical, political, personal, and intellectual commitments to Newark's queer community. The hope here is not that *Queer Newark* be the final word on this rich history—indeed, there are *so* many histories left to uncover, and topics from religion to municipal politics could use further attention.[32] Instead, all involved hope this book will be generative of even more research and investigation, but most of all, that *Queer Newark* be seen as honoring those LGBTQ Newarkers who paved the way for our current moment, and that it might inspire those younger readers who hold in their hands the future.

It's offered in solidarity; reader, please enjoy, mourn when necessary, learn, and take action!

Notes

1. Gateways to Newark website, https://gatewaystonewark.com/portraits/gallery/.

2. Tatyana Fazlalizadeh artist page, https://gatewaystonewark.com/portraits/artists/tatyana-fazlalizadeh/.

3. Khari Johnson-Ricks artist page, https://gatewaystonewark.com/portraits/artists/khari-johnson-ricks/.

4. Darnell Moore, quoted on the Queer Newark Oral History Project's statement of purpose, https://queer.newark.rutgers.edu/about. For a more thorough explication of QNOHP principles and goals, see Moore, Beryl Satter, Timothy Stewart-Winter, and Whitney Strub, "A Community's Response to the Problem of Invisibility: The Queer Newark Oral History Project," *QED: A Journal in GLBTQ Worldmaking* 1, no. 2 (2014): 1–14.

5. Nan Alamilla Boyd and Horacio N. Roque Ramírez, eds., *Bodies of Evidence: The Practice of Queer Oral History* (New York: Oxford University Press, 2012); Elizabeth Lapovsky Kennedy and Madeline D. Davis, *Boots of Leather, Slippers of Gold: The History of a Lesbian Community* (New York: Routledge, 1993); Twin Cities GLBT Oral History Project, *Queer Twin Cities* (Minneapolis: University of Minnesota Press, 2010); Harrison Apple, "The $10,000 Woman: Trans Artifacts in the Pittsburgh Queer History Project Archive," *Transgender Studies Quarterly* 2, no. 4 (2015): 553–564; Rochella Thorpe, "'A House Where Queers Go': African-American Lesbian Nightlife in Detroit, 1940–1975," in *Inventing Lesbian Cultures in America*, ed. Ellen Lewin (Boston: Beacon Press, 1996), 40–61; E. Patrick Johnson, *Sweet Tea: Black Gay Men of the South, an Oral History* (Chapel Hill: University of North Carolina Press, 2008); Johnson, *Black. Queer. Southern. Women.: An Oral History* (Chapel Hill: University of North Carolina Press, 2018).

6. This paragraph is from Whitney Strub, "No Sex in Newark: Postindustrial Erotics at the Intersection of Urban and Adult Film History," *Journal of Cinema and Media Studies* 58, no. 1 (2018): 175–182; for full citations to the works mentioned, see p. 177, footnotes 6–9.

7. Andrew Jacobs, "In a Progressive State, a City Where Gay Life Hangs by a Thread," *New York Times*, December 2, 2007.

8. Susan Hirsch, *Roots of the American Working Class: The Industrialization of Crafts in Newark, 1800–1860* (Philadelphia: University of Pennsylvania Press, 1978), xix.

9. Hirsch, *Roots*, 36–38; Daniel W. Crofts, "Re-Electing Lincoln: The Struggle in Newark," *Civil War History* 30, no. 1 (1984): 54–79. On early abolitionist work in

Newark, see Noelle Lorraine Williams's remarkable digital history project *Black Power!: 19th Century,* https://blackpower19thcentury.com/ and Lauren O'Brien, "Ghosts of the Brick City: The History of Black Dispossession, Public Memory, and Urban Renewal in Newark, NJ" (PhD diss., Rutgers University, 2022), chapter 1.

10. Clement Price, "The Beleaguered City as Promised Land: Blacks in Newark, 1917–1947," in *A New Jersey Anthology,* ed. Maxine N. Lurie (Newark: New Jersey Historical Society, 1994), 11, 15, 19; Curtis Lucas, *Third Ward, Newark* (New York: Lion, [1946] 1952).

11. Paul Stellhorn, "Boom, Bust, and Boosterism: Attitudes, Residency and the Newark Chamber of Commerce, 1920–1941," in *Urban New Jersey Since 1870,* ed. William Wright (Trenton: New Jersey Historical Commission, 1975), 46–77; Warren Grover, *Nazis in Newark* (New Brunswick, NJ: Transaction Publishers, 2003).

12. Kevin Mumford, "Double V in New Jersey: African-American Civic Culture and Rising Consciousness against Jim Crow, 1938–1966," *New Jersey History* 119, no. 3 (2001): 22–56; Harold Kaplan, *Urban Renewal Politics: Slum Clearance in Newark* (New York: Columbia University Press, 1963).

13. On the competing narratives of 1967 in Newark, see Mark Krasovic, *The Newark Frontier: Community Action in the Great Society* (Chicago: University of Chicago Press, 2016).

14. For a nuanced assessment of Gibson and James, see Robert Curvin, *Inside Newark: Decline, Rebellion, and the Search for Transformation* (New Brunswick, NJ: Rutgers University Press, 2014), 145–215; on city decline, see Brad Tuttle, *How Newark Became Newark: The Rise, Fall, and Rebirth of an American City* (New Brunswick, NJ: Rutgers University Press, 2009), 236.

15. Eileen Maura McGurty, "City Renaissance on a Garbage Heap: Newark, New Jersey, and Solid Waste Planning," *Journal of Planning History* 2, no. 4 (2003): 311–330; Elizabeth Strom, "Let's Put on a Show! Performing Arts and Urban Revitalization in Newark, New Jersey," *Journal of Urban Affairs* 21, no. 4 (1999): 423–435.

16. Andra Gillespie, *The New Black Politician: Cory Booker, Newark, and Post-Racial America* (New York: New York University Press, 2012), 57, 84.

17. Curvin, *Inside Newark,* 227.

18. On Booker, see Jonathan Wharton, *A Post-Racial Change Is Gonna Come: Newark, Cory Booker, and the Transformation of Urban America* (New York: Palgrave Macmillan, 2013); on the Zuckerberg donation, see Dale Russakoff, *The Prize: Who's in Charge of America's Schools?* (New York: Houghton Mifflin Harcourt, 2015).

19. Tom Wiedmann, "Newark Remains NJ's Largest City, 2020 Census Data Shows," *Tap Into Newark,* August 12, 2021, https://www.tapinto.net/towns/newark/sections/essex-county-news/articles/newark-remains-nj-s-largest-city-2020

-census-data-shows; Nicole Torres, "Newark's 1974 Puerto Rican Riots through Oral Histories," *New Jersey Studies* 4, no. 2 (2018): 212–229.

20. "Spina Assails Homosexual Edict," *Star-Ledger*, November 9, 1967; Alfred Richlan, "Your Child's Health Today," *Italian Tribune News*, February 20, 1970. Thanks to Mark Krasovic for both of these articles.

21. Anthony Heilbut, *The Gospel Sound: Good News and Bad Times*, 25th anniversary ed. (New York: Limelight Editions, [1971] 1997), 145, 149; Heilbut, *The Fan Who Knew Too Much: Aretha Franklin, the Rise of the Soap Opera, Children of the Gospel Church, and Other Meditations* (New York: Knopf, 2012), esp. 37–40; Archbishop Carl Bean with David Ritz, *I Was Born This Way* (New York: Simon & Schuster, 2010).

22. Gary Jardim, *Blue: Newark Culture*, vols. 1 and 2 (Orange, NJ: De Souza Press, 1990 and 1993).

23. Karen McCarthy Brown, "Mimesis in the Face of Fear: Femme Queens, Butch Queens, and Gender Play in the Houses of Greater Newark," in *Passing: Identity and Interpretation in Sexuality, Race, and Religion*, ed. Maria Carla Sanchez and Linda S. Schlossberg (New York: New York University Press, 2001); Peter Savastano, "'St. Gerard Teaches Him That Love Cancels That Out': Devotion to St. Gerard Maiella among Italian American Catholic Gay Men in Newark, New Jersey," in *Gay Religion*, ed. Scott Thumma and Edward R. Gray (Walnut Creek, CA: Altamira Press, 2005), 181–202; Savastano, "Changing St. Gerard's Clothes: An Exercise in Italian-American Catholc Devotion and Material Culture," in *Italian Folk: Vernacular Culture in Italian-American Lives* (New York: Fordham University Press, 2011), 171–187; Aryana Bates, "Religious Despite Religion: Lesbian Agency, Identity, and Spirituality at Liberation in Truth, Unity Fellowship Church" (PhD diss., Drew University, 2001); Bates, "Liberation in Truth: African American Lesbians Reflect on Religion, Spirituality, and Their Church," in *Gay Religion*, 221–237; Eugenia Lee Hancock, "AIDS Is Just a Four Letter Word: An Ethnographic Study of Theodicy and the Social Construction of HIV/AIDS in Newark, New Jersey" (PhD diss., Drew University, 2002).

24. Ana Ramos-Zayas, *Street Therapists: Race, Affect, and Neoliberal Personhood in Latino Newark* (Chicago: University of Chicago Press, 2012), 246–281; Arlene Stein, "What's the Matter with Newark? Race, Class, Marriage Politics, and the Limits of Queer Liberalism," in *The Marrying Kind?: Debating Same-Sex Marriage within the Lesbian and Gay Movement*, ed. Mary Bernstein and Verta Taylor (Minneapolis: University of Minnesota Press, 2013), 37–66.

25. Zenzele Isoke, *Urban Black Women and the Politics of Resistance*, The Politics of Intersectionality series (New York: Palgrave Macmillan, 2013).

26. Anna Lvovsky, *Vice Patrol: Cops, Courts, and the Struggle over Urban Gay Life before Stonewall* (Chicago: University of Chicago Press, 2021).

27. "In the Matter of Disciplinary Proceedings against One-Thirty-Five Mulberry St. Corp.," Bulletin 892, No. 2, December 1950; "In the Matter of Disciplinary Proceedings against Hub Bar," Bulletin 1423, No. 5, February 1962. The ABC's bulletins are available at https://dspace.njstatelib.org/xmlui/handle/10929/51416.

28. Yoland Skeete-Laessig, *When Newark Had a Chinatown: My Personal Journey* (Pittsburgh: Dorrance Publishing, 2016).

29. Yamil Avivi, "Queering Political Economy in Neoliberal Ironbound Newark: Subjectivity and Spacemaking among Brazilian Queer Immigrant Men," *Diálogo: An Interdisciplinary Journal* 18, no. 2 (2015): 105–118; Avivi, "Betina Botox and Lobixomen 'Tão Engraçados!' Queer Brazilian Televisual Representations Shaping Spatial (Im)possibilities in Newark," *The Bilingual Review/La Revista Bilingüe* 33, no. 4 (2017): 45–59.

30. George Kelling and James Q. Wilson, "Broken Windows," *Atlantic Monthly*, March 1982.

31. Alecia McGregor, "Politics, Police Accountability, and Public Health: Civilian Review in Newark, New Jersey," *Journal of Urban Health* 93, no. 1 (2016): 141–153. On the targeting of transgender sex workers—and an example of unsympathetic and sensationalized media coverage—see "Six Arrested in Prostitution Bust in Newark," *RLS Media*, October 10, 2017, https://www.rlsmedia.com/article/six-arrested-prostitution-bust-newark.

32. Indeed, "queer" itself may not be the final word on this subject. While its selection to name the QNOHP emerged from extensive community dialogue sessions in 2011, social science research undertaken among LGBTQ Newark youth of color a few years later found that few used the term to self-identify and many were confused or ambivalent about its meaning. Vanessa R. Panfil, "'Nobody Don't Really Know What That Mean': Understandings of 'Queer' among Urban LGBTQ Young People of Color," *Journal of Homosexuality* 67, no. 12 (2019): 1713–1735.

CHAPTER 1

Sodom on the Passaic

Excavating Early Queer Histories of Newark, 1870s–1940s

PETER SAVASTANO AND TIMOTHY STEWART-WINTER

THE EARLY QUEER HISTORY of Newark, New Jersey, was structured by its industrial and immigrant character and its proximity to New York City. This essay provides a series of glimpses at queer Newark through the first half of the twentieth century. It has three broad aims: to situate the reader in Newark and thus set the stage for later chapters; to introduce major themes and concepts in queer history of this period, revealing Newark as a stage or laboratory for working out ideas about homosexuality; and to introduce some key figures and moments we hope other scholars will explore in further detail.

Newark in the first half of the twentieth century was a city of industrial workers, many of them European immigrants, the vast majority white. It was a big city for the period—one of the nation's fifteen largest in each decennial census from 1850 to 1940—and it benefited from its proximity to the nation's commercial and cultural capital, New York. In 1900, Newark had a population of a quarter million people, which nearly doubled to 442,000 by 1930 at its peak. Spurred partly by Civil War production needs, Newark became known in the late nineteenth century for its industries, especially leather goods and metal refining. By the early twentieth century Newark workers manufactured goods ranging from sewing machines to beer, and the city was increasingly a nexus for rail transportation.[1] Marshes were dredged in the Passaic River to construct a major port, and during World War I the U.S. military built a major shipbuilding center.[2] The city's population remained predominantly working class. In 1955, manufacturing

FIGURE 1.1. Rebuilding a dock destroyed by fire, 1918. New Jersey Picture Collection, Newark Public Library.

FIGURE 1.2. Port Newark, connecting the city to international flows of commerce and culture, 1916. New Jersey Picture Collection, Newark Public Library.

had begun to decline but was still "the principal source of employment in Newark."[3]

Ten miles from New York and easily accessible by ferries and bridges, Newark's leisure and sexual economy was, like its manufacturing and commerce, deeply interwoven with that of the larger metropolis across the Hudson. During one crackdown on vice in New York at the turn of the twentieth century, for example, Newark's police commissioner expressed a concern that "some members of the undesirable classes of society in New York might take refuge in this city" and urged that his officers "keep a strict watch hereafter on the saloons of the city."[4] As in nearby Jersey City, commuting to New York for work or leisure became even more accessible after 1911, with the opening of "tubes" dug under the Hudson River. Some New Jerseyans likely traveled to New York in search of queer nightlife as the latter grew during the 1920s "pansy craze."

Far from a mere waystation, Newark could be a queer destination even for denizens of the city then becoming known as the "Big Apple." When the raucous blues singer Bessie Smith returned to the Northeast after a period touring the South in 1926, New Yorker Carl Van Vechten traveled to hear her at Newark's Orpheum Theater.[5] It could even be a place where New Yorkers went in search of freedom from the conformities of home. Consider nineteen-year-old Arthur Houston, who on a fall evening in 1928 left home in East Flatbush, Brooklyn, and, borrowing the clothing of a sister, traveled to Newark and spent one night in the Young Women's Christian Association before checking into Newark's Hotel Lucerne under the name of Miss Dorothy Dix of Hollywood, California. Hotel staff, apparently thinking the guest might be a runaway girl, called the police department's missing persons bureau. Soon arrested on the charge of impersonating a woman, Houston reportedly told officers that "during his short stay in Newark [he] had enjoyed himself by flirting with men on the streets," and "had made an appointment to meet one of the men who had taken him automobile riding." By one account, at the time of the arrest, "Houston, who is a slim blond, was attired in a pink dress and a white coat and hat."[6] Queer travel between New York and Newark was never unidirectional, despite the metropolitan bias in available sources.

The evidence surrounding Houston raises another problem for queer historians: What was Houston's "identity"? The first generation of scholars in gay and lesbian history might have seen Houston as a gay man who cross-dressed, while more recently scholars of trans history have pointed out that there is little basis for emphasizing the desire for sex with men on the part of a figure such as Houston rather than the decision to wear feminine clothing, or to assume that the latter was done merely as a tactical means to pursue the former. The evidence recorded by others allows us only to conjecture about Houston's self-understanding.[7] Figures such as Houston are thus not easily assimilated to our contemporary distinctions between sexual orientation and gender identity.

Thus, queer historians have typically emphasized not that gay and trans people always existed in the past, but instead that our familiar contemporary categories for sorting people by sexual orientation and gender identity—including the gay/straight and trans/cisgender binaries—did not necessarily correspond to how people lived before World War II. For American men in this period, sex between men was typically regulated and understood based not on who a man's sexual partner was but on the role they played in a sexual encounter. "Many 'normal' men in black and immigrant working-class neighborhoods in particular," George Chauncey has argued, "did not need to perform as 'heterosexuals,' nor did anyone consider them members of the 'gay world,' so long as they performed normative masculinity and made it clear that their partner would play the 'woman's' part in the sexual encounter." Some of these men, though by no means all, understood themselves to be women born in the wrong body.[8]

Because oral histories and other first-person narratives of queer life are largely unavailable for this period, and because, unlike Germany, the United States did not have a queer political movement before World War II, much of what we know about LGBTQ life in this period comes from records produced by hostile institutions. Nightlife is especially well documented, not only because lively streets, bars, and clubs were places where people could encounter strangers and seek sex, but also because it was intensively policed. Newark's downtown also grew with the opening of movie palaces, hotels, and department stores such as Hahne's and Bamberger's, though middle-class whites began to move to the suburbs.[9]

Immigration and internal migration drove Newark's growth. Irish and German immigrants were the first wave, followed by Italians and Jews from Germany, Russia, and Poland. Newark's foreign-born population was 32 percent in 1910[10] and 26 percent in 1930.[11] Many other Newarkers were second-generation Americans who lived in German, Italian, or Jewish enclaves. In 1930, fully 12 percent of Newark's total population were children of Italian immigrants.[12] Due to migration from the rural South, the city's Black population rose to 4 percent in 1920; by 1940 it was nearly 11 percent.[13]

The question of who should "count" as part of a history of early queer Newark is tricky. Gender and sexual nonconformity are universal but the way they are organized socially changes over time. While there have likely always been people with same-sex erotic desires and behaviors, historians have traced the emergence of gay identity and community to the early twentieth century. John D'Emilio argues that the rise of wage labor and concomitant decline of household-based production let people live outside nuclear families, separating sex from procreation and making it "possible for homosexual desire to coalesce into a personal identity." By around 1900, "a class of men and women existed who recognized their erotic interest in their own sex, saw it as a trait that set them apart from the majority, and sought others like themselves."[14]

The limitations of the known archive also leave us with more questions than answers about such figures as Robert Ballantine, bachelor scion of Newark's wealthy brewery-owning family, who committed suicide in 1905 after being blackmailed over his "personal habits"; or Marcus Ward, son of New Jersey's Civil War–era governor and lifelong bachelor, who left his hefty fortune to establish the Marcus L. Ward Home for Aged and Respectable Bachelors and Widowers in the 1920s. Press accounts referred to a "southern girl" loved by Ballantine (hardly a blackmailable offense) but also more cryptically attributed his suicide to "habits of dissipation and drink," while Ward was described as a "strange, austere, lonely old man." Without more information, we cannot claim them as part of Newark's LGBTQ history, but neither is there reason to default to assumptions of straightness.[15]

Many biases have shaped what we know about Newark's queer history. To the extent that policing served a political imperative to protect white citizens from danger, this often meant a concern less with suppressing queer life among Black people than with confining deviance within the segregated Black ghetto that emerged in Newark's Third Ward after World War I. By the late 1920s, as illicit nightlife grew in the Third Ward, Newark police strove to prevent interracial mixing after midnight by keeping white people out. And yet, with the continuing influx of southern migrants during the Great Depression, the nightlife scene only continued to grow.[16]

We also know more about queer men's lives than those of queer women as a result of men's greater access to public space, money, and power. With women, "you really didn't know," recalled Amina Baraka of her childhood among Black Newarkers in the late 1940s; "you would have [to] find that out after you've been friends with them for a while. But the men were much more open. They had more power, I guess, to announce what their sexuality was."[17] Two female followers of Father Divine's idiosyncratic Peace Mission Movement—a Black-led religious movement that required sex segregation and the celibacy of its members—Happy S. Love, who was Black, and Dorothy Moore, who was white, met at the Newark Peace Mission in 1948. While little is known about their relationship, the surviving poems that Love wrote professing her love for Moore convey, in the words of one scholar, "the complex religious contours of her celibate same-sex desire."[18] Given the collision of subcultures in the early twentieth century city and the fuzzy boundaries of queerness in this period, it can be useful for queer historians to examine the sexually marginalized more broadly, particularly sex workers, who were frequently the object of highly systematic policing.[19]

The remainder of this chapter will discuss two major themes in the history of early queer Newark: first, the encounter between queer and other sexually marginalized people and the police who sought to confine or eradicate them; and second, Newark as a stage or laboratory for conceptualizing knowledge about homosexuality. In Newark as in other U.S. cities in this period, queer people clashed against an emerging, contradictory set of legal and scientific regimes for producing knowledge about homosexuality. Margot Canaday has argued that at the federal level the "straight state" shifted in the twentieth century from what she calls "nascent policing" toward "explicit regulation," and we can similarly witness at the local level the emergence of efforts to comprehend and map emerging queer minorities in Newark.[20]

Policing the City

As U.S. cities grew in size and complexity in the late nineteenth century, so too did municipal police departments. Among the signal concerns of these agencies was enforcing gender and sexual norms in public places, especially places where strangers congregated. Policing shaped queer life in urban America in this period and produced some of the most important available sources regarding the texture of life among working-class people.

The surveillance of city streets encompassed the control of what Clare Sears has aptly called "problem bodies," with people who transgressed gender norms treated increasingly as likely or actual criminals.[21] A list of "representative crooks" included in an early history of the Newark police department included

Etta M. Lewis, alias Gertrude Townsend, aged twenty-one, who was arrested in 1885 on a charge of entering and stealing, and was "dressed in male attire, and passed at her boarding house as a boy," at the time of her arrest. After serving time, Lewis went to Cincinnati and again masqueraded as a young man.[22] Police were preoccupied with gender; men passing as women and women passing as men, by dramatizing the possibility of deceiving strangers, seemed to reveal and epitomize the perils of urban life.

The Progressive Era, as historians label the first decades of the twentieth century, was marked by nascent queer visibility and emerging efforts by reformers and police to clamp down on it. Police records (particularly a logbook kept by Newark police detective Frank C. Brex) illustrate the rise of places in Newark—including Prince Street, Broome Street, Howard Street, South Orange Avenue, and Springfield Avenue—where a carnival life emerged at the end of the nineteenth century and proceeded well into the twentieth. Queer life in Newark was policed as part of the broader regulation of gender and sexuality. Brex conducted an undercover sting operation to arrest an abortion provider in 1915, for example.[23] That same summer, he worked to track down one Harold Gruber and, on finding him in Newark's Lyric Theatre, arrested him "for Buggary which he permitted Walter Ross to commit on him," a rare example of men facing criminal charges under the laws that prohibited sex between men and thereby cast a pall of criminality over queer existence.[24] The Lyric, which hosted boxing matches and musical performances, may also have been a cruising spot for gay men.[25] It had also been the site of a shocking crime in which a woman in a box seat was allegedly jabbed by a needle dipped in a "white slave poison agent" after a movie screening (early twentieth-century reformers were gravely concerned with the possibility of "white slavery," their term for what is today called sex trafficking).[26]

After the construction of the Hudson Tubes, Newark became a key stop on northeastern circuits for performers, and its nightlife burgeoned.[27] As in other cities, the business elite responded by sending investigators to report on "conditions" in the city's bars and clubs. On a January 1914 visit to a burlesque theater, a woman investigator found that "the dialogue on the stage was very suggestive. When a certain female impersonator appeared, some of the men in the audience near the investigator declared that they knew him and described his habits in loud tones so that women in their vicinity heard."[28]

During World War I, the federal government and private reform agencies reached into localities in an effort to protect servicemen from venereal disease and, to a lesser extent, immorality. This surveillance dovetailed with and bolstered local regulations. An investigator from the New York–based Committee of Fourteen, dispatched across state lines for undercover reporting on Newark's nightlife, reported that on his four visits to the city he "found conditions very bad in every section that I covered, particularly amongst the colored crowd." He described "Saloons and cabarets running wild, street walkers, private houses and speak-easys."[29] A man who had recently migrated to the region and worked as a superintendent in a Newark shipyard told him "that Newark is the only open town and he prefers to stay here then [*sic*] in New York."[30]

Yet the emphasis on preventing heterosexual intimacies meant that same-sex encounters might draw comparatively less attention. Soldiers and sailors gathered near Broad and Market Streets told one investigator that "none of the hotels will let them in with a woman." In one tavern the investigator found "about 20 unaccompanied men, 4 couples, no unescorted women," adding that "the majority of the men appeared to be a lot of foreigners, were mostly speaking German." The investigator's worry on seeing these men together was not that they might be cruising, but rather that they might be engaging in unpatriotic talk in a foreign tongue.[31] As in the committee's reports on New York City nightlife, the overwhelming concern was with female prostitution and the threat it posed to men. Queer intimacy between women was even more invisible. Police assumed that women standing or drinking unescorted on the street were sex workers, not that they were lesbians—though the investigators for the 1914 report on "social evils" in Newark did make occasional note of "perverts," a term capacious enough to include sexually assertive or nonconforming women of various sorts that sometimes seems to indicate lesbians, such as one "pervert from choice" described as "very pretty, but tough," and another simply listed as "pervert-fear of pregnancy."[32]

By this period, prostitution flourished in Newark much as it did across urban America, a function of demographic density and the relative anonymity of city life. Historians have noted the intimate relationship between the history of sex work and that of LGBTQ life, with their shared criminalization and illicit social spaces.[33] By the 1910s authorities had certainly honed their methods of sexual surveillance and repression in Newark, which would later blossom into antigay policing. The ways the 1914 report on social evils described female sex workers—"They loiter about the streets, usually in pairs, and flirt with strangers . . . They are weak, frivolous and often eager to hear obscene stories and look at vulgar and indecent pictures"—would echo across decades of derisory descriptions of queer Newarkers, many of whom supported themselves through sex work.[34] Most importantly, sex workers and queer Newarkers would share a long struggle for access to the public sphere, as several later chapters will show.

Knowledge Production

The turn from nascent policing to explicit regulation, as Canaday terms it, involved not only municipal police departments but a wide variety of other actors—vice reformers, legislatures, the courts, the press, federal military police, and civilian authorities who claimed the right to regulate city streets during World War I and II. It was reflected in the creation, after the repeal of Prohibition in the early 1930s, of state-level bureaucracies to regulate the sale of alcohol (see chapter 2). Indeed, the head of New Jersey's new state liquor regulator, the Alcoholic Beverage Control agency, announced in 1934 that he was formulating new regulations to ban female impersonators in all establishments.[35]

Two particularly vivid cases illustrate how, as urban America prospered in the 1920s, Newark was the scene of multiple complex and contradictory debates over the boundaries and significance of homosexuality. The first of these cases unfolded in the courts—specifically in the Essex County Courthouse in downtown Newark in November 1925, in a high-profile criminal trial involving a wealthy young defendant from Upper Montclair, a suburb of Newark, who confessed to killing a Black taxi driver to steal his car, then kidnapping and murdering a six-year-old white girl, Mary Daly, and burying her body. Many white-owned newspapers initially assumed the suspect was a Black man.[36] Harrison Noel, twenty, whose father was a prominent New York attorney, had briefly attended Harvard University the previous fall, then was confined in a hospital for the insane in February 1925, from which he escaped in June.[37]

The context of this episode was a burst of obsessive and sensational media attention on "sex fiends," a category that broadly lumped together erotic deviance and violent criminality and focused on crimes against children in particular.[38] Scientific experts in the study of sexuality often fueled this coverage. In newspapers across the country, Noel was frequently compared to Nathan Loeb and Richard Leopold, similarly wealthy and highly educated young men in Chicago whose trial the previous year had been the object of tremendous public fascination and insinuations of sexual perversion, forging a link in public discourse between homosexuality and crimes against children. In that case, historian Paula Fass notes that, crucially, "rumors about the mutilation of the body and the body as the site of perverse practices started almost immediately after the discovery of the unclothed child," before Leopold and Loeb were even suspects. These rumors were "subsequently inflamed by psychiatric reports and wide-ranging interviews that suggested boyish compacts and alluded to perversions (a code word for homosexuality) between Leopold and Loeb."[39]

Journalists and psychiatrists, for whom the trial of Leopold and Loeb had been a boon, pounced on the Mary Daly kidnapping and then on Noel, with the *New York Times* running front-page articles for six consecutive days.[40] "Both are classed as 'thrill' murders," according to a front-page story in a Kansas newspaper: Noel, like Leopold and Loeb, was the "son of well-to-do parents and a youth of intellectual attainments" who "maintained a nonchalant demeanor" during questioning and killed out of "sheer blood lust," yet at least briefly "thought of ransom."[41] Another reporter wrote that word of Noel's confession had led to a mob gathering outside the Montclair police station. Rumors that Noel was jailed "for impairing the morals of little girls" reportedly drew two thousand people to the Montclair police station, where "rumblings of a lynching" were only quelled when doctors asserted that in fact Noel had not raped the girl but only killed her. The same story claimed, obviously based on a leak by a public official, that in his cell Noel "shows not the slightest sign of remorse."[42] Police called Noel "a fiend"[43] and the case quickly led to demands to curtail parole in New Jersey and New York.[44]

Despite the lack of an accomplice who could be cast as Noel's perverted intimate, reporters grasped for other means to suggest there was something queer about him. For instance, they interviewed his former Harvard roommate, who said he "was not like the other fellows."[45] They asserted that he was "convinced of his difference from normal boys."[46] Journalists published the findings of experts, such as one phrenologist's detailed analysis of Noel's facial features: "He has a small development of combativeness," she concluded, "which would make him cowardly."[47] Still another reporter was convinced that Noel was "considered simply eccentric" by family members, and that his mother "was his best friend and the one who had most influence with him."[48]

The case of Leopold and Loeb "had attached categories of normality and abnormality to definitions of childhood," and Noel "may have suffered from the connection with Leopold and Loeb," according to Fass.[49] The case's queer resonances sometimes broke through to the surface. At trial, his "untidy and filthy habits" were detailed, including his refusal to keep his clothes on, sitting hours without moving, refusing to eat for fear of poisoning, and "insist[ing] that he be called 'Tessie' because he was a female." Perhaps it was this last detail that led the prosecutor to assert that Noel had "homosexual proclivities."[50] The jury, largely made up of Newark residents, most of them "workingmen and tradesmen" according to the *New York Times*, were unmoved by defense claims of insanity and convicted Noel after a five-day trial, sentencing him to death, though a higher court reversed this sentence and instead sent him to an asylum.[51]

As Daniel Hurewitz shows, courtrooms operated as critical sites for forging public understandings of homosexuality in this era.[52] While definitions of sexual identity remained inchoate rather than coherent, the dense webs of associative connections among homosexuality, deviance, pathology, and perversion were on ample display in Newark's Harrison Noel case, as well as in the more famous Leopold and Loeb trial.

A different sort of Newark-based knowledge production came from the prolific author William J. Fielding, whose short 1925 tract *Homo-Sexual Life* anticipated some aspects of the later, more famous Kinsey reports of 1948 and 1953. Born in Morris County, New Jersey, in 1886, Fielding was largely raised in Newark, which he recalled fondly for its "picturesque Branch Brook Park" and the "unrivaled Newark Public Library."[53] After leaving school in eighth grade, he did skilled repair work for the company that built the Hudson Tubes and took business courses at a school in Newark. In 1909 he secured a job at Louis C. Tiffany and Company, the New York City jewelry firm, where he went on to work for fifty years as a white-collar employee.

While working at Tiffany's, he began writing poetry; served as editor of a socialist newspaper, *The Newark Leader*; and eventually turned his attention to sex and sexuality, spurred on by what he saw as the hypocrisy of such puritanical reformers as anti-obscenity activist Anthony Comstock. "In the warped minds of these people," Fielding later wrote, "the very fact of sex was equated with vice."[54] In the preceding decades, early sexologists including Havelock Ellis, Richard von Krafft-Ebing, and John Addington Symonds developed and published new theories of human sexuality. Fielding read them and other influential thinkers from Freud to radical birth-control advocate Margaret Sanger, and in his first book, *Sanity in Sex* (1920), he popularized their ideas, calling for birth-control access, education about venereal disease, and an end to sexual ignorance.[55]

After *Sanity in Sex,* Fielding published most of his later writing on sexuality in a book series edited by Emanuel Haldeman-Julius, whom he knew through their shared work on socialist publications. The Little Blue Book series—five-cent pamphlet editions published by the Haldeman-Julius publishing house in Girard, Kansas—were "a ubiquitous presence in working-class homes and farms during the 1920s and early 1930s" and "emerged . . . into the space left by the Espionage Act's suppression of the radical press."[56] While living at 13 South 12th Street in Newark, west of the base of Branch Brook Park, Fielding began writing for Haldeman-Julius, eventually publishing thirty books that sold five million copies, most of them in the Little Blue Book series, earning a flat $100 per title (no royalties). *What Every Married Woman Should Know,* for instance, sold half a million copies.[57]

Homo-Sexual Life belonged to this flurry of writing but stood out for its forward-thinking and progressive analysis. Two decades before the Kinsey scale, which rejected binary sexuality, Fielding applied a similar spectrum to gender (not yet conceptualized as wholly distinct from sexuality). "No individual is wholly of one sexual character," he asserted, "The most masculine man is not one hundred per cent masculine, nor is the most feminine woman one hundred percent feminine."[58] Describing homosexuality as part of adolescence, he quoted a range of experts but showed clear sympathy for pioneering queer German sexologist Magnus Hirschfeld, "one of the greatest of contemporary authorities on the sex question in all its phases," who "is convinced that homosexuality is a normal state, and that genuine homosexuality is always an inborn condition."[59]

While homosexuality (or "inversion") had often been described in pathologizing terms by medical professionals, Fielding pushed back against this framework: "after all, the psychiatrist and neurologist get the sick and pathologic cases, and rarely the better kind."[60] While "the homosexual has some special problems to meet" resulting from his sexual acts, "the heterosexual also has his problems which not infrequently lead to dire results," and "in both cases" these difficulties "are due in no small degree to the obstacles put in the way by others, through lack of understanding."[61] On an affirmative note, Fielding concluded, "There are and have been a great many inverts who have not only enjoyed average mental and physical health—but have been versatile and productive in their accomplishments."[62]

Homo-Sexual Life sold approximately 130,000 copies.[63] For Fielding, it was one Little Blue Book among many, with others covering psychoanalysis, auto-suggestion, rejuvenation, and in another proto-Kinseyian framing, *Man's Sexual Life* and *Woman's Sexual Life*. For particular readers, though, it struck a powerful chord, and Newark became the site of robust dialogue about homosexuality as Fielding corresponded with readers who were moved to contact him. Responding to a man inquiring about his wife's possible lesbianism, Fielding told him, "Your wife, of course, is a homosexual. . . . The modern, scientific stand is to recognize this as a situation which cannot be eliminated."[64]

One grateful reader celebrated *Homo-Sexual Life*, telling Fielding, "At last intelligent comment is now available to the layman, and I hope that your little volume will find its way into the hands of the suffering thousands who are struggling for light and help in their mental topsiturviness."[65] To a gay man who contacted him, Fielding noted the necessary secrecy around gay communities in the United States—presumably including Newark. In "the leading cities of continental Europe," he noted, there are gay clubs whose "existence is well known" and where homosexual gatherings "are at least semi-public . . . In this country, however, where there is less tolerance about any phase of the sex question, Homosexual clubs or social groups, if they exist—and I imagine they do in some of the large cities—are forced to keep their existence absolutely private, as otherwise public opinion would hound them and the authorities would prosecute them."[66]

Fielding himself appears to have lived a fairly conventional heterosexual life. Married three times, he maintained a lifelong intimate friendship with Joseph Lewis, a founder of the Freethinkers of America, a relationship Fielding described as "closer and of longer duration than that with any other individual in any activity" (in comparison, none of his wives receives more than a brief paragraph in his memoir).[67] But decades worth of preserved correspondence between Fielding and Lewis contain no passionate or erotic content and merely reflect a deep friendship based on shared political and intellectual interests. "I was always reticent, really secretive," Fielding wrote of his childhood, and it's possible that he purged his archives. But more likely, he was simply a nongay man whose cutting-edge work on homosexuality developed as a corollary to his broader inquiries into sexuality at large.[68] In 1952, in the wake of Kinsey's blockbuster books on American sexual practices, the *New Yorker*'s Talk of the Town column profiled Fielding and described his unusual combination of day job and evening-and-weekend sexology. "Kinsey has my sex history, and my wife's," he told the magazine—though Kinsey's individual sex histories remain inaccessible to researchers.[69]

Regardless of his personal life, William J. Fielding made Newark a critical hub of knowledge production about homosexuality in the 1920s. Major figures such as Havelock Ellis took notice, writing him in 1927, "It is satisfying to know that such writings as yours, with their sane outlook, have so wide a circulation," and the two later met when Fielding visited Europe in 1934. Fielding also knew Dr. Harry Benjamin, who paved the way for understanding transgender identity.[70] While less a trailblazing theorist than a popularizer and translator of theory to a wider public readership, Fielding was at the forefront of queer-affirmative conceptualizations of homosexuality.

In the 1940s, Fielding and his third wife moved to Long Island. The timing coincides with the earliest period covered by Queer Newark Oral History Project interviews. It is to the available glimpses of queer life in the 1940s which this chapter now turns.

Toward a Queer Newark

It is primarily in the post–World War II era that we begin to see a more visible queer Newark come into focus, though it is largely through the eyes of straight observers at first. As noted in chapter 2, the largest archive of queer Newark life from the late 1930s to the 1960s comes from the repressive state bureaucracy of the Alcoholic Beverage Control agency and its aggressive surveillance. From the 1950s onward, accounts recorded by the Queer Newark Oral History Project have begun filling in history as experienced from queer perspectives. Before that, we have mostly incomplete yet valuable fragments.

For example, Amiri Baraka was born Everett Leroy Jones in Newark in 1934. He later became an icon of the Black Arts Movement and Black Power politics. As chapter 3 shows, Baraka's sexuality and sexual politics were complex and shifting, but he lived most of his life as a straight man, with evolving views that circled from overt homophobia to support for LGBTQ rights. In his 1984 autobiography, Baraka recalled the casual presence of "fags and bulldaggers" on the streets of Black Newark neighborhoods during his youth. He described "Danny whose brother was gay in those days when we called them 'sissies,'" and elaborated about the unnamed brother: "the dude did pitch and switch when he walked and his hair was done up rococo and curled up." Danny also had a cousin who was "funny," who "fanned up and down the street like he was on his way to mind the seraglio." While they are little more than glimpses, Baraka's memories offer evidence of a visible, and to some extent accepted, queer presence in 1940s Newark.[71]

Amina Baraka, who grew up in Newark as Sylvia Robinson and would later marry Amiri in 1966, held similar memories. Growing up on Howard Street, which cut through the Third Ward and served as the title of Nathan Heard's gritty 1968 novel, she lived in a building managed by her grandparents. Her grandmother in particular "was a very open person," and "everybody came to visit us and sit and talk. She made hot biscuits with syrup and greens and stuff for everybody." The guests included a lesbian couple, Mary and Ruth. "Nobody said anything. They used to take me to the movies. They were very nice to me," Baraka explained. A gendered asymmetry marked her memories of queer Newarkers:

> The ones I knew, if you came after them, you was gonna be in some trouble—particularly the males. They would definitely fight back. The women was a little different because you really didn't know. I mean, they weren't overtly—you would have [to] find that out after you've been friends with them for a while. But the men were much more open. They had more power, I guess, to announce what their sexuality was. The women were not . . . it was understood. Nobody had to talk about it. . . . Some of 'em were masculine and some dressed in feminine. Actually, they dressed the way I dressed and everybody else dressed, generally.[72]

Baraka also recalled the touring Jewel Box Revue, which "used to have programs downtown Newark here," with one performer, Bobby Lee, of whom she said, "Actually, Bobby Lee, I didn't know she was a man. I swear I didn't. She was able to—she was just beautiful. I mean, like you say, it's a pretty man. She was beautiful. Of course, my grandfather, it was a little different. My mother wanted to go. She wanted to go down there because everybody could attend 'em. He told her he didn't want her to go. But she went anyway."[73]

Meanwhile, Gail Malmgreen was born in 1942 to children of immigrants—Russian and Jewish on her mother's side and Norwegian on her father's. Growing up mostly in Weequahic—a neighborhood later made famous by novelist Philip Roth—her parents "had a circle of friends, radical Jewish friends," including tacitly understood queer members. Her older cousin Arnold, for instance, "would come to visit us quite a lot. . . . I knew he was gay, and I can't quite understand how people knew someone was gay in those days, since the word was never mentioned, it was never talked about. . . . It was just obvious, he wasn't getting married, and whatnot." A "kind of a Bohemian respect" helped make sense of the social relations, though much went unspoken. After Arnold moved to Florida in the late 1940s, Malmgreen's parents had other gay friends, such as Bernie and Irving, a couple who "always came over together. Again, we liked them, treated them sort of like uncles, and so on." Bernie and Irving worked as furriers, which led to a highlight of Malmgreen's childhood when they made her a "beautiful teddy bear that was made out of scraps of fur." In the immediate postwar years when "everyone was buying houses and having children," she saw "no gap" in her parents' treatment of their straight and gay friends.[74]

Almost as quickly as this gay visibility blossomed, so too did hostile reaction, which mirrored rising antigay sentiment across the nation as the Cold War took shape. The local *Star-Ledger* ran the syndicated "Worry Clinic" column of Chicago-based Dr. George W. Crane, who repeatedly warned parents of burgeoning homosexuality—"all too common nowadays"—among youth and advocated preventing it through the forging of proper heterosexual romantic attachments by "letting boys and girls attend school and social affairs together." This would help avoid such outcomes as the cautionary tale of thirty-two-year-old teacher Sarah and her "gym teacher" girlfriend, or a college-aged daughter and her roommate who "hug and kiss like two newlyweds. Their behavior is so sentimental and mushy as to be nauseating."[75]

As in other industrial cities in the early twentieth century, Newark's queer life emerged in tandem with efforts to regulate, control, and suppress it. During World War I, the militarization of the Port of Newark and of the city's downtown led indirectly to a flood of police and investigators who have bequeathed us troves of documents about gender and sexual nonconformity in Newark. After World War II, as nonconformity of all stripes came under attack across the United States, queer life was a key target. Newark was no exception. At the turn of the 1950s, the head of Newark's police department, Public Safety Director John Keenan, called for "strict registration of known sex perverts," claiming that sex crimes had increased to "pose a threat to the health, welfare and safety of the citizenry of New Jersey."[76] The available archives of queer life in early twentieth-century Newark are limited and dispersed across a wide range of sources. For the midcentury period, by contrast, two distinct and rich sets of material come into view. On the one hand, at the edge of living memory we can begin to access recorded oral history accounts by narrators who either participated in or sympathetically observed LGBTQ life in Newark. On the other hand, we can turn to the extensive print record maintained by hostile agents of the state, who documented its texture only inadvertently in the course of condemning and curtailing it.

Notes

1. See, among other works, Samuel H. Popper, "Newark, N.J., 1870–1910: Chapters in the Evolution of an American Metropolis" (PhD diss., New York University, 1952); Clement Alexander Price, "The Afro-American Community of Newark, 1917–1947: A Social History" (PhD diss, Rutgers University-New Brunswick, 1975); Brad R. Tuttle, *How Newark Became Newark: The Rise, Fall, and Rebirth of an American City* (New Brunswick, NJ: Rutgers University Press, 2009).

2. "Diversified Industry Aids Newark Growth," *New York Times*, April 21, 1929; "Port Newark Celebrates 50 Years of Progress," *Herald-News* (Passaic, NJ), October 20, 1965.

3. Chester Rapkin, Eunice Grier, and George Grier, *Group Relations in Newark—1957: Problems, Prospects, and a Program for Research*, 1957, Newark City Documents Collection, Charles F. Cummings New Jersey Information Center, Newark Public Library, 11–15.

4. "Vice Crusade in Newark," *New York Times*, November 24, 1900.

5. Carl Van Vechten, "Negro 'Blues' Singers," *Vanity Fair* 26, no.1 (1926): 67, 106, 108.

6. "Impersonated Girl, Local Lad Held in Newark," *Brooklyn Citizen*, October 20, 1928; "Newark 'Girl' Proves to Be Local Youth," *Standard Union* (Brooklyn), October 20, 1928; "Find Fugitive Wearing His Sister's Clothing," *Gaffney Ledger* (Gaffney, SC), November 8, 1928.

7. Clare Sears, *Arresting Dress: Cross-Dressing, Law, and Fascination in Nineteenth-Century San Francisco* (Durham, NC: Duke University Press, 2015); Jen Manion, *Female Husbands: A Trans History* (Cambridge, UK: Cambridge University Press, 2020).

8. George Chauncey, "Preface to the 2019 Paperback," in *Gay New York: Gender, Urban Culture, and the Making of the Gay Male World* (New York: Basic Books, [1994] 2019), xxi–xxii.

9. Price, "The Afro-American Community."

10. In 1910 the largest fractions of Newark's foreign-born population were born in Germany and Russia (20 percent each), followed by Italy (19 percent), Austria (12 percent), and Ireland (10 percent). Percentages calculated from Table 12, p. 586, in the file named 41033935v29-34.pdf at https://www2.census.gov/prod2/decennial/documents/.

11. See the file named 10612982v3p2ch03.pdf at https://www2.census.gov/prod2/decennial/documents/. Percentage calculated from Table 18, p. 207.

12. In 1930, the largest fractions of the foreign-born were from Poland (14 percent), Germany (11 percent), and Ireland (7 percent). Percentages calculated from Table 19, p. 210, in the file named 10612982v3p2ch03.pdf at https://www2.census.gov/prod2/decennial/documents/.

13. Price, "The Afro-American Community," 15.

14. John D'Emilio "Capitalism and Gay Identity," in *Powers of Desire: The Politics of Sexuality*, ed. Ann Snitow, Christine Stansell, and Sharon Thompson (New York: Monthly Review Press, 1983), 101–113, here 105.

15. "Hounded to His Death," *Washington Post*, December 11, 1905; "Rutgers Loses Rich Trustee," *Central New Jersey Home News* (New Brunswick), December 11, 1905; "Itinerant Peddler Living Like a King," *Baltimore Evening Sun*, September 23, 1927.

16. Price, "The Afro-American Community," 50, 63.

17. Kristyn Scorsone, Christina Strasburger, Whitney Strub, and Mi Hyun Yoon, interview with Amina Baraka, March 2, 2018, Queer Newark Oral History Project (QNOHP), 2, https://queer.newark.rutgers.edu/sites/default/files/transcript/2018-03-02%20Amina%20Baraka.pdf.

18. Judith Weisenfeld, "Real True Buds: Celibacy and Same-Sex Desire across the Color Line in Father Divine's Peace Mission Movement," *Devotions and Desires: Histories of Sexuality and Religion in the Twentieth-Century United States*, ed. Gillian Frank, Bethany Moreton, and Heather R. White (Chapel Hill: University of North Carolina Press, 2018), 90–112, here 107.

19. Julio Capó Jr., *Welcome to Fairyland: Queer Miami before 1940* (Chapel Hill: University of North Carolina Press, 2017).

20. Margot Canaday, *The Straight State: Sexuality and Citizenship in Twentieth Century America* (Princeton, NJ: Princeton University Press, 2009).

21. Sears, *Arresting Dress.*

22. *History of the Police Department of Newark* (Newark: The Relief Publication Co., 1893), 392.

23. Log Book of Detective Frank C. Brex, New Jersey Collection, Newark Public Library, 89, 134, 138–139.

24. Log Book of Detective Frank C. Brex, 70. The facts of the case merit recitation: On June 19 a Lieutenant Daly made a complaint against Ross for committing sodomy on Harold Gruber. Ross, however, was immediately "paroled for the grand jury" whereas Gruber was not, perhaps because—as the receptive partner in the alleged sexual encounter—his transgression was deemed more minor. In a bizarre twist, Ross claimed that he was instructed by a Mr. Werkman, a saloonkeeper on Chapel Street, to lie about having committed sodomy on Gruber in exchange for Werkman forgiving $2.50 that Ross owed for clothes sold to him by Werkman. The surviving police record entangles the alleged criminal sexual act between two men with other scenarios—resentment, revenge, extortion, slander—and it is impos-

sible today to discern what actually happened. We can discern, however, the capacity and willingness of Newark police at least occasionally to wield against gay men the criminal code prohibiting same-sex acts.

25. "Lyric Theater, Newark," *Passaic Daily News*, April 24, 1909. On New York theaters as cruising sites, see Chauncey, *Gay New York*, 194–195.

26. "Arrest Man at Theater after Woman Drugged with Needle," *Buffalo Times*, December 5, 1913; "Rare Drug Used, It Is Thought, in Capturing Women," *St. Louis Post-Dispatch*, December 6, 1913.

27. Price, "The Afro-American Community"; Barbara J. Kukla, *Swing City: Newark Nightlife, 1925–50* (Philadelphia: Temple University Press, 1991).

28. Newark Citizens' Committee, *Report on the Social Evil Conditions of Newark, New Jersey, to the People of Newark, 1913–1914*, American Vigilance Association, 111.

29. David Oppenheim, "Newark, N.J.: Investigation Report, D.O.," September 28, 1918, box 25, New Jersey folder, Committee of Fourteen Records, New York Public Library.

30. H. K., "Newark, N.J.," October 5, 1918, p. 4, box 25, New Jersey folder, Committee of Fourteen Records, New York Public Library.

31. Oppenheim, "Newark, N.J.: Investigation Report, D.O.," August 29, 1918, box 25, New Jersey folder.

32. Newark Citizens' Committee, *Report on the Social Evil Conditions of Newark*, 166, 169. The lack of further detail makes it difficult to parse these terse descriptions with precision; the word appears over thirty times in the report and "perversion" from fear of pregnancy could also invoke sex workers who only engaged in oral sex with male patrons. Still, the report's enumeration of "the growing tendencies toward pervert practices, on the part of professional prostitutes" as a "medical question" posed by its findings (119, 121) suggests that it includes lesbians. On the Committee of Fourteen's New York reports, see Chauncey, *Gay New York*, 367.

33. See, for example, Nan Alamilla Boyd, *Wide-Open Town: A History of Queer San Francisco to 1965* (Berkeley: University of California Press, 2005).

34. Newark Citizens' Committee, *Report on the Social Evil Conditions of Newark*, 75.

35. "Jersey Liquor Czar Frowns Upon Female Impersonators at Bar," *Herald-News* (Passaic, NJ), July 27, 1934; "Burnett to War on Female Impersonators," *Daily Record* (Long Branch, NJ), July 28, 1934.

36. "White Press and Crime," *Chicago Defender*, October 17, 1925.

37. "Youth of 20 Kidnapped and Killed Girl; Confesses, Reveals Mary Daly's Body; Also Admits Killing Negro to Get Auto," *New York Times*, September 7, 1925.

38. Estelle B. Freedman, "'Uncontrolled Desires': The Response to the Sexual Psychopath, 1920–1960," *Journal of American History* 74, no. 1 (1987): 83–106; Paula S. Fass, "Making and Remaking an Event: The Leopold and Loeb Case in American Culture," *Journal of American History* 80, no. 3 (December 1993), 919–951.

39. Fass, "Making and Remaking an Event," 924.

40. "Noel's Father Will Fight to Save Son; He Blames Asylum," *New York Times,* September 9, 1925; "Murder Indictment Found against Noel," *New York Times,* September 10, 1925.

41. "Parallel to Franks Case," *Kansas City Times,* September 7, 1925, front page; see also "Brutal Death of Mary Daly Parallels Killing of Bobbie Franks," *New York Daily News,* September 13, 1925.

42. "Evidence Links Insane Boy with Upstate Crimes on Girls; Probe Dual Roles," *New York Daily News,* September 10, 1925.

43. "Noel Murder Trial Demanded by State," *New York Daily News,* September 9, 1925.

44. "State to Probe Freeing of Maniacs by Doctors," *New York Daily News,* September 10, 1925.

45. "Man Who Roomed at Harvard with Insane Slayer Says He Had 'Inferiority Complex,'" *Des Moines Tribune,* September 9, 1925.

46. "Girl Victim's Mother Faints at Noel Trial," *New York Daily News,* November 11, 1925.

47. "Criminal Tendencies Bared in Face Chart of Kidnaper," *New York Daily News,* September 8, 1925.

48. George Britt, "Noel-Daly Murder Spurs Demand for Larger Asylums," *Messenger-Inquirer* (Owensboro, KY), September 10, 1925.

49. Fass, "Making and Remaking an Event," 939.

50. "Strange Actions of Noel Related by Asylum Aides," *Brooklyn Times-Union,* November 12, 1925.

51. "On Trial for Life, Noel Is Apathetic," *New York Times,* November 10, 1925; "Noel's Father Will Fight to Save Son," *New York Times,* September 9, 1925; "Father Will Not Hire Lawyer to Aid Noel," *Washington Post,* October 18, 1925; "High Court Saves Noel from Chair," *New York Times,* May 18, 1926.

52. Daniel Hurewitz, *Bohemian Los Angeles and the Making of Modern Politics* (Berkeley: University of California Press, 2007).

53. William J. Fielding, *All the Lives I Have Lived* (Philadelphia: Dorrance and Co., 1972), 40.

54. Fielding, *All the Lives,* 107.

55. Fielding, *Sanity in Sex* (New York: Dodd, Mead and Co., 1920).

56. Eric Schocket, "Proletarian Paperbacks: The Little Blue Books and Working-Class Culture," *College Literature* 29, no. 4 (Fall 2002): 67–78, here 68, 69.

57. William F. Ryan, "The Biblio-File," review of *All the Lives I Have Lived,* by William J. Fielding, *The Rosslyn Review* 6, no. 8, issue 138 (April 5, 1973). Copy in William John Fielding Papers, Tamiment Library & Robert F. Wagner Labor Archives, New York University.

58. William J. Fielding, *Homo-Sexual Life*, Little Blue Book no. 692 (Girard, KS: Haldeman-Julius Company, 1925), 6.

59. Fielding, *Homo-Sexual Life*, 14.

60. Fielding, *Homo-Sexual Life*, 58.

61. Fielding, *Homo-Sexual Life*, 55.

62. Fielding, *Homo-Sexual Life*, 25.

63. Fielding, *All the Lives*, 151.

64. Citing Hirschfeld, he continued, "The problem is not considered one of morality at all . . . the conditions would seem to indicate that your wife is congenitally predisposed to homosexuality, and therefore it would be hopeless to attempt to create a normal sexual constitution in her case. If by any chance, however, it is an acquired condition, it is of such long standing that it would be extremely difficult to overcome . . . my advice would be to let your wife go her own way, consider her a closed episode, and turn your mind elsewhere. I would recommend a quiet divorce, if possible, without casting any stigma on your wife—as I do not believe it is a moral problem at all—which would leave you free to remarry when you think it desirable." Fielding to James C., December 21, 1923, "Series I. Case Histories," Case C1, box 1, folder 6, Fielding Papers.

65. E.R.B. to Fielding, September 19, 1925, box 1, folder 5, Fielding Papers.

66. Fielding to R. D., August 21, 1926, "Series I," Case B5, box 1, folder 8, Fielding Papers.

67. Fielding, *All the Lives*, 161.

68. Fielding, *All the Lives*, 4.

69. "Tiffany's Sexologist," *The New Yorker*, March 29, 1952, 23–24.

70. Havelock Ellis to Fielding, March 2, 1927, "Series II. Correspondence," box 1, folder 81, Fielding Papers; Fielding, *All the Lives*, 165–166.

71. Amiri Baraka, *The Autobiography of LeRoi Jones* (Chicago: Lawrence Hill, [1984] 1997), 23, 25.

72. Scorsone et al., interview with Amina Baraka, 2, 3.

73. Scorsone et al., interview with Amina Baraka, 3.

74. Whitney Strub, interview with Gail Malmgreen, November 30, 2017, QNOHP, 2, 4–5, 5, 6, https://queer.newark.rutgers.edu/sites/default/files/transcript/2017-11-30%20Gail%20Malmgreen.pdf.

75. Dr. George W. Crane, "The Worry Clinic," *Star-Ledger*, December 15, 1947; also September 26, 1947.

76. "Urges Registration of Sex Perverts," *Paterson News*, March 7, 1950.

CHAPTER 2

The View from Mulberry and Market

Revisiting Newark's Forgotten Gay and Lesbian Nightlife

ANNA LVOVSKY

ALLOW ME TO TAKE YOU on a tour of Mulberry Street in downtown Newark in the spring of 1961. Sprawling out just beside the city's commercial center, between Pennsylvania Station to the east and Newark's proudest shopping district, Broad Street, to the west, Mulberry emerged in the 1950s as a hub of queer life. On this particular day, start heading north from Green Street. Pass Ding Ho, the Chinese restaurant, and on your right is Skip's Bar, a fairly recent fixture where gay men mingle among a larger mixed-gender crowd. Walk another block, past the fire station and the appliance repair shops, and look both ways: to the left, at 153, is Hy and Sol's, where patrons drop in to flirt and banter at late hours, while 146 houses the Hub, around since the early 1950s but waning in popularity with younger cruisers. From there, look right on Edison Place: you should just be able to make out Skippy's Hideaway, a lively bar with a dance floor and a jukebox playing the day's radio hits, catering to queer men and a handful of women. Or head across the intersection to Murphy's Tavern, crowded and inefficiently laid out, with a large canoe-shaped bar taking up the main part of the floor, but still unquestionably the crown jewel of Newark's gay bar scene, drawing tourists and fiercely loyal regulars alike. Another 250 feet and on your right, past Market Street, is Sam and Anne's, a dive bar spilling out across three storefronts, known for the stench of beer that hits you long before you step into the place, where queer men and women, Black and white, can stop in for a cheap drink. Or take a

FIGURES 2.1 AND 2.2. Some of the only known images of midcentury Newark gay bars were captured incidentally by Samuel Berg's systematic photographs of city blocks. Seen here, the Hub bar and Skippy's Hideaway. Samuel Berg Collection, Newark Public Library.

left on Market. About three-quarters down the block is the Four Corners, a massive bar commonly serving over a hundred patrons a night, a steady clientele of gay men among them.

Alternately, you could continue down Mulberry Street to Raymond Boulevard, where, taking a right, you'd find yourself in front of New Jersey's Division of Alcoholic Beverage Control (ABC)—the agency that tried to shut these places down.[1]

Histories of 1960s Newark often evoke visions of white flight and segregation, of urban decay and dwindling opportunity, of police harassment and abuse of Black residents all erupting, in the summer of 1967, in waves of violence and fury in the Central Ward. But Newark in these years was also, less famously, home to a remarkable patchwork of gay and lesbian nightlife, dotted with dives, clubs, and cocktail bars that drew queer, predominantly white crowds from across New Jersey and even nearby Manhattan. Newark's queer bars were places of comfort, of camaraderie, of personal experimentation and sexual possibility. They also waged daily battle against the liquor board, an aggressive agency that would pride itself, in 1966, on making New Jersey "the toughest state in the United States on liquor enforcement." That agency never quite succeeded in quashing Newark's queer life, and today its records offer an ironically vibrant window into that forgotten past.[2]

Drawing on the ABC's administrative files, supplemented by court records, photographs, city directories, and interviews collected by the Queer Newark Oral History Project, this chapter reconstructs Newark's gay and lesbian bar scene from the 1930s through the 1960s. A closer look at the many places where Newark's men and women spent their evenings illuminates the sheer richness of queer nightlife in a small, rapidly diversifying northeastern city, where the steady ebb of white, middle-class families left space not just for growing Black neighborhoods but also for a commercial culture that flouted traditional sexual norms. It offers visibility into the countless small moments and daily encounters—nascent romances and heartbreaks, celebrations, spats, and petty annoyances, reunions among lovers and game nights among friends—of a community often lost to the historical record. It expands our sense of the geography of queer life following World War II, as not necessarily confined to discrete pockets of the city but permeating the broader spaces of urban commerce. Against a backdrop of pervasive regulation, a thriving social world arose, offering a home to queer men and women from Newark and beyond. This is a look back into that world.

Newark's gay bars continued a rich lineage of queer life in the United States. From the turn of the twentieth century onward, in cities like Los Angeles, San Francisco, New York, and Chicago, taverns were among the most reliable sites of queer community, semi-private spaces that nurtured boundary-pushing behaviors that might have drawn more hostility on the streets. Although few records capture such early spaces in Newark itself, the city's saloon culture offered a frequent setting for ostensibly scandalous sexual cultures. A 1914 report produced by the Citizens Committee, a local civic group that investigated urban vice, recounted a range of "evil conditions" including not just prostitution but also interracial mingling, promiscuous working-class dating habits, and gambling—all traceable, in its opinion, to Newark's robust network of bars.[3]

By the early 1930s, that nightlife had unquestionably grown to include a queer element, as a Depression-era craze for "pansy" entertainments—floorshows and cabarets featuring overtly gender-bending performers—introduced urban audiences across the country to the outward traces of sexual difference. The fad originated in New York, and New Jersey critics decrying the phenomenon often presumed their readers' familiarity with Manhattan's biggest stars. But New Jersey residents hardly needed to cross the river to experience such entertainments. By the middle of the decade, the state was home to multiple venues featuring "female impersonators," from glamorous casinos along the Jersey Shore to beer parlors in smaller towns like Keansburg.[4]

With the repeal of Prohibition in 1933, which both legalized alcohol and left its oversight to the state-operated Department (later Division) of Alcoholic Beverage Control, those spaces began to draw more scrutiny. Charged with protecting the public morals, liquor officials looked askance at a range of transgressive behaviors in licensed bars, from racial mixing to gender nonconformity. Not yet a year into his tenure, the ABC's first commissioner, the deeply moralistic D. Frederick Burnett, received a letter from New Jersey's Licensed Beverage Association expressly warning that the "evil" of "female impersonators" would revive the same immoral conditions that led to Prohibition in the first place. Sharing the group's outrage, Burnett drafted a regulation banning bars from hosting "any known . . . prostitutes, female impersonators, or other persons of ill repute," a provision the agency would apply liberally to venues serving "fairies," "fags," and "perverts."[5]

Charges under Burnett's regulation emerged in small cities like Saddle River and Absecon as soon as 1935, though these early cases generally targeted hired performers. The rule's expansion to target gay patrons really began in Newark.[6]

The first major case originated at a tavern run by Peter Orsi at 112 Bank Street, known among locals by the spring of 1939 for its unorthodox crowds. For gay men themselves, visiting Orsi's was not an entirely pleasant experience. Arriving patrons sometimes had to weather jeers from local youths, who gathered by the doors to harass customers. Inside, they faced the disdain of Orsi himself, who claimed, at least, that he never sought his queer patrons and "had been trying to get rid of them" for some time. Still, Orsi's tavern was a lively scene. The night of March 4 found some forty men crowded in the front room, sipping drinks, talking with friends, flirting with strangers. A handful were vividly made up in lipstick, rouge, mascara, and nail polish. In a back room, a piano player—himself dolled up in makeup—provided live music as two couples swayed in the center of the floor.[7]

Confronted by two liquor agents, Orsi wasted no time in pointing out five especially flamboyant men and asking the agents to eject them. But at the hearing, he changed his strategy, denying that he had recognized any queer customers to begin with. Even his most conspicuous patrons, Orsi insisted, might have been actors wearing stage makeup or men covered in talcum powder from a recent shave.

Commissioner Burnett was not persuaded. "Possible—yes! But not at all probable!!" he countered. "I am not at all squeamish in imputing knowledge to a licensee of the character of these persons when anyone can tell objectively and most of us know what they are." Burnett suspended Orsi's operations for thirty days, a relatively modest punishment as they came, but in this case it doomed the bar. Unusually for a first violation, the local liquor board declined to renew Orsi's license. Burnett affirmed the decision, agreeing that venues "where these denizens of Sodom congregate are particularly abhorrent." Desperate, Orsi petitioned the New Jersey Supreme Court, but it summarily dismissed his case. The liquor board's decision to deny a license to a man who welcomed "perverts" at his bar, Justice Charles Wolcott Parker surmised, was simply not "something that concerns the Supreme Court."[8]

Orsi's jousts with the liquor board set the terms of New Jersey's crackdowns on queer bars in the coming decades. Those terms included, first and foremost, the profound moral opprobrium that attached to the ABC's campaigns, vividly on display in Burnett's opinions but also echoed by judges and other commissioners after him. As Burnett's successor would decry in 1941, "the mere thought" of queer patrons at a bar was "repugnant," both because it offended the public morals and because it risked sparking more violent disturbances, encouraging "normal red-blooded m[e]n" to impose a "heavy-fisted penalty." Officials would rely on similar rhetoric to justify charges well into the 1960s.[9]

Those terms also included the assumption that bar owners recognized their queer crowds. Prohibiting licensees from serving "known" female impersonators—revised, in later years, to "apparent homosexuals"—the ABC's campaigns did not primarily target actual gay or lesbian patrons at a bar. They targeted patrons outwardly visible as such, a quirk that invited liquor agents to invoke popular stereotypes about queer bodies to prove that the defendants must have known their patrons for who they were. Ironically, the very liberality of New Jersey's leisure culture during Prohibition laid the groundwork for the state's crackdowns following Repeal, identifying queer bodies as something that all bartenders—and, for that matter, all patrons—had presumably encountered before. That dynamic would make the ABC an unusually prolific agency, filling its docket with charges against bar owners whose crowds departed from conventional gender norms.[10]

Still, Orsi's tavern on Bank Street was just the beginning of queer nightlife in Newark. Not fourteen months after that case wound down, the ABC brought charges against another bar on Central Avenue, where crowds of men embraced, kissed, and danced by the counter.[11] The trail then goes cold for some years, but after World War II, as servicemen and single professionals flocked to the nation's cities, Newark found itself home to burgeoning pockets of queer life. From 1952 through roughly 1967, bars catering to gay men included the Torch on Clinton Avenue, the Four Corners on Market Street, the Polka Club on Springfield Street, the Blue Note on Branford Place, the Promenade on Park Avenue, the Waldorf Cafeteria on Broad Street, Club Coronet on 13th Street, Jack's Star Bar on Tichenor Street, the Bunny Hutch on Verona Avenue, and Skippy's on Edison Place. Mulberry Street emerged as a particular destination, housing Sam and Anne's at 120, Murphy's Tavern at 135, the Hub at 146, Hy and Sol's at 153, and, for a time, Skip's at 204. Lesbian bars were not exactly as pervasive, but queer women, too, had their pick of venues. Alongside frequenting Jack's, the Torch, the Bunny Hutch, Skippy's, and Sam and Anne's, lesbians gathered at the Pelican Bar on Broad Street, Club Delite on Bank Street, and—a little further from downtown—the OK Corral, Latin Quarter, and Club Tequila on Pennington Street. By 1960, Newark was sufficiently well recognized for its queer life that, when Manhattan authorities cracked down on gay bars that spring, New Yorkers began taking the bus to visit Murphy's and Skippy's. In 1961, a prosecutor for the ABC would express some incredulity that anyone living in Newark could claim not to have "seen homosexuals walking around Mulberry Street or Market Street."[12]

The bars themselves were a diverse collection. For one thing, they varied in size, from massive dance spaces like the Four Corners or Skippy's, where the near-exclusively gay crowds swelled as high as 150 people, to smaller venues like Hy and Sol's, where evening numbers ran as low as twenty even on Fridays.[13] They also varied by class. On the one extreme was the Promenade, an upscale bar known for its art deco interior and muted atmosphere, conducive to thoughtful conversation. Not quite as elite though still making some pretensions to middle-class respectability was the immensely popular Murphy's, which catered largely to white-collar workers, salesmen from local department stores (Bamberger's, Hahne's, Kresge's), and journalists from the nearby *Newark Evening News*.

On the other end were dives like Jack's Star Bar, a rowdy watering hole whose customers' antics—entirely aside from any apparent gay men or lesbians—drew multiple charges of obscenity in 1965 alone, or Sam and Anne's, a seedy operation emitting a stench of alcohol, one patron recalled, that "pervaded the whole block." Known for its anything-goes atmosphere, Sam and Anne's embraced a broad slice of Newark street life, from local reporters to aging burlesque stars, to alcoholics and "skid row types" battered by Newark's dwindling fortunes, to gay teenagers grateful for the bar's lax policy on serving minors—as well as, one remembered, for the escape it offered from their classmates' "square" fantasies of suburban barbecues and picket fences.[14]

The bars' racial composition shifted over the 1950s and 1960s, though not quite fast enough to keep pace with Newark's changing demographics. A comparatively small city, Newark was reconfigured after the war by a stream of Black migration and by aggressive patterns of white flight. By the mid-1960s, over half the city's residents were Black, alongside a growing Latino population. In theory, New Jersey banned segregation in 1949, but the reality lagged substantially behind those aspirations, and gay and lesbian bars were no different. At least one bar in the late 1950s, the Blue Note on Branford Place, was known among gay circles for catering specifically to Black men. But between persistent social divides and economic hurdles that limited the spending power of Black residents, many bars, including Murphy's, were essentially white-only through the 1950s. Murphy's expanded in the 1960s to welcome a significant Latino patronage; a small raid in 1965 yielded a roster of names that included a Manuel Fernandez, Carlos Miranda, and Joseph Martinez alongside a Gilbert Caplan and Carmine Marino. But it did not precisely cater to Black crowds.[15]

Larger bars and dive bars could be more hospitable. Jack's, especially popular with lesbians in the mid-1960s, employed a Spanish-speaking bartender on its staff and drew enough Spanish-speaking patrons to post its signs in both English and Spanish. Skippy's was popular primarily with white men but, unlike Murphy's, it routinely welcomed at least some Black customers—as well as, for that matter, women. Sam and Anne's, known for its eclectic clientele, served a steady stream of Black patrons, male and female, gay and straight. Among the bar's regulars in the late 1950s was an older woman named Nell, "a large black woman," a patron named John recalled, who was "like a mother to all the gay black boys," welcoming them to her apartment off Mulberry Street when the bar was closed. A frequent and generous host, Nell threw storied parties, inviting both Black and white gay youth to mingle, drink, dance, and sometimes spark more intimate encounters. But even live-and-let-live Sam and Anne's was hardly a place of reliable racial harmony. Often oblivious to the city's racial tensions, John recalled being shocked by the reactions of other white patrons when he brought two Black friends to visit. One acquaintance "wouldn't come near me," John recounted. "He said, 'I'm ashamed of you.'"[16]

Bars like Murphy's and Skippy's served a largely—sometimes entirely—gay clientele. But the sheer breadth of Newark's queer nightlife also owed to the fact that its boundaries could be surprisingly porous. Hy and Sol's, for instance, welcomed groups of gay men alongside a diverse mixed-gender crowd, more often attracting the ABC's attention for permitting prostitution or employing female hostesses than for serving "apparent homosexuals." Men flocked to Sam and Anne's precisely because they could trust, as John put it, that "nobody gave a shit" about their private lives, sharing the space with a sundry crowd of straight men and women. At Jack's, gay men and lesbians often mingled with other patrons and varied in number over the course of a week. Though butch lesbians and "effeminate" men dominated on Fridays, liquor agents hoping to discover the same crowd on a Saturday found a lone pair of gay men and no lesbians at all. "You are here on the wrong night," the bartender explained. Even bars that drew queer crowds from afar were not always exclusively queer. In the late 1950s, the Pelican Bar prided itself for its popularity with lesbians, including not just local factory workers and saleswomen but also showgirls from New York. But it was not a "lesbian bar" per se, serving queer women alongside—and often deliberately segregating them from—its straight patrons.[17]

As the Pelican Bar's precautions suggested, the prevalence of mixed venues meant that gay men and women's nights out often included flights of casual derision from straight customers and staff. John remembered that nobody at Sam and Anne's "gave a shit" if you were gay, but at least one patron patently did. Spotting two effeminate men in the winter of 1959, he complained to the bartender. Asked by two patrons to move their drinks so they could "get away from the lesbians and fags," a bartender at Club Delite happily complied. "I don't like them myself," he admitted.

Beyond such generic displays of contempt, lesbians faced a more particular hazard: straight men resentful of their sexual unavailability. The bartender at Club Delite, indeed, may have taken particular objection to the women who drank and danced together by the bar. "You can't trap any of the single broads in here with all of these lesbians," he complained. Even bars that welcomed queer patrons sometimes did little to protect them from other customers. At the Latin Quarter in the summer of 1962, one woman had the misfortune of attracting the attention of an older patron named Tony. For several days, Tony tried to persuade her to sleep with him, until finally, facing a series of rejections, he erupted in anger and frustration, cursing the woman and the "perverted" tendencies that allegedly stopped her from requiting his interest. A bartender derided Tony's foolishness in provoking the woman's friends, but he did not ask Tony to leave.[18]

The prevalence of Newark's mixed bars expands our understanding of the geography of queer nightlife following World War II. Historians have commonly portrayed gay and lesbian bars at midcentury as trending toward increasing insularity. Buoyed by an influx of young professionals, by this view, queer communities amassed both the numbers and the economic power to support their own network of bars as havens against the outside world—spaces where queer men and women could be themselves without the judgment of a hostile public. Many bars resisted opening their doors to straight patrons, screening out new arrivals, offering shoddy service, or relying on informal methods of harassment to discourage interlopers from staying inside.[19]

FIGURES 2.3 AND 2.4. Sam and Anne's on Mulberry Street, just visible on the right; a rare image of Murphy's Tavern. Photographer Berg took his shots in the early morning when few people were on the streets. Samuel Berg Collection, Newark Public Library.

In Newark, bars like the Blue Note and Murphy's likely played a similar role. Yet Newark's queer men and women did not constrain themselves to their "own" designated pockets of the city. They staked out a place for themselves within Newark's broader commercial life, routinely entering and occupying spaces that also served straight crowds. The porous geography of Newark's queer nightlife reveals the impressive robustness of the gay and lesbian community by the late 1950s, confident enough not only to walk openly along Mulberry and Market Streets but also to gather with friends in shared public spaces. It illuminates the many overlapping circles of otherness that shaped queer individuals' experiences of the city. From the gay youth who identified with Sam and Anne's rejection of suburban values to the butch women at Jack's Star Bar, who shared drinks and bawdy jokes not just with each other but also with the eponymous Jack himself, gay men and lesbians used Newark's bars to foster a range of relationships grounded in their sense of difference from mainstream social norms. Not least, this pattern suggests the surprising visibility of sexual difference in Newark's leisure culture. Certainly, most of the city's bars featured no obvious queer presence. But the substantial number that did suggests that, whether or not they approved, many straight Newarkers were well aware of their city's queer subcultures, coexisting with those cultures in their own travels through Newark's commercial life.[20]

Even without offering a perfect buffer against the outside world, Newark's bars nurtured a vibrant social scene, inviting patrons to cast off societal and gender norms. At places like Murphy's, Club Tequila, and Jack's, gay men playfully swished their hips, experimented with scare drag, and bandied about camp nicknames and slang. Butch women cursed, downed shots of whiskey, wore their hair in trims and pompadours, and showed off masculine fashions, from rugged cowboy boots and denim jackets to formal suits, dress shirts, and ties.[21]

More than sites of self-expression, of course, bars were essentially social spaces. At the Latin Quarter and Jack's, crowds of women gathered together, squeezing in as many as eight to a table. One evening at Club Delite, a tight-knit trio—Janet, an attendant at a girl's reformatory; Judy, a color chemist; and Dorothy, Judy's roommate ("roommate"?)—dropped in for a nightcap after an evening at the bowling alley. At a short-lived bar on Mulberry Street in 1950, groups of men traded affectionate insults. "You look like you're pregnant," one teased a newcomer about his outfit. "Maybe I am pregnant," the newcomer replied, pulling his shirt out in an approximation of a bulge. "Maybe he"—pointing to another friend—"is the father." After Murphy's Tavern took over the space some years later, its patrons carried on the same traditions, singing along to their favorite songs, whispering secrets into each other's ears, and playing shuffleboard and pinball. When one regular returned after a surgery in 1965, two friends rushed over to embrace him, guiding him back to a larger group where a third offered up a precious seat.[22]

Bars were also romantic spaces. At a time when many expressions of same-sex desire were criminalized and the very possibility of lasting romance derided as a fantasy, bars offered a space for both passionate attractions and deep emotional commitments to flourish and be celebrated. Just a few glimpses of Newark nightlife in the 1960s: Around 1 A.M. at the Latin Quarter, a woman named Mickey, dressed like a greaser with sideburns and rolled-up sleeves, dances the Twist with another woman by the jukebox. At the Club Tequila, several pairs of women sway together on the dance floor, drawing each other close, their hands resting on each other's necks. At Murphy's, a young patron named Carlos, known to his friends as Brenda, pulls in another man by the waist, leaving a trail of kisses on his cheek and neck. Drop in again, and two slightly intoxicated patrons—unusually for Murphy's, one white and one Black—rise from the bar, jostling each other as they fumble to the door. Or, if you catch yourself in the thronging crowd, look up toward the back corner: two patrons, eager for a moment of quiet intimacy, have stretched up their arms and interlaced their fingers just beneath the ceiling, and in that pose they continue their conversation, leaning against the wall and holding hands. Even the ABC's agents could not help acknowledging the tenderness of such scenes. "To me," one observed of two women dancing at the Latin Quarter, "they look like they're really in love."[23]

More than gathering places for lovers, bars were settings for nascent romance: places to take chances, to flirt with strangers, to approach secret crushes. One Friday night at Murphy's, an artist named Jules pulled aside a recent acquaintance to ask if his friend, Ray, were single. "I said it and I'm glad," he insisted to Ray afterward. "It took me three weeks." Another evening, a computer programmer named Jimmy Geddings was sitting alone at the bar when blond, athletic David DeOlden took a seat beside him. A recent transplant from Massachusetts, Jimmy was still getting his bearings in the city. He lived at the local YMCA but, at thirty years old, found the other residents too young for meaningful friendship. In the evenings, he frequented Newark's gay bars, including Murphy's, of course, but also Skippy's, the Hub, and Sam and Anne's. That night, Jimmy and David struck up a conversation that lasted an hour and a half. Their knees brushing beneath the counter, they talked about David's engineering training in Georgia, about water-skiing behind David's uncle's motorboat, about Jimmy's recent trip south sightseeing with his mother. A week later, when Jimmy spotted David again, he immediately waived him over to the bar, where the two continued talking about pedestrian topics—a dreaded dentist's appointment—as well as, eventually, more intimate ones.[24]

And, of course, bars witnessed the collapse of romances. The perennial backdrop of queer social life, bars were places where people sought comfort in the throes of heartbreak, or where once-promising relationships stalled and withered away. At Murphy's, the same night that Jimmy lit up upon recognizing David in the doorway, a patron nearby confided to a friend about a recent breakup. "I don't go out with him anymore. We are incompatible," he explained. And then, after a pause: "It is better this way." At Jack's one evening, two women sitting in a booth began to argue over when to leave, bickering and finally cursing each other in frustration. Another rose and, perhaps drunk, heckled a fellow patron named Dorothy sitting by the bar. The two had used to date before Dorothy broke off the affair, leaving the two suddenly struggling to navigate a once-familiar shared space.[25]

These are the moments that beckon, across half a century, from Newark's queer downtown. Bars were places where queer men and women drank and danced, met one-night stands and celebrated with committed partners, caught up with trusted confidants and made new friends, greeted old friends and bumped into people who frankly annoyed them. They were spaces where patrons shared inside jokes and adopted camp nicknames, reinvented themselves and sought new homes in unfamiliar cities, sang songs, gossiped about new arrivals, drank away heartbreak, were generous, affectionate, and funny but also jealous, angry, impatient, and peevish. Gathered as evidence of the depravity that justified shutting these spaces down, the ABC's own records preserve a vision of queer bars as sites of palpable humanity and emotional richness.

And bars were also, sometimes, sites of terror. However boisterous or self-consciously respectable their crowds, bars that welcomed queer men and women all operated in violation of the liquor codes, and all were vulnerable to surveillance, harassment, and discipline.

Sometimes, the ABC based its charges simply on patrons' unconventional conduct. Such conduct included overt sexual overtures, but mostly it consisted of the sorts of stereotypes that liquor agents claimed all bartenders should have recognized as queer. Evidentiary reports often read like catalogues of gender-nonconforming behaviors, from women who wore pants, spoke in gruff tones, or "drank their beer roughly" to men who "swayed as they moved," raised their pinkies, or simply acted in an overly "friendly" manner.[26]

Some investigators also relied on a more insidious tactic: the deliberate entrapment of unwary patrons. When Jules revealed his crush to Ray at Murphy's Tavern in the spring of 1965, he was not just talking to a new acquaintance. He was speaking to a liquor agent. So was Jimmy Geddings in his two nights of flirtation with the charming, handsome David DeOlden. After the two men finally left Murphy's together on their second night, a pair of agents intercepted them and David revealed his true identity. The investigators led Jimmy back to Murphy's, back past the familiar bar and into a small stock room in the rear, where they demanded his full name and address. Luckily, his employer never learned of the encounter, but within a month Jimmy had declared his brief experiment with Newark over. "I didn't like Newark," he later explained. "I wanted to go home." That fall, he returned briefly to testify on behalf of Murphy's at its hearing, eager "to clear [his] name" of any lingering accusations. Recounting his ill-fated move on the stand—with the once charming, promising David watching him the entire time from across the room—Jimmy painted a picture of such abject, relatable loneliness that, when the ABC's attorney pressed him on his "habit" of talking to strange men at bars, the presiding judge himself objected. "This is getting out of line," he protested. "A man alone in a strange city is glad to talk to anybody, I assume."[27]

Throughout the 1950s and 1960s, bar owners challenged this regime of surveillance. In doing so, they raised a variety of objections, from accusing agents of fabricating evidence to denying that their patrons were truly "homosexuals." Most, however, exploited the particular burden of proof at the heart of the liquor law, insisting that they had no way of knowing which customers were gay. As the owner of Jack's Star Bar protested in 1966, harnessing the medical rhetoric that often trailed discussions of homosexuality in his favor: "Just because a girl wears slacks she is a lesbian? I am no doctor."[28]

A few mounted particularly bold campaigns of resistance. A surprising standby in the lesbian bar scene of the early 1960s was the male, straight Anthony

Faliveno, a former bookmaker, a committed scofflaw, and, by his own admission, a bit of a hothead. For years, Faliveno managed the Latin Quarter, a bar catering largely to lesbians and some gay men. Accused of serving "apparent homosexuals" in 1961, Faliveno denied that he had recognized any lesbians and received a forty-five-day suspension. Six months later, liquor agents confronted him again, and this time Faliveno reacted more aggressively. Breaking away, he made his way briskly through the bar, directing his most vulnerable patrons to disperse, before turning back to confront the investigators. "Show me the lesbians," he challenged. (The ABC's director was unimpressed; he suspended the bar's license for another four months.) Far from learning his lesson, Faliveno soon moved up in the world, leasing the space next door and opening it as Club Tequila, a bar catering, once again, to lesbians. Or, more accurately, to lesbians and liquor agents. The bar attracted so much attention that, in its first week of operation, two investigators dropping in found a pair of colleagues already there. Confronted a third time, Faliveno played innocent. "It's absolutely hard to believe," he insisted, "but I don't know what a lesbian is and I never did." That being the case, the director concluded, "it would seem to be the better part of wisdom that he get out of the tavern business at the earliest possible moment." But Faliveno didn't, at least not voluntarily. In the winter of 1964, Club Tequila attracted another set of charges. Outraged, the director finally revoked Faliveno's license, bringing an end to one proud pocket of Newark's lesbian life.[29]

The city's most protracted battle against the ABC, however, was waged by none other than Murphy's Tavern. A five-minute walk from the ABC's headquarters, Murphy's was a small space, some 20-by-40 feet, with a double-sided bar holding a store of whiskey, chips, and pretzels anchoring the room, and a jukebox, cigarette machine, pinball machine, and shuffleboard table sharing the left wall. Despite its cramped layout, the bar was immensely popular with gay men—a fact that, starting in 1959, would bring it in for multiple encounters with the ABC.[30]

The first stretch of surveillance began on October 24, when a series of visits over seven months—including by Investigator David DeOlden—resulted in two separate charges of serving homosexuals. Murphy's owners fought the accusations up to New Jersey's appellate court, insisting, first, that they could not recognize a patron's sexuality, and second, that the only ones engaging in overt obscenity were agents like DeOlden himself. Among their many witnesses, they called a longtime director of the Newark Athletic Club—a professional connoisseur of manly men—to testify that he found nothing uncommon about men speaking in high voices, walking elegantly, or even reaching for each other's privates. Sometimes, he confided, "I do it myself." Still, the ABC director suspended Murphy's license, and the appellate panel affirmed.[31]

For the next five years, Murphy's never quite left the ABC's sights. In January 1963, it changed hands, passing to new owner Al Hirschorn. That fall, Hirschorn quietly handled a third round of charges, pleading no contest and weathering an additional two-month suspension.[32]

By 1965, the situation had grown more dire. That spring, the ABC brought two more sets of charges, and Hirschorn realized that its patience was at an end. Waging an extensive defense that occupied four days of hearings, he called a parade of witnesses, including multiple bartenders, several patrons, and a psychiatrist who testified, in his expert opinion, that the liquor board's evidence in no way proved the patrons' homosexuality.[33] But the most memorable part of the proceeding was the testimony of a loyal patron named Manuel Fernandez, known to his friends at the bar simply as Man. A thirty-two-year old clerk at a local paper company, Man was a regular at Murphy's, having visited the bar each weekend and, in the warmer months, several times a week for the past two years. On the stand, his testimony was a master class in dry humor and camp, visited mercilessly on the prosecutor and on Hirschorn's attorney alike. Asked if he took notes of the agents' visits: "No, I don't take notes when I go to a bar." Asked whether he changed his hair from time to time: "It's very hard to change a toupee from time to time unless you buy a new one." Asked about the use of the word *kids* as gay slang: "I suggest you say that to my mother, because my mother calls me a kid, but she's not a homosexual." Asked about his conversation with a liquor agent: "I thought [he was] a little strange myself. He kept hopping up and down like a toad." Asked about men raising their pinkies: "My father lifts his pinkie in the air when he drinks"—and "No, I don't find anything peculiar about my father."[34]

Hirschorn had guessed correctly; given the bar's history, the ABC revoked his license. Undeterred, he appealed to the New Jersey Supreme Court, joined now by two other bars from Atlantic City and New Brunswick. Some thirty years ago, that august legal body had rejected Peter Orsi's challenge as "not something that concerns the Supreme Court." But in the intervening decades, a good deal had changed. By the mid-1960s, the California courts had repeatedly affirmed the right of queer men and women to gather peacefully in bars. Sustained criticism of entrapment by gay activists and civil libertarians, often imbedded in broader criticisms of police abuses against marginalized groups, convinced police departments in Washington, DC, and New York to retreat from their undercover tactics. The U.S. Supreme Court's 1965 decision in *Griswold v. Connecticut,* recognizing a right to marital privacy, emboldened legal defenses of consensual sexual acts. And growing media coverage of homosexuality, often informed by interviews with gay men themselves, increasingly recast public understandings of gay life not as an illness or a crime but as a benign subculture.[35]

Against that backdrop, Hirschorn and his co-petitioners doubled down, defending not just their inability to recognize queer patrons but also those patrons' right to gather openly in bars. In November 1967, the New Jersey Supreme Court agreed. Rejecting the ABC's long-standing claims that gay bars threatened either the public morals or the public peace, the court ruled that gay men and lesbians "have the undoubted right to congregate in public" on the same terms available to straight men and women. The ruling effectively halted the ABC's campaigns. In the coming months, the director summarily dismissed a handful of lingering appeals. By the end of 1968, proceedings targeting bars for serving queer customers disappeared from the liquor board's records. Although police surveillance and harassment of New Jersey's queer men and women would continue in other forms for decades to come,[36] the ABC largely removed itself from those operations. And thus, just as the liquor board's antigay campaigns effectively began in Newark, so they, in key part, ended there.[37]

By the time the New Jersey Supreme Court issued its decision, Newark's downtown felt very different than it had in the spring of 1961. Just a few months earlier, in July 1967, much of the city west of Mulberry erupted in flames and gunfire, as long-brewing tensions between Newark's police and its Black citizens spilled over into one of the deadliest conflagrations in a decade of protest. As Newarkers waited for the violence to subside, the governor temporarily closed the city's bars, and soon afterward the city's crumbling economy would shutter many for good. Theaters shut down. Stores grew dilapidated. In 1975, a national survey would remark on Newark's few remaining sites of leisure in all but anointing it the "worst American city."[38]

Many of Newark's gay and lesbian bars followed the same fate, though a few resisted. A bustling venue in its heyday, Skippy's closed before the Supreme Court even heard Murphy's appeal, gone by 1966. The Pelican Bar hung on through 1967, while Hy and Sol's made it to 1969. Jack's provided a home for brawls and bar fights until 1970, while Sam and Anne's perfumed Mulberry Street with beer through 1974. Club Delite lingered into the 1980s. Proud, indefatigable Murphy's relocated and remained a beacon for queer crowds, slowly diversifying in spite of itself, until the early 2000s.[39]

Starting in the late 1970s, Newark's queer bar scene would rebuild—increasingly, reflecting the city's demographics, not as a white-centered commercial destination but as a nexus of local Black and Brown life. Kristyn Scorsone picks up this story in chapter 4, documenting the queer cultural renaissance that blossomed along Halsey Street, in particular, during the city's purported post-1967 decline.

Ironically, however, the very end of the ABC's campaigns makes the early history of these bars hard to reconstruct. Individuals from those days are hard to locate. Few remember details of particular bars, or necessarily visited them at the time. The strange legacy of the ABC's charges is that we have far richer records of Newark's white queer culture in the years when gay bars were illegal than of the more diverse spaces that emerged afterward.

In 2021, New Jersey made a different kind of history: That summer, it became the first state in the nation to apologize for its crackdowns against gay bars. "We cannot simply ignore this history," Attorney General Gurbir Grewal insisted, but must "acknowledge the pain caused by the ABC's past actions."[40] And rightly so. But neither should we forget the vibrant social world that flourished despite the state's best efforts to repress it, and that reminds us, a half-century later, of the complexity and richness of midcentury queer life.

Notes

1. *Skip's Bar v. ABC*, Bulletin 1392, No. 1, 1962, 1–3; *In re Hy and Sol's Bar*, Bulletin 1356, No. 3, 1960; *In re Sol's Tavern*, Bulletin 1587, No. 1, 1964; *In re Hub Bar*, Bulletin 1423, No. 5, 1961; *In re Skippy's Hideaway*, Bulletin 1580, No. 5, 1964; *Murphy's Tavern, Inc. v. Davis*, 70 N.J. Super. 87 (App. Div. 1961), Transcript of Testimony, 24a; Whitney Strub and Kristyn Scorsone, interview with John, August 3, 2016, Queer Newark Oral History Project (QNOHP), 13, 18, 20, 22, 26, https://queer.newark.rutgers.edu/sites/default/files/transcript/2016-08-03%20John%20final%20version%20to%20post.pdf; *In re Anna Siegel*, Bulletin 1293, No. 3, 1959; *In re Anna Siegel*, Bulletin 1493, No. 1, 1962; *In re Four Corners Bar*, Bulletin 1475, No. 3, 1962. My research into the ABC's bulletins and appellate court records on related cases was conducted in the New Jersey State Law Library in Trenton. The bulletins have

since become available online at https://dspace.njstatelib.org/xmlui/handle/10929/51416.

2. Charles Sergis, "State Rated Toughest in Liquor Control," *Hackensack Record*, November 25, 1966, 18. For accounts of social turmoil in Newark, see Kevin Mumford, *Newark: A History of Race, Rights, and Riots in America* (New York: New York University Press, 2007), 98–148; Brad R. Tuttle, *How Newark Became Newark: The Rise, Fall, and Rebirth of an American City* (New Brunswick: Rutgers University Press, 2009), 142–170. Although the term can be anachronistic, for clarity I use *queer*, and sometimes *gay*, as an umbrella category referring to Newark's diverse gay and lesbian bars.

3. On emergent gay nightlife, see Lillian Faderman and Stuart Timmons, *Gay L.A.: A History of Sexual Outlaws, Power Politics, and Lipstick Lesbians* (New York: Basic Books, 2006); Nan Alamilla Boyd, *Wide Open Town: A History of Queer San Francisco to 1965* (Berkeley: University of California Press, 2003); George Chauncey, *Gay New York: Gender, Urban Culture, and the Making of the Gay Male World, 1890–1940* (New York: Basic Books, 1994); Chad Heap, *Slumming: Sexual and Racial Encounters in American Nightlife, 1885–1940* (Chicago: University of Chicago Press, 2009). On Newark, see Tuttle, *How Newark Became Newark*, 90–97; Barbara J. Kulka, *Swing City: Newark Nightlife, 1925–1950* (Philadelphia: Temple University Press, 1991), 4.

4. On the pansy craze, see Chauncey, *Gay New York*; Heap, *Slumming*. For New Jersey, see O. O. McIntyre, "New York Day by Day," *Passaic Daily News*, January 7, 1932, 8; "Burnett Prepares to 'Clamp Down,'" *Asbury Park Press*, July 27, 1934, 1; "'Feminine Men' at Inn Cause Grief to Proprietress," *Vineland Evening Times*, April 26, 1935, 1; "K'Burn Tavern Owners Face Council Hearing," *Matawan Journal*, September 20, 1935, 3; "Liquor War: Second Phase," *Hackensack Record*, December 16, 1935, 5.

5. "New Jersey Loses a Valuable Public Servant," *Red Bank Daily Register*, April 25, 1940, 6; "Liquor War: Second Phase," 5; "Burnett Prepares to 'Clamp Down,'" 1; "Bars—Where Men Are Men and Women Must Be Women," *Camden Morning Post*, July 28, 1934, 1, 11. For the regulation, see *In re Peter Orsi*, Bulletin 326, No. 1, 1939, 2. For terms used interchangeably, see *In re Log Cabin Inn*, Bulletin 279, No. 8, 1938, 11; *McCracken v. Caldwell*, Bulletin 456, No. 3, 1941, 3–5; *In re M. Potter, Inc.*, Bulletin 474, No. 1, 1941, 1–2; *Orsi v. ABC*, Bulletin 352, No. 2, 1939, 3. On concerns over racial mixing, see "Newark Awaits Decision from Beverage Board," *New York Amsterdam News*, April 23, 1938, 7.

6. "'Feminine Men' at Inn Cause Grief," 1; "K'Burn Tavern Owners Face Council Hearing," 3; "Shupack Loses License," *Bergen Evening Record* (Hackensack, NJ), November 13, 1937, 1; "Liquor War: Second Phase," 5.

7. *In re Peter Orsi*, Bulletin 326, 1. An earlier Newark case also mentioned two men identified as a "married" couple within a longer list of offenses. *In re Log Cabin Inn*, Bulletin 279, 10–12.

8. *In re Peter Orsi,* 1–2; *Orsi v. ABC,* Bulletin 352, 3; *Orsi v. D. Frederick Burnett,* Bulletin 359, No. 13, 1939, 11.

9. *In re M. Potter, Inc.*, Bulletin 474, 1 (quoted); Sergis, "State Rated Toughest in Liquor Control," 18.

10. Anna Lvovsky, *Vice Patrol: Cops, Courts, and the Struggle over Urban Gay Life before Stonewall,* chapter 1.

11. *In re M. Potter, Inc.*, Bulletin 474, 1.

12. For these bars and others, see note 1; *In re the Torch,* Bulletin 945, No. 5, 1952; *In re Polka Club,* Bulletin 1045, No. 6, 1955; Strub and Scorsone, interview with John, 18, 23; Dan Russo, *Downtown* (Indiana: iUniverse, 2010), 3–4; Advertisements, "Asst. Managers," *Newark Star-Ledger,* July 20, 1958, 33; *In re Club Coronet,* Bulletin 1123, No. 2, 1956; *In re Jack's Star Bar,* Bulletin 1667, No. 3, 1966; *In re Bunny Hutch,* Bulletin 1722, No. 2, 1967; *In re Pelican Bar,* Bulletin 1242, No. 3, 1958; *In re Club Delite,* Bulletin 1495, No. 6, 1963; *In re OK Corral,* Bulletin 1562, No. 1, 1964; *In re Latin Quarter,* Bulletin 1471, No. 2, 1962; *In re Club Tequila,* Bulletin 1557, No. 1, 1964; Strub and Scorsone, interview with John, 13. Quote is from *Murphy's Tavern, Inc. v. Davis,* Transcript of Testimony, 59a, 145a.

13. *In re Four Corners Bar,* Bulletin 1475, 9; *In re Skippy's Hideaway,* Bulletin, 1580, 12; *In re Hy and Sol's Bar,* Bulletin 1356, 4–6; Strub and Scorsone, interview with John, 26.

14. *In re The Promenade,* Bulletin 1381, No. 8, 1961; Strub and Scorsone, interview with John, 21. *In re Murphy's Tavern,* Bulletin 1677, No. 1, 1966, 4; *Murphy's Tavern, Inc. v. Davis,* Transcript of Testimony, 55a, 65a, 80a. *In re Jack's Star Bar,* Bulletin 1667, 5–6, 9–11. *In re Anna Siegel,* Bulletin 1493, 1–2; Strub and Scorsone, interview with John, 20.

15. For shifting demographics, see Kulka, *Swing City,* 3, 7; Tuttle, *How Newark Became Newark,* 4. On desegregation, see Brian Alnutt, "'Another Victory for the Forces of Democracy': The 1949 New Jersey Civil Rights Act," *Pennsylvania History,* vol. 85 (2018), 363–393; Milton Honig, "Non-Whites Rise 109% in Newark," *New York Times,* April 3, 1959. For spending power, see Tuttle, *How Newark Became Newark,* 154. For bars, see Strub and Scorsone, interview with John, 18, 23. *Murphy's Tavern, Inc. v. Div. of Alcoholic Beverage Control,* Supreme Court of New Jersey, No. 5433 (1967), Appendix, 603a, 644a; *Murphy's Tavern, Inc. v. Davis,* Transcript of Testimony, 117a.

16. *In re Jack's Star Bar,* Bulletin 1667, 10–11; Strub and Scorsone, interview with John, 23, 27; Whitney Strub and Tim Stewart-Winter, interview with John, March 29, 2017, QNOHP, 11, 16, https://queer.newark.rutgers.edu/sites/default/files/transcript/2017-03-29%20John%20interview%202%20final%20to%20post.pdf.

17. For dedicated gay bars, see *In re Hub Bar,* Bulletin 1423, 11; *In re Skippy's Hideaway,* Bulletin 1580, 12; *In re Murphy's Tavern,* Bulletin 1563, No. 4, 1964, 10; *In re Club Coronet,* Bulletin 1123, 3. For mixed crowds, see *Skip's Bar v. ABC,* Bulletin

1392, 2; *In re Hy and Sol's Bar,* Bulletin 1356, 4; *In re Sol's Tavern,* Bulletin 1587, 1–2; *In re Anna Siegel,* Bulletin 1293, 4; *In re Anna Siegel,* Bulletin 1493, 2; Strub and Scorsone, interview with John, 20; *In re Club Delite,* Bulletin 1495, 11–12; *In re Jack's Star Bar,* Bulletin 1667, 5–8; *In re Pelican Bar,* Bulletin 1242, 7.

18. *In re Anna Siegel,* Bulletin 1293, 4. *In re Club Delite,* Bulletin 1495, 10. *In re Latin Quarter, Bulletin,* Bulletin 1471, 4.

19. Lvovsky, *Vice Patrol,* 34–35, 147–48; John D'Emilio, *Sexual Politics, Sexual Communities: The Making of a Homosexual Minority in the United States, 1940–1970* (Chicago: University of Chicago Press, 1983), 32–33; Boyd, *Wide Open Town,* 125–126; David K. Johnson, *The Lavender Scare: The Cold War Persecution of Gays and Lesbians in the Federal Government* (Chicago: University of Chicago Press), 150–151.

20. *In re Snug Harbor Inn,* Bulletin 1161, No. 3, 1957, 6–8; *In re Garden State Club,* Bulletin 1153, No. 1, 1957; *In re Paddock Bar,* Bulletin 1202, No. 5, 1958. *In re Jack's Star Bar,* Bulletin 1667, 9.

21. For gay bars, see *In re One-Thirty-Five Mulberry Corp.,* Bulletin 892, No. 2, 1950, 3–4; *In re Hub Bar,* Bulletin 1423, 11–12; *In re Latin Quarter,* Bulletin 1471, 4; *In re Murphy's Tavern,* Bulletin 1677, 2; *Murphy's Tavern, Inc. v. Davis,* Transcript of Testimony, 26a, 93a. For lesbian bars, see *In re Club Delite,* Bulletin 1495, 9–10; *In re Jack's Star Bar,* Bulletin 1667, 7–8; *In re Latin Quarter,* Bulletin 1471, 3; *In re Club Tequila,* Bulletin 1557, 2–3.

22. *In re Latin Quarter,* Bulletin 1444, No. 3, 1962; *In re Club Delite,* Bulletin 1495, 11; *In re Jack's Star Bar,* Bulletin 1667, 7. *In re One-Thirty-Five Mulberry,* Bulletin 892, 3. The agent's notes appear to substitute "mother" for "father." *In re Murphy's Tavern,* Bulletin 1677, 3; *Murphy's Tavern, Inc. v. Davis,* Transcript of Testimony, 93a; *Murphy's Tavern, Inc. v. Div. of Alcoholic Beverage Control,* Appendix, 519a.

23. *In re Latin Quarter,* Bulletin 1471, 3; *In re Club Tequila,* Bulletin 1557, 2; *In re Club Delite,* Bulletin 1495, 10. *Murphy's Tavern, Inc. v. Div. of Alcoholic Beverage Control,* Appendix, 386a, 117a; *Murphy's Tavern, Inc. v. Div. of Alcoholic Beverage Control,* Brief for Respondent, 5; *In re Latin Quarter,* Bulletin 1471, 4.

24. For Jules, see *In re Murphy's Tavern,* Bulletin 1677, 3; *Murphy's Tavern, Inc. v. Div. of Alcoholic Beverage Control,* Appendix, 378a, 386a–389a, 461a. For Jimmy, see *Murphy's Tavern, Inc. v. Davis,* Transcript of Testimony, 94a–97a; 138a–146a, 150a–151a.

25. *Murphy's Tavern, Inc. v. Davis,* Transcript of Testimony, 106a; *In re Jack's Star Bar,* Bulletin 1667, 7–8.

26. *In re Jack's Star Bar,* Bulletin 1667, 7, 8; *In re Club Tequila,* Bulletin 1557, 2; *Murphy's Tavern, Inc. v. Div. of Alcoholic Beverage Control,* Appendix, 387a; *Murphy's Tavern, Inc. v. Davis,* Transcript of Testimony, 26a, 47a–49a.

27. *In re Murphy's Tavern,* Bulletin 1677, 3. *Murphy's Tavern, Inc. v. Davis,* Transcript of Testimony, 99a–100a, 141a–143a, 146a, 149a. Liquor board hearings were

technically adjudicated by "hearing officers" rather than traditional judges, though their function was roughly analogous.

28. The quote is from *In re Jack's Star Bar,* Bulletin 1667, 9, 12–13. *In re Club Delite,* Bulletin 1495, 11.

29. *In re Latin Quarter,* Bulletin 1444, 6–7; *In re Latin Quarter,* Bulletin 1471, 4–6, 8. *In re Club Tequila,* Bulletin 1557, 1–2, 4, 5–6; *In re Club Tequila,* Bulletin 1570, No. 1, 1964, 1–2.

30. *In re One-Thirty-Five Mulberry,* Bulletin 892, 2. For a description, see *Murphy's Tavern, Inc. v. Davis,* Transcript of Testimony, 24a, 82a; *Murphy's Tavern, Inc. v. Div. of Alcoholic Beverage Control,* Appendix, 445–449a. Size estimates vary, so I've roughly averaged them.

31. *In re Murphy's Tavern,* Bulletin 1374, 5–8; *Murphy's Tavern, Inc. v. Davis,* Brief for Appellant, 2, 7–8. *Murphy's Tavern, Inc. v. Davis,* Transcript of Testimony, 84a–88a. *Murphy's Tavern v. ABC,* Bulletin 1395, June 26, 1961, 13.

32. *In re Murphy's Tavern,* Bulletin 1563, 9–10.

33. *In re Murphy's Tavern,* Bulletin 1677, No. 3, 1961, 4–6; *Murphy's Tavern, Inc. v. Div. of Alcoholic Beverage Control,* Appendix, 484a–582a, 575a.

34. *Murphy's Tavern, Inc. v. Div. of Alcoholic Beverage Control,* Appendix, 486a, 488a, 493a, 495a, 508a, 510a, 514a–515a, 517a.

35. *One Eleven Wines & Liquors, Inc. v. Div. of Alcoholic Beverage Control,* 50 N.J. 329 (1967). Lvovsky, *Vice Patrol,* chapter 1, footnote 47; chapter 6; epilogue.

36. See chapter 10 in this book.

37. *One Eleven Wines & Liquors, Inc. v. Div. of Alcoholic Beverage Control,* 339–342. *In re Jet Set Bar & Lounge,* Bulletin 1776, No. 3, 1967, 5; *In re Val's Bar,* Bulletin 1804, No. 6, 1968, 15; *In re Paddock Inn,* Bulletin 1804, No. 7, 1968, 16.

38. Tuttle, *How Newark Became Newark,* 142–166; Mumford, *Newark,* 215–216; Bobbie Barbee, "Riot or Revolt? Report on Newark Violence," *Jet,* August 1967, 17–18; Arthur M. Louis, "The Worst American City," *Harper's,* January 1975, 67–71, here 71.

39. New Jersey Bell Telephone Directory for Newark for September 1965, 388; September 1966, 382; September 1967, 312; September 1969, 350 (as "Sol's"); September 1970, 181; September 1971, 177; September 1974; September 1975, 303; September 1980, 55. For Murphy's, see *Out Magazine,* June 2003, 126; Beryl Satter, interview with Yvonne Hernandez, May 29, 2014, QNOHP, https://queer.newark.rutgers.edu/interviews/yvonne-hernandez.

40. Office of the New Jersey Attorney General, Attorney General Executive Directive No. 2021-8, June 29, 2021, 3–4.

Oral History Excerpt #1

John

John preferred not to use his last name. One of our oldest interviewees, born in 1938, he grew up in an Irish Catholic family. Here he narrates some of his childhood memories.

NEWARK WAS A GREAT place to grow up. I'm still in touch with a lot of the people I went to grammar school with. We all sort of agree what a great place it was to grow up. One of the great things about Newark—and I'm sure that's still true today—is the easy access to New York, particularly, say, with my family. My family were theatergoers. They were really into going to the theater. You just got on a bus, and went to New York, and there was nothing to it. Of course, we took all of that for granted. We lived in a very rich cultural atmosphere. We assumed that the whole rest of the country was experiencing what we were experiencing. Well, I found out later in life that we actually had been kind of privileged without knowing it. But it was a very good place to grow up. That's what I think.

I was the youngest of five. My mom was a stay-at-home mom. My father was really a mechanic, but he did really a lot of things. North Newark was exclusively white.

As far as the cultural world of Newark, I'd say going downtown was always pretty exciting. Because that's where the movie theaters were. There were neighborhood movie theaters, as well. The first run movie theaters were downtown. It was Loew's State on Broad Street, and then RKO Proctor's, the Paramount, Adams, and the Warner's Branford. They were the big movie palaces. The Paramount was especially—I think we qualified it as a movie palace. But I mean, you didn't go into downtown Newark for theater. Theater was someplace you went to

New York for. If you want to see movies, if you want to do some shopping, or if you just wanted to be in a place where there were a lot of people having a lot of fun, that was downtown Newark, at least in the forties.

Eighth grade was when I started to have a sex life. It was with a classmate. We continued having sex right up to high school graduation. I mean, I don't know whether I was typical. I probably wasn't. I hate to say this, but I didn't think much about it. It felt natural to me. It didn't seem like—I didn't feel I was doing anything wrong. I don't think he did, either. It was part of—I don't know. I think I'm being truthful in saying this, I don't think I made a big thing out of it when I was a teenager. I didn't have a lot of shame or anything.

Believe it or not, it was a great place to be gay, lots of cruising spots. Since the drinking age was twenty-one, a lot of us weren't able to get into the bars until we were older. In the meantime there was plenty of cruising at Penn Station, Central Station on Broad Street, the Globe Theater also on Broad Street, the Penthouse Theater of the RKO Proctors on Market Street, the Bickford Cafeteria on Broad Street near Market, and most sensationally the north end of Branch Brook Park.

Lightly edited for cohesiveness. Listen to or read the whole oral history at https://queer.newark.rutgers.edu/interviews/john.

CHAPTER 3

Toward a Queer Newark Left

Sexuality and Activism in the New Left and Black Power Eras

WHITNEY STRUB

When Raymond Proctor passed away in October 1988, the obituary in the Newark *Star-Ledger* noted his work as director of the Urban Institute at Essex County College. It detailed his earlier accomplishments, including military service in the Korean War and a term as leader of the Newark-Essex branch of CORE, the Congress of Racial Equality. The obituary listed no cause of death.[1]

Nothing about Raymond Proctor's obituary marked him as gay. But a photocopy of it saved in the archival files of the Newark Community Project for People with AIDS carried with it a handwritten note that, during his funeral services, members of his family asked that, "in lieu of flowers or monetary contributions to the family," donations instead be made to the People with AIDS group. Eager to learn more about him, members of the Queer Newark Oral History Project contacted his brother Richard and Richard's three children in 2016, resulting in a rich collective accounting of Raymond's life and death.[2] Without that one stray annotated obituary, thankfully preserved by parties unknown, the memory of Raymond Proctor would likely have remained unconnected to LGBTQ Newark history. While he lived much of his adult life outside of any closet, he did so without necessarily publicly or verbally identifying as gay, posing challenges to historians interested in the intersections of the Black freedom struggle and queer Newark history because he so easily eludes detection. As such, Proctor offers a productive window into the larger history of Newark's left, where for much of the 1960s and beyond activists had a choice of identifying as queer *or* left, but rarely both at once. This story also acts as a useful counterweight to the larger history of heteronormativity in Newark, so often enforced by conservative agents of the state or the church; here, it was often internal sexual regulation that foreclosed openly queer leftism, routing such activists as Raymond Proctor into carefully cultivated situational identities.

This chapter explores Proctor's navigation of the Newark left, along with the travails of white New Leftists Carl Wittman and Carol Glassman, Puerto Rican lesbian feminist Hilda Hidalgo, and others. It also considers the career of the poet and playwright, who later became a Black nationalist and communist, Amiri Baraka, whose notoriously antigay politics of the 1960s and 1970s concealed the queerness of his earlier literary work, arguably the major cultural representation of midcentury queer Newark life. I employ a capacious framework of the liberal-left spectrum to best capture the unwieldy and sometimes inchoate organization of local resistance politics, but with anticapitalism and antiracism as the conjoined gravitational centerpieces of most of the ideological formations at play.[3] Radical politics around race and class in 1960s–1980s Newark rarely also involved radical sexual or gender politics, leaving unresolved contradictions for queer Newark leftists to confront.

At the national level, the early gay rights movement that emerged in the 1950s had deep and complicated roots in the left. Harry Hay, founder of the pioneering Mattachine Society, brought a fiercely leftist consciousness honed within the Communist Party before his expulsion for homosexuality, and much of the early members of the society shared a history in communism, even adopting a secret-cell-based organizing strategy. Even as overt Marxism went underground within the homophile movement as it turned toward patriotism and assimilation, it never wholly vanished from early gay and lesbian politics, reappearing with gay liberation in the 1970s. With roots as much in the antiwar movement against the United States' imperialist intervention in Vietnam as in homophile groups, gay liberationists generally adopted anticapitalist values, and as the Black lesbian, socialist, and feminist Combahee River Collective declared in its influential 1977 statement, "the liberation of all oppressed peoples necessitates the destruction of the political-economic systems of capitalism and imperialism as well as patriarchy."[4]

Meanwhile, though the left shaped the trajectory of queer liberation, LGBTQ members of straight-dominated leftist organizations often struggled for inclusion in frequently hostile spaces. "The traditional Marxist Left," wrote Dennis Altman in 1971, "has been as contemptuous, as disregarding, as oppressive, once given the chance, of homosexuals as anyone else." Historians have begun to document the gaps and fissures that prevented left-heteronormativity from rendering the movement wholly suffocating to queer people, uncovering a rich lineage of queer 1910s anarchists, sexually unconventional and bohemian midcentury Trotskyists, and more. By 1970, Black Panther Party cofounder Huey Newton declared that "maybe a homosexual could be the most revolutionary" among the oppressed, and the first openly gay presidential candidate was David McReynolds of the Socialist Party in 1980. These breakthrough moments, however, remained exceptional and precarious rather than consistent and secure.[5]

In Newark, only the most fleeting glimpse of a pre-1960s queer left currently exists. The city's radical roots run deep; some of the earliest U.S. emissaries of Karl Marx's ideas were German immigrants who settled in Newark in the 1850s.[6] As Peter Savastano and Timothy Stewart-Winter note in chapter 1, before authoring *Homo-Sexual Life* in 1925, William Fielding edited the *Newark Leader*, a socialist newspaper, suggesting some intersection between radical sexual and class politics. But only in Newark's Trotskyist left of the 1940s can we begin to locate a concrete local convergence of leftism and queerness, and barely at that. George Breitman, a straight leader of the Socialist Workers Party, recounted decades later that "I did not know of any prohibition or proscription" against homosexuality in that era, adding, "there were homosexuals there in the membership and the leadership." However, he offered no further detail, confessing, "I never thought about the matter then because no one ever advised me it was of concern to the party," leaving the history tantalizingly elusive. Only in the 1960s does a queer Newark left begin to come into focus, and the activists discussed below all walked a delicate tightrope in finding community within a left that was rarely radical enough to affirm their queerness.[7]

Newark's Queer New Left: CORE and NCUP

The burgeoning radicalism of the 1960s arrived in Newark through a multitude of groups, but the two that most challenged entrenched political power were CORE, the Congress of Racial Equality, and NCUP, the Newark Community Union Project. Both emerged out of multiracial left organizing but were unable to sustain it, and historian Kevin Mumford reads them as a joint reflection of "the limits of interracial activism" in that decade.[8] CORE and NCUP also both briefly had queer leaders in the 1960s, and neither sustained this leadership. In the case of NCUP, gay leader Carl Wittman was driven out, and in CORE, the brevity of Raymond Proctor's chairmanship is less clearly explainable but carries hints of heteronormative anxieties. Proctor, Wittman, and NCUP member Carol Glassman illustrate the challenges for gay and lesbian activists navigating the 1960s Newark left.

Carl Wittman, born in 1943 and raised not far from Newark in suburban northern New Jersey, played a foundational role in the direction taken by the leading campus group of the 1960s New Left, Students for a Democratic Society (SDS). With SDS heavyweight Tom Hayden, he coauthored a 1963 strategy document, "An Interracial Movement of the Poor?" While SDS found its primary base in what Hayden's famous 1962 Port Huron Statement framed as "people of this generation, bred in at least modest comfort, housed now in universities, looking uncomfortably to the world we inherit," Wittman had looked beyond his own idyllic campus at Swarthmore College in southeastern Pennsylvania to organize in nearby Chester, a working-class town where white college students and poor Black residents attempted to forge cross-class and interracial solidarity. From this a strategic vision developed of moving SDS beyond the homogeneity of its university setting and into impoverished and disfranchised communities. "Nothing less than a wholly new organized political presence in the society is needed to break the problems of poverty and racism," Hayden and Wittman argued. SDS's Economic Research and Action Project (ERAP) was launched shortly thereafter.[9]

Wittman and Hayden arrived in Newark in the summer of 1964 to build the local ERAP branch, the Newark Community Union Project. NCUP's ambitious yet faltering program began with employment demands, but its methods centered on listening closely to community members' needs, and a focus on housing justice quickly rose to the forefront. Members helped tenants navigate complicated municipal bureaucracies to assert their rights and fought exploitation by organizing rent strikes and pickets of landlords' suburban homes. While the 1966 documentary *Troublemakers* shows how challenging it was to win even the most modest campaigns for things like a stoplight at a dangerous intersection, NCUP's deep organizing helped empower many local residents to assert themselves politically for the first time, including such future leaders as eventual city councilman Jesse Allen.[10]

Along the way, NCUP lost Carl Wittman. He had been sexually active with men since his early teens, but like most gay leftists of the time, he was not explicitly out at this point, nor did he register as gay to community members while door-knocking and canvassing. Perceptions among his comrades varied; straight NCUPer Norman Fruchter recalled that he "sort of always knew Carl was gay," but fellow gay Newark activist Derek Winans "didn't know it at the time."[11] At NCUP's cramped, makeshift headquarters, where compressed groups sleeping in close proximity raised few eyebrows, he and male companion Vernon Grizzard "were always sleeping in the back of Carl's station wagon" or in sleeping bags together on the floor, Hayden later recalled. Precise details of what followed remain hazy, but at some point Hayden apparently issued an edict against homosexuality. At an NCUP meeting, recounted gay activist Derek Winans (also not yet out at the time), Hayden "made the statement that the presence of any gay people was going to distract from the purpose of the movement," and "therefore anybody involved should leave." Wittman's own later account corroborates this, though in his published memoirs Hayden simply observed that "upon discovering that Carl Wittman was gay . . . I noticed in myself a tendency to withdraw from him."[12]

In a 2014 interview, Hayden offered his most substantive comments on Wittman's departure from NCUP. Noting that he had been personally familiar with gay couples and at the time found them "weird, but not threatening," he also explained, "If you're knocking on doors about poverty, you wouldn't say, 'By the way, we support gay rights,' because no one even knew what gay rights were or they thought it was something obscene." And indeed, during that same era, when NCUP invited Bayard Rustin to Newark for a rally, their opponents posted gay-baiting neighborhood flyers calling attention to Rustin's jail term on a bathroom-cruising morals charge, showing how antigay sentiment could be weaponized against radicals in Newark, just as Mississippi officials during the Freedom Summer of the same moment harnessed homophobia to discredit civil rights organizing. But even by Hayden's account, Wittman was "a very good organizer. He had lot of empathy for people." Losing him undermined NCUP, and for Wittman, the sting lingered. After he publicly came out in 1968, his landmark 1969 essay "A Gay Manifesto" recounted how "some years ago a dignitary of SDS on a community organization project announced at an initial staff meeting that there would be no homosexuality (or dope) on the project." Over time, his bitterness grew, and by 1978, when he wrote about the incident again, he noted that

Hayden's declaration "left me stunned and terrified"—and also displaced him from his own room, as Hayden promptly "proceeded to borrow my room to bed down with his latest woman," calling attention to the hypocrisy of straight promiscuity at a time of antigay repression enacted in the name of NCUP's reputational standing.[13]

Meanwhile, Wittman's time in NCUP coincided precisely with Raymond Proctor's leadership of the Newark-Essex CORE branch. Proctor, born and raised in New Orleans, headed north to New York City at eighteen, following his slightly older brother Richard. They lived with their father in Washington Heights and the Bronx, and both served terms in the army when they were drafted. Richard remembered Ray as rebellious, arguing with their mother as an adolescent and "in constant fights with the authorities" of the army, where he traveled widely to Germany, Morocco, and elsewhere. Returning to the US, the brothers followed their father to New Jersey, where Ray attended Seton Hall University, graduating in 1960 before taking a position as a case worker for the Essex County Welfare Board. Richard also recalled that his charismatic brother dated women in this era. "I remember Ray brought this beautiful girl to visit," he noted; "I thought he was straight."[14]

The Black freedom struggle in Newark dated back to the era of slavery, though by the early twentieth century it took the form of elite-led "patron-client politics," as historian Clement Price details. Desegregation of local hospitals and department stores in the 1930s and 1940s sometimes involved picketing, but movement leaders showed a clear "preference for bourgeois reform," excluding labor, leftists, and militant nationalists.[15] When the national Congress of Racial Equality's Freedom Rides drew widespread attention in spring 1961, it sparked the organization of what became the Newark-Essex CORE branch and a newly militant attitude. Ray and Richard both participated in the group from its earliest moments, and Ray joined Freedom Rides into Maryland. His steadfast work was recognized and he was elected second vice chairman in August 1962, the next year advancing to first vice chair. He threw himself into the cause, getting arrested with six other CORE members for "creating a disturbance by singing too loudly" while protesting segregation at a Newark White Castle restaurant in 1963, when he was twenty-nine years old. Another arrest a few years later resulted from a city hall sit-in. With Richard directing a sustained campaign against major Newark employer New Jersey Bell's discriminatory hiring policies, the Proctor brothers played leading roles in Newark-Essex CORE, alongside founding chairman Robert Curvin. When Curvin stepped down in May 1964, Ray was elected chair.[16]

While Newark's CORE had fought aggressively against racist employment and promotion practices, it was widely (and to a large extent accurately) perceived as a middle-class organization, which undermined its local community standing as Newark's Black bourgeoisie, like their white counterparts, evacuated the city for the suburbs in the 1960s. Ray Proctor strove to bring a radical community spirit to CORE's work. Shortly after taking over, he told the *New York Times* that the construction of Rutgers-Newark's law school was employing an "inadequate" number of Black and Puerto Rican workers and announced plans to picket. Proctor promised the protests would be peaceful but "we consider ourselves free to utilize any methods we see fit if we don't get satisfaction by next weekend."[17]

Recognizing that employment gains had not always benefited the more impoverished residents of Newark's Central Ward, Proctor outlined a new vision in May 1965, which involved intensive weekly free school programs for local children. In order for CORE "to build a more solid base in the Negro community," it was time "to become more identified with the people there." This sounded closer to the kinds of community organizing the controversial NCUP was undertaking (as well as those the Black Panther Party would shortly commence), and indeed, Proctor explicitly defended NCUP's right to protest at a time when many other Newark-based groups held NCUP at arm's length. Until his tenure, CORE had avoided electoral politics, which were often a losing proposition within the deeply entrenched Democratic machine of Essex County, but in 1965 it endorsed the same oppositional United Freedom Ticket that NCUP threw itself into.[18]

And then, as quickly as he took charge, Raymond Proctor departed the Newark-Essex CORE. In May 1965, *Newark News* reported his move to Sweden for graduate study in social work. Reporter Douglas Eldridge observed that Ray was "tired of this grueling pace," but hinted at other causes too. "When Proctor became chairman last May," he wrote, "there was a little uneasiness in the CORE ranks. Some members wondered if anyone who dressed and spoke as meticulously as Proctor could be an effective leader." Describing Ray as a "slim, intense young man," Eldridge found him "sitting in his bachelor apartment." These effeminizing phrasings dripped with insinuation, never moving beyond coded language but resonating with the sorts of description that permeated gay pulp fiction of the era (in Richard Amory's nearly contemporaneous 1966 novel *Song of the Loon*, one man remembers fondly the "dark, lithe body, the intense, darkly handsome face" of a lover). Whether or not CORE members recognized Ray as gay—and Richard did not think they did, though he acknowledged, "if people had negative things to say about him, or about his sexuality, they wouldn't have said it to me"—he clearly deviated from normative hetero-masculinity in ways that caused some implicit discomfort, and possibly experienced more overt pressure left out of the historical record from the unnamed members of the CORE ranks cited by Eldridge.[19]

While the Newark left lost important leaders in Proctor and Wittman, other queer leftists remained and struggled to incorporate both their politics and their identities into their organizing spaces. Carol Glassman of NCUP offers an illustrative example of how the left could at times be more exclusionary than the broader Newark community. Born in Brooklyn in 1942, the middle child of a first-generation Jewish immigrant family, Glassman attended Smith College, where she found her way to the New Left, spending the summer of 1964 in the Philadelphia ERAP branch before arriving in Newark later that year. "Up to that point," she recalled in an oral history, "I was heterosexual." But in NCUP, she met a young Black woman from the neighborhood named Judy. In her own words, she recounted:

> There were a lot of kids in the neighborhood who hung around in our office . . . and there was one young woman, she—really a kid, well, who . . . I don't know how to describe her, she was a little bit of a wild child, and she was what in those days would've been called butch, and she became very attached to me and me to her. And she got arrested, she would—she started to—we had a house where people—an apartment where people just stayed, I mean a lot of kids in the neighborhood would, and I don't remember exactly when Judy started to stay but she did, and when she stayed she would often sleep in bed with me . . . we weren't sexually involved, but there was clearly—but I had no language for it. So, I think she probably did [know she was gay] but I didn't.

Witnessing Judy handcuffed to a radiator after her arrest aroused powerful feelings in Carol, and "I think I started to become a little bit more aware of how attached to her I was at that point, although, again, I don't think I had any language or any words for it exactly." Judy was sentenced to the Clinton Reformatory for Women—"really for nothing, for being black and poor and a little out of control"—and only upon attempting to visit her did Carol have her burgeoning identity named, in a classic example of state interpellation: "I was essentially denied the right to visit her and what I was told was that she was a known lesbian and why would these women have tried to visit her."[20]

Carol's and Judy's developing relationship went unspoken but was recognized within both NCUP and the Clinton Hill community of south Newark. Judy's butch appearance set her apart from normative feminine gender presentations, though not wholly—Glassman described 1960s Newark butch style as involving "pointy men's shoes" and "slickened hair," while Judy fashioned hers in "a bit more of an Afro." The couple found some private space in NCUP's small short-wave radio studio. Not quite settled into a lesbian identity—indeed, decades later Glassman would note with a laugh, "maybe I really *am* the B in LGBT, I don't know"—Carol quickly picked up on the banal everyday homophobia within the movement, as when she was arrested with a group picketing an exploitative grocer and, in the holding cell, one of the other women from the protest made a casual comment about the police matron, "'that bitch' or 'that dyke' or that . . . something or other." The comment came from "somebody I knew and cared about," she recalled, "I can remember my own chill at that."[21]

While nobody in Newark *approved* of the relationship, Glassman encountered varying degrees of soft censure. Terry Jefferson, a Black Newarker who became active with NCUP, "completely got it, and was fine with her but she sort of gave me a little warning that, you know, essentially people were gonna talk and I needed to be a little careful." Tom Hayden, with whom Glassman had an affair that overlapped with her time with Judy, later wrote in his memoir, "When I learned that a woman I'd slept with was lesbian, I was shocked," though Glassman herself noted, "I had no experience of him being cold towards me when he found out." Her most painful encounter came from her white female NCUP roommate, who asked her to move out, being "very explicit that she didn't want people to think that she was a lesbian."[22]

None of this deterred Glassman from remaining active in NCUP. Her community organizing appears in *Troublemakers,* where she helps a Black couple navigate Newark's convoluted bureaucracies, and when the white NCUP contingent relocated to Newark's mostly white Ironbound neighborhood after 1967 on the principle of organizing one's own people, she went along, staying active on the Newark left for several more years before leaving for New York and graduate studies in social work. Wittman and Proctor also stayed active in radical politics, though Wittman's exile from Newark was effectively permanent. He went first to nearby Hoboken, later to San Francisco, where he wrote his pioneering gay liberation manifesto, and ultimately to North Carolina.

Ray Proctor's brother Richard recalls his time in Sweden as a "turning point," during which he eased into his sexuality. He returned wearing flared pants and carried himself with a new self-confidence. Proctor's family recalled slightly different versions of his actual coming out. Richard detailed a dinner with his wife and a few other friends, where Ray "announced that he was gay," but his wife gave their children a variation on the story, in which she eventually asked Ray. "He started laughing," recounted Ray's niece Angela, saying "everyone knows but you!" His nephew Kevin added, "She said he fell on the floor, his feet were kicking up in the air, and he was laughing. 'I can't believe—you're the only one that doesn't know!'"[23]

From that point on, around the late 1960s, Ray was generally quite open about his sexuality. He took his nieces and nephews along on a vacation to Fire Island ("All I remember was there was nothing but men there," said his niece Debra with a laugh),[24] and he took a position at the new Essex County College in Newark teaching sociology and directing its Urban Institute. There, he took militant positions against the administration when they attempted to divert resources toward a suburban branch campus. He was fired in early 1970 along with some other faculty, ostensibly for lacking a master's degree, but students and faculty organized in rebellion with a People's Council, whose ten-point program (clearly modeled on the Black Panther Party's own such document) explicitly demanded his reinstatement. Students called a strike, and Ray was rehired, going on to move the Urban Institute into the community as if picking up where he had left off with CORE, and opening a Third World Community Center on Springfield Avenue, site of much of the worst destruction during the 1967 Newark rebellion, in late 1970. Committed to radically community-based hiring practices, Ray sent job candidates not just through traditional academic interviews, as one participant recalled, but also to interview with a group of welfare mothers whose assessment played a critical role in the decision.[25]

Ray didn't verbally inform his colleagues that he was gay, but he didn't need to. Colleague Steve Block, who considered him "an incredibly fun person to be with," with a great sense of humor and a "huge smile when he was into something," considered Ray "always out"; "there was no attempt to hide who [he was] that I'm aware of."[26]

FIGURE 3.1. Raymond Proctor in the 1970s, courtesy Proctor family.

In the cases of Proctor, Wittman, and Glassman, then, left heteronormativity lacked the power and violence of state-enforced antigay policies or the deeply suffocating impact of religious oppression, but it still hurt queer leftists in various ways. All three still found places on the left, and while Wittman and Hayden never reconciled, Glassman's roommate apologized a half-decade later and they resumed their close friendship for decades to come. Her girlfriend Judy, however, self-medicated with alcohol to cope with the interlocking oppressions of being Black, female, gay, and poor. Without access to the resources that middle-class and white activists often had, Judy had a tragic accident, falling down a set of stairs and dying in young adulthood, a loss that still haunted Glassman many decades later.

Queer Baraka and the Black Power Closet

As Proctor and Wittman were leaving Newark, LeRoi Jones was returning. Under the name he would shortly take, Amiri Baraka, his momentous importance to Newark history could hardly be overstated.[27] Only novelist Philip Roth rivals his stature as Newark's most iconic writer. Baraka played central roles in organizing Black Power politics locally and nationally, including his contributions to the election of Newark's first Black mayor, Kenneth Gibson. Those stories appear in every account of modern Newark. In a far less familiar story, Baraka also served as the foremost midcentury literary scribe of queer Newark through his poems, plays, and novels. As such, his complicated role in radical and queer Newark history requires some attention.

Baraka was born Everett Leroy Jones in Newark in 1934. He attended Rutgers University-Newark and Howard University, joined the Air Force, and was stationed in Puerto Rico, with extensive time to read. Discharged as an undesirable after being anonymously accused of communist sympathies, he fell in with the Greenwich Village bohemian scene, where he quickly emerged as a literary phenomenon, writing a string of plays and poems that won national acclaim (he changed the name Leroy to the more artsy LeRoi here). He was already committed to radical leftist politics, and a trip to Cuba shortly after the revolution in 1959 cemented a commitment to both Third World anticolonial movements and the "ultramasculinist ideology" embodied by Fidel Castro.[28] Married to the white Hettie Cohen, he settled into well-lauded literary stardom, until the assassination of Malcolm X brought him to a racial reckoning. Confronting his Blackness by abandoning his wife and children, he relocated to Harlem, where he played a pivotal role in shaping the emergent Black Arts movement. In late 1965, he returned to Newark, which served as his home base for the rest of his life.

Rarely is Baraka's story told from the perspective of LGBTQ history, and when it is, the vicious homophobia that marked his Black Power years tends to occupy center stage. In that era, Baraka deployed "faggot" as an insult with particular vitriol, notoriously labeling NAACP leader Roy Wilkins "an eternal faggot" in his "Civil Rights Poem" (1966). A chilling open letter to the gay Bayard Rustin in 1971 called him a "nigger traitor" who, "through your sickness, alienated the Black community," and he threatened, "one day, you will even be eliminated." Scholars have attended to this "cruel hostility toward homosexuals," as Daniel Matlin calls it.[29]

Less familiar than Baraka's antigay rhetoric is his personal and literary immersion in queer bohemia before his 1965 shift in politics. In fact, a fascination with homosexuality marked Baraka's youth, as he candidly admitted in a 1970 interview. "It's a subject I have always been very serious about," he explained; "I was always curious about it because there were so many 'fags' in our neighborhood, all the time." Indeed, as Savastano and Stewart-Winter note in chapter 1, Baraka's later recollections offer some of the earliest glimpses of queer Black life in Newark.[30] This makes Baraka a complicated figure, certainly oppressive within the Newark left of the late 1960s and 1970s, but as gay Black critic Ron Simmons put it in a landmark essay, "the tragic irony is that the 'faggot' Baraka attacks so viciously is in reality himself. He has never reconciled his homosexual past [discussed below] with his persona as the clenched-fist black militant."[31]

Baraka's ambivalent, contradictory feelings about homosexuality were on display in his first volume of poetry, *Preface to a Twenty Volume Suicide Note*, published in 1961. In "Hymn for Lanie Poo," the Jones-like narrator scorns his sister's boyfriend for being "a faggot music teacher" (who furthermore "digs Tchaikovsky"). But as Ben Lee notes, the poem also solicits "the poet's adoption of his own queer voice" at one point, as "he sashays toward a hypocritical preacher," which "complicates the force of the epithet 'faggot' in the poem's concluding section."[32]

That same year, Jones and Diane Di Prima launched *Floating Bear*, a mimeographed experimental poetry newsletter. Reflecting the social mores of the Greenwich Village literary community, the second issue carried "four casually gay love poems" by Frank O'Hara, and transgressively queer novelist William Burroughs's work appeared shortly thereafter.[33] The notorious *Naked Lunch* author was upstaged by LeRoi Jones himself, whose short play *The Eighth Ditch Is Drama* erupted in graphic gay sex. Set in a military embankment, its language was so blunt ("I never sucked no cock" one man tells another, before succumbing to his advances) that Jones was arrested in October 1961 and charged with distributing obscenity.[34]

He beat the charges when a federal grand jury declined to indict him, and despite this attempted state persecution, Jones defiantly returned to homosexuality time and again in his early work. His play *The Toilet* (1963) centered on a group of teenage boys mobbing another boy, Karolis, for allegedly sending one of their gang, Foots, a love letter. As the play's agonizing gay-bashing plays out, Karolis insists that "right here in this filthy toilet," Foots had "put [his] hand on me" and said to call him by his real name, Ray. The boys beat Karolis, leaving him battered on the bathroom floor, but after they exit, Ray/Foots returns, and the play ends as he "kneels before the body, weeping and cradling the head in his arms."[35]

Queer themes continued in *The Baptism* (1966), a less searing and more satirical play about three characters simply called a Boy, a Minister, and a Homosexual. The Minister offers predictable fire-and-brimstone bromides, the Boy masturbates while he prays, and the Homosexual is the effective hero of the chaotic play, offering catty commentary ("Quiet, you obnoxious mediocrities!" he hisses at offended churchgoers) and getting the play's final words. Surveying the wreckage left after an explosive, violent catharsis, he quips, "Damn, looks like some really uninteresting kind of orgy went on in here." Unperturbed by moral dilemmas, the Homosexual exits, musing to himself, "think I'll drift on up 42nd Street and cruise Bickford's."[36]

Jones published his first novel, *The System of Dante's Hell*, in 1965. Queer imagery saturates the book, with a visit to "the fag's house," an acquaintance with a "faggot brother who is probably sucking a cock right this moment," and a "closet queen" in Newark, among numerous other allusions. Written in brittle modernist prose, the book's fractured narrative models Jones's own, from Newark to the Air Force and beyond. Deliberately grotesque set pieces include the violent misogyny of an attempted rape (in which the Jones-like character and his friends pick up a desperate, destitute woman in their car) and homosexuality, creating a hellish Dantean vision. The narrator recounts his travels: "In Chicago I kept making the queer scene. Under the 'El' with a preacher." He calls himself Stephen Dedalus when meeting men (James Joyce's personal avatar in his novels, to which *The System of Dante's Hell* is heavily indebted). He keeps a journal, wondering, "Am I like that?" and says of one man, "He loved me because he knew I'd sucked his cousin off."[37]

These currents of queerness and dystopian heterosexuality collide in a climactic scene in which the protagonist encounters Peaches, a female prostitute in

Shreveport, Louisiana, while he is stationed in the South. As he fails to perform sexually, Peaches taunts him, asking of the Air Force, "they let fairies in there now?" He wants to tell her, "I can't think. I'm sick. I've been fucked in the ass." Instead, the scene extends to cartoonish desperation, until finally, as she shouts, "Fuck me, you lousy fag," he thinks back to "a black man under the el who took me home in the cold" and completes the act. The novel ends with the narrator beaten up by some local men.[38]

The System of Dante's Hell presented a daunting challenge to critics, who largely sidestepped its extensive engagement with homosexuality. The *New York Times*, for instance, called it "fragmentary, allusive, private," but never explained what that entailed.[39] One thing seemed clear, though: Jones affirmed an interpretation of his work as autobiographical. *The Toilet* "came so much out of my memory, so exact," he said in a 1964 interview, and the next year a *Los Angeles Times* profile described *The System of Dante's Hell* as "drawn from his own adolescence."[40] But his reflexive engagement with queerness remained largely unresolved and unremarked upon, aside from occasional homophobic dismissals, as when the *New York Herald Tribune* called a staged version of *Eighth Ditch* a "crude, distressingly vulgar segment of sodomistic vainglory" or another critic labeled *The Toilet* "a barely stageable homosexual fantasy." Police also busted stagings of Jones's plays in Los Angeles and Detroit.[41]

The overtly autobiographical nature of Jones's work raises questions about his actual sexual practices, to which there are few concrete but several suggestive answers. Certainly he was highly sexually active with women, including his wife Hettie Jones, collaborator Diane Di Prima (with whom he had a child), and many others. Ishmael Reed, who carried on a decades-long combative friendship with Baraka, recalled that his then-girlfriend Vashti "told me she was stunned by the revelations about Amiri's gay past" when she read *Dante's Hell*, clearly taking it literally. Hettie Jones wrote that "he'd once confessed to me some homosexual feelings, though never any specific experiences." Perhaps more revealingly, poet Allen Ginsberg's lover Peter Orlovsky wrote to him in 1963, "I hope Leroy is happey and alright. Sorrey I dident make love with him when he wanted me to."[42]

All of this put LeRoi Jones at the forefront of queer Newark cultural representation. While queer characters graced the margins of Nathan Heard's pulpy Newark novel *Howard Street* (1968), only Jones wrote sustained depictions of queer Newark life, often in granular geographic detail. *The System of Dante's Hell* was rife with Newark locations, and in *The Eighth Ditch*, one of the soldiers lives on Morton Street. Even his interracial heterosexual psychodrama *The Slave* (1964) pauses for a *Toilet*-like memory when lead character Walker reflects about "when we used to chase that kind of frail little sissy-punk down Raymond Boulevard"—a knowingly precise detail, since one narrator of 1950s downtown life for the Queer Newark Oral History Project described gay in-jokes calling the street "Miss Raymond" and "the Road to Ruin" for its centrality to Newark cruising.[43]

The tone regarding queerness in Jones's work was ambivalent at best, but this resonated with other queer authors of the moment. In addition to publishing O'Hara and Burroughs, Jones edited and befriended poet Allen Ginsberg, included John Rechy in a 1963 collection, and drew on French writer Jean Genet in his plays. Aside from Ginsberg's often effusive celebrations of gayness, most of these authors also dwelt in complicated affective spaces; Rechy's landmark hustling novel *City of Night* (1963), for instance, framed homosexuality as part of an alienated and often exploitative social world.

As such, Jones's racial reckoning of 1965—as he moved to Harlem and then Newark and helped conceptualize the Black Arts movement—was as much a sexual transformation as a racial one, in which homosexuality went from serving as a complex site of both disgust and desire to one laden with crude racialized tropes. His 1965 essay "American Sexual Reference: Black Male" laid out the new terms, opening with the assertion, "Most American white men are trained to be fags."[44] From this point on, "faggotry" served as a marker of white decadence or failed Black masculinity. Once dispossessed of layered meaning, it became a blunt tool of weaponized homophobia, which is how he deployed it in Newark throughout the late 1960s and 1970s.

Rechristening himself Amiri Baraka in 1968, Jones played an outsized role in Newark Black Power politics. By no means the only participant committed to antigay positions, his leading intellectual role as both organizer and theorist nonetheless meant that he acted as a central enforcer of an intensifying queer-bashing regime in Newark left politics. As later recounted by his wife Amina Baraka, this hurt his friendships with gay writers James Baldwin and Allen Ginsberg. It also left no space for queer leftists in the Black Power nexus—which by 1970 was *the* primary framework for radical politics in Newark. Asked whether there were gay or lesbian members of United Brothers or Committee for a Unified Newark, two Baraka-led organizations, Amina recounted, "I don't know because they were so homophobic and sexist." When the Black lesbian, feminist, and socialist Combahee River Collective cited an example of regressive gender politics in their influential 1977 statement, it came from a pamphlet written by the women in the Baraka-led Committee for a Unified Newark.[45]

Only with the rise of Black gay studies in the 1990s, such as Ron Simmons's aforementioned "Some Thoughts on the Challenges Facing Black Gay Intellectuals," did questions about Baraka's own suppressed queer affinities receive serious attention. After reading *Dante's Hell,* Simmons wrote that "one's anger toward Baraka's homophobia is replaced with sympathy." Indeed, to this day the question of queer *desire,* so evident within Baraka's early work, remains almost wholly absent from the enormous literature generated about him, with the few exceptions coming from what became known as queer of color critique, such as Marlon B. Ross's analysis of the "queer resources of Black nationalist invective" and José Esteban Muñoz's locating of utopian queer futurity in *The Toilet.*[46]

In Newark, this overwhelming framework left little space for contestation. Perhaps the only public challenge to the pervasive antigay attitude of Black Power politics came from a short "Commentary on Being a Black Lesbian," published by Marie Teresa in the debut summer 1972 newsletter of the newly formed Gay Activists Alliance of Essex and Union Counties. In three brief paragraphs, Teresa detailed her oppression as a Black person at the hands of white supremacy, but then specified her gendered oppression within Black society, as Black women were "burdened with the responsibilities of reproducing armies of black children." Within this framework of women as babymakers, Teresa argued that lesbianism was "regarded not only as a deviation, and a 'sick' behavior needing to be changed, but as a traitorship needing to be wiped out in order to save the pride of the Black Race." Indeed, she was echoing Baraka's own language. While the essay is short, it stands out as a rare queer refutation of what scholar Zenzele Isoke later termed the "Black heteropatriarchal politics" that came to dominate Newark.[47]

For queer-oriented Black Newark activists of this era, the safest option seemed to be the closet. Documenting Newark's Black Power closet remains challenging, but Frank Hutchins allows us one glimpse. Originally from Philadelphia's Germantown, Hutchins came to Newark via Morristown, New Jersey, in the early 1960s. Connecting with Black political organizing, he joined the campaign for Kenneth Gibson, Newark's first Black mayor, who was elected in 1970. Hutchins worked for Gibson briefly, though his "ideas were considerably to the left of Gibson's," white fellow organizer Bob Cartwright recalled. Hutchins played a leading role in advancing Newark's first rent control laws in 1972, but after falling out of favor with the mayor, Hutchins joined the radical nexus around Baraka. He spoke at a 1973 Afrikan Liberation Day rally that also included Baraka, and that year he ran in a failed bid for the New Jersey State Assembly on the Black "Unity Movement" ticket, promoted in Baraka's newspaper *Black New Ark*. Later, Hutchins found his calling as a tenants-rights organizer, becoming director of the Greater Newark Housing and Urban Development (HUD) Tenants Coalition. When tenants won a city council vote against a proposed sewer surcharge that would be passed on to renters in late 1983, Hutchins delivered the victory address, condemning the austerity policies of then federally dominant Reaganomics and demanding that "rich corporations and property owners" pay their fair share. He continued this work into the twenty-first century, and passed away in 2009.[48]

Throughout his years of political work, Hutchins kept his personal life private. He sang in the choir of his Baptist church, sometimes a queer-coded activity but hardly definitively so, and when he was interviewed in 1998 for a local African American oral history project and asked his marital status, he simply stated, "I'm single," with a slight chuckle that frequently accompanied his speech.[49] Most other activists left it at that—with one exception. Bob Cartwright, a straight white man who had worked under Raymond Proctor at Essex County College and recalled his sexuality as something that went both understood and unverbalized, said of gay Newarkers on the left, "Frank is the one that we actually did speak about." The issue arose out of a protracted effort to forge a citywide coalition of community organizers. Hutchins was already leading tenants-rights work, and as such he joined the coalition's board. But as Cartwright explained, around 1982,

> Frank was on the board. We also were able to get volunteers from various organizations . . . the Jesuit Volunteers, and there were a couple of other similar things at that time. At one point, it became an issue that Frank was sleeping with two of the young men who had come in through one of those volunteer programs. Given the fact that it had been difficult to include Newark Tenants Organization in the Newark Coalition for Neighborhoods, it just provided fuel that people could use. Now, the way things turned out, we were able to defuse it. It [didn't] become an issue. It's one of the few times that I can recall that we actually talked about a person's sexual preferences with regard to the political work that we were

> doing. At that time, gay rights was not on the table for us. There were these other issues involving neighborhood stuff, and environmental issues, and taxes and whatnot. Gay rights was not one of them. . . . It was a distraction, and it was a distraction that could be used against Frank and the Newark Tenants Organization.[50]

The logic here was the same as that Tom Hayden had used: an apprehension about homosexuality, which was rooted in anxiety about community reaction and which placed the onus of antigay sentiment on the broader Newark community but also acknowledged the harsh realpolitik that such sentiment was indeed widespread. It was a move undertaken well beyond Newark, as when Martin Luther King Jr. distanced himself from Bayard Rustin on similar grounds in the early 1960s. And indeed, Cartwright also recalled an activist with the Ironbound Committee Against Toxic Wastes who left the organization after coming out in the 1980s—not due to homophobia within the group but out of an expressed concern that his gay identity would be weaponized against the cause by the local political establishment.[51]

In Frank Hutchins's case, though, the issue was resolved in his favor through a strategic silence that was also his own preferred approach. The sex crisis was not so much resolved as buried, and Hutchins went on to decades of committed tenants-rights activism, his sexuality held in perpetual abeyance but not invisible, just unmentioned. And yet, like the Brazilian immigrant men examined by Yamil Avivi in chapter 9, the notion of the closet proves less useful than Carlos Ulises Decena's conceptualization of "tacit subjects," for whom sexuality is "something present yet not remarked upon, something understood yet not stated, something intuited yet uncertain, something known yet not broached by either person in a given exchange."[52]

Richard Cammarieri, a straight longtime housing organizer in Newark, confirmed this. Fondly recalling Hutchins as a friend and comrade, he "never considered Frank closeted," as he "never seemed to be hiding anything." In years of working together, they never explicitly discussed Hutchins's sexuality. But in the 1980s Hutchins comfortably invited Cammarieri and others to Murphy's, Newark's storied gay bar, where he was clearly known as a regular, and Cammarieri visited his Weequahic apartment and met a younger man introduced as Hutchins's nephew. "Most of us either assumed or knew he was gay," Cammarieri said. The version of Black Power politics that governed Newark in the 1970s and 1980s prevented Frank Hutchins and others from living openly gay lives to some degree—but the metaphor of the closet ultimately fails to capture the nuances of the tacit queerness he and others on the Newark left carefully cultivated. It was a suffocating form of sexual policing, one that obscured the historical record but could not, in the end, snuff out queer life on the Newark left.[53]

Hilda Hidalgo and the Place of Puerto Rican Lesbian Feminism

No figure better embodies the delicate negotiations with public visibility required of LGBTQ Newark leftists than Hilda Hidalgo. As a pioneering Puerto Rican lesbian feminist, she contributed to each of those categories both holistically and separately, mastering the art of situational identity when expressing her full intersectional identity seemed strategically unsound. Hidalgo was in a committed relationship with her partner Joan McEniry from the mid-1960s until McEniry's death from cancer in 1995 and out as a lesbian from the mid-1970s onward. She tended to emphasize her lesbian identity in national women's studies and social work scholarly communities, while in Newark her public image hewed closer to a Puerto Rican ethnic identity, with her sexual identity left somewhat suspended. Far from any sort of closet, this approach instead showed a savvy understanding of the survival strategies required of queer Newark leftists.

Hidalgo's political and career accomplishments were prodigious, as even a paragraph summary indicates. Born in Río Piedras, Puerto Rico, in 1928, she graduated high school early and joined a convent, spending eleven years in Philadelphia and on a mission in Puerto Rico before leaving to earn her bachelor's degree at the University of Puerto Rico in 1957. Hidalgo then found employment at the Girl Scouts of America. Her drive and intellect won her a scholarship to Catholic University in Washington, DC, for a master's degree in education, and the Scouts then appointed her district director of Greater Essex County in New Jersey, bringing her to Newark in 1960. While she headed up to Smith College in Massachusetts for a master's degree in social work in 1968 and joined the faculty of the Department of Urban Planning and Community Development at Rutgers University's Livingston College in 1969, her political home was Newark, where she cofounded ASIPRA, Inc., La Casa de Don Pedro, the United Community Corporation, and other community organizations.[54]

While pragmatic about organizing for power, Hidalgo was unambiguously on the Newark left. By 1965, she was already frustrated enough with the local Democratic machine to join the United Freedom Ticket that was endorsed by both CORE and NCUP (she ran for county freeholder on a platform for a $2/hour minimum wage, affordable housing, and the building of the community college that would later employ Ray Proctor). She chaired the first Puerto Rican convention in New Jersey and served on the planning committee and as secretary of the 1969 Newark Black and Puerto Rican Convention, the latter of which helped forge some of the coalitional bonds needed to elect Ken Gibson in 1970. Apparently in response to her outspoken work, she received threatening calls, and her car was firebombed outside her home in North Newark in October 1969.[55]

Once ensconced in academia, Hidalgo wrote extensively, and *The Puerto Ricans in Newark, N.J.*, a 1971 booklet that grew out of her course on Puerto Rican lifestyles and the American experience, offered the most thorough examination of Puerto Rican Newark undertaken at the time, rife with data and analysis of the community, most of whose members had resided in Newark for over five years but remained politically alienated, more likely to vote in elections back on the island than locally. Reflecting the frustrations Puerto Rican Newarkers felt as the Black Power politics they had helped build largely ignored them once installed, the report contended they would no longer serve as "an invisible minority that can be 'taken care of' by attaching them to programmatic interventions designed for 'Blacks' or [the] 'Spanish-speaking.'" These were sentiments Hidalgo also expressed in a blunt letter to Mayor Gibson the next year after she and others were "maltreated and physically attacked by your personnel staff" after a meeting in his office. While *The Puerto Ricans in Newark* included a brief discussion of "sex roles," it did not challenge the prevailing heteronormativity of its moment—though Hidalgo offered a tacit queer nod in her acknowledgment, "To my friend Joan L. McEniry I owe a great debt of gratitude for her expert and generous editorial aid."[56]

During this era, Hidalgo navigated lesbian visibility carefully. Carol Glassman met her through NCUP's involvement in the 1965 United Freedom campaign but only gradually "would start to run into her in gay things" in New York. She recalled crossing paths with Hidalgo at the New York lesbian bar the Duchess ("or at some tea party") to their mutual surprise—anticipating Hidalgo's coming out in the 1970s, which would always remain more visible outside of Newark.[57]

Vote The United Freedom Ticket Nov. 2, 1965

HILDA HIDALGO

- FOR A $2.00 AN HOUR MINIMUM WAGE
- FOR JOBS AND APPOINTMENTS OPEN TO ALL CITIZENS
- FOR GOOD HOUSING AT REASONABLE RENTS
- FOR A COMMUNITY COLLEGE NOW
- FOR VOCATIONAL SCHOOLS THAT WILL TRAIN YOUTH FOR TODAY'S JOBS

GET ACTION!

Elect **HILDA HIDALGO**

Freeholder of Essex County

 11

FIGURES 3.2 AND 3.3. Hilda Hidalgo campaign flyer, 1965 United Freedom Ticket; Hidalgo and partner Joan McEniry, July 1994. Courtesy Puerto Rican Community Archives, New Jersey Hispanic Research & Information Center, Newark Public Library.

After coming out, Hidalgo ventured into queer Puerto Rican sexuality more openly. Her landmark article (cowritten with her straight sister Elia Hidalgo Christensen) "The Puerto Rican Lesbian and the Puerto Rican Community" appeared in an early issue of *The Journal of Homosexuality* in 1976. Declaring the existing literature on Puerto Rican lesbians "nonexistent," it was based on sixty-one interviews about the attitudes of women from the community, as well as of a larger sample of straight Puerto Ricans. The article found that, while young women were coming out in greater numbers and their families frequently offered "silent tolerance," they also found a disconnect between their community and the white-dominated gay and lesbian movement.[58]

Hidalgo's work put her at the forefront of what was then self-described as Third World lesbian feminism, and indeed, in a 1980 talk on "Third World Lesbians: Organizing at the National Level to Combat Oppression," she delivered what would become known as intersectional analysis, critiquing the women's and gay and lesbian movements for their whiteness while also noting that queer women of color faced oppression in their home communities, even as socialists primarily concerned with class were eager to downplay the emerging homophobia of the Republican New Right. Very much engaged with the work of Audre Lorde, the Combahee River Collective, and other contemporaries, she brought impassioned critique and organizing to the field of social work in particular. At the 1982 National Association of Social Workers (NASW) Conference on Gay/Lesbian Issues, she lambasted by name various NASW members who had engaged in antigay rhetoric and actions, and her success in fostering more inclusive practices was recognized in a 1985 Distinguished Service Award from the NASW's National Committee on Gay and Lesbian Issues.[59]

She went on to publish work in several pioneering Latina lesbian collections, culminating in her edited 1995 book *Lesbians of Color: Social and Human Services,* which used standpoint epistemology (basically, the argument that one's analysis and knowledge are heavily determined by one's positionality) to demand a more attentive and intersectional professional praxis in social work. This time, the dedication was not coded: "for thirty-five years you have been my loving companion, and our relationship has helped me to be a better person," she wrote to McEniry.[60]

As a pioneer in Puerto Rican lesbian scholarship, cited regularly into the twenty-first century, Hidalgo was by no means closeted.[61] Yet her work frequently observed the professional costs out Puerto Rican women paid; in her

1976 article she noted that the interview sample included twelve "prominent Puerto Rican women" who did not wish to put their names on the record and "expressed great fear that their leadership position vis-à-vis the Puerto Rican community would be jeopardized if their sexual orientation and preference were discovered." Two decades later, *Lesbians of Color* began with essentially the same observation.[62] In Newark, Hidalgo seems to have made a similar calculation. While she was certainly out, she rarely highlighted queer or lesbian issues within Newark. The same year she won an award for her lesbian organizing at the national level within NASW, Hidalgo and McEniry coedited the collection *Hispanic Temas: A Contribution to the Knowledge Bank of the Hispanic Community,* published by the Rutgers-Newark Puerto Rican Studies Program. Nowhere did the book acknowledge their relationship or queer sexuality; essays dealt with single mothers and abortion, among other topics. Hidalgo's own essay "The Puerto Rican Family in the U.S.A." covered gender roles within the traditional patriarchal family; she did not cite her own work on Puerto Rican lesbians. When she was chosen as New Jersey's representative for *Ladies Home Journal*'s "50 American Heroines" in 1984, the article highlighted her contributions to Hispanic social work but said nothing of her lesbianism.[63]

Hidalgo's personal papers, left to the Puerto Rican Community Archives at the Newark Public Library, shed more light on her political work than her personal life. But they sustain the impression that her Newark-facing identity differed in emphasis from her national academic profile, as a Puerto Rican voice with some of its intersectional layers downplayed. After the Los Angeles riots of 1992, she appeared on a New Jersey News television panel of community leaders alongside former and current mayors Gibson and Sharpe James, where she contended that Newark hadn't changed that much since 1967 and rued the "growing Hispanic community who still remains unrepresented."[64] Her continued radicalism was fully on display in 1993 when she was arrested after refusing to leave the Morton Street School while inspecting it for the state education commission (she was later acquitted on all charges).[65] But like the Puerto Rican lesbians she alluded to in her scholarly work, Hidalgo apparently assessed Newark as a place where pushing for LGBTQ rights might work to the detriment of her concurrent struggle for Puerto Rican and women's rights. The different ways in which she represented her identity were a choice forced on her by the failure of the broader multiracial left to foster a space for more intersectionally informed queer demands.

Epilogue

When sustained LGBTQ activism in Newark emerged in the aftermath of Sakia Gunn's murder in 2003, its base was not radical or leftist groups but rather the queer-friendly Liberation in Truth Church (today Unity Fellowship Church). The historical hostility of the Newark left to openly queer participants helped secure that trajectory, and also made the presence of queer leftists less visible, often forcing them to choose between queer and left identities within movement spaces.

Among the main characters of this chapter, the parallels between Raymond Proctor's and Carl Wittman's trajectories continued beyond their overlapping time in the Newark left. Wittman, alienated by the hostile environments of NCUP and SDS, first went to Hoboken and Jersey City, where he simultaneously came out and married his female companion Mimi Feingold. Soon he relocated to San Francisco, where he risked jail time as a draft-resistance organizer and helped spearhead gay liberation, while at times supporting himself through sex work. In Oregon and later North Carolina, he spurred rural queer organizing and LGBTQ health resistance to the medical establishment. Proctor also pursued alternative forms of knowledge. After leaving Essex County College, his jobs included a stint as business manager at New York City's Studio 54, and he immersed himself in theosophy, numerology, and other spiritual paradigms. The tragic final parallel came in the form of the AIDS epidemic. As noted, it took Proctor's life in 1988. His nephew Kevin helped shave him when he grew too weak, and remembered his heartbreaking attempts at denial as he would repeat, "I don't have AIDS. I don't have AIDS." Carl Wittman died two years earlier, committing medical suicide as his body gave out from AIDS, surrounded by friends and departing after a listening to Bach's Goldberg Variations with his lover Allan Troxler.[66]

Meanwhile, as white NCUP members regrouped in the Ironbound neighborhood, Carol Glassman and Derek Winans played important roles in forging what eventually emerged as the long-standing Ironbound Community Corporation, whose ongoing work in the twenty-first century on environmental justice, immigrant rights, and other issues therefore has roots in the queer Newark left. Glassman wrote extensively, including a chapter in the landmark 1970 feminist anthology *Sisterhood is Powerful* and a dissertation about gay couples coping with AIDS (completed in 1991 for a doctorate in social work from Columbia

University). She remained engaged with left politics through the Trump era, cosigning a 2020 open letter in *The Nation* from the "Old New Left" calling on the "New New Left" of the Democratic Socialists of America to support the presidential campaign of Joe Biden.[67]

By that point, Amiri Baraka was gone, having passed away in 2014. Baraka was always a dynamic thinker, re-evaluating his anti-Semitism, anti-feminism, and homophobia, albeit slowly. By 1981, he acknowledged that his use of "faggot" "does come from the denigration of homosexuals, and I think that, as I said, gratuitous attacks on homosexuals have to be opposed," though he still added that "homosexuality is a social aberration . . . a product of a class society." He also didn't "want the child to *be* a homosexual"—a view he learned to renounce when his daughter Shani turned out to be a lesbian. In a horrifying turn, Shani Baraka and her partner Rayshon Holmes were murdered in 2003 by the estranged husband of another of Baraka's daughters. In the wake of this shattering family tragedy, Amiri and Amina Baraka joined an effort to create a Newark PFLAG (Parents and Friends of Lesbians and Gays) chapter, though in the tumult of the ensuing trial and grief, it never got off the ground. By the time of his own death, Baraka openly supported LGBTQ rights, and in a generational passing of the torch, his son Ras was elected mayor of Newark shortly after his passing. As mayor, Ras Baraka introduced a major series of programming on queer nightlife by the Queer Newark Oral History Project in 2014.[68]

This chapter began with an obituary, and it concludes with more. When Joan McEniry passed away from cancer in 1995, her obituary in the Newark *Star-Ledger* recognized Hilda Hidalgo as "her companion of 36 years."[69] Hidalgo retired to Florida, where she met a new partner, Cheryl Lamey, who was with her when she passed away from pancreatic cancer in 2009. Instead of a conventional obituary, the *Star-Ledger* ran a piece in their opinion section, which commended her courage in coming out; according to the NewsBank database, it was the first time she was explicitly identified with the word *lesbian* in the *Star-Ledger*.[70]

But not all of Newark's queer left history followed this arc toward public visibility. Frank Hutchins remained active in the struggle for housing justice until his declining health stopped him. He passed away in 2009, in the same year as Hidalgo and also from cancer, at the age of seventy-five. A stirring *Star-Ledger* article commemorated his activism, and mayor Cory Booker dedicated part of a South Ward street in his name the next year, honoring the "warrior of the people." In his 2016 book *United*, Booker, now in the U.S. Senate, dedicated an entire chapter to Hutchins, calling him "a father to me, one of my most cherished teachers, a man who changed the course of my life." Nowhere did he even obliquely address Hutchins's personal life.[71]

Writing about sexually unconventional Trotskyists during this same era, Alan Wald has observed that "secrecy turned out to be habit-forming; much was never recorded at the time, and then it was forgotten." In words that resonate with Frank Hutchins's own story, Wald concludes, "the biographical study of many postwar activists is partly an exercise in speculation because institutionalized forgetting has obscured research."[72] Hopefully this essay challenges that erasure, while also observing the limits of historical knowability. How many more Frank Hutchinses navigated Newark's left closets? Can the queer histories of Black Power, the Newark Socialist Workers Party, and later radical movements for environmental justice, prison abolition, immigrant rights, and anti-imperialism be recovered? One thing is clear: by pulling together the disparate threads of radical queer Newarkers, we can better see the compromises forced upon them, the limitations of the postwar left, and the courage they showed in retaining their commitments to the leftist politics and queer liberation that are both necessary for any better future.

Notes

1. "Raymond Proctor, College Instructor," *Star-Ledger*, October 22, 1988, with handwritten notes, in Newark Community Project for People with AIDS Collection, box 1, Charles F. Cummings New Jersey Information Center, Newark Public Library.

2. Whitney Strub and Mary Rizzo, "Raymond Proctor (Family Interview)," with Richard Proctor, Angela Proctor Weaver, Deborah P. Carter, and Kevin Proctor, August 6, 2016, Queer Newark Oral History Project (QNOHP), https://queer.newark.rutgers.edu/interviews/raymond-proctor-family-interview.

3. Historian Doug Rossinow argues that a left-liberal coalition dominated radical U.S. politics between the 1880s and 1940s before its destruction during the Cold War, though at the local level in Newark it persisted much longer, arguably through the present day, as seen in the organizing for Kenneth Gibson's 1970 mayoral election and Ras Baraka's in 2014. See Rossinow's *Visions of Progress: The Left-Liberal Tradition in America* (Philadelphia: University of Pennsylvania Press, 2008).

4. Stuart Timmons, *The Trouble with Harry Hay: Founder of the Modern Gay Movement* (Boston: Alyson Publications, 1991); Justin David Suran, "Coming Out

against the War: Antimilitarism and the Politicization of Homosexuality in the Era of Vietnam," *American Quarterly* 53, no. 3 (2001): 452–488; "The Combahee River Collective Statement" (1977), https://www.blackpast.org/african-american-history/combahee-river-collective-statement-1977/.

5. Dennis Altman, *Homosexual Oppression and Liberation* (New York: New York University Press, [1971] 1993), 227; Terence Kissack, *Free Comrades: Anarchism and Homosexuality in the United States 1895–1917* (Oakland: AK Press, 2008); Christopher Phelps, "A Neglected Document on Socialism and Sex," *Journal of the History of Sexuality* 16, no. 1 (2007): 1–13; Alan Wald, "Cannonite Bohemians after World War II," *Against the Current*, July/August 2012, 25–35; Huey P. Newton, "The Women's Liberation and Gay Liberation Movements" (1970), https://www.blackpast.org/african-american-history/speeches-african-american-history/huey-p-newton-women-s-liberation-and-gay-liberation-movements/; Martin Duberman, *A Saving Remnant: The Radical Lives of Barbara Deming and David McReynolds* (New York: New Press, 2011). For brilliant recent works on the collisions of left and queer history, see Emily Hobson, *Lavender and Red: Liberation and Solidarity in the Gay and Lesbian Left* (Berkeley: University of California Press, 2017); Aaron Lecklider, *Love's Next Meeting: The Forgotten History of Homosexuality and the Left in American Culture* (Berkeley: University of California Press, 2021).

6. Bruce Levine, "Immigrant Workers, 'Equal Rights,' and Anti-Slavery: The Germans of Newark, New Jersey," *Labor History* 25, no. 1 (1984): 26–52.

7. George Breitman to Alan Wald, March 14, 1985, in author's possession. My gratitude to Alan Wald for sharing this document with me, which I learned about from Christopher Phelps, "The Closet in the Party: The Young Socialist Alliance, the Socialist Workers Party, and Homosexuality, 1962–1970," *Labor: Studies in Working-Class History of the Americas* 10, no. 4 (2013): 11–38.

8. Kevin Mumford, *Newark: A History of Race, Rights, and Riots in America* (New York: New York University Press, 2008), 76–97.

9. Students for a Democratic Society, "The Port Huron Statement" (1962), http://www.progressivefox.com/misc_documents/PortHuronStatement.pdf; Tom Hayden and Carl Wittman, "An Interracial Movement of the Poor?" (SDS, 1963), https://www.sds-1960s.org/Interracial-Movement-Poor.pdf. On ERAP, see Jennifer Frost, *"An Interracial Movement of the Poor": Community Organizing and the New Left in the 1960s* (New York: New York University Press, 2001). The most substantive treatment of Wittman's life comes from the memoir of his onetime lover, D. E. Mungello, *Remember This: A Family in America* (Lanham, MD: Hamilton Books, 2016).

10. *Troublemakers*, directed by Robert Machover and Norman Fruchter (Alpha-60, 1966). The best accounts of NCUP are Frost, *"An Interracial Movement"*; Mumford, *Newark*; and Mark Krasovic, *The Newark Frontier: Community Action in the Great Society* (Chicago: University of Chicago Press, 2016).

11. Author interview with Norman Fruchter, October 24, 2014, New York City; David Gerwin, interview with Derek Winans, transcript, September 24, 1995, Derek Winans Papers, box 1, folder 11, New Jersey Historical Society, Newark.

12. Gerwin, interview with Winans, 1995; Tom Hayden, *Rebel: A Personal History of the 1960s* (Los Angeles: Red Hen Press, 2003), 119.

13. Wittman, *The Gay Manifesto* (New York: The Red Butterfly, 1969), 6; Wittman, "Us and the New Left," *Fag Rag*, Fall 1978, 22. On the Rustin flyers, see Mumford, *Newark*, 90; Charles Francis, "Freedom Summer 'Homos': An Archive Story," *American Historical Review* 124, no. 4 (2019): 1351–1363.

14. Strub and Rizzo, "Raymond Proctor (Family Interview)," 3, 5, https://queer.newark.rutgers.edu/sites/default/files/transcript/2016-08-06%20Proctor%20Family.pdf.

15. Clement Price, "The Struggle to Desegregate Newark: Black Middle-Class Militancy in New Jersey, 1932–1947," *New Jersey History* 99, no. 3/4 (1981): 215–222, here 218, 224.

16. "Newark-Essex CORE Chapter Elects Officers," unidentified clipping, Proctor Family album, Hillsborough, New Jersey; Newark-Essex CORE meeting minutes, August 13, 1962, Robert Curvin Papers, box 2, Newark Public Library; Newark-Essex CORE minutes, March 11, 1963, Curvin Papers, box 2, Newark Public Library; "Precinct Picketed," *Newark News*, August 3, 1963; "City Hall Closes, 10 Sit-Ins Jailed," clipping in Proctor family album; "CORE Sets Moves against N.J. Bell," *Newark News*, March 25, 1964; "Newark CORE Unit Elects Proctor Head," *Newark News*, May 12, 1964.

17. "CORE Set to Picket Rutgers on Hiring," *New York Times*, May 24, 1964. The dean of the law school with whom Proctor negotiated, Willard Heckel, lived fairly openly with his partner, Rutgers-Newark Vice President Malcolm Talbott, though no known records indicate whether Proctor and Heckel recognized one another as gay men.

18. Douglas Eldridge, "CORE Going to 'the People,'" *Newark News*, March 21, 1965; "Protest Unit Is Defended," *Newark News*, February 11, 1965.

19. Douglas Eldridge, "Proctor Leaving CORE Post," *Newark News*, May 9, 1965. Eldridge also referenced Proctor's bachelor status upon his assuming the chairmanship in 1964. Excerpt from Richard Amory's *Song of the Loon* (1966) included in Michael Bronski, *Pulp Friction: Uncovering the Golden Age of Gay Male Pulps* (New York: St. Martin's Griffin, 2003), 215. Unfortunately, Eldridge passed away in 2016 before I could ask him about his reporting, and Robert Curvin agreed to an interview about Proctor before falling ill, with his passing in 2015 also foreclosing commentary from CORE's most central figure.

20. Whitney Strub, interview with Carol Glassman, December 4, 2014, QNOHP, 2, 3, https://queer.newark.rutgers.edu/sites/default/files/transcript/GlassmanCarol_Session1_2014-12-04_transcript_final.pdf.

21. Strub, interview with Glassman, 4, 9, 10, 24.

22. Hayden, *Rebel*, 119; Strub, interview with Glassman, 12, 13.

23. Strub and Rizzo, "Raymond Proctor (Family Interview)," 5, 7.

24. Strub and Rizzo, "Raymond Proctor (Family Interview)," 40.

25. "People's Council Ten Point Program," January 8, 1970, Essex County College collection, Newark Public Library Digital Repository; "Third Word Store Front," *ECCO* (Essex County College student paper), November 5, 1970, Essex County College collection, Newark Public Library Digital Repository; Whitney Strub, interview with Bob Cartwright, October 28, 2016, QNOHP, https://queer.newark.rutgers.edu/interviews/bob-cartwright.

26. Author interview with Steve Block, March 6, 2015, Newark.

27. The scholarly literature on Baraka is immense, but for the most in-depth analysis of his political work in Newark, see Komozi Woodard, *A Nation within a Nation: Amiri Baraka (LeRoi Jones) & Black Power Politics* (Chapel Hill: University of North Carolina Press, 1999).

28. Cynthia A. Young, *Soul Power: Culture, Radicalism, and the Making of a U.S. Third World Left* (Durham, NC: Duke University Press, 2006), 34.

29. LeRoi Jones, "Civil Rights Poem," *Black Arts* (Newark: Jihad Productions, 1966). Baraka's open letter is quoted in Daniel Matlin, "'Lift Up Yr Self!' Reinterpreting Amiri Baraka (LeRoi Jones), Black Power, and the Uplift Tradition," *Journal of American History* 93, no. 1 (2006): 91–116, here 110.

30. Theodore Hudson, "A Conversation between Imamu Amiri Baraka and Theodore R. Hudson," (1970), in Charlie Reilly, ed., *Conversations with Amiri Baraka* (Jackson: University of Mississippi Press, 1994), 76.

31. Ron Simmons, "Some Thoughts on the Challenges Facing Black Gay Intellectuals," in *Brother to Brother: New Writings by Black Gay Men*, ed. Essex Hemphill (Washington, DC: RedBone Press, 1991), 273.

32. LeRoi Jones, *Preface to a Twenty Volume Suicide Note* (Totem Press, 1961), 11; Ben Lee, "LeRoi Jones/Amiri Baraka and the Limits of Open Form," *African American Review* 37, no. 2–3 (2003), 38.

33. Lee, "Limits of Open Form," 37.

34. LeRoi Jones, *The Eighth Ditch Is Drama, Floating Bear* #9 (July 1961), 1–7. Copies of the newsletter can be accessed through Jed Birmingham's very useful Floating Bear Archive, https://realitystudio.org/bibliographic-bunker/floating-bear-archive/. On Baraka's obscenity charges, see Jerry Gafio Watts, *Amiri Baraka: The Politics and Art of a Black Intellectual* (New York: New York University Press, 2001), 46; Werner Sollors, *Amiri Baraka/LeRoi Jones: The Quest for a "Populist Modernism"* (New York: Columbia University Press, 1978), 101.

35. LeRoi Jones, *The Baptism and The Toilet* (New York: Grove Press, 1966), 59, 60, 62.

36. Jones, *The Baptism*, 27, 32.

37. LeRoi Jones, *The System of Dante's Hell* (New York: Grove Press, 1965), 52, 56, 64, 57, 62.

38. Jones, *The System of Dante's Hell*, 139, 131, 140.

39. Emile Capouya, "States of Mind, of Soul," *New York Times*, November 28, 1965.

40. Judy Stone, "If It's Anger . . . Maybe That's Good: An Interview with LeRoi Jones" (August 1964), in *Conversations with Amiri Baraka*, 10; Cecil Smith, "Angry Young Playwright Seeks Reality," *Los Angeles Times*, March 21, 1965.

41. Both quotes are from Sollors, *Amiri Baraka/LeRoi Jones*, 280, footnote 3; 283, footnote 38.

42. Hettie Jones, *How I Became Hettie Jones* (New York: Grove Press, 1990), 86; Peter Orlovsky to Allen Ginsberg, September 25, 1963, in Ginsberg and Orlovsky, *Straight Hearts' Delight: Love Poems and Selected Letters, 1947–1980*, ed. Winston Leyland (San Francisco: Gay Sunshine Press, 1980), 216.

43. LeRoi Jones, *The Slave*, in *Two Plays by LeRoi Jones: Dutchman and The Slave* (New York: William Morrow & Co., 1964), 53; Whitney Strub and Kristyn Scorsone, interview with John, August 3, 2016, QNOHP, https://queer.newark.rutgers.edu/interviews/john.

44. LeRoi Jones, "American Sexual Reference: Black Male" (1965), in *Home: Social Essays* (New York: William Morrow & Co., 1966), 216.

45. Kristyn Scorsone, Christina Strasburger, Whitney Strub, and Mi Hyun Yoon, interview with Amina Baraka, March 2, 2018, QNOHP, 5, https://queer.newark.rutgers.edu/sites/default/files/transcript/2018-03-02%20Amina%20Baraka.pdf; "The Combahee River Collective Statement."

46. Simmons, "Some Thoughts on the Challenges Facing Black Gay Intellectuals," 273; Marlon B. Ross, "Camping the Dirty Dozens: The Queer Resources of Black Nationalist Invective," *Callaloo* 23, no. 1 (2000): 290–312; José Esteban Muñoz, "Cruising the Toilet: LeRoi Jones/Amiri Baraka, Radical Black Traditions, and Queer Futurity," *GLQ* 13, no. 2–3 (2007): 353–367. See also Julius B. Fleming Jr., *Black Patience: Performance, Civil Rights, and the Unfinished Project of Emancipation* (New York: New York University Press, 2022), 132–181.

47. Marie Teresa, "Commentary of Being a Black Lesbian," *GAA-Essex Union Newsletter* (Summer 1972): 3; Zenzele Isoke, *Urban Black Women and the Politics of Resistance* (New York: Palgrave Macmillan, 2013).

48. Strub, interview with Cartwright, 15, https://queer.newark.rutgers.edu/sites/default/files/transcript/2016-10-28%20Bob%20Cartwright.pdf; Cheo Hekima, "A.L.D. Success," *Black New Ark* (June 1973): 1; "Unity Movement Candidates Denounce Gasparinetti Assassination Threat," *Black New Ark* (September 1973): 8; "Victory Party for Tenants!" *Ironbound Voices* (January 1984): 1.

49. Pauline Blount, interview with Frank Hutchins, June 29, 1998, Krueger-Scott African American Oral History Collection, Rutgers University Libraries, https://doi.org/doi:10.7282/T3JS9SFR.

50. Strub, interview with Cartwright, 17.

51. Cartwright, email to author, January 13, 2022.

52. Carlos Ulises Decena, *Tacit Subjects: Belonging and Same-Sex Desire among Dominican Immigrant Men* (Durham, NC: Duke University Press, 2011), 18.

53. Author interview with Richard Cammarieri, January 25, 2022, Zoom.

54. This account draws primarily on Elizabeth Parker, "Hilda A. Hidalgo: Ph.D., Puerto Rican, Latina, Lesbian, Feminist, New Jerseyan," *Garden State Legacy* 23, March 2014, https://gardenstatelegacy.com/files/Hilda_A-Hidalgo_Parker_GSL23.pdf, an excellent overview of Hidalgo's life and work.

55. Parker, "Hilda A. Hidalgo"; Douglas Eldridge, "Puerto Rican Leader Blames Vigilantes for Burning Car," *Newark News*, October 9, 1969. On Hidalgo's role in the convention, see Lauren O'Brien, "¡Venceremos! Harambee!: A Black & Puerto Rican Union?" *New Jersey Studies* 4, no. 1 (2018): 130–146. A 1965 campaign flyer lists her platform in the Hilda Hidalgo Papers, oversize box 6, Puerto Rican Community Archives, Newark Public Library.

56. Hilda Hidalgo, *The Puerto Ricans in Newark, N.J.* (Newark: Aspira, 1971), 8, 16, 1; Hidalgo to Kenneth Gibson, March 9, 1972, Hilda Hidalgo Papers, box 5, folder 9.

57. Strub, interview with Glassman, 28.

58. Hilda Hidalgo and Elia Hidalgo Christensen, "The Puerto Rican Lesbian and the Puerto Rican Community," *Journal of Homosexuality* 2, no. 2 (1976): 109–121, here 110, 115.

59. Hidalgo, "Third World Lesbians: Organizing at the National Level to Combat Oppression," August 1980, Hidalgo Papers, box 1, folder 10; Hidalgo, "On Oppression and Fighting Back," 1982, box 1, folder 22.

60. Hidalgo, ed., *Lesbians of Color: Social and Human Services* (New York: Harrington Park Press, 1995).

61. For one example of many, see Lawrence La Fountain-Stokes, *Queer Ricans: Cultures and Sexualities in the Diaspora* (Minneapolis: University of Minnesota Press, 2009), 67.

62. Hidalgo and Christensen, "The Puerto Rican Lesbian," 116; Hidalgo, *Lesbians of Color*, 4.

63. Hilda Hidalgo and Joan McEniry, *Hispanic Temas: A Contribution to the Knowledge Bank of the Hispanic Community* (Puerto Rican Studies Program, Rutgers University-Newark, 1985); *Ladies Home Journal* clipping, July 1984, Hidalgo Papers, box 6, folder 16.

64. "Rage in America: Voices from Newark," New Jersey News, May 14, 1992, VHS tape in Hidalgo Papers, oversize box 2.

65. Evelyn Nieves, "Official and 3 Journalists Arrested in Newark," *New York Times*, October 21, 1993.

66. Strub and Rizzo, "Raymond Proctor (Family Interview)," 56; Mungello, *Remember This*, 184. See also Ian Lekus, "Health Care, the AIDS Crisis, and the Politics of Community: The North Carolina Lesbian and Gay Health Project, 1982–1986," in *Modern American Queer History*, ed. Allida Black (Philadelphia: Temple University Press, 2001), 227–252.

67. "An Open Letter to the New New Left from the Old New Left," *The Nation*, April 16, 2020.

68. D. H. Melhem, "Revolution: The Constancy of Change" (1981), in *Conversations with Amiri Baraka*, 199–200; Scorsone et al., interview with Amina Baraka.

69. "Joan L. McEniry, 65, Rutgers Professor," *Star-Ledger*, August 4, 1995.

70. "Restless for Justice," *Star-Ledger*, December 10, 2009.

71. David Giambusso, "Legendary Community Organizer, Frank Hutchins Dies at 75," *Star-Ledger*, November 21, 2009; Street dedication flyer, April 13, 2010, Ironbound Community Corporation Collection, Newark Public Library Digital Collection; Cory Booker, *United: Thoughts on Finding Common Ground and Advancing the Common Good* (New York: Ballantine Books, 2016), 96.

72. Alan Wald, "Cannonite Bohemians," 26, 33.

Oral History Excerpt #2

Yvonne Hernandez

Yvonne is from a Puerto Rican family. Here she narrates how she came into her lesbian identity gradually.

I WAS ALWAYS FASCINATED with the girl that sat in front of me. Her hair would smell so good, and I just uh . . . you know. As a child I didn't realize it, until I got to high school, and we're talking about the early 1970s where you can get beat up or made fun of or ostracized, so I never really told any of my friends.

So my mother knew, and so she was telling me, "You've gotta stop hanging out with these girls, going to these places, because people are going to start thinking that you're like *them*." And I said to my mom, "Well . . . you know, mom, I *am* like them." And she froze and she looked at me, she said, like, "Come again?" I said, "Yeah, I—I'm, I'm, I'm one of those." I said, "Yeah, I'm—I'm a lesbian," I used that word. "And Joyce, you know, she's my girlfriend." My mother held her head [and] walked out of the room. And I remember as I was saying it, I felt all this . . . no fear, like, it was like a relief, like *ahh*!

She comes back, and she said, "You know what?" She said, "I would"—she came, all in my face, I thought she was gonna slap me or something. She said, "I would rather"—I mean, nails out—"I would rather you had told me that you were a whore in the street than *that*." And I felt really guilty after that, because I remember seeing a picture of my mother in school with the graduation, the kindergarten graduation, and in the picture, my mother looked so sad, in the picture. And I just started crying, I said, "I have to stop doing this. I have to . . . get a grip on myself, uh, this is a phase." Um, and I actually convinced myself that, yes, this is a phase, I'm just—I got rid of all my friends . . . I said, "I'm killing my mom, and I can't do this," and I just completely got out of the life. *Completely.* I didn't go to any of the gay clubs or *anything.*

So, after a couple of years, I stayed by myself, I didn't date anyone. I met this really nice guy. And he asked me one day, we went to a place called the Blue Ribbon Inn in Hillside, 'cause I like country music. So we went to the Blue Ribbon Inn, it's a country western bar, and we were sitting there, and he said, "You know, I heard something about you." I said, "I know what it is, I know what it is." But he said, "I don't care," and that it's fine, you know, "my love." So we wound up getting married.

Had two children, my son now is thirty, and my other son is twenty-nine, we had two back-to-back. But after they were about five years old, I just, I left him, I said, "I can't do this. I can't sleep in the same room with him, I can't look at him naked, I can't stand the smell of this man." He didn't stink, I mean, he was—his hygiene was beautiful. But, in my psyche, he smelled like a man.

I took my children, they were babies, to Independence Park in the Ironbound section in Newark. And I went to the water fountain, and there was this girl standing there and I thought she was with her kids, but it turns out that she worked for the park, and when I went over there, she helped me pick up my son so that he could drink water, and her hand kinda touched my hand, and I just lost it 'cause she was so cute with her little tool belt. So *[Laughs]* I was like, oh my god, this is great, so we were talking for a while, and when I went home that night I was quiet and my husband kept looking at me. And it's almost like he knew that I was feeling something.

Lightly edited for cohesiveness. Listen to or read the whole oral history at https://queer.newark.rutgers.edu/interviews/yvonne-hernandez.

CHAPTER 4

Glitter on Halsey Street

Queer and Trans World-Making in Newark, 1970s–Present

KRISTYN SCORSONE

IN THE SUMMER OF 1967, after a Black cab driver named John Smith was beaten by Newark police officers, the city's Black community took to the streets in anger. Their rebellion was fueled by long-standing issues of police brutality, a lack of economic opportunity, substandard housing, and poverty. For five days the city streets became a battleground. At the urging of then Mayor Hugh Addonizio, the governor deployed the state police and the National Guard to quell the so-called "riots." According to Tracey "Africa" Norman, "We were almost in the heart of things because the army was all around up and down Clinton Avenue. Then the tanks came down Johnson Avenue . . . I remember my father [and] we were all standing there, my father would yell, 'Duck!' *[Laughs]* We all just laid down on the patio until they all passed."[1]

The unrest ended with twenty-six dead; one of whom was a fire captain, another a police detective. But the rest were Black residents, including several children. President Lyndon B. Johnson employed the Kerner Commission to determine the reason for civil unrest. The commission's conclusions confirmed that racial oppression was to blame. The report states, "Our nation is moving toward two societies, one black, one white, separate and unequal." Among the remedies listed are the creation of new jobs and training programs, better social services and increased public assistance, improvements in the education system, better housing, and an end to de facto segregation. Despite the opportunity for a national reckoning with issues of race, the president shelved the report. Since then, the city of Newark has engaged in remembrances at the anniversary of the rebellion. News media has largely sensationalized the uprisings as violent and irrational riots, while historians have re-examined this history and challenged the public to understand the social and structural issues of racism as well as racist federal and local policies that caused the rebellion to happen.[2]

Newark experienced economic decline during the Great Depression and deindustrialization that began in the 1950s. This hit everyone in the city hard, but the Black community was particularly affected. During the postwar era, the city engaged in a program of urban renewal using federal funds; developers using these funds displaced Black residents from their neighborhoods. Due to discrimination and segregation, jobs were scarce for Black people. After the 1967 Newark uprising, also known as the Newark rebellion, decline rapidly increased as white people and white-owned businesses fled the city, and jobs became scarcer. By the 1970s and 1980s, beginning with President Richard Nixon and accelerating under President Ronald Reagan's administration, the War on Drugs disproportionately targeted Black communities with high rates of incarceration. This was combined with the HIV/AIDS epidemic, which worsened under the George H. W. Bush and Bill Clinton administrations and further devastated communities.[3]

By all accounts, the post-1967 period is considered the nadir of Newark's history. By 1975, for instance, *Harper's* famously measured "America's Worst City" through a series of metrics (crime, health, wealth, housing, etc.) and concluded that "Newark stands without serious challenge as the worst of all."[4] By the early twenty-first century, the city was the butt of jokes by late-night television comics.[5] Although Newark did indeed go through an economic decline, the people who have made it their home are not the sensationalized representations often portrayed in the media. Moreover, the city's history is not a simple declension narrative of the fall of another postindustrial northern city. By widening the typical historical lens to incorporate sexuality, the city's history looks much different. The majority Black queer and transgender community who started to come together and build queer institutions during the 1970s, while the city was commonly understood to be entering its darkest days, shifts our understanding and challenges the conventional history of Newark. For Tracey "Africa" Norman, who witnessed the 1967 unrest as an adolescent, the 1970s offered newfound freedoms to explore gender and sexuality as the city's queer bar and club scene began to take root. Queer bars and clubs that opened in the 1970s also laid the groundwork for the city's queer and transgender community to engage in later kinds of queer institution-building, such as entrepreneurial businesses. As community hubs, these spaces would enable the formation of collective power through social connection, while also offering what theorist J. Jack Halberstam describes as a queer subculture and placemaking practices that challenge heteronormative ideas about labor, production, and reproductive and familial time. Bars, clubs, and businesses provide alternative pathways for Black queer and transgender people in Newark to mobilize resources; take on leadership roles; and exist outside of and lay challenge to a heteronormative and racist society that has historically excluded the majority of Black queer and transgender people, who do not typically adhere to heteronormative and patriarchal standards, from social citizenship and its protections. Predominantly Black queer and transgender bars, clubs, and businesses were—and in many ways continue to be—an act of world-making to erect social, political, and economic structures as a means of survival in a white supremacist and heteropatriarchal system.[6]

Halsey Street is a lens through which we can think of two generations of Newark LGBTQ history, in a way that helps make gender visible as it shifts from a male-dominated to female-run space. Bars and clubs are known for providing sanctuary spaces in a world historically hostile to queer and transgender individuals. In part, the shift to virtual space and social networking apps, which provide easy connections for community and relationships, has made LGBTQ bars and clubs less necessary. Perhaps even more impactful, however, are the effects of gentrification in urban areas, making the cost of running large bars and clubs prohibitive in smaller cities where there are not enough queer and transgender patrons to sustain them. Instead, small businesses provide a form of sanctuary through civic-minded owners, predominantly Black queer women who are active in the fight for equality. Consequently, the nature of queer and transgender space in and around Halsey Street has changed over time, but it has remained an important hub of the city's LGBTQ community.

Nightlife on Halsey Street in the 1970s and 1980s

In the 1970s, Halsey Street in the Central Ward of Newark became a queer hub, with bars and clubs located on or adjacent to this downtown strip. Halsey's bars and clubs did not appear out of thin air. There were already a few established gay bars scattered around the city—as Anna Lvovsky shows in chapter 2, a midcentury downtown queer bar and nightlife scene had dwindled by the late 1960s, though longtime staples such as the legally pioneering Murphy's Tavern remained open. What changed in the 1970s was the appearance of clubs in addition to the bars, and most significantly, the remaking of Newark nightlife as predominantly Black-centered. Most of the clubs emerging at this time were queer-owned and staffed and often featured drag performers, live DJs, and even theatrical shows. Some were predominantly Black queer and transgender hangouts, while others had mixed straight and gay clientele. Overall, the appearance of these clubs in a central area of the city made the queer and transgender community increasingly visible and predated the area's ballroom scene, which gained steam in the 1980s and 1990s.

What's more, Halsey Street's legacy as a queer area has continued to the present day. Many people interviewed for the Queer Newark Oral History Project archive commonly associate Halsey Street with the queer and transgender community; however, instead of queer bars and clubs, queer-owned businesses now lay in and around the area. As the earlier nightlife scene coalesced, Black queer and transgender individuals found ways to connect, support each other, and express Black queer culture through the club scene. This ultimately strengthened Newark's LGBTQ community and paved the way for new economic opportunities for Black queer and transgender people to build institutions within the city.

One of the most crucial architects of Newark's 1970s club scene was club owner, promoter, and manager Albert Murphy. As a community leader, Murphy was a progenitor of Newark's gay fashion and club scene. He was initially known for throwing extravagant Mother's Day fashion shows that featured high fashion models like Beverly Johnson, the first Black model to make the cover of the world's foremost fashion magazine, *Vogue,* in 1974. That same year, Murphy opened Le Joc at 36 Halsey Street, a two-level, loft-style Black gay club where Johnson and other top models such as Iman and Pat Cleveland would socialize.[7] With Le Joc, Murphy set out to create an ultra-hip club influenced by underground dance parties, rent parties, and house parties. Gary Jardim, editor of *Blue,* a two-volume book on Newark art, life, and style, writes: "Al [Murphy] didn't invent the ecstatic, all out, all-night party approach, the fruit-bar and non-alcoholic format, the concept of the club as sanctuary, or the vision of the club as a theatrical environment for the expression of free black subjectivity—all of that can be traced back to the early-70s private gay clubs, but he was part of that original crowd, and it was his genius to imagine and execute the club as a house of style, indeed, as a sanctified house party, which is what he pulled off at Le Joc."[8]

In the early 1970s, across the Hudson River in New York City, an underground party known as The Loft was largely frequented by the gay community, including Murphy, who was friends with Loft creator David Mancuso. Murphy was likely influenced by what he saw happening at Manhattan parties when he conceived Le Joc.

More than just cutting-edge, the underground nature of Black queer parties helped to avoid police harassment and raids while also providing alternatives to majority-white gay bars and clubs that were alienating and could even be dangerous for queer and transgender people of color. In downtown Newark, Murphy's Tavern was frequently targeted by police for surveillance. In 1967, Murphy's, along with two other New Jersey gay bars, took the state's Alcoholic and Beverage Control (ABC) Commission all the way to the state Supreme Court to fight against revocation of their liquor license for serving, as the ABC put it, "apparent homosexuals." Ultimately, in a landmark victory, the gay community of Newark won the right to congregate in bars. Yet not all gay bars in the city were safe spaces for everyone. Several years later, about a mile north of Murphy's, an interracial couple were shot at by a group of white men as they left The Other World, a gay bar with a mostly white clientele. The Other World was in what was then the predominantly Italian North Ward neighborhood of North Newark. The Black partner in the couple, James Credle, referred to the area as "Imperiale country." His remark gestures at the racial tensions in Newark at the time, as Italian Americans became emboldened by local politician Anthony Imperiale's racist rhetoric. Imperiale, known for race-baiting, openly advocated for armed white self-defense and vigilantism during and following the 1967 unrest. By crossing a racial boundary to frequent a gay bar, Credle and his white boyfriend risked violent retribution in an area of Newark known for its nighttime street patrols by white residents.[9]

On Halsey Street, Le Joc was the first Black and queer owned and operated underground club in Newark, and as such it created financial opportunities for other Black queer individuals who knew Al Murphy. Murphy was known for giving jobs to his friends, so when he started Le Joc he recruited close friends Darryl Rochester, Erica Harrison, Tommy Garrett, and Shelton Hayes to work at and design the club to rival the hippest spots in New York City. As part of the ambience, no alcohol was served. Instead, punch and a fruit plate were set out by

Harrison, who ran concessions. At the entrance to Le Joc was a subversively gendered life-size painting of model and Newark native Sherry Gordon's face with the body of a man wearing a jock strap, hence "Le Joc." Gordon had been discovered walking down a local street by Garret, who had connections in the fashion industry. According to Rochester, after you passed the painting of Gordon, "Then you walked in and it had a staircase that went up and it was live white doves . . . real doves . . . in cages . . . this was spectacular back then. And then you went to the disco booth, and it was just chairs and lounge. It was nothin' to see Pat Cleveland lounged out on one of the chairs."[10] Ultimately, Le Joc lasted only two years, closing in 1976, but it set the tone for a vibrant queer club scene in Newark where Black queer culture flourished and employment opportunities were available.

Several blocks south from Le Joc, on the corner of William and Halsey Streets, the Doll House opened in 1976 as a unique club space that infused elements of the Black Arts Movement with high fashion, camp, and ballroom culture. The Black Arts Movement was a Black-led arts, literature, and theater movement during the sixties and seventies that emphasized Black Power and used culture as a vehicle for Black self-determination. Newark native Amiri Baraka founded the movement when he established the Black Arts Repertory Theater (BARTS). BARTS was established in Harlem in 1965 after the assassination of Malcolm X and used theatrical performance as a form of political engagement that centered Black history and experiences. The movement spread to other cities and was embodied in the work of writers and poets like Larry Neal, Ntozake Shange, Nikki Giovanni, and others. Yet despite the proximity of famous queer writers James Baldwin and Audre Lorde, sexism and homophobia were a pervasive element within masculinist aspects of the Black Arts Movement and were accepted by many of the more militant Black cultural nationalists, as Whitney Strub demonstrates in chapter 3 when he discusses the queer Newark left and the shifts in Baraka's sexual politics over time. As a result, spaces like the Doll House enabled the Black queer and transgender community to carve out their own cultural version of queer and gender-nonconforming Black Power through drag performance and camp theater productions.[11]

While gay bars like Murphy's were not always tolerant of transgender people, Doll House was a venue where Black transgender women could socialize, work, and perform. Owners Bobby White and Dorian Paris (formerly Dorian Smith), described as beautiful gay men who could pass for women, owned several small clubs in Newark over the years and were considered leaders in Newark's LGBTQ community. Moreover, White was a very popular female impersonator in Newark for both gay and straight audiences. They hired transgender women like Angela Raine and Pucci Revlon to work in the Doll House, which was above a well-known nightclub on the jazz circuit, Sparky J's. Both women describe how White and Paris mentored them on aspects of the entertainment industry, including background work and promoting shows. Raine started out doing janitorial work and waiting tables, then worked behind the scenes on costuming and props. Eventually, she would perform on the Doll House stage in drag shows and plays. She did lip sync performances as Grace Jones, was a member of the Doll House Dolls, and did a small tour in the Bobby White Revue. The Doll House Dolls and White's Revue were both populated by predominantly Black and Brown transgender women. Similarly, Revlon did some background work as well as performance. According to Revlon,

> In the Doll House. In the club. We had everybody sit around and we used the center of the floor. We roller skated around. Bobby White played Dorothy. I played the mother. We had the little minions running around, these little flying little monkey things. We did the whole *Wiz* on roller skates inside the Doll House. We did a show, a little play, *Is My Family Turning Gay?* That was a whole little two-hour little production in the back of it. We did the [Ziegfeld] Follies like from—the follies back in the 1930s I think, where the show girls came out with the big hats and stuff.

Revlon also participated in the ballroom competitions—or "walking in" shows—in New York City and New Jersey to win prize money. Revlon later appeared in the ballroom documentary *Paris Is Burning* (1990) along with other members of Newark's LGBTQ community. The influence Newark's club and ballroom scene had on New York City's scene has yet to be fully studied and appreciated.[12]

An important part of queer and transgender institution-building is claiming public spaces where queer and transgender individuals can find affirmation of their own identities as they meet others like them. The founding of collective spaces and identity formation in the 1970s was critical to queer and transgender individuals who, if they had been isolated, may have had only a limited window into their identity. Without much representation in the larger society and media, queer and transgender people used bars and clubs as avenues for identity formation and shared connections. Meeting others could expand the possibilities of existence and ways of moving through the world. Angela Raine described how working at the Doll House enabled her to meet transgender women from various parts of the city and state. Prior to her time at the Doll House, the transgender women she knew were, as she describes them, "night girls."

> You didn't see them as women in the daytime, or you didn't see them in the daytime. The ones I met after I got to the Doll House were realistic, they were daytime women. I mean, day or night, they were the same person. . . . I learned that we were all not the same because you had tall trans women and you had short trans women. Every makeup of woman there was; it was weird because they looked like women. It was shocking to me because there was a few that had great bodies, and I was like, wow, weird and how did that happen? . . . With me, I was young, just starting out, so I had no sense of fashion, I had no sense of what it was like to be a woman. I just thought I was a girl. That was as good as it got.

Witnessing many different forms of transgender womanhood while working and performing at the Doll House enabled Raine to radically envision her own Black womanhood and other ways of living despite society's denial of the full spectrum of transgender lives.[13]

As an entrepreneur, Raine would go on to represent transgender identity and issues through her writing. In 2006, she began to self-publish Newark's first transgender-owned and edited magazine, *La'Raine*, every three months. Within the pages of *La'Raine*, topics ranged from beauty tips for trans women to healthy recipes to poetry submissions. Raine watched for decades as transgender women in and outside her social circle were murdered, which led her to include a column on "Transgender Deaths: Why Are We Misunderstood?" Her husband began to write erotic stories for the magazine featuring queer and transgender sexual encounters (as Dominique Rocker notes in chapter 8), thereby providing a rare public outlet for frank sex talk within Newark's trans and lesbian communities. Raine continues to print each issue herself and distributes them to local LGBTQ organizations and at special events like Newark Pride, in addition to individual purchases that go directly through her. Her readers became so invested in Raine's fictional transgender love stories that community members were demonstrably upset when she killed off one of her main characters. Raine's magazine is the only one of its kind, not only in Newark, but in the entire state, and as such provides a unique historical record of Newark's transgender history.

In the second half of the 1970s, Le Joc closed its doors, but Al Murphy continued to be a prominent figure in Newark's gay club scene. He promoted a gay night at a local club called Docks and then was hired to manage Miles Berger's club on Broad Street, Zanzibar. Berger's aim was to create a flashy Studio 54–style club, but with gay Black men as the main clientele, unlike the largely white crowd at Studio 54. With Berger's money and Murphy's creative vision Zanzibar became legendary for its wild parties with elaborate decor, an outdoor pool in the back, and exotic animals in cages. Shelton Hayes would work with Murphy on Zanzibar's decor just as he did at Le Joc. One infamous night, Hayes filled the entire club with mounds of glitter. According to Darryl Rochester, for days afterward the downtown area was covered in glitter as it was spread by patrons leaving Zanzibar. Those tiny glimmering specs clung to sweaty bodies moving through the boundary between the queer club space and the rest of Newark, leaving evidence of queer joy and embodiment behind on the city's streets. Such was the milieu of the city's gay and transgender nightlife in the 1970s and 1980s.[14]

Although bars and clubs were important to the coalescence of Newark's LGBTQ community, these spaces also had their shortcomings. Because, in general, queer and transgender nightlife historically centers on the consumption of alcohol, issues such as alcoholism can be pervasive in the community. In clubs like Le Joc, where alcohol was not served, recreational drugs were often popular. What's more, none of the clubs were owned by queer or transgender women. Gay establishments were usually owned by straight or gay men. To date, no evidence has been found of any bars or clubs in the city being owned by queer or transgender women. There is only scant mention in oral histories of a lesbian-identified woman named Irma who managed the Majestic. And it was not until the 1980s that parties for lesbians began to be held on different nights, usually at bars that otherwise served a straight clientele, like First Choice in the Ironbound section of Newark.[15]

The impact of the AIDS epidemic, the city's continued economic decline, and later forces of gentrification ended the heyday of Newark's gay club and bar scene. In the 1980s, there were a small handful of bars and clubs that appeared. The Cactus Club in the Ironbound section of Newark was a dance club featuring go-go boys where, according to Peter Savastano, "everybody was gay, everybody was white, the music was horrible. It was all that dreadful, high energy, gay white boy music that only makes it possible for you to move your elbows and your shoulders." SRO (which stood for "Standing Room Only") on Halsey Street was

FIGURE 4.1. Business card for SRO at 199 Halsey Street, owned by Nelson and Scottie, a gay couple, ca. 1980. While not flashy, the card subtly includes paired-off same-sex symbols, signifying its status as a gay and lesbian club. From the International Gay Information Center ephemera collection, New York Public Library.

owned by a Black gay couple identified only as Nelson and Scottie. It was known for being a space where lesbians hung out. SRO could not compete with the popularity of Murphy's Tavern. These smaller clubs usually closed within a year or two and never reached the prominence of the earlier clubs. Zanzibar managed to stay open until the early 1990s, but after Albert Murphy died from AIDS and Shelton Hayes left, the clientele shifted, and the club became less popular, eventually closing around 1993. In the 1980s and 1990s, the ballroom scene gained popularity and clubs acted as "houses" that provided health care for those in the community affected by HIV/AIDs, at a time when municipal, state, and federal government agencies collectively turned a blind eye on the epidemic, dismissing it as solely a "gay disease."[16]

Without its robust club scene, Halsey Street still maintained a visible queer presence through the sex workers who populated it; by 1996, Peter Savastano described the street as "known for its male hustler scene." Looming gentrification reversed that. In 2007, then mayor Cory Booker, as part of his plan to revitalize the city, personally rode a bulldozer into the building that used to be

Zanzibar. Around the same time, as Rutgers University-Newark aspired to become a more residential college, Rutgers police began asserting a new and hostile presence, acting "very nasty to people on the stroll" along Halsey, as Aaron Frazier recounted.[17]

The Leadership of Black Queer Women in Newark

In the early twenty-first century, leadership of Newark's LGBTQ community shifted and Black lesbian-identified women moved to the forefront of queer institution-building, especially in and around Halsey Street. Although queer culture in Newark dates back to the advent of its urbanization, not until the twenty-first century did an organized LGBTQ movement, largely led by Black queer women, coalesce. Recognizing the need for political mobilization due to rising violence against the Black queer and transgender community, especially queer youth, Black queer women came together to push for changes through grassroots mobilizations. In the face of municipal neglect, they claimed spaces for LGBTQ youth and adults and began to hold annual weeklong Pride events. Their efforts resulted in various queer institutions, including a community center, a nondenominational church, and a drop-in health center. Black lesbian-owned businesses began to flourish as well. In many ways they too would function as queer sanctuary spaces, while also providing avenues for the women who owned them to participate in economic, cultural, and political activism as queer community leaders. According to historian Joe William Trotter Jr., "from the beginning, African Americans used the unique conditions of the urban environment to open up pathways to their own emancipation." Black queer and transgender women are included in the history of African Americans who, Trotter argues, "built on their economic contributions to forge vigorous movements for freedom, independence, and access to civil and human rights." What's more, Black queer women played a significant role in shaping the Queer Newark Oral History Project (QNOHP), a historical reclamation project to document and preserve the life stories of LGBTQ individuals in and of Newark. Their mobilizations have furthermore paved the way for LGBTQ equality statewide and nationally.[18]

The murder of a young butch lesbian named Sakia Gunn in 2003 galvanized Newark's LGBTQ community. Black lesbians were at the forefront of mobilizations in the wake of her death. Gunn was on her way home to Newark from

Greenwich Village in Manhattan. Upon reaching the bus stop at the intersection of Broad and Market Streets, two men began to sexually harass Gunn and her friends. After Gunn told the men she was gay, one of them, Richard McCullough, attacked her. Gunn fought back, but McCullough fatally stabbed her. Tragically, she died in the arms of a friend on the way to the hospital. When the news reached the LGBTQ community in Newark, thousands of young people gathered for Gunn's funeral. Gunn's friends continued to fight for change and Black queer women mobilized to demand safe spaces for LGBTQ youth. Women like Laquetta Nelson and June Dowell-Burton took charge of attempts to persuade the city to provide a city-sponsored LGBTQ community center, but they were dismissed by then mayor Sharpe James. Frustrated, Nelson told *The Advocate,* a national gay magazine, that Newark's city government would only pay "lip service" to the community's needs and that her attempts to draw attention to events in Newark "always fell on deaf ears." Even worse, when June Dowell-Burton approached the mayor, he stated, "There are no gay people in Newark," essentially denying the existence of queer people as his constituents.[19]

In the face of government stonewalling, Black queer women forged ahead on their own. June Dowell-Burton founded Newark Pride, Inc., a community-based and volunteer-run organization to enhance LGBTQ life through annual Gay Pride Week events. The first weeklong Newark Pride celebration was held in 2005. The following year, the city raised the gay pride flag for the first time in front of the Essex County Courthouse and, in 2007, then mayor Cory Booker raised the flag with Dowell-Burton and Dana Rone, the city's first out lesbian elected official, at the entrance to Newark City Hall. During his term, Booker also formed the LGBTQ Advisory Concerns Commission; Newark was the first city in the state to do so. It was followed by the Essex County LGBTQ Advisory Board. In later years, Newark Pride continued to grow under the leadership of president Sharronda "Love" Wheeler. The LGBTQ community marched from City Hall down Broad Street for the first time during Newark's 2016 Gay Pride Parade, and at the 2018 parade Amina Baraka, wife of the late poet-activist Amiri Baraka and mother of Newark mayor Ras Baraka, rode on one of the parade's floats.[20]

Despite moments of progress, the city promised but ultimately failed to deliver a community center for LGBTQ youth. Gary Paul Wright, executive director of the African American Office of Gay Concerns in Newark and member of both the Newark and Essex County LGBTQ advisory boards, wrote a scathing op-ed on the tenth anniversary of Gunn's murder for the *Star-Ledger*, decrying that the annual flag raisings and both advisory commissions were empty gestures dressed up as progress. Similarly frustrated with government inaction, Reverend Janyce Jackson Jones and Reverend Alicia Heath-Toby bypassed the city to open the Newark LGBTQ Community Center on Halsey Street in 2013. According to Heath-Toby, "the community said, 'Enough.' Because there were killings of trans folks, and sexual abuse happening, and the rise of health issues in the community, wrongful arrest, and all those things were happening to LGBTQ folks. Particularly young folks, and so a group of leaders said, 'Enough is enough.' . . . That's really how it came to be. It came as a result of people just being fed up."[21]

Black queer women were not going to wait around for the city to protect the LGBTQ community. As a member of the city's LGBTQ Advisory Concerns Commission, Jones was part of the conversations concerning the need for a safe space for the LGBTQ community. She led the effort to establish the space on Halsey Street in collaboration with Gary Paul Wright of the African American Office of Gay Concerns (AAOGC), Darnell L. Moore, co-founder of the Queer Newark Oral History Project, Brian McGovern at North Jersey Community Research Institute (NJCRI), and other community folks like the late James Credle, former dean at Rutgers-Newark.

Years later, the Newark LGBTQ Community Center continues to be a vital community resource, providing programs, services, advocacy, and events under the leadership of two Black queer women, Beatrice Simpkins, executive director, and Denise Hinds, board chair.[22]

Reverend Jackson Jones was also instrumental in establishing safe spaces for Newark's LGBTQ community to worship under the leadership of Senior Bishop Jacquelyn Holland, one of the first women Bishops in the Unity Fellowship Church Movement. In April of 1995, she worked with Bishop Holland to establish the LGBTQ affirming Liberation in Truth Unity Fellowship Church (L.I.T.) in Newark.[23] In 2012, Jones co-founded its successor Unity Fellowship Church NewArk, a merging of L.I.T.'s congregation and Unity Fellowship, New Brunswick's, with their Pastor Kevin E. Taylor. The history of the Unity Church Fellowship Church Movement dates back to 1982 when Bishop Carl Bean, known for the 1977 pro-gay dance anthem "I Was Born This Way," which inspired Lady Gaga's 2011 "Born this Way," founded the first Unity Fellowship church in Los Angeles, California. Bean recognized the need for a spiritual space welcoming to gay men of color who were frequently ostracized from their churches after testing positive for HIV/AIDS. Subsequently, many Unity Fellowship churches were established in several cities as places of worship welcoming to LGBTQ people of color. Jones was similarly concerned about the stigma people living with HIV/AIDS faced when she decided to become a reverend at L.I.T. and, after Bishop Holland retired in 2005, was consecrated as pastor. Because L.I.T. was known for female leadership and had a mostly female congregation, in 1998 the State of New Jersey approached the church to do HIV prevention work with Black and Brown women. A few years later in 2002, under L.I.T., Holland and Jones opened a state-funded HIV/AIDS drop-in center on New Street called Loving in Truth, which grew to provide not only HIV and AIDS prevention education, but also showers, laundry services, condoms, and snacks for community members in need, many of whom were trans women engaging in sex work to survive and queer youth who were kicked out of their homes. When state funding ran out, the New Street location closed, but L.I.T. had an additional space around the corner on Halsey Street, the Liberation in Truth Social Justice Center, which survived solely on their fundraising efforts. This was the space that Jones ultimately secured for the Newark LGBTQ Community Center in 2013.[24]

Unity Fellowship Church NewArk provides a pivotal institutional base for Black lesbian empowerment, creating opportunities for collaborative entrepreneurship and grassroots organizing. Many Black queer women cite the church as their main reason for moving to Newark. The welcoming nature of the congregation enabled many Black queer women interested in entrepreneurship to form friendships that ultimately led to business partnerships and involvement in local activism. Lesbian-owned businesses like the Artisan Collective, Off the Hanger, ANE Clothier, Diamondz N Da Ruff, FEMWORKS, and the Essex County RAIN Foundation, a shelter for homeless LGBTQ youth in the neighboring town of East Orange, were all started by current or former members of Unity Fellowship.

Peggie Miller, a longtime member of the church, co-owned Diamondz N Da Ruff, a local restaurant that served the community regardless of ability to pay and became a community hub predominantly for lesbians. Miller established the space in 2014 with two other Black queer women, Debra Holmes of Jersey City and Gloria Carter, well-known as the mother of billionaire and award-winning rap artist and record producer, Jay-Z. Miller, Holmes, and Carter made patrons feel at home and welcomed those who lacked a stable residence, providing free meals to individuals experiencing homelessness. According to Miller, "We felt that everyone in Newark is a diamond. No matter how rough it is, there's diamonds, and they deserve to be treated with royalty." While every night was described as a wall-to-wall party with delicious food, D.J.s, and live singing, there were also times when local organizers like Newark Pride, Inc. president, Sharronda "Love" Wheeler, would hold Newark Pride meetings there. When it closed in 2019, Holmes lamented the loss of such a loving communal space. "I've always thought of Diamondz N Da Ruff like being the *Cheers* of Newark. When you came in there everybody knew your name and everybody was family. That was the place to be."[25] Holmes has since partnered with Ms. Theresa Randolph, well-known for her Black lesbian parties, to create an annual dinner, award, and fashion show event to honor community members called Just Being Us, held in Newark's Robert Treat Hotel. Their first event in 2022 honored masculine-identified women. The following year, they honored couples like Reverend Alicia Heath-Toby and her wife Saundra Toby-Heath, who fought for, and won, the right for same-sex couples to marry in New Jersey as notable plaintiffs in the New Jersey Supreme Court case, *Lewis v. Harris* (2006). In 2024, they plan to honor a broad spectrum of Newark's LGBTQ community.[26]

In 2000, Peggie Miller created PMP Enterprises, an entertainment company for music and fashion that celebrates Black butch identity. Under PMP Enterprises, Miller holds annual New Millennium Butch Fashion Shows featuring aggressive Black lesbians—"aggressive" or "AG" are other terms for butch lesbians primarily used within the Black community—from Unity Church NewArk and her all-butch Newark fraternity, Pi Lambda Phi (PLP). In collaboration with other Black lesbians in the city, Miller self-published *New Millennium Butch* in 2009, a coffee table book and calendar. The book and calendar are unique, featuring only photographs of dapper Black butch lesbians in tailored suits captured by photographer Tamara Fleming. According to Miller, Black butch visibility is essential to her work: "My focus has always been on the aggressive women because I've never felt the aggressive woman got all the attention that's needed. Not only that, since we are always hid because of who we are . . . I wanted to make sure we're shown in our best light. You know what I mean? That's why I love showing them or showing myself. I don't model, but I just put it together, showing how beautiful, that we are beautiful, regardless, and that we should be seen."[27]

Miller exhibited the photographs in 2011 at the Queer Newark Oral History Project's first conference, "Queer Newark: Our Voices, Our Histories." The audience was a wide mix of people ranging in age, class, gender, sexuality, and race. Some of them were perhaps seeing Black butch women positively represented for the first time. With the exception of well-known Black women like actress Lena Waithe, Black butch women rarely walk major runways or appear in magazines, television, and film. Miller's work serves to correct the historic invisibility of Black butch women. Until the COVID pandemic in 2020, Miller continued to hold fashion shows in Newark and outside of New Jersey. With more widespread vaccination and less community spread, Miller, with the help of Jae Quinlan, brought back the New Millennium Butch fashion show for a chic community audience at Rutgers-Newark during Newark Pride week in July 2023.[28]

Similarly, Anita Dickens established a gender-inclusive boutique to disrupt the prevalence of gender-binary clothing stores. Dickens started Off the Hanger, a fashion and furniture store, with her spouse Lynette Lashawn in 2010. Lashawn curates one half of the store with femme-style high-fashion clothing, while the other half of the store includes masculine-of-center or unisex clothing either sourced elsewhere or created by Dickens under her own brand, ANE Clothier. Dickens, who prefers to dress in menswear, resents using traditional clothing store fitting rooms where she often experiences "the look," in which, she explains, other customers or employees make it clear that a queer and gender-nonconforming person is not welcome in a space where gender is specifically demarcated in binary terms.[29]

Discrimination that occurs in fitting rooms falls along the same lines as movements to block transgender individuals from using public bathrooms that correspond to their gender identity. Che Gossett places anti-trans bathroom legislation in the context of "racial slavery" and the Jim Crow era, when bathrooms were segregated by male/female and Black/white binaries. Gossett writes, "The bathroom, with its gender-binary regime of sexual difference, is one of the signatures—along with hyper-incarceration, mass deportation, and racial capitalism—of the afterlife of slavery." In resistance to the historical legacy of violence against Black and transgender bodies, which includes discrimination and harassment in various public spaces, Dickens's store provides an alternative space outside the limits of heteronormative society where gender-nonconforming individuals are able to shop without social or legal judgment. To make clear her mission, Dickens has a sign inside Off the Hanger that reads, "All Genders." It sits directly below a mirror, where it serves to underscore the reflected image of each person as they read it. Moreover, by modeling all of the clothes herself on her website and social media accounts, she uses her Black queer body to demonstrate how masculine

FIGURE 4.2. Anita Dickens, co-owner of Off the Hangar, which serves a queer and gender-nonconforming clientele, in early 2023. Courtesy Queer Newark Oral History Project.

clothing is not exclusive to cisgender male consumers while also interrupting the presumed whiteness of queer and transgender identity.[30]

Although it closed in 2020, for nearly a decade the Artisan Collective stood in defiance of the whitewashing process inherent in a city undergoing the forces of gentrification. The Artisan Collective was a small shop featuring handmade items created by the co-owners, five Black queer women: Jae Quinlan, Burley Tuggle, Saundra Toby-Heath, Juanita Martin, and Leslie Peterson. It also served as a sanctuary space for lesbian creators and artists. All of the co-owners regularly provided space in their shop for other local queer artists to sell their artwork and have remained heavily involved in the local art community. Quinlan currently serves on the board of Art Front Galleries, an organization that helps local artists gain visibility through pop-up art shows, and has been involved in Newark Pride, the Newark LGBTQ Community Center, Unity Fellowship

Church NewArk, and the Queer Newark Oral History Project. Much of Quinlan's artwork draws on a historical understanding of the Black queer urban experience, which she translates into artistic and cultural expressions that destabilize racist, sexist, and homophobic ideas in society.

Artisan Collective became a hub for Black lesbian expression, not only through artwork and craft, but also through Quinlan's open mic night, "Crack the Mic." These reoccurring events would feature spoken word and musical performances chiefly by local Black women, many of whom were queer and gender-nonconforming. Unlike other lesbian spaces, which tend to cater to white lesbians, "Crack the Mic" validated and fostered the voices, ideas, history, and desires of Black queer women who varied in their socioeconomic status and gender identity. Despite the shop closing, Quinlan remains active in Newark's queer art scene and local LGBTQ activism and organizing.[31]

Black queer women have been pivotal to the inception and shaping of the Queer Newark Oral History Project. They have been critical contributors to the project's publicly accessible archive of historical research by sharing their stories and other archival materials. Jae Quinlan facilitated the project's acquisition of a set of pioneering safer-sex materials and nineties ballroom videos shot on camcorder, making her an integral part of preserving LGBTQ Newark history. Professional photographer and entrepreneur Tamara Fleming photographed the project's early planning meetings with local LGBTQ community leaders, including Quinlan and Peggie Miller. These images remain an important part of QNOHP's archive. Fleming's work as a photographer serves as an intervention in Black queer erasure and includes a historical consciousness. Conceived of as an ongoing image study and archive, Fleming has photographed approximately twenty leaders in Newark's LGBTQ community. Her portraits include physically disabled queer people of color and delve into issues of mental illness and explore emotionality. Along with the images she took of butch lesbians for Miller, Fleming's LGBTQ leaders portraits were displayed on large screens at Queer Newark's 2011 conference, providing another window into Newark's LGBTQ community to a rapt audience. What's more, June Dowell-Burton, Janyce Jackson Jones, Miller, and Quinlan took part in the conference as panelists. Queer Newark held its second conference, "Sanctuary: A History of Queer Club Spaces in Newark," a monthlong series of public programs exploring the city's queer bar and club scene, with notable Black lesbian party promotor Theresa

FIGURE 4.3. Ad for the Artisan Collective on Halsey Street, in *NMB: New Millennium Butch,* vol. 1, issue 1 (September 2012).

Randolph as a panelist. Known in Newark and nationwide for her work as a club promoter, Ms. Theresa founded B.L.I.S.S. Entertainment as well as the Ms. Full-Figured USA Pageant and Ms. Theresa Productions. For over twenty-five years her lesbian nightlife parties served as community institutions where Black lesbians could safely meet when the majority of LGBTQ bars and clubs only catered to gay men. The conference helped situate Black lesbian entrepreneurs like Ms. Theresa at the center of queer history and gave voice to other Black queer women panelists who found refuge in these spaces.[32]

Newark's Queer Futurity

Understanding the impact of gentrification on other cities, current mayor Ras Baraka wants to revitalize Newark without displacing poor and working-class residents. He has emphatically refuted any assertions that Newark might be "the next Brooklyn." His plan is to repurpose empty space abandoned since the 1950s as well as carve out affordable housing within all new housing developments. Yet, despite his approach, the risk remains that the rent prices will increase beyond the means of many current residents, organizations, and small business owners, including for spaces rented by Newark's LGBTQ community. As Christina Strasburger and Mary Rizzo show in their discussion of Queer Newark walking tours (chapter 11), Newark's queer history is already largely a history of absences. Bars, clubs, and organizations that once provided sanctuary no longer exist. The Newark LGBTQ Community Center, led by Beatrice Simpkins and Denise Hinds, almost permanently closed its doors in 2017 when developers purchased the entire block as part of the corporatization of downtown Newark. Fortunately, then director Jeffrey Trzeciak, as a prominent gay man with the power to intervene, provided space within the Newark Public Library for the center in what would otherwise have been a devastating blow to Newark's LGBTQ community. During the height of the COVID pandemic and subsequently when the library came under new leadership after Trzeciak resigned, the community center's future became precarious. As of 2022, however, Simpkins and Hinds were able to secure a new location in downtown Newark on Market Street.[33]

Although the forces of gentrification and the COVID pandemic will likely result in the loss of more queer institutions, the Newark Black queer community can still be found amidst displacement. Black queer women continue to lead as they reimagine the city's queer future. They brought queer-institutions to the streets and to the virtual spaces of the internet. Simpkins and Hinds continued to host much-needed community events during the pandemic on online platforms like Zoom and YouTube. They also took to the streets to fight for the lives of Black transgender women alongside volunteers like Angela Raine. Together they have held public candlelight vigils where the names of transgender individuals who were tragically murdered were read aloud as part of the Transgender Day of Remembrance. Their advocacy includes transforming harmful police practices, such as how the city's officers handle interactions with members of the LGBTQ community. This work has led to the Newark Department of Public Safety appointing a police officer in a new role as an LGBTQ community liaison. When a local Black transgender woman named Ashley Moore was found deceased on a street downtown and her death was not properly investigated by Newark police, Simpkins led the fight for justice for Moore and her family. What's more, during the summer of 2020, twenty-four queer organizations in and around Newark signed on to participate and hundreds took to the streets despite pandemic fears to show support for the Black queer and transgender community in the March for Queer Black Lives, an outgrowth of continuing Black Lives Matter protests.

In his oral history, Darryl Rochester shared a story about club Zanzibar in Newark in the 1970s. He describes glitter falling off queer and transgender bodies as they walked to and from club Zanzibar in Newark, sweaty from dancing with queer friends and family.

> DARRYL ROCHESTER: [W]hen you walked in the door, there was glitter piled up like this. A foot high of glitter. All through the club, upstairs and downstairs, so people was walking through glitter and at the end of the night, everyone was sparkling! . . . I know glitter stays with you forever.
>
> TIMOTHY STEWART-WINTER: Forever.
>
> DARRYL ROCHESTER: Forever! My roommate had to come home with me in glitter and I was in the cab—the only thing I can say is downtown Newark had glitter all up Broad Street for two days! For two days, glitter, glitter. Everyone was laying and rolling in it and just crazy. Could you imagine, sweat and glitter![34]

Just when you think glitter is gone, it shows up again and again in odd places: in your clothes even after you washed them, in your hair, on your pillow, embedded in your carpet. It has a sort of impermanent permanence. Zanzibar's glitter certainly blew down Halsey Street, a few blocks away, and it can be found all over the city. Queer theorist José Esteban Muñoz once wrote that "queerness exists for us as an ideality that can be distilled from the past and used to imagine a future. The future is queerness's domain." What's left of Newark's queer and trans past may not be easily apparent, but like tiny bits of glitter, it has left fabulous traces. Newark's queer bars and clubs, businesses, and other institutions may at times vanish, but the capacity for queer and trans world-making will continue.[35]

Notes

1. Naomi Extra, interview with Tracey "Africa" Norman, October 31, 2016, Queer Newark Oral History Project (QNOHP), 2, https://queer.newark.rutgers.edu/sites/default/files/transcript/2016-10-31%20Tracey%20Africa%20Norman%20interviewed%20by%20Naomi%20Extra.pdf.

2. On Newark activism and the 1967 Newark uprising, see Mark Krasovic, *The Newark Frontier: Community Action in the Great Society* (Chicago: The University of Chicago Press, 2016); Robert Curvin, *Inside Newark: Decline, Rebellion, and the Search for Transformation* (New Brunswick, NJ: Rutgers University Press, 2014); Junius Williams, *Unfinished Agenda: Urban Politics in the Era of Black Power* (Berkeley, CA: North Atlantic Books, 2014); Kevin Mumford, *Newark: A History of Race, Rights, and Riots in America* (New York: New York University Press, 2008); United States Kerner Commission, *The Kerner Report: The 1968 Report of The National Advisory Commission on Civil Disorders* (New York: Pantheon, 1968).

3. Mumford, *Newark*; Krasovic, *The Newark Frontier*; Curvin, *Inside Newark*.

4. Arthur Louis, "The Worst American City," *Harper's*, January 1, 1975, 71.

5. Rohan Mascarenhas, "YouTube Spat Breaks Out between Late-Night Comedian Conan O'Brien, Newark Mayor Booker," nj.com, September 30, 2009, https://www.nj.com/news/2009/09/spat_breaks_out_between_late-n.html.

6. J. Jack Halberstam, *In a Queer Time and Place: Transgender Bodies, Subcultural Lives* (New York: New York University Press, 2005).

7. Gary Jardim, ed., *Blue: Newark Culture/Volume Two* (Orange, NJ: De Sousa Press, 1993), 148; Timothy Stewart-Winter and Esperanza Santos, interview with Darryl Rochester, September 19, 2019, QNOHP, https://queer.newark.rutgers.edu/interviews/darryl-rochester; *Vogue* magazine cover, August 1, 1974, https://archive.vogue.com/issue/19740801.

8. Jardim, *Blue*, 146.

9. For groundbreaking histories of gay and lesbian bar culture in New York and San Francisco, see Nan Alamilla Boyd, *Wide Open Town: A History of Queer San*

Francisco to 1965 (Berkeley: University of California Press, 2003) and George Chauncey, *Gay New York: Gender, Urban Culture, and the Making of the Gay Male World*, 1890–1940 (New York: Basic Books, 1994). For insight on how white lesbian bars could be hostile places for Black queer women, see Rochella Thorpe, "'A House Where Queers Go': African American Lesbian Nightlife in Detroit, 1940–1975," in *Inventing Lesbian Cultures in America*, ed. Ellen Lewin (Boston: Beacon Press, 1996), 40–61; David M. Halbfinger, "Anthony Imperiale, 68, Dies; Polarizing Force in Newark," *New York Times*, December 28, 1999; Candace Bradsher and Whitney Strub, interview with James Credle, May 3, 2014, QNOHP, https://queer.newark.rutgers.edu/interviews/james-credle; Whitney Strub and Timothy Stewart-Winter, "Remembering One Eleven Wines, a Pre-Stonewall Win against Homophobic State Surveillance," *Slate.com*, November 30, 2017, https://slate.com/human-interest/2017/11/remembering-one-eleven-wines-liquors-a-pre-stonewall-win-against-homophobic-state-surveillance.html.

10. Steward-Winter and Santos, interview with Rochester, 33, https://queer.newark.rutgers.edu/sites/default/files/transcript/Darryl%20Rochester_REDACTED%20Transcript.pdf.

11. Amiri Barka, *The Autobiography of LeRoi Jones* (New York: Freundlich Books, 1984). According to Amiri Baraka's wife, Amina Baraka, in his later years Baraka began to rethink some of his homophobic and sexist beliefs. See Kristyn Scorsone, Christina Strasburger, Whitney Strub, and Mi Hyun Yoon, interview with Amina Baraka, March 2, 2018, QNOHP, https://queer.newark.rutgers.edu/interviews/amina-baraka.

12. Anna Alves and Whitney Strub, interviews with Angela Raine, October 20, 2016, and February 6, 2018, QNOHP, https://queer.newark.rutgers.edu/interviews/angela-raine; Whitney Strub and Craig Blunt, interview with Pucci Revlon, April 12, 2017, QNOHP, 6, https://queer.newark.rutgers.edu/sites/default/files/transcript/2017-04-12%20Pucci%20Revlon%201.pdf. Revlon did not consent to be in *Paris Is Burning* and felt betrayed by director Jennie Livingston.

13. Alves and Strub, interview with Raine, February 6, 2018, 3, https://queer.newark.rutgers.edu/sites/default/files/transcript/2018-02-06%20Angela%20Raine.pdf.

14. Jardim, *Blue*, 1993; Steward-Winter and Santos, interview with Rochester. Zanzibar stayed open until the early 1990s, but after Albert Murphy died from AIDS and Shelton Hayes left, the clientele shifted, and the club became less popular.

15. Kristyn Scorsone, interview with Tiney Pringle, February 22, 2018, QNOHP, https://queer.newark.rutgers.edu/interviews/tiney-pringle.

16. Kristyn Scorsone, Timothy Stewart-Winter, and Whitney Strub, interview with Peter Savastano, July 15, 2015, QNOHP, 4, https://queer.newark.rutgers.edu/sites/default/files/transcript/2015-07-15%20Peter%20Savastano%202-Final%20

to%20post.pdf; Whitney Strub, interview with Walter Newkirk, February 26, 2018, QNOHP, https://queer.newark.rutgers.edu/interviews/walter-newkirk; Strub and Blunt, interviews with Revlon; and Stewart-Winter and Santos, interview with Rochester.

17. Peter Savastano, "Some Initial Reflections on HIV/AIDS and HIV/AIDS Related Deaths in the Gay and Lesbian Communities of Newark and in 'The Houses of Newark,'" June 1996, 7, in Queer Newark Oral History Project files; Whitney Strub, interview with Aaron Frazier, November 21, 2017, QNOHP, 21, https://queer.newark.rutgers.edu/sites/default/files/transcript/2017-11-21%20Aaron%20Frazier%203_1.pdf.

18. Joe William Trotter Jr., *Workers on Arrival: Black Labor in the Making of America* (Oakland: University of California Press, 2019), xvi–xvii; see also Kevin Mumford's *Newark*, in which he notes that in the wake of the Great Migration there were upwardly mobile African American entrepreneurs in Newark, but there is little evidence they were involved in activism, especially in the face of Jim Crow. Zenzele Isoke, *Urban Black Women and the Politics of Resistance* (New York: Palgrave Macmillan, 2013). Isoke is one of the few scholars to date who has written extensively about Black lesbians in Newark and their grassroots activism using oral history.

19. "A Movement Grows in Newark," *The Advocate*, October 14, 2003; Whitney Strub, interview with June Dowell-Burton, December 1, 2015, QNOHP, https://queer.newark.rutgers.edu/interviews/june-dowell-burton.

20. "History of Newark Pride," Newark Pride website, https://newarkpride.org/about-us/historic/; Timothy Stewart-Winter and Whitney Strub, "The Murder of Sakia Gunn and LGBT Anti-Violence Mobilization," *Queer Newark, 1885–Present*, Outhistory.org, 2014, https://outhistory.org/exhibits/show/queer-newark/murder-of-sakia-gunn; Scorsone et al., interview with Amina Baraka.

21. Author interview with Alicia Heath-Toby, January 27, 2017, QNOHP, 1–2, https://queer.newark.rutgers.edu/sites/default/files/transcript/2017-01-27%20C.%20Alicia%20Heath-Toby%20interviewed%20by%20Kristyn%20Scorsone.pdf; Gary Paul Wright, "Remembering the Murder of Sakia Gunn, and Newark's Lost Opportunity: Opinion," nj.com, May 23, 2013, https://www.nj.com/njv_guest_blog/2013/05/remembering_the_murder_of_saki.html.

22. Author interview with Janyce Jackson Jones, December 27, 2022, QNOHP, https://queer.newark.rutgers.edu/interviews/janyce-jackson-jones.

23. Liberation in Truth is abbreviated as "L.I.T." rather than LIT, because the Newark community refers to it as L.I.T., with each letter spoken, and not "lit." Reverend Janyce Jackson Jones explained that to refer to the church as "LIT" is historically incorrect. Author interview with Jones, December 27, 2022, QNOHP.

24. Archbishop Carl Bean with David Ritz, *I Was Born This Way: A Gay Preacher's Journey through Gospel Music, Disco Stardom, and a Ministry in Christ* (New

York: Simon & Schuster, 2010), 196, 213; Anna Alves, interviews with Janyce Jackson Jones, March 9 and May 13, 2016, QNOHP, https://queer.newark.rutgers.edu/interviews/janyce-jackson-jones; author interview with Jones, December 27, 2022, QNOHP; Esperanza Santos interview with Senior Bishop Jacquelyn Holland, November 25, 2019, QNOHP, https://queer.newark.rutgers.edu/interviews/bp-jacquelyn-d-holland.

25. *Cheers* was an American television show, set in a bar where, according to the theme song, "everyone knows your name." It ran on NBC from 1982 to 1993 and is considered one of the most popular television series in history.

26. Author interview with Peggie Miller, March 7, 2017, QNOHP, 12, https://queer.newark.rutgers.edu/interviews/peggie-miller; Author interview with Debra Holmes, August 15, 2023, QNOHP, interview in author's possession.

27. Author interview with Miller, 21.

28. Author interview with Miller.

29. Author interview with Anita Dickens, December 8, 2016, QNOHP, https://queer.newark.rutgers.edu/interviews/anita-dickens.

30. Che Gossett, "Blackness and the Trouble of Trans Visibility," in *Trap Door: Trans Cultural Production and the Politics of Visibility*, ed. Reina Gossett, Eric A. Stanley, and Johanna Burton (Cambridge, MA: The MIT Press, 2017), 184.

31. Author and Monica Liu, interview with Jae Quinlan, October 19, 2016, QNOHP, interview in author's possession; The Robert Treat Hotel in Newark has been an important space for LGBTQ Newarkers who have held ballroom competitions there in the 1990s, such as the late James Credles' Fireball, Peggie Miller NMB Fashion Shows, and now Holmes and Randolph's Just Being Us events. Some community members, like Peter Savastano, claim to have heard about drag shows happening there as far back as circa the 1950s.

32. Darnell Moore, Beryl Satter, Timothy Stewart-Winter, and Whitney Strub, "A Community's Response to the Problem of Invisibility: The Queer Newark Oral History Project," *QED: A Journal in GLBTQ Worldmaking* 1, no. 2 (2014): 1–14; "Queer Newark: Our Voices, Our Histories," Conference, Queer Newark Oral History Project website, https://queer.newark.rutgers.edu/queer-newark-our-voices-our-histories.

33. Karen Yi, "Is Newark the Next Brooklyn? Mayor Says No," nj.com, February 19, 2017, http:// https://www.nj.com/essex/2017/02/is_newark_the_next_brooklyn_mayor_says_no.html; Tony Gallotto, "Newark's LGBTQ Community Center Opens on Market Street," tapinto.net, January 22, 2022, https://www.tapinto.net/towns/newark/sections/giving-back/articles/newark-s-new-lgbtq-community-center-opens-on-market-street.

34. Steward-Winter and Santos, interview with Rochester, 49.

35. Eric Keifer, "Newark Police Department Appoints LGBTQ Community Liaison, patch.com, March 31, 2021, https://patch.com/new-jersey/newarknj

/newark-police-department-appoints-lgbtq-community-liaison; Kayla Rivas, "Newark LGBTQ Community Center Honors Slain Transgender, Gender Non-Conforming People," *Tap Into Newark,* November 22, 2019, https://www.tapinto.net/articles/newark-lgbtq-community-center-honors-slain-transgender-gender-non-conforming-people; "Walk with Us for Black Queer Lives," Queer Newark Oral History Project website, June 7, 2020, https://queer.newark.rutgers.edu/walk-us-black-queer-lives; José Esteban Muñoz, *Cruising Utopia: The Then and There of Queer Futurity* (New York: NYU Press, 2009).

Oral History Excerpt #3

Angela Raine

Angela Raine recalls being confused for Grace Jones, and also some of the violence inflicted on transgender women.

WHEN A LOT MORE STARS started doing real hard disco, we would have the show on the dance floor. Once we did that, I started doing Grace Jones. I was great at Grace Jones. We actually had a lot of fun doing shows. In the Doll House, I was okay, I was comfortable. If I took that persona out of the Doll House cuz I had my hair cut like Grace Jones and I dressed outrageously like her on stage, my thinking wasn't that you can't do that in society. I actually would go out in full makeup, full gear, high heels and everything like Grace Jones, not knowing the ramifications that were coming with it.

I retired at twenty-one because I went out one night with this guy, we was on the motorcycle, we went out to, I think, Turtle Back Zoo or West Orange somewhere. They had a carnival. We got there at night, so it's tons of light. First and foremost, I didn't know white people knew Grace Jones *[Laughs]*. I didn't know that they knew who Grace Jones was. I got off the motorcycle and took off the helmet, and somebody screamed, "It's Grace Jones!" We were swarmed, and it was freaking me out. I didn't even get to enjoy this carnival. We ended up getting back on the motorcycle and being escorted out of there cuz it was so frightening, it was like I didn't know that this is her life, this is what she has to go through.

It happened to me on Broad Street at Newark. I took a cab [to] downtown Newark from where I lived because I was in full gear, it was summertime—this was broad daylight. I was going out, and dressing up was my thing. I always had to be dressed. With the haircut—and I wasn't big on wigs—with the haircut, it's summertime, I'm all right, I'm comfortable. I jumped in the cab from where I lived—cuz everybody where I lived, I lived in the projects, everybody knew me there, most of the people in my building knew I did Grace Jones stuff. For me to come out looking like Grace Jones, it was, "Hey, Angie." I jumped in the cab, and I got off on Broad Street. I crossed the street, and I was mobbed. It freaked me out because I felt trapped, and there was nowhere to run. I mean, I was used to a little attention, and sometimes it was negative attention, but this was all positive, but it was just too many damn people. After that, I gave up doing shows, period. I would do it periodically at the Doll House. Other than that, no.

The stroll is the red-light district, and that's where the trans women went to make their money. That was located on West Kinney and Broad. Very few trans women went [elsewhere downtown] because the men, if they found out you were trans, they were violent. At least in the Kinney area, they knew.

Down here where the baseball stadium is there was the Lincoln Motel, which has Zanzibar's, and maybe a block or so over, there was another hotel called the Benzell. That's where a lot of trans women lived. It was a beautiful hotel back yonder when. One or two of my friends got killed in there. I can tell you a whole bunch of tragic deaths now, but we won't go there.

Pepsi, she was six-foot-one maybe, light-skinned, beautiful. Lived in her red lipstick. She was a nice person in her own way. She was murdered. She had got a settlement from a car accident or something, and her boyfriend was an active drug user, and she gave him a nice chunk of money, and he went out and blew it. When he came back and asked her for some more money, and she didn't give it to him, he killed her.

There was a trans woman killed in Military Park. They would just say a male dressed as a woman. My girlfriend Mona, she got hit and dragged almost a block. When she died, she died three weeks later, there was nothing said. There was no kind of investigation. It was nothing. This girl up in Military Park and my girlfriend at the Benzell, even this young girl that I used to hang out with during her transition, she was murdered. That was horrible, but there was no press, no investigation about that.

Lightly edited for cohesiveness. Listen to or read the whole oral history at https://queer.newark.rutgers.edu/interviews/angela-raine.

CHAPTER 5

Project Fire

AIDS, Erasure, and Black Queer Organizing in Newark

JASON M. CHERNESKY

ON APRIL 5, 1988, a protest was held in Wanaque, New Jersey. The residents of this bucolic, semirural suburban community, not far from the New York state border, were upset about a proposed state-run convalescent home for 120 New Jerseyans living with HIV/AIDS. Ken Higgins, a civic leader in Wanaque, told the *New York Times*, "these AIDS people come from a decadent society.... I'm talking about sex and degenerates passing needles in Newark. They don't want them in Newark. Newark says Nimby [Not in my backyard]. Well, don't put them in our backyard. We believe Nimby too!" Other protestors, like an eight-year-old child and her father, held signs reading "Keep AIDS out of Wanaque," and "Don't bring the city to the suburbs."

Mike Ryan, another local civic leader, further underscored the sentiments expressed by the protestors. "I don't have anything against them, but why should they be next to my house? Who's going to visit a drug addict? Who's going to visit a homosexual? Another homosexual! They go after your child." He added, "if they are drug abusers, they belong in the city and who knows where they're from if they're homosexual."[1] Leaving aside the veiled racialized grievances, NIMBY-ism, and homophobia voiced by the Wanaque residents, their comments about Newark speak to an important popular perspective about how New Jerseyans came to view where and who was most impacted by HIV/AIDS in the state. Most importantly, Mr. Ryan's specific comment about not knowing from where the gay convalescents derived represented a common popular framing about how the

AIDS epidemic's impact on Newark's LGTBQ communities went unrecognized or was marginalized in public and public health discussions about the disease.

This chapter explores and analyzes how this particular cultural erasure structured how many people living outside Newark's gay and queer communities understood, and responded to, the HIV/AIDS epidemic in New Jersey's largest city during the 1980s and 1990s. In this chapter, cultural erasure refers to the ways in which the problem of HIV/AIDS among Newark's LGBTQ communities was largely left unrecognized in mass media narratives about the disease and in some public health initiatives that sought to address the epidemic—which was especially the case at the local level. As we will see, Newark's LGBTQ communities were either left out or marginalized in HIV/AIDS surveillance in New Jersey, public health decision-making surrounding the disease, and mass media accounts about the epidemic in Newark.[2]

An important component of this erasure stemmed from the epidemiological profile of HIV/AIDS in New Jersey. As the epidemic unfolded in the state during the 1980s, public health experts noted how—unlike many other parts of the United States that saw higher reported cases among gay men or men who have sex with men (MSM)—New Jersey, and particularly the greater Newark region, experienced higher cases and rates among intravenous (IV) drug users, heterosexual women, and children born with the disease. This helped shape public health agendas and priorities in the state. Often reported as a unique phenomenon, the state's epidemiological profile also helped shape and reinforce narrowly constructed mass media narratives about the real and imagined problems in underserved urban communities of color in the age of HIV/AIDS—narratives that excluded how these same interconnected phenomena impacted the lives of gay communities of color. The chapter concludes by highlighting how Newark's first gay-men-of-color AIDS service organization, Project Fire, successfully educated gay men and women about how to protect themselves from HIV from the early 1990s to the early 2000s. Project Fire's AIDS service work, moreover, must be understood within the context of the cultural erasures that framed popular and public health responses to HIV/AIDS in Newark.

By exploring and interrogating the interplay between the cultural erasure of HIV/AIDS among Newark's LGBTQ communities and their response to the epidemic, this chapter aims to historicize and amplify (where sources allow) once marginalized and/or ignored voices, experiences, and actions of Newark's gay men as they coped with HIV/AIDS during the first two decades of the epidemic.[3] While this story is certainly *not* a comprehensive history of HIV/AIDS in Newark more broadly, or how the disease impacted the city's LGBTQ communities specifically, my second goal is to use this story to facilitate scholarly engagement that will further amplify this largely forgotten chapter in the history of Newark and HIV/AIDS in America.[4]

Origins: The Rise of New Jersey's Unique HIV/AIDS Profile

From the beginning of the epidemic, HIV/AIDS has disproportionately impacted communities of color in New Jersey more broadly and in Newark specifically. Moreover, in New Jersey at least, HIV/AIDS was also concentrated in the state's urban environments. The underlying causes that led to the HIV/AIDS crisis among Black and Latinx urban communities in Newark began decades before the virus appeared in North America.

The deprivation—the structural racism—endured by Black and Latinx communities in Newark, as described throughout this book, resulted in what psychologist and urban studies scholar Mindy Fullilove calls "root shock"—the social, emotional, and environmental upheaval that was brought on by urban renewal policies, increased race-based segregation, and concentrated poverty in Newark and other cities.[5]

HIV, the virus that causes AIDS, appeared in North America at some point in the 1970s, and it was in this disrupted urban ecology that the virus eventually thrived. By the late 1970s, men, women, and children living in Newark were becoming exposed to the virus—though no one knew it at the time. The intricate details of HIV transmission are complicated, but for the purposes of this chapter, there are essentially four prevalent modes of transmission. These include sexual intercourse; the transfusion of, or exposure to, contaminated blood or blood products, including via shared syringes for drug use; and, for children, the exposure to contaminated blood and bodily fluids before or at birth (if the mother is HIV-positive during pregnancy).[6] In short, the structural inequalities that placed marginalized Newark residents at greater risk of experiencing "root shock"—and its attendant negative consequences—made these populations equally more vulnerable to HIV infection. This was compounded by urbanized and racialized segregation in New Jersey (decades of racist housing policies helped to concentrate populations of color in the state's cities). Many of the counties hardest hit by HIV/AIDS were anchored by majority Black and

Latinx cities. Such phenomena thus resulted in higher rates and more cases of HIV/AIDS among the state's Black and Latinx populations—particularly in the state's underserved cities.[7]

On June 5, 1981, the first official cases of what would come to be known as HIV/AIDS were reported to and by the Centers for Disease Control and Prevention (CDC). In their *Morbidity and Mortality Weekly Report*, the CDC reported that five gay men in Los Angeles had acquired a rare form of pneumonia called *Pneumocystis carinii* pneumonia (PCP).[8] What would become known as the HIV/AIDS epidemic had begun. Over the course of the epidemic in the 1980s and 1990s, gay men and MSM were statistically the most affected by the disease at the national level. The CDC reported the highest cases among gay white men and MSM during this period. This began to change in the 1990s, however, and by mid-decade, higher numbers of Black Americans with HIV/AIDS would be reported to the CDC.[9]

Like many gay men at the time, Aaron Frazier, a Black man living in Newark, knew that a new disease was sickening and killing gay men in the early 1980s. As the outbreak unfolded during this period, gay men and MSM across the United States were grappling with, and were important witnesses to, the high rates of illness and death among their friends and neighbors. In Newark, many of the surviving accounts about the disease's impact are from oral histories provided by men who have survived the epidemic, such as Frazier. Reflecting on those early years, Frazier remembers how he became aware of the disease's impact, as he noticed that a number of people he knew "just started dying." He remembered that at one time during these early years somewhere between "5 to 10 people . . . died in the course of a week. I'm talkin' about from Murphy's" (a popular downtown gay bar); this did not include some of the people he knew that frequented "the stroll." In another oral history, speaking about the toll the disease took on Newark's gay communities, Bernie McAllister recalled that "When the epidemic was at its worst, [there were] two funerals a day for years," and that he alone lost "about 150 friends."[10]

Frazier's experience with the disease also provides important insight into how HIV/AIDS manifested in New Jersey. For seven years, Frazier was in a relationship with a man who was an IV drug user. The man eventually died from AIDS. Though the epidemiological profile of the disease has shifted since the beginning of the twenty-first century, New Jersey consistently saw higher reported cases (and rates) among IV drug users during the first two decades of the epidemic. This was largely due to two factors: the disrupted urban ecologies in which HIV thrived and an increased supply of heroin.[11]

In the greater Newark/New York City region, a particular infrastructure for using heroin also contributed to the spread of HIV. First, because the use and possession of drugs and drug-using material was illegal—coupled with several other issues that placed drug users in danger—some drug users were forced into using "shooting galleries," specifically the "cash galleries," since they offered a safe place for taking drugs. Second, these facilities were often located in abandoned properties and near drug marketplaces. Those concerned about carrying drug-using equipment could rent syringes, for example, in cash galleries. This meant multiple usages of a single syringe on any given day. Since HIV was (is) a blood-borne pathogen, the shooting gallery became an efficient system in which the virus thrived and traveled.[12]

Beginning in the late 1980s, New Jersey public health officials often cited the unique way the disease unfolded in the state. The New Jersey Department of Health was the primary public health institution that responded to HIV/AIDS in the state during this period. In 1987, it published its first public report about the epidemic, *AIDS in New Jersey: A Report from the Department of Health,* which stated, "in other parts of the country, the vast majority of people with AIDS have been homosexuals, and intravenous drug abusers constitute what is being called the second wave' of the epidemic. But in New Jersey, drug abusers—along with their sexual partners and their children—have comprised most of those affected by the epidemic since its onset."[13] Of course, state health officials were also intent on educating all New Jerseyans about how the disease was a serious and deadly sexually transmitted disease, regardless of one's sexual orientation. The report did emphasize the increased risk the disease posed to gay men, and showed (albeit implicitly) how the disease disproportionately affected New Jersey counties that had higher populations of Black and Latinx residents (e.g., Essex, Hudson, and Passaic Counties).[14]

What was most notable was the emphasis state health officials put on this "special" epidemiological characteristic—the reported high rates of the disease among IV drug users. To fully understand the complex phenomena that influenced the ways in which the Department of Health responded to HIV/AIDS in the 1980s and 1990s requires more analytical space than is available in this chapter. However, it is important to note that while state health officials were dedicated to controlling the spread of and mitigating the effects related to HIV/

AIDS during this period, their rhetorical emphasis on increased rates among IV drug users was nonetheless a defining feature in how state health officials publicly discussed the overall impact of the epidemic in New Jersey.

As the epidemic entered its second decade, the highest number of reported cases and rates of the disease were still seen among IV drug users, heterosexual women, and children born with HIV. Yet roughly a third of all reported cases in New Jersey—34 percent—were among gay men and MSM. It is unclear what percentage of that third were Black and Latinx men, but we know that 70 percent of all reported adult and adolescent cases in the state were among populations of color.[15] In addition, given the segregated racial geography of the state, HIV/AIDS was significantly concentrated in the counties that housed cities near the greater Newark area (which included Jersey City and Paterson).[16]

In short, the hegemony of HIV/AIDs statistics—especially the slightly higher numbers and rates among IV drug users—overdetermined the way New Jerseyans and others came to understand the epidemic in Newark. The epidemiological picture of HIV/AIDS in Newark would also factor into restrictive narratives about American "inner cities" during this era—narratives that were hyperfocused on racialized urban poverty and its attendant problems, most notably drug use. This same phenomenon also reinforced the cultural erasure of gay men and MSM of color in the growing public discourse surrounding how the disease impacted communities of color in the late 1980s and early 1990s.

Erasure of the Epidemic's Impact on Newark's Gay Community

As the epidemic entered its second decade, the overall erasure of gay men in Newark essentially operated on two registers. The first was related to how the unique epidemiological profile of HIV/AIDS in Newark became inextricably linked to dominant, racialized mass media narratives about urban poverty and its attendant problems. Stories about the statistical realities of HIV/AIDS in Newark reflected not only the close connections made between racialized urban poverty and how HIV/AIDS affected heterosexuals, but also the restrictive nature of such narratives. If stories help us make sense of the world, high-profile mass media narratives about HIV/AIDS in Newark were structured around familiar "conventions of representation" that tightly framed the epidemic in terms of how Americans saw the connections between the rise of this new disease and the underserved urban communities of color it affected.[17]

As the epidemic gained greater public visibility in the United States in the mid-1980s, we can see how mass media narratives about HIV/AIDS in Newark took form. In 1984, the *Chicago Tribune* ran a front-page story about Dr. James Oleske, a prominent pediatric AIDS specialist working in Newark. In the article, Oleske was quoted as saying: "It's not surprising that this is a what we are seeing in Newark" (referring to the problem of HIV/AIDS among children and their mothers). "The city has a lot of poverty. . . . People turn to drugs. Newark does not have a lot of homosexuals, but it does have a lot of drug abusers. That often goes with poverty."[18] While it is unclear the degree to which Oleske was aware of Newark's gay communities, his remarks are nonetheless representative of how AIDS was framed as a disease associated with urban poverty in Newark.

By the late 1980s and early 1990s, a similar framing came to dominate national mass media coverage of HIV/AIDS among urban communities of color in the U.S. writ large. It was common to find national news stories that highlighted how the number of HIV/AIDS cases were increasing among populations of color—particularly among heterosexual men, women, and children. Most importantly, such stories about AIDS merged with another topic that dominated the public agenda during this period: the American inner city. This was evidenced by a 1987 article published in *Time* about the so-called changing face of AIDS. Not only was the epidemic becoming "younger, darker, [and] more feminine," the article stated, it was also "becoming common in inner-city ghettos."[19]

This particular framing of HIV/AIDS within the context of real and imagined inner-city problems helped reinforce (or even helped shape) a segmented cultural perception about the epidemic by the late 1980s. This was exemplified in a 1987 article published in the *Chicago Tribune* titled "Underclass Falling Victim to AIDS Siege." The article stated that "AIDS is no longer the disease of homosexual middleclass white men, it is increasingly prevalent among impoverished minority men, women, and children . . . among the underclass."[20] Equally unsurprising were the ways in which public presumptions about sexuality were grafted onto discussions about the racialized geography of the epidemic. This represents a fixed set of narratives about the epidemic that cast HIV/AIDS in gay enclaves as primarily affecting white men. As the nation turned its attention toward HIV/AIDS among communities of color—especially in the inner city—the epidemic was, in essence, often seen as a "heterosexual disease."

In Newark, Peter Savastano—a gay white man who worked with people coping with HIV/AIDS—saw things with more nuance. On the one hand, he understood that (statistically speaking), the epidemic had a larger impact on IV drug users, as well as "the heterosexual population . . . primarily women and children." On the other hand, in a reflective essay he wrote in 1996, Savastano also underscored that many gay Newarkers faced the same structural inequalities and problems that affected the lives of heterosexual populations coping with the disease. Gay men and MSM were not only coping with the disease and death, but the "daily drama of HIV/AIDS" was also spun out "against the background of incredible poverty, government corruption . . . racial tension, and the deep festering wounds from the 1967 uprising." There were, however, some media accounts about AIDS in Newark that attempted to unpack similar problems in the city that were related to the disease. A case in point is Lena Williams's 1989 *New York Times* article titled "Inner City Under Siege: Fighting AIDS in Newark."[21] Williams made similar connections to how HIV/AIDS was predominantly affecting IV drug users, heterosexual men and women, and children. She discussed how AIDS was "not sending shock waves through neighborhoods that are already suffering from drugs, crime, poverty, illiteracy, unemployment and deteriorating housing." In other words, for some Newark residents, AIDS had not become a problem that took top priority in their lives—particularly if they felt it did not affect them. While the article provided nuance in discussing the lived reality of people in Newark in the age of HIV/AIDS, it did not discuss how the disease impacted the city's gay community.[22]

This pattern continued through the early 1990s, at which point it became clear that Newark had become one of the most important urban representatives in media coverage that focused on HIV/AIDS among heterosexual IV drug users, women, and children born with the disease. As part of a series titled "AIDS in the 90s" in March of 1990, *NBC Nightly News* reported from Newark on how HIV/AIDS was inextricably linked to IV drug use and poverty in American "inner cities." Standing on a Newark street, a reporter explained how IV drug use was at the center of the outbreak in "poverty-stricken urban neighborhoods," where male "addicts [were] infecting their female sex partners."[23] That same year, the *New York Times* published an article titled "In Newark, a Spiral of Drugs and AIDS, Urban Epidemic: Addicts and AIDS." The piece informed readers about Newark's unique epidemiology. "The epidemic in Newark has always been," the article stated, "a disease that strikes intravenous drug users more than any other group."[24] As was the case through the middle of the 1990s, Newark's unique epidemiology remained at the center of mass media stories about AIDS in that city.[25]

But the erasure of how the epidemic impacted gay men in Newark was not just a mass-media phenomenon. The second mode (or register) by which this erasure occurred was at the city government level—specifically at the city's Department of Health and Human Services (HHS). The city's public health leadership response to HIV/AIDS is largely absent from the historical record. But what we can glean from the handful of sources indicates that city leadership did not prioritize addressing HIV/AIDS specifically or proactive public health initiatives more broadly. As part of her testimony in a congressional hearing in 1989 titled "AIDS in Newark and Detroit" (which was part of a series of hearings that would eventually inform the writing and passage of the largest AIDS relief legislation in the country, The Ryan White CARE Act of 1990), the Director of Newark's HHS, Callie Foster Struggs, stated where the city placed public health in the catalogue of municipal priorities: "In developing . . . municipal budgets, you will find that the first and second priorities are police and fire with the third being streets and sanitation. Health and human service[s] do not normally come very high in the priority list."[26] Though Struggs also highlighted that Newark HSS was involved in HIV/AIDS educational initiatives, the details about the totality of those programs require further investigation by scholars.[27]

Fiscal constraints might help to explain why Newark's HHS did not develop and enact a robust proactive response to HIV/AIDS, but their use of statistics in the same hearing raises more questions than answers as to why gay men and MSM were left out of that presentation. Strugss presented, and submitted to the congressional record, a table showing a statistical breakdown of cases of HIV/AIDS gathered by Newark's HHS. The table displayed the adult cases, pediatric cases, IV drug user cases, heterosexual cases, and "other [HIV] statistics." What makes the omission of gay men curious is that it was a standard category used by public health and HIV/AIDS surveillance experts at the national, state, and local levels at this time. Moreover, this data could have been acquired from the New Jersey Department of Health. In fact, public health worker David Byrnes, in a 1990 HIV/AIDS statistical report compiled for East Orange, New Jersey, demonstrated that gay men in Newark were recorded in the statistical record—these numbers were derived from New Jersey AIDS surveillance data. Regardless, the omission of gay men in Newark also seems to fit with the city's under-recording AIDS data more broadly. In an internal annual report written for the end of the year 1986, Newark's HHS did not record any HIV/AIDS data.[28] While this is a single report written nearly three years before the congressional hearing, the lack of HIV/AIDS data in the report is striking.

The reasons for these omissions are unclear given the historical information currently available, but we might consider how the power of place, coupled with the city leadership's refusal to recognize Newark's gay communities of color, may have played a role here. First, we might consider how the lack of resources, the residents' mistrust of institutions, and other larger structural conditions potentially led to the local health department's inability to record and respond to HIV/AIDS among the city's gay communities of color. In her important study "AIDS is Just a Four-Letter Word," the scholar and activist Eugenia Lee Hancock demonstrates how a combination of limited resources and other endemic problems in the city constrained the work of Newark's HHS. Moreover, mistrust in public health and medical institutions in Newark was arguably another barrier to data collection among health workers already stretched thin. Secondly, and perhaps most importantly, the ability of Newark's LGBTQ communities to be seen by the city's leadership was greatly constrained by, as Hancock so tersely states, "institutional racism and homophobia"—two important social processes that were "hardwired into the social systems and structures of Newark." This was compounded by the fact that the "gay community [was] not identified as a *constituency* in Newark, in stark contrast to their counterparts in New York City." Indeed, Newark mayor Sharpe James denied the presence of LGBTQ people in Newark, even to queer activists, into the twenty-first century, as Kristyn Scorsone notes in chapter 4.[29]

The refusal of powerful institutions and actors to recognize the plight of gay men of color and their subsequent actions are well known. Such erasure was part of, and shaped by, the politics of race, racism, place, class, and homophobia in the decades leading up to and including the emergence of HIV/AIDS.[30] If attention was going to be paid to AIDS in Newark's queer community, it would have to come from the community itself.

Unpacking Project Fire's Duffle Bag: Black Gay Men Respond to AIDS

Project Fire emerged at a time when there were well-established national grassroots AIDS service organizations that provided HIV/AIDS educational materials to gay men. Since the early days of the epidemic, some of these organizations were particularly important in helping to develop and provide educational campaigns geared toward gay men of color. These groups included, for example, Blacks Educating Blacks about Sexual Health Issues (BEBASHI) in Philadelphia and the National Association of Black and White Men Together (NABWMT), which operated in a number of cities.[31] But Newark lacked grassroots HIV/AIDS advocacy organizations through much of the 1980s.

This began to change in the late 1980s and early 1990s. One of the first grassroots organizations established in Newark was the Newark Community Project for People with AIDS (NCPPWA), officially formed in 1988. The group was chaired by Derek T. Winans, a white and politically connected Newark activist who worked on antipoverty programs, civil rights, and welfare and tenants' rights initiatives in the city during the 1970s and 1980s—issues of the queer Newark left discussed by Whitney Strub in chapter 3.[32] As part of a growing number of AIDS service organizations during this period, NCPPWA organized to fill a gap in community-based AIDS advocacy in the city. The group's primary mission, along with other AIDS service organizations, was to educate the community about the disease, help those with HIV/AIDS get the services they needed, and promote prevention strategies.

Much of NCPPWA's leadership was gay, and according to Winans, 83 percent of the group's members were Black or Latinx. Though the group was primarily made up of people of color from Newark, its overall stated goals were to help *all* Newarkers affected by or at risk for HIV/AIDS. It established connections to city and state politicians and secured modest funds for HIV education and prevention. But in what appears to be a tacit concession to the antigay *realpolitik* of the late 1980s, it downplayed gay-specific concerns in order to make the broadest—and most politically palatable—demands. NCPPWA dwindled as the 1990s began; ultimately, it made crucial strides toward mitigating the epidemic but acted as a precursor to explicitly queer AIDS activism in Newark.[33]

Shortly after the formation of NCPPWA, the city saw the emergence of the first HIV/AIDS advocacy groups devoted specifically to educating gay men and MSM of color about the disease. In 1990, James Credle (who was an NCPPWA subcommittee member) helped form People of Color Together (PACT) in the greater Newark area. The group was established, in part, as a support group for gay men and lesbians living in and around the city.[34] For nearly a decade Credle was involved with—and one of the founding members of—NABWMT in New York City.[35] It was in 1990 that Credle was approached by Pattie PenDavis, who was looking to provide AIDS education for gay men of color in Newark. She heard of Credle's involvement in AIDS advocacy and activism in New York as a member of NABWMT and Men of All Colors Together (MACT). According to Credle, PenDavis "said there were too many people in the community [Newark] who were dying, and they were not getting the information around HIV." After their meeting, Credle, along with Eric Perez of MACT, held an AIDS education workshop at a local bar. It was at that point that Credle decided to try and educate gay men and MSM in Newark about HIV/AIDS and harm-reduction techniques by importing much of what he learned while active in AIDS and gay activist initiatives in New York City.[36]

A few years after Credle and Perez held this initial harm-reduction workshop, Credle applied for and received a grant from the New Jersey Department of Health to fund their work.[37] Their grant application came at a time when there were some funds and attention allocated toward safe-sex and HIV prevention education for Black communities in the United States. In 1987, the CDC set aside $177.7 million for fiscal year 1988 to address AIDS education in Black communities. According to a New Jersey Department of Health memo, the funds were allocated to address "issues identified in the 'Black resolution' . . . delivered at the August 7–9 CDC Conference on AIDS in Minority Populations."[38] New Jersey health officials also recognized—in their 1991 strategic AIDS plan *New Jersey: A State Organizing to Fight AIDS, a Plan for the 1990s*—that there were few "adequate prevention education [efforts that] specifically targeted" gay and lesbian communities in the state. "This may be attributed, at least in part," the plan stated, "to New Jersey's distinction as the only state in which reported AIDS cases in [IV drug users] exceeded those among gay and bisexual men." The plan also indicated that, contrary to some epidemiological assumptions, HIV/AIDS was increasing among the state's gay populations.[39] At present, there is no evidence linking the state's recognition of the need to provide more harm-reduction resources to LGTBQ communities to a rise in national funding for HIV prevention. Nevertheless, the AIDS plan signaled a slight shift in how the state prioritized prevention. Most importantly for Credle and his colleagues, there was now much-needed funding that helped them form their HIV/AIDS-service organization in Newark.

Between 1992 and 1993, Credle and others formed Project Fire, which drew its name and inspiration from a Harlem Renaissance periodical. Growing out of a meeting held by PACT, the advocacy group wrote that their name was in tribute of the 1926 magazine *Fire!!*, which featured "stories of open homosexual love between Blacks." According to Project Fire, "those pioneers dared to speak openly and publicly about homosexual relationships at a time when public rejection was at its height." These same conditions, the group stated, faced the gay and bisexual communities of Newark, who feared for their lives and where "HIV infection runs rampant [in a place] with few services and little outreach to people . . . other than [those] of heterosexual orientation."[40] Over the next decade, Project Fire worked to educate gay men and MSM about safer sex practices in the greater Newark area.[41]

Though it is difficult to discern how many people Project Fire reached, we know it did so through two primary methods. One of these involved a duffle bag and a safer-sex program developed by the National Task Force on AIDS Prevention (NTFAP). Developed by members of NABWMT, and funded through money from the CDC, the NTFAP program produced and taught what they titled the *Hot, Horny and Healthy Curriculum: An HIV Prevention Playshop for African American Gay and Bisexual Men*. This curriculum was the educational cornerstone for Project Fire's safer-sex advocacy mission. Used elsewhere, the *Hot, Horny and Healthy* manual centered on providing safer-sex education in intimate settings, called playshops, that were often held in someone's home. According to the curriculum, the playshop approach helped men learn about HIV/AIDS and prevention techniques, while simultaneously exploring "new ideas of sexual enjoyment and gratification" that sought to "replace their old high-risk activities with safer, but still satisfying alternatives." Along with this curriculum, Project Fire volunteers also carried with them, in a duffle bag, other pieces of essential equipment.[42]

Part of the *Hot, Horny and Healthy* curriculum ensured that men left the meetings more knowledgeable about how to have pleasurable and safer sex, which meant demonstrating how to use particular technologies. For instance, Project Fire's duffle bag held several different lubes, eleven dildos, condoms, and latex gloves. Such technologies were important—alongside educational material about how to properly use condoms, for example—because the curriculum emphasized "safer" sex over "safe" sex. The NTFAP understood that messages about "safe" sex did not always resonate with all men, but in demonstrating how to have both "safer" and enjoyable sex, they felt more men might partake in less risky sexual practices. This meant providing men with the tools necessary to have safer sex and use certain toys or other techniques that made sex fun and pleasurable as well.[43]

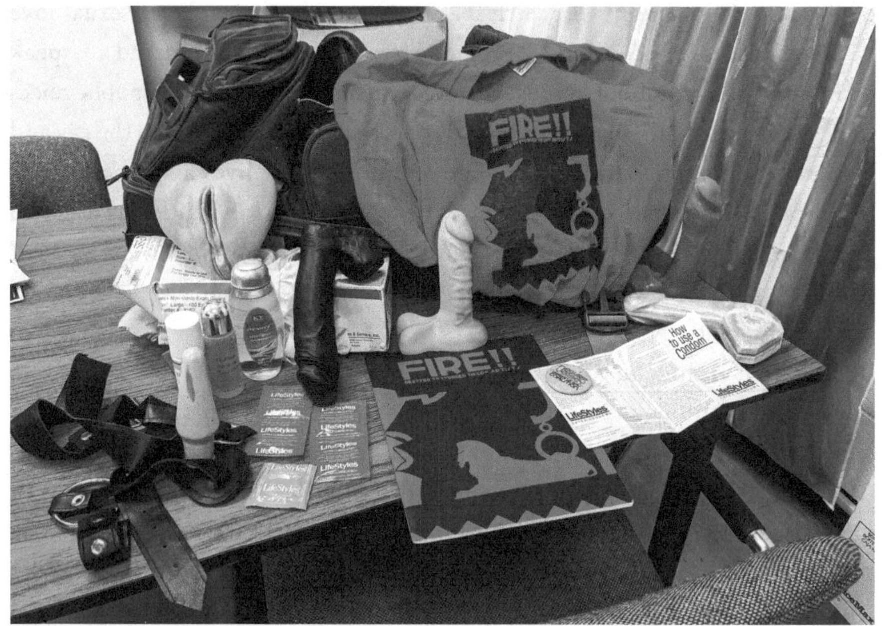

FIGURE 5.1. Project Fire's safer-sex education duffel bag, unpacked in the Queer Newark Oral History Project archives, courtesy QNOHP.

FIGURE 5.2. Don Ransom at the Fire Ball, Robert Treat Hotel, April 15, 1995. Organizer James Credle noted that audiovisual documentation of these events was very sparse, so this image comes from best available source, Project Fire Ball, Part II, James Credle VHS Collection, Queer Newark Oral History Project archives.

Project Fire was also devoted to educating lesbians about safer-sex practices. Similar to the NTFAP's curriculum for men, Project Fire volunteers used the *Wet, Wild and Well: Lesbian Sex in the 1990s* curriculum, which discussed everything from how to use safer-sex technologies (like dental dams) to dating tips. According to the curriculum guide, which was produced by the Whitman-Walker Clinic in Washington, DC, *Wet, Wild and Well* targeted lesbians because they were largely absent from HIV/AIDS harm-reduction programming. "Lesbians, due to their perceived low risk sexual activities," the guide stated, "have been pigeon-holed as 'islands of immunity' and subsequently left [out] of HIV risk reduction educational efforts." Project Fire's duffle bag contained toys, tools, and information useful to lesbian audiences as well.[44]

While Project Fire's harm-reduction training mirrored that of larger organizations that provided HIV/AIDS education to gay men and women of color, their engagement with *Fire!!* presented a unique, creative, and important use of this piece of Black American culture. It was an *essential* tool in their HIV prevention efforts. The magazine was not just the namesake or inspiration for the group. The fact that *Fire!!* was part of a panoply of safer-sex technologies in the group's duffle bag reveals how Project Fire's harm-reduction educational work was inextricably linked to messages of personal empowerment and the historical legacy of queer identity-making that, in this case, they linked to the Harlem Renaissance. In a 2015 public talk, Credle, while holding a copy of *Fire!!*, told the audience that they thought the magazine was a "very important . . . symbol that was crucial to our people and crucial to our survival," which was tied to "remembering our history."[45] In a city where it was difficult to establish safe public spaces for LGBTQ communities, Project Fire's playshops and other initiatives helped provide spaces where queer identity-making and empowerment could occur. These were critical to Project Fire's public health agenda.

This was also the case with Project Fire's marquee public event: their "Fireball." From the early 1990s to the early 2000s, the organization hosted this annual gala to promote safer-sex practices in the greater Newark area. The Fireball was a drag and runway show where, according to Credle, participants "would be in competition around a safer sex message and we would provide [prize] money for them in terms of who did the best safer sex message [in their] presentation."[46] By all accounts, these were well-attended events, integrated into Newark's thriving ballroom scene, as discussed in chapter six of this book. "We used to have a thousand people who came to our balls," Credle stated in an oral history.[47] Though the Fireballs were structured and performed as typical ballroom competitions, they uniquely fused grassroots HIV/AIDS service work and queer Black and Latinx cultural expression. Along with their use of *Fire!!*, Project Fire used a creative artistic endeavor to not only make their HIV prevention messaging accessible to their peers, while simultaneously fostering empowerment, partly by claiming a queer space in the genealogy of Black cultural history that went under-recognized in the straight Newark of Ken Gibson, Sharpe James, and Amiri Baraka.

The Fireballs were also, therefore, a subtle form of HIV/AIDS and queer activism. While these events did not confront power in the mode of large-scale protests or other public displays of civil disobedience, these collective actions can be seen as a kind of disruptive event that contested the cultural erasure of HIV/AIDS among Newark's LGBTQ communities during the 1980s and 1990s.[48]

Project Fire would operate its playshops and Fireballs from around 1992 to some point in the early 2000s. According to Credle, the group lost funding after ten years of operating because the "federal bureaucracy told us that our way of doing the work in terms of our home health parties was not getting enough feedback [and] that we actually couldn't show that we were having people change their behavior."[49] Though the Fireballs stopped and the duffle bag was stored in James Credle's home closet for years, until he donated it to the Queer Newark Oral History Project, HIV prevention work continues in the greater Newark area. Since at least the early 2000s, longtime AIDS advocates such as Gary Paul Wright, a founder of the African American Office of Gay Concerns in downtown Newark, and groups like Project WOW continue to educate LGBTQ communities of color about HIV/AIDS prevention strategies. Their work, like that of Project Fire and NCPPWA before them, remains crucial as the problem (one of many) of HIV/AIDS has disproportionately affected communities of color in New Jersey and the greater Newark region.

Coda

Project Fire's harm-reduction initiatives were an important intervention in the larger landscape of HIV/AIDS work in Newark. For a decade, they represented one of the only organizations developed by and for gay men of color, and for such a small, volunteer-run group, they were able to have an outsized presence in the city. Their relationship to the larger geography of cultural erasure in which they operated is also an important component of this story—one that requires further investigation. This chapter has provided some analytical suggestions as to how they may have contested this erasure, but questions remain. In what ways did Project Fire or other LGTBQ communities in Newark *explicitly* contest their cultural erasure in the 1980s and 1990s? How might the work of Project Fire fit within a larger story of other under-recognized or forgotten AIDS service/activist groups that operated in other marginalized American cities? In what ways can the cultural erasure of gay communities impacted by HIV/AIDS help inform contemporary urban and political histories of Newark?

Regardless of how future scholars engage with these historical phenomena, the story told here also stands as a reminder that HIV/AIDS is still a problem affecting LGTBQ communities of color. The rates of new infections are higher among gay men and MSM of color nationally, and in New Jersey the epidemiological portrait of the disease has flipped. As of 2019, reported cases of HIV/AIDS among gay men and MSM of color have surpassed reported cases among IV drug users and heterosexual women. While the epidemiological profile has changed in New Jersey, the disease remains—as it has from the beginning of the epidemic—an endemic problem among the state's communities of color, especially in the greater Newark region.[50] Given the long history of racialized health disparities in the United States, the disparity in HIV/AIDS rates in New Jersey (and the nation as a whole) is undoubtedly the result of race-based structural inequalities, unequal access to health care and prevention methods, and persistent poverty.

Like HIV/AIDS before it, the COVID pandemic has yet again made visible those structural inequalities that are linked to, and in many cases are the causes of, such health disparities. Whether this new epidemic will overshadow the continuing problem of HIV/AIDS in the greater Newark area—especially among LGBTQ communities of color—is presently unclear. Nevertheless, more work remains to be done in educating LGBTQ communities about, and providing needed resources for, HIV/AIDS prevention in the region. Some of that work continues to be done by local HIV/AIDS advocates who seek to mitigate the impact of a disease that remains largely under-recognized outside Newark's LGBTQ communities of color.

Notes

1. Michael Winerip, "Our Towns; Nimby Views on People with AIDS, *New York Times*, April 5, 1988.

2. Though HIV/AIDS has long been understood to be a pandemic disease event, many of the actors during this period referred to the disease outbreak as an epidemic. Since this is an actor's category, and for reasons related to consistency in the prose, I will be using epidemic in the chapter.

3. The scholarship on the history of HIV/AIDS is vast; among the key works this chapter draws from are Sander L. Gilman, *Disease and Representation: Images of Illness from Madness to AIDS* (Ithaca, NY: Cornell University Press, 1988); Steven Epstein, *Impure Science: AIDS, Activism, and the Politics of Knowledge* (Berkeley: University of California Press, 1996); Paula A. Triechler, *How to Have Theory in an Epidemic: Cultural Chronicles of AIDS* (Durham, NC: Duke University Press, 1999); Cathy J. Cohen, *The Boundaries of Blackness: AIDS and the Breakdown of Black Politics* (Chicago: University of Chicago Press, 1999); Jennifer Brier, *Infectious Ideas: U.S. Political Responses to the AIDS Crisis* (Chapel Hill: The University of North Carolina Press, 2011); Sabrina Marie Chase, *Surviving HIV/AIDS in the Inner City: How Resourceful Latinas Beat the Odds* (New Brunswick, NJ: Rutgers University Press, 2011); and Dan Royles, *To Make the Wounded Whole: The African American Struggle against HIV/AIDS* (Chapel Hill: The University of North Carolina Press, 2020).

4. I want to thank the Queer Newark Oral History Project and all of the individuals who provided their oral histories. Without their stories, this chapter would not have been possible. I also want to thank Wangui Muigai, Ezelle Stanford III, Antoine Johnson, and Whitney Strub for their insight and editorial suggestions.

5. Mindy Thompson Fullilove, *Root Shock: How Tearing Up City Neighborhoods Hurts America, and What We Can Do about It* (New York: Ballantine/One World, 2004).

6. This information is derived from Jason M. Chernesky, "'The Littlest Victims': Pediatric AIDS and the Urban Ecology of Health in the Late-Twentieth-Century United States" (PhD diss., University of Pennsylvania, 2020), 19–61.

7. Chernesky, "'The Littlest Victims,'" 19–61.

8. Centers for Disease Control, "*Pneumocystis* Pneumonia—Los Angeles," *Morbidity and Mortality Weekly Report* 30, no. 21 (June 5, 1981): 250–252.

9. See, for example, Centers for Disease Control and Prevention, *HIV/AIDS Surveillance Report: U.S. HIV and AIDS Cases Report through December 1995* 7, no. 2, 1995. This specific report highlighted the shifting demographics of HIV/AIDS. This is not to suggest that national public health officials were not aware of the changes in its epidemiology prior to 1995.

10. Whitney Strub, interview with Aaron Frazier, February 27, 2018, Queer Newark Oral History Project (QNOHP), 3, https://queer.newark.rutgers.edu/sites/default/files/transcript/2018-02-27%20Aaron%20Frazier_Part4.pdf; Esperanza

Santos, interview with Bernie McAllister, October 25, 2019, QNOHP, 14 (transcript not available online).

11. Strub, interview with Frazier. Information about the number of cases among IV drug users is derived from "AIDS Cases, State of New Jersey as of December 31, 1990," The New Jersey State Library.

12. There is a vast amount of social science and public health literature on needle-sharing practices in the United States during this period; see, for example, Don C. Des Jarlais, Samuel R. Friedman, and David Strug, "AIDS and Needle Sharing within the IV-Drug Use Subculture," in *The Social Dimensions of AIDS: Method and Theory*, ed. Douglas A. Feldman and Thomas M. Johnson (New York: Praeger, 1986), 111–125; Don. C. Des Jarlais, Thomas Kerr, and Patrizia Carrieri et al., "The Sharing of Drug Injection Equipment and the AIDS Epidemic in New York City: The First Decade," in *Needle Sharing among Intravenous Drug Abusers: National and International Perspectives, NIDA Research Monograph 80*, ed. Robert J. Battjes and Roy W. Pickens (Rockville, MD: National Institute on Drug Abuse, 1988), 167. It is important to note that not every drug user frequented shooting galleries; see Bill Hanson, George Beschner, James M. Walters, and Elliott Bouvelle, eds., *Life with Heroin: Voices from the Inner City* (New York: Lexington Books, 1985). The extent of abandoned properties in Newark is difficult to assess. However, the city of Newark sought to institute a comprehensive health plan for the city, in which they mapped significantly deteriorated properties; see James A Buford, *Newark Comprehensive Health Plan, 1976–1977, Newark Health Planning Agency* (Newark, NJ: Department of Health and Welfare, 1977), Rutgers University Special Collections, Medical Library (hereafter cited as NJ AIDS Collection).

13. State of New Jersey Department of Health, *AIDS in New Jersey: A Report from the Department of Health*, April 1987, box 2, folder 4, NJ AIDS Collection.

14. Chernesky, "'The Littlest Victims,'" 19—61; see also *AIDS in New Jersey*.

15. New Jersey Department of Health, "AIDS Cases in New Jersey as of July 31, 1990," New Jersey State Library; New Jersey Department of Health, "AIDS Cases in New Jersey as of December 1992," New Jersey State Library; see also "Recommendations of State Commissioner of Health Frances J. Dunston to Governor Jim Florio," *New Jersey: A State Organizing to Fight AIDS, a Plan for the 1990s* (1991), box 5, folder 8, NJ AIDS Collection.

16. This is informed by Chernesky, "'The Littlest Victims,'" 35–47, and Lizabeth Cohen, *A Consumers' Republic: The Politics of Mass Consumption in Postwar America* (New York: Knopf, 2003).

17. This idea about how stories help us make sense of the world, as they pertain to disease phenomena, is informed by Priscilla Wald, *Contagious: Cultures, Carriers, and the Outbreak Narrative* (Durham, NC: Duke University Press, 2008).

18. Dennis L. Breo, "'The Cure Will Come from the Kids': Children of AIDS, Children of Hope," *Chicago Tribune*, January 1, 1984.

19. Richard Stengel, "The Changing Face of AIDS," *Time Magazine*, August 17, 1987.

20. Wes Smith, "Underclass Falling Victim to AIDS Siege," *Chicago Tribune*, February 16, 1987.

21. Peter Savastano, "Some Initial Reflections on HIV/AIDS and HIV/AIDS Related Death in the Gay and Lesbian Communities of Newark and in 'The Houses of Newark,'" 1996, in Queer Newark Oral History Project files.

22. Lena Williams, "Inner City Under Siege: Fighting AIDS in Newark, *New York Times*, February 6, 1989. In fact, Williams's article was one of the rare journalistic accounts that captured the complexities of HIV/AIDS in Newark during the late 1980s.

23. The quotes are derived from "AIDS in the 90s, Women and Infants," March 28, 1990, *NBC Nightly News*, Vanderbilt Television News Archive. The other parts in the series "AIDS in the 90s" include "The Gay Community," March 27, 1990, and "The Care Crisis," March 29, 1990.

24. John Tierney, "In Newark, a Spiral of Drugs and AIDS, Urban Epidemic: Addicts and AIDS," *New York Times*, December 16, 1990; *NBC Nightly News*, "AIDS in the 90s."

25. See Chernesky, "'The Littlest Victims,'" 106–147.

26. *Hearings before the Human Resources and Intergovernmental Relations Subcommittee of the Committee on Government Operations*, 101st Cong., Day 2 (1989) (statement of Callie Foster Struggs, Director of Newark Department of Health and Human Services), quote is from page 51.

27. Testimony of Callie Foster Struggs, 49.

28. "Information from David Byrnes, East Orange Health Officer, June 5, 1990," box 7, folder 6, NJ AIDS Collection; *Newark Department of Health and Human Services Annual Report*, Department Box, No. 0391, City of Newark Records Management Center, Newark, NJ.

29. Eugenia Lee Hancock, "AIDS Is Just a Four-Letter Word: An Ethnographic Study of Theodicy and the Social Construction of HIV/AIDS in Newark" (PhD diss., Drew University, 2002), 63–68; quotes are from page 65 (emphasis in original).

30. This analysis is informed by Cohen, *The Boundaries of Blackness*; Darius Bost, *Evidence of Being: The Black Gay Cultural Renaissance and the Politics of Violence* (Chicago: University of Chicago Press, 2019); Royles, *To Make the Wounded Whole*; Kevin J. Mumford, *Not Straight, Not White: Black Gay Men from the March on Washington to the AIDS Crisis* (Chapel Hill: University of North Carolina Press, 2016); Mae Henderson and E. Patrick Johnson, *Black Queer Studies: A Critical Anthology* (Durham, NC: Duke University Press, 2005).

31. For other organizations, see Brier, *Infectious Ideas*. For Black AIDS activism and advocacy, see Royles, *To Make the Wounded Whole*.

32. Kasi Addison, "Derek T. Winans, 65, Newark Activist," *Star-Ledger*, June 23, 2004.

33. This information is derived from "Mission Statement," Newark Community Project for People with AIDS, 1988, Newark Community Project for People with AIDS (NCPPWA) Collection, Newark Public Library Digital Repository, https://archive.org/details/NwkAids027. See also "The AIDS Epidemic in Newark and Detroit," *Hearing before the Human Resources and Intergovernmental Relations Subcommittee of the Committee on Government Operations*, 101st Cong., first session (1989) (statement of Derek T. Winans, Chairperson of the Newark Community Project for People with AIDS). This overall assessment is based on the small but valuable archive NCPPWA left behind, housed at the Newark Public Library and digitally available at: https://archive.org/details/NwkAids027.

34. "About PACT and Project 'Fire,'" Project Fire Training Manual, African American AIDS History Project, James Credle Papers, accessed August 1, 2021, http://afamaidshist.fiu.edu/omeka-s/s/african-american-aids-history-project/item-set/731.

35. Royles, *To Make the Wounded Whole*, 55.

36. Candace Bradsher, interview with James Credle, Queer Newark Oral History Project (QNOHP), 27; https://queer.newark.rutgers.edu/sites/default/files/transcript/JamesCredleQNOHP.pdf. For more on Credle's connections to other AIDS service and gay organizations, see Royles, *To Make the Wounded Whole*, 47–72.

37. This information is derived from James Credle's presentation at a Queer Newark Oral History Project event; see "Ballroom Scene and HIV/AIDS Education in Newark: Project Fire Credle," 2015, Queer Newark, https://www.youtube.com/watch?v=CuD6wNsEyPc (accessed January 1, 2020); hereafter cited as Credle Ballroom Scene interview. see also Bradsher, interview with Credle.

38. Memo, "Blacks Choose County Minority Task Force," Silas Mosley Jr., Senor Training Technician AIDS Program, New Jersey Department of Health to Black Groups, Clubs, Organizations and Individuals, October 16, 1987, NCPPWA Collection.

39. *New Jersey: A State Organizing to Fight AIDS*; quotes are from pages 95–96.

40. "About PACT and Project 'Fire,'" James Credle Papers.

41. Bradsher, interview with Credle, 28.

42. National Task Force on AIDS Prevention (NTFAP), *Hot, Horny and Healthy Curriculum: An HIV Prevention Playshop for African American Gay and Bisexual Men*, October 1992, James Credle papers. For the contents of the Project Fire duffle bag, see "Safe Sex Duffle Bag," Credle papers. For more information about the work of the NTFAP, see Royles, *To Make the Wounded Whole*, 47–72. In the mid-2010s, James Credle discussed some of Project Fire's work and the contents of the duffle bag, as well as some of the other individuals involved in Project Fire's work; see

"Ballroom Scene and HIV/AIDS Education in Newark: James Credle Introduction (Part 1)," 2015, Queer Newark, https://www.youtube.com/watch?v=FPlEiDTooUo.

43. NTFAP, *Hot, Horny and Healthy Curriculum.*

44. *Wet, Wild and Well: Lesbian Sex in the 1990s,* A Heart Project Workshop, January 1991, James Credle papers; quote is from page 2.

45. Credle Ballroom Scene interview. This analysis is informed by Bost, *Evidence of Being*; Royles, *To Make the Wounded Whole,* 73–102; and Anne Elizabeth Carroll, *Word, Image, and the New Negro: Representation and Identity in the Harlem Renaissance* (Bloomington: Indiana University Press, 2007), 191–220.

46. Bradsher, interview with Credle, 28.

47. Descriptions of the Fireball are derived from Bradsher, interview with Credle, 28, and video clips of the balls archived by the Queer Newark Project: "Fireball 1996," https://www.youtube.com/watch?v=6oylGFvrTMY; "Fireball 1998," https://www.youtube.com/watch?v=JyU7X3Ov7_w.

48. This argument is informed by Bost, *Evidence of Being.*

49. Bradsher, interview with Credle, 28.

50. New Jersey Department of Health, "County and Municipal HIV/AIDS Statistics, 2018," accessed October 1, 2021, https://www.nj.gov/health/hivstdtb/hiv-aids/statmap.shtml.

CHAPTER 6

Ballroom Interlude

QUEER NEWARK ORAL HISTORY PROJECT

Newark's ballroom scene is the crown jewel of its queer culture, recognized and respected nationally for its creativity and competitiveness at the cutting edge of style and performance. From the drag and gender-nonconforming underground of the 1950s and 1960s, to the grassroots origins of organized ballroom houses in the 1980s, and on through Newark's connection to the New York scene documented in the iconic film *Paris Is Burning* (1989) and the popular series *Pose* (2018–2021; in which Michaela Jaé Rodriguez provided the Newark backround), Newark has long been an epicenter of ballroom culture.

Ballroom culture consists of houses, whose members compete by walking the runway in a series of categories centered on gender, fashion, and style. Indicating its centrality to queer Newark life, the ballroom scene was the subject of one of the first published scholarly studies of queer Newark, Karen McCarthy Brown's "Mimesis in the Face of Fear: Femme Queens, Butch Queens, and Gender Play in the Houses of Greater Newark" (2001). Bringing an anthropologist's eye to the community, she sees the ballroom as a ritual, one in which queer members rejected by their biological families reconstitute family in the houses, and where gay and trans participants reeling from the social violence of bigotry, AIDS, and condemnation find strength and power in their runway performances. The fierce stylings of vogueing—a technique born in the Black and Latinx ballroom and appropriated for mass culture by the pop star Madonna—serve as an expression of "performative anger," Brown contends. The ballroom also allows space for mourning; in a legendary 1998 Fireball, which featured a "Memorial Runway," Angel Vizcaya walked shortly after his brother had died from AIDS. With a "feather-encrusted hoop" beneath on oversized skirt that concealed a birdcage within his costume, he paused upon striking a pose and held a white dove "aloft, its wings flapping," which Brown reads as an act of "pour[ing] his grief and his pressing need to transcend suffering, if only temporarily, into this startling runway performance."[1]

Newark also appears in the definitive study of ballroom culture, Marlon Bailey's *Butch Queens Up in Pumps: Gender, Performance, and Ballroom Culture in Detroit* (2013). Bailey expands upon Brown's analysis, meticulously showing how, "through gender and sexual performativity, ballroom members create a wider range of gender and sexual subjectivities than is recognized and legitimized in the heteronormative world." Such categories as the Butch Queens Up in Pumps of the title (cisgender gay men who perform as women) and Femme Queens (transgender women) compete within a standard of *realness*—which is based, ironically, on understanding gender *as* performance, in some ways an embodied queer theory. Bailey's landmark book is an ethnography of the Detroit ballroom scene, but reflecting Newark's prominence within the national ballroom nexus, his second chapter opens with a vignette at Newark's Robert Treat Hotel, frequent site of highly regarded balls for which houses travel great distances to compete.[2]

Newark's ballroom scene is not well preserved in traditional archives, aside from some 1990s flyers thankfully collected by archivist Steven Fullwood as part of the Black LGBTQ In the Life Archive at New York Public Library's Schomburg Center for Research in Black Culture. But it is a recurring motif of Queer Newark Oral History Project interviews. Thus, this chapter (put together collectively by members of QNOHP) acts as an interlude: instead of a sustained single-authored piece, it offers some glimpses of the precursors to the ballroom scene and then lets participants and observers tell the story in their own rich words.[3]

Prehistory: Before the Ballroom

One such early glimpse of gender-bending performance in Newark comes from Reese LaRue, a local dancer and entertainer who put on shows such as *Gay Paree* at the Kinney Club in the Third Ward in the 1940s. In her book *Swing City*, about Newark nightlife from the 1920s to 1950, Barbara Kukla describes LaRue's shows as being "as lavish and torrid as his terpsichore," with "glamorous costumes and a touch of nudity." Though not explicitly queer, LaRue's style nonetheless hinted at something beyond conventional gender roles.[4]

We can see the groundwork for a later world of gender-nonconforming queer performance being laid in the 1950s, largely through the reports of the Division of Alcoholic Beverage Control (ABC) that Anna Lvovsky uses to chart queer Newark nightlife in chapter 2. In one striking example, the Polka Club at 324 Springfield Avenue (located at the heart of the later 1967 Newark rebellion) held an Autumn Jamboree in September 1954. An ABC investigator reported that a bartender told him it was to be a "faggy" show, adding, "You know, when all the men change into women." Tickets cost $1.25, and ABC agents noticed a number of (people they identified as) men "wearing mascara, lipstick, rouge, and eyebrow make-up and attired in the shirts and 'slacks' of the type designed for women." Some other "male patrons wore evening gowns," with "at least twenty males in the audience who dressed and acted like females." The show involved singing, dancing, burlesque, and "bumps and grinds" that were "lewd and suggestive." Additionally, some "simulated intercourse" affronted the liquor board spies. The Jamboree cost the Polka Club its liquor license for six months—but thanks to that act of state oppression, we can witness Newark's drag culture in action.[5]

The Jewel Box Revue, a popular touring female-impersonator show, came through Newark regularly in this era, as recalled by Amina Baraka in chapter 1 of this book. It advertised freely in the local papers—a 1968 booking at RKO Proctor's in downtown Newark promised, "you won't believe your eyes as you watch the most amazing, most glamorous, most exciting deception in the world!"[6] But while the Jewel Box Revue allowed trans and gender-nonconforming performers a chance to make a living, its target audience was clearly the broader straight world, who were invited to marvel at the art and magic of gender-bending. Newark also had a queer underworld not intended for straight consumption, as Peter Savastano recalled in a QNOHP interview:

> There was this Black Richie Havens kind of guy who had an apartment in the area of Newark where I lived in at the time [circa 1969]. A friend of mine, a white girl I hung out with, took me to his apartment. And I remember Jimmy Hendrix's first album . . . was playing on the record player and I was given pot to smoke. So somehow through this group of people I ended up in this place in Newark that was kind of like a factory and it was two o'clock in the morning and there was this incredible

> dance going on there with all these beautifully dressed women, or so I thought at the time. I was among the few white people there, maybe there was four of us. And I only realized shortly after when someone told me that most of those women were not women! They were men dressed as women. And somehow over that period of time, which I'd say was about a year or so, I ended up in about five or six of these, what I now know, was a kind of moving party . . . one of them was somewhere down University Street over where The Goodwill Hope and Rescue Mission was and all of these meatpacking things and these little side streets. And the other one I remember, which doesn't make any sense to me now, but here's what I remember. So where Macy's was, so corner of Halsey and Market Street, right across from Macy's was a place called DMI Drafting Supplies, it was an art supply store and I remember going to one of these happenings in this huge empty loft dance studio across from Macy's above from DMI.[7]

Two figures who played a pivotal role in building Newark's queer infrastructure were Bobby White and Dorian Paris, who "really made Newark what it is for the gay people," according to longtime community member Craig Blunt. As Pucci Revlon, a transgender Newarker who eventually joined the ballroom scene, added:

> Mm-hmm. Yeah. Then Paris and Bobby White became friends somewhere in the 1950s. They used to tell me how when they'd go out in drag, they used to have to run from the police and hop the fences and hide in the yards and stuff cuz the police catch them out in drag they'd get beat up and thrown in jail. They did they own little ball things here that were just central in Jersey. They had several different clubs. They had one over here on West Market. The one on Twelfth Street. The one on Elizabeth Avenue. One on William Street, that's the Doll House. I worked for them at the Doll House at the time [see chapter 4 for more on the Doll House and its trans performances].
>
> We started taking hormones back when I was about eighteen. I think Niecy started, she was about fifteen. We started growing boobs back then. That's when we start hanging out late at night walking up and down the street in negligees and stuff, acting like we were pretty because that's what we did back then. Then we started going to balls about a year later. I think the first ball I went to was in New York. I think it was up in Harlem. It wasn't a crystal ball. It was something else. I know it had big pedestals in the middle of the floor. The big columns. It was nice back then. Then it was just mainly Fem-Queens. They had a couple of Butch-

Queen categories. I think it was Cunty Butch-Queen or the Mod Boy and Face and the Executive Look and probably something else. Then the grand prize was Fem-Queen. That's when grand prize started, like I think it was $300. Then it went to $500. Then they started doing this $1,000 grand prize. The first $1,000 grand prize was held in Irvington Manor. I remember that because I sold tickets for that for the girl that was doing it at the time . . . [8]

Okay, there was balls here in New Jersey, but there was just a few people that can actually do a ball. You need to have money to rent a club. You need to have money to buy the trophies. You need to have money to print up the flyers and then have them distributed, and then you need to have tickets. . . . But only several people . . . had balls back in the 70s in New Jersey. That's when we started branching out to New York, 'cause the ballroom scene started to get bigger. . . . They have more categories over there than they did over here. . . . We had Femme Queen Face, Butch Queen Face, Model's Effect, Femme Queen Models Effect, Mod Boy on the Butch Queen side. Then you had Business Woman, Housewife. Yeah, like about, maybe, fourteen categories on this side. When you got to New York, they start expanding categories.

Certain people that could actually afford to have these balls was having these balls in these clubs. Matter of fact, most of the time it was in Bobby White's club. It was on a smaller scale. Grand Prize could have been no more than about $250. They used to have Evening Gown Wears . . . , and we also had a five-hundred-pound stripper. Yeah, La Contessa De Francisca com Bella Ce Soir. This child was wide. That butt had to be about that big, in a bikini, more or less, and will strip down. Yeah. I know she's in a nursing home now. We had fun when we did go to the balls. Then Donna came, Lady Donna. She started having the ballrooms and she started with $500, the next day you know it's $1,000, and all the kids from New York started coming.[9]

Another staple of Newark's early drag ball culture was Trudy's Ball, described as an "almost legendary event" in a late-1970s issue of *Female Impersonator News*. Cheekily declaring in its title that "Transvestites Have Two Balls," the article celebrated Trudy's in Newark and the "Beach Drag Ball" at the M&K Discotheque in Atlantic City. Explaining that "the drag ball is an institution in the drag world," the uncredited author noted, "some of the prettiest 'girls' from New York and New Jersey come out for Trudy's Ball, many accompanied by very handsome and debonair escorts." Drag, the article concluded, "is alive and well in New Jersey."[10]

TRANSVESTITES HAVE TWO BALLS

FIGURE 6.1. "Transvestites Have Two Balls," *Female Impersonator News,* no. 10 (n.d., ca. 1976–1978).

A Scene Takes Shape

Aaron Frazier dated the emergence of a more formalized Newark ballroom scene to about 1980, which was spurred on by the organization of houses:

> The original balls only occurred once a year in Newark . . . and it was a girlfriend thing, but when houses became houses then you can look for a ball like maybe once a month. But then new kids wanted to have practice before the real ball. So then people started doing mini balls at places like Birds Lounge, the Blue Swan back during the day, Black Box, Zanzibar, The Honey Hole, which used to be on Broad Street; Laurel's Garden that used to be on Clinton Avenue; Irvington Manor. It was a lot of outlets to have a mini ball. You don't have that today. If we want to have a ball in Jersey, in Newark, you're going to spend close to anywhere from $5,000 to $10,000, and . . . that's just for the rental of the space for the venue. You're talking about security, that's another say $1,500. You might as well round it to an even $2,000. You're doing trophies, another thousand. You doing like cash prizes, that's another five. So then you've got people that you got to pay, the MC, the DJ, a couple of performers, you might as well say that's an additional five. So the

price, it went up, so it's not that prevalent. If you're not in with an organization or get a sponsorship, it's costly. . . . [My first ball] was at the Terrace Ballroom; it was a girlfriend ball. This was in, I'm going to say, 1980. . . . And it just was a fab time.[11]

I was just coming out of the closet. When I went away to school, I went to Virginia Union University. I came out of the closet basically down here from a suicide attempt and I met some people from New York, DC, Maryland, and even some people in Richmond. They took me to my first gay club. In Richmond. I was, "Wow. I never been to one." Who do I see when I first—I don't even know the name of the club. I didn't even know what the street was. All I know is the person who was performing was Ms. Divine [a drag actor famous from such John Waters films as *Pink Flamingos*]. She was performing and she had that red, white, and blue thing. I said, "I saw that bitch. I was there for—" I was like that. I was looking at her like this. In all honesty, . . . —that's where my house name come from, is from her. Yes. From Divine. The name of my house is Divine.[12]

Bernard McAllister was a key source for Karen McCarthy Brown's scholarly piece, and a central figure in Newark's ballroom scene as house mother for the House of Jourdan, which was established in 1985. When the house's annual gala fundraiser appeared on the local evening news in 2000, the television anchors smirked. But by 2005, mayoral candidate Cory Booker campaigned at a ballroom event, and in 2007 the *Star-Ledger,* New Jersey's largest newspaper, featured the House of Jourdan on its cover. In 2021 *Pose* star Rodriguez credited a member for introducing her to the ballroom scene.[13] McAllister said:

I approached ballroom family much like I approach my family. All my family aren't blood cousins to me, but we were raised in the same crib. We ate the same food. We got the same spankings. We had the same experiences. . . . The New York houses, and if you didn't hang with the New York girls, you weren't fab, you weren't anybody. We were walking this ball, our first ball as Jourdan's, as a house. They had this thing called runway, but it was runway as a house where you have to be in sync in a group walking the runway, and do precision and all that stuff. Well, [when] we went there we were the underdogs, we left there we were champs.

And from then on it just grew, and the House of Jourdan was wonderful, for me, because it allowed me to test my chops. It allowed me to make mistakes, and it allowed me to grow with my recovery. 'Cause I had one year clean by the time I got to the house of Jourdan, I had maybe a year and a half. They followed me up until then, and it was a beautiful thing. I've created almost more legends and icons than anybody in the ballroom scene. We were the first house to feed the homeless. We were the first house in the country to go to a state assembly and speak. . . . We did a lot of stuff, like when we fed the homeless people, we literally cooked the food in our homes, put it in plates, wrapped it up, and gave it to them. That was Elaina Jourdan's idea and from there, I think we were the precursor to ballroom today. Now, did we have our issues? Yeah, we were considered a gang once.

ESPERANZA SANTOS (QNOHP): By who?

BERNIE MCALLISTER: By the city of Newark and the State of New Jersey.

ESPERANZA SANTOS: Well, how could they slap that label on you?

BERNIE MCALLISTER: Because we were a gang, honey.[14]

McAllister continued:

Dean [James] Credle, used to be the Dean of African American Affairs here at Rutgers. And they started this thing called, oh my God, the Fireball. They were the first ones that ever come to the ballroom scene people. This is before New York even started [giving] talks about safer sex. And it would have these safer sex parties, and you would get $50 for each party. I had twenty kids and you only needed four people at a party. So we can have a party over and over and over and over and over again. And it was with Dean Credle cuz at first we didn't trust in Credle, no, cuz the ballroom scene was so . . . this was the 80s and early 90s. We didn't trust those people because again, they were outsiders and nobody took care of us but us.

They got us to be more political. And New York noticed what we were doing here in New Jersey because they had the Latex Ball in New Jersey and New York, but it was nothing like the Fireball. And so it was a big deal. Cuz South Jersey/North Jersey is basically two separate states, okay?

I think getting clean gave me a voice in a whole different way. I met Dean Credle and I had maybe eight, nine years clean. I found my voice where my grandmother said that you were gonna help people. I found that Ballroom bein' the mother of a house at that time because I've been the mother and the father. It gave me a voice to help because when you're in charge of a house and you know you have people under you, and you know that they depend on you for guidance, and you're clean, it gives you inspiration. It motivates you.

Tracey "Africa" Norman, born and raised in Newark, became an international model and the first Black trans woman to appear on a Clairol box, among numerous other achievements. Because of her travels, she entered the ballroom scene a bit late, primarily in New York, and she encountered some initial resistance:

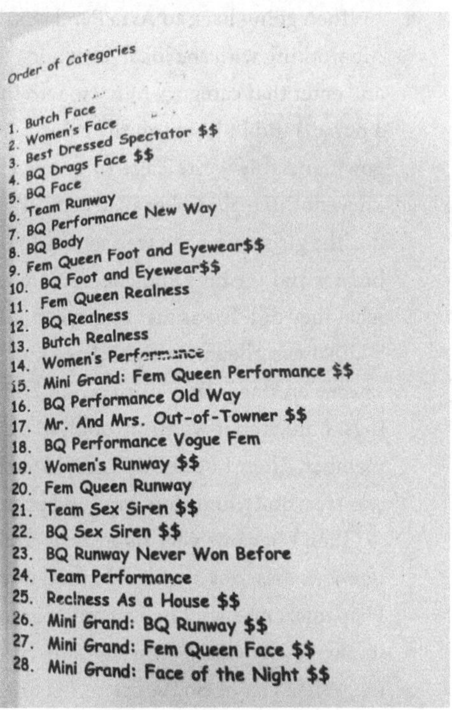

Order of Categories

1. Butch Face
2. Women's Face
3. Best Dressed Spectator $$
4. BQ Drags Face $$
5. BQ Face
6. Team Runway
7. BQ Performance New Way
8. BQ Body
9. Fem Queen Foot and Eyewear$$
10. BQ Foot and Eyewear$$
11. Fem Queen Realness
12. BQ Realness
13. Butch Realness
14. Women's Performance
15. Mini Grand: Fem Queen Performance $$
16. BQ Performance Old Way
17. Mr. And Mrs. Out-of-Towner $$
18. BQ Performance Vogue Fem
19. Women's Runway $$
20. Fem Queen Runway
21. Team Sex Siren $$
22. BQ Sex Siren $$
23. BQ Runway Never Won Before
24. Team Performance
25. Reclness As a House $$
26. Mini Grand: BQ Runway $$
27. Mini Grand: Fem Queen Face $$
28. Mini Grand: Face of the Night $$

FIGURES 6.2 AND 6.3. House of Jourdan flyer (1999) with categories, courtesy House Ballroom Scene Collection, Schomburg Center for Research in Black Culture, New York Public Library.

I got back from Paris in, I would say in '87. I didn't start doing the ballroom scene until '89. What happened is that I was living with mom and some friends of mine had told me that Paris Dupree was giving this ball. At the time, I was broke as a doornail. I was going for the grand prize, which was $1,000. Prior to all of that, I used to go to it in the 70s before the modeling thing took off. During my transformation and being young and a teenager, I would just go up to Harlem with a group of other girls and not participate, but to look and be amazed.

One day they pushed me out on the floor and asked me my name. I said that I was Tracey and I'm from New Jersey. I wasn't popular. I was not well received by the ball community in the 70s. They didn't, I don't know. I can't tell you till today, but I was not popular. It might have been a Jersey thing. . . .

In Harlem, in New York, I was not welcomed every time that I hit the floor. That only last for a minute because I got bored with it and so I left the community. . . . That's when my modeling thing and training started, so my life was different.

Then going back to Avis Pendavis. That was her ball. Grand prize was $1,000. Me working with the local designers, I was able to get a dress and go that evening and enter that category to try to win the money. I didn't win because I didn't have a purse. I didn't know all the rules. I just knew that I had on this beautiful white gown and this white cape to go over it. I'm doing my modeling walk that they knew nothing about because I stood out because I only did what I was trained to do. The girls back then were doing this shoulder thing and it was like shaking the breasts and pushing the cheeks. It was just crazy. Any walk that they did, that's what they did. It was just so gay I couldn't stand it.

That was the same night that I met the people from the House of Africa. They saw me on stage. They liked me and they wanted me to come to one of their meetings. I did, and it was in Brooklyn. They asked me to join their house, so I was a member. Then I became Tracey Africa, a member. I would walk. My categories was face, body, and runway grand prize.

Then I became very popular as Tracey Africa because I was winning because one, I was dark-skinned so I stood out from my lighter-skinned sisters who were Hispanic, and two, I had so much grace on the runway they couldn't understand it. The guys picked up on my walk before the females started trying to walk like me. When I came on the scene, I changed the whole community of how to present yourself to the judges.

Then another member moved from New York into Newark. There was maybe two or three of us eventually, but I was the first original member who lived in Newark. Everybody that was a part of the House was in New York. These people from the House of Africa, they were all good friends. We were a mixed group. We were Black, Hispanic, white, and Jamaican. The members were all mixed. The two white females that participated in the female categories, they had some experience with modeling. I just polished it a little with posture and poise.

When 1990 came around, that's when my career as Tracey Africa started. Eventually the two original members, Stella and the original father, decided that they didn't want to be mother and father anymore so they voted me as mother and then Eddie Smith was going to be the father of the house. That's how I became the mother of the House of Africa. I was mother for maybe about two, three years at the most because Eddie had gotten ill and he didn't survive his illness. Eddie was the glue that held the house together. Once Eddie's passing, the majority of the members just started going their separate ways. I just continued not really participating, but just going to the balls. If they saw me in the audience, they would call me out. Some balls I participated wholeheartedly in because the prize money was big.[15]

James Credle served as assistant dean of students at Rutgers University-Newark for many years and was one of the very earliest out gay leaders on campus. His extensive gay activism included the ballroom-related AIDS education work of Project Fire, discussed by Jason Chernesky in chapter 5. Credle explained:

> In 1990 I decided I needed to move back to Newark, that I didn't need to be going over on that subway, that there were too many people in Newark getting sick and dying. So I worked with Barbara Ford to write a grant to the state that was monies coming from Washington, the CDC, where we did what we called home health parties with people teaching them about how to be safe and doing safe sex practices. And that project was called Project Fire and it started around 1992 and it went for ten years until the federal bureaucracy told us that our way of doing the work in terms of our home health parties was not getting enough feedback [and] that we actually couldn't show that we were having people change their behavior. So they were doing more quantitatively looking at how people were changing their behavior. So the funding ceased to be available to us for our work. But we were written up in the *Trenton Times* because they claimed that we were buying wigs and stiletto heels for our group, and actually what we were doing, we had started balls. We used to have a thousand people who came to our balls. At our balls . . . the houses would be in competition around a safer sex message and we would provide money for them in terms of who did the best safer sex message. . . . But the point was the money came from ticket sales and came from money that we had raised, and we never used a dime of any monies that we got from the federal bureaucracy to do that work. But, of course, it gets all, the health department and the state didn't want to have anything to do with us after that in terms of HIV. And so it was very successful and if you ever want to see, I still have tapes from the balls, a whole list of tapes [now held by the Queer Newark Oral History Project].[16]

Douglas Says, fashion designer, offered a critique of the ballroom scene:

> I walked Butch Queen in Drag and I walked on [the] runway, but the ballroom has never been my scene. I never understood their politics. I think it's a lot of unfair favoritism that goes on there, and it's so odd because now I have—maybe two years ago, I got an icon ring from one of the balls, now I'm considered an icon and I'm considered a legend and this is ridiculous to me, because I really have not even participated in the balls.[17]

FIGURES 6.4 AND 6.5. Fire Ball runways in 1995 and 1998, courtesy James Credle VHS collection, Queer Newark Oral History Project. Note that these are low-resolution images but constitute some of the only visual documentation of the 1990s Newark ballroom scene.

The Twenty-First-Century Ballroom

Kysheif DeGraffenreid built a reputation for "schoolboy realness" and ultimately attained "legendary" status as the Legendary Scooda Balenciaga. He recounted his entrance into the community:

> Born and raised here in Newark, New Jersey. Attended local schools. I was a graduate of St. Benedict's Preparatory High School. During that time, it was like my senior year in high school when I really started getting a sense of my sexuality.... I was just feeling like there was a disconnect with me in the presence of that school. And I couldn't really identify with no one because it was like a Catholic high school and no one was really out about their sexuality or never even spoke about it. So I had to look elsewhere to identify with others like me.
>
> I had known about vogueing but I didn't know really too much about it. So it was like my senior year in high school, and as I was starting to get more comfortable with myself. There was a local nightclub called The Globe and it was [in] downtown Newark. It was located next to Symphony Hall.
>
> And I'd heard that was like the hotspot that was like the place to go. It was... the gay spot. That was where you could just be yourself. So one night me and my best friend, he went to Technology High School, he was like you want to go, and we was like okay. So he had got his mother's car and came and picked me up....
>
> Soon as we went to the door, it was like this drag queen who had greeted us... and was collecting our money. That was... my first culture shock. And I embraced it. I was like wow. I always wanted to know what it felt like to be in the presence of just the all-gay community and I was like bam! It just hit me in the face with a drag queen. So that night I didn't see anything really too much out the ordinary and I was like okay. There was a drag queen there, there were transgenders there, there were straight-looking guys, there were straight-looking girls there. So I was like okay there was nothing out the ordinary. It just feels like the same club, they listen to the same music.... So I started just jamming, just chilling, doing my two step.... So me and my friend we are just standing there and enjoying it, we are having fun [and] they are playing house music.
>
> So at one particular time, everybody just cleared the floor and just moved out the way and I was like, what's going on? All we just heard was this beat. It was like pirika, pirika, pirika ha, pirika.... And they had broken out into a circle like it was about to be a breakdance battle or something. But when we had looked into the circle to see what was going on it was these two drag queens and they was voguing. They was like going wild and I was, oh my God! I was so fascinated because...

this is my first time actually seeing live voguing and action and somebody know what they are doing and they was just spinning and twirling and dipping all over the place. It was so fascinating with the lights on in the club. This is the experience I wanted.

So that night I'd left and was more than satisfied. I was so satisfied. That week, later, I was trying to find the vogueing beats. They didn't have YouTube back then so everything was on CDs. I think we had MySpace back then [2004]. So I was trying to find stuff on MySpace through people's Facebook pages. I would try to find like the voguers, but was like I don't know nobody.[18]

Rejean "Tornado" Veal was born and raised in Newark and discovered vogueing while attending Malcolm X Shabazz High School. Since then, he has built a career as a professional dancer, performing in a number of venues in the United States, including the Brooklyn Academy of Music and the Drawing Center in New York City, and touring abroad in countries like France, Russia, and China. Veal is a member of the House of Revlon. He recounted discovering the community:

My sophomore year in high school, there was this one guy that was in my class, we were real cool and cordial. I knew he was in the life but at the time I knew about myself but I was still hiding it from everyone because I didn't want to be the stereotypical gay guy who they think everyone has to wear rainbow and tights and I wasn't like that. I was just a regular guy and me and him would hang out a lot. I actually marched in the high school marching band so I was around a lot of openly gay guys who would dance and things like that. That summer going into junior year, I got introduced to a few other guy friends. I would see them vogue all the time and I would be doing stuff. I first thought—I was just like kind of laughing. I was like, "Oh my God, what are y'all do—did you just drop like that on the ground?" Like I wouldn't . . . drop in these clothes.

When I entered into the scene, I noticed that they were really harsh—my first time I remember actually walking they were really harsh on me. It was just like, "Oh no." . . . A lot of people would get discouraged by it. And they would just feel like they wouldn't want to be a part of the scene anymore. But for me, that made me go home and perfect my craft and let them know, like listen, "Oh, no, no. Y'all are not gonna air and tell me that I wasn't good." Like if y'all don't think I'm good, I'm going to go home and show you how much better I can get. So it was a challenge for me. That's what made me step into the scene.

And to have these balls that started out in New York and branched off from New York to New Jersey and now DC, Philadelphia, Boston. Things started to get . . . just really popular. It was . . . to me, it's still not an underground scene anymore, like it's so well known. Being able to travel to different states and you get to see their venues now, you get to see how people would do things and cathedrals and stuff like that. You would be so amazed that just being able to travel to DC for a ball, it is like, "Hey, when I get off the bus, I'm gonna go see the White House." Now you can go and be a tourist for a second and then go to the venue and be like, "Wow, this is really nice."[19]

Tyra Gardner highlighted the family aspects of the scene:

Ballroom, listen, ballroom saved a whole host of lives. Whether people would admit it or not, ballrooms, you create your own family. You create your mothers, your fathers, and all of that kind of stuff. It's a creative expression that you set for yourself. It's literally a family.

People don't really understand my kids are my kids. They didn't come outta me, but they are my—I had 'em tatted like, those are *my* kids. Period. They mothers even know like, "Go to your mother house." I be like, "Baby mother, your child over here acting up. I'm gonna need you to get 'em"—they respect the fact that they leaving their kids or their kids are a part of me and I'm representing 'em. . . . These kids come from all walks of life and from all over the world. . . . I can talk about ballroom, girl. It was the thing that molded everything.

In ballroom, it molded me to have that sternness in a sassy way, I guess we can put it like the "snaps, honey" and the "miss things" and the "gurl." That came from there. That's where we learned how to do those things and sashay of the walks. . . . Ballroom was and is key, although you have your ups and down in ballrooms, now.[20]

Kiyan Williams is an artist and writer whose work has been widely exhibited at such venues as SculptureCenter, The Jewish Museum, Brooklyn Museum, and more. They were active in the formation of the Queer Newark Oral History Project. As a young person in Newark, Williams got their early understanding of gender fluidity from the ballroom scene:

I just started to like that experience of participating in fashion shows and meeting gay people. For the first time, I seem to hang around gay men, and being introduced to the ballroom scene and men who deviated from hegemonic unlimited masculinity was definitely inspiring. It mostly gave me the inspiration to continue expressing myself through fashion. Even though I didn't—I wasn't quite ready, I didn't [go] into my gender embodiment yet.[21]

Dinean Robinson wrote about her experiences working with young people in Newark's ballroom community:

I came to Newark in 2007. Taking up residence in Newark was a return to my familial roots. My grandfather was raised in Newark. My great-grandmother migrated to the bustling hub from Virginia with my grandfather and his siblings in tow. My great-uncle talks fondly of their time living on Walnut Street "down neck." When I moved to Newark from Buena Vista Township in South Jersey, I landed in Newark's South Ward. With then -mayor Cory Booker leading the City, LGBTQ Newarkers had an elected official whose administration would address our needs.

I spent my first few years in Newark nurturing my connection to local organizations, pouring into the community (and letting the community pour into me) and unexpectedly, with a front-row seat to Newark's Kiki ballroom scene. I found an affordable two-bedroom apartment on S. 16th Street and Avon Avenue. That's an address that to this day triggers audible reactions from anyone with whom I share my Newark story. The apartment was on the top floor of a multi-family house. Poor upkeep combined with relatively low rent meant that I would inevitably share the apartment with a community of rodents that freely scurried through the walls. It wasn't a good apartment by any stretch of the imagination. Still, one of its best attributes was the people living on the first floor. I didn't know it at the time, but my neighbors were a group of friends, all of them young, gay, and Black. They were regular participants and members of NJCRI's LGBTQ youth program Project WOW. NJCRI, the North Jersey Community Research Initiative, is one of New Jersey's largest and most comprehensive HIV/AIDS community-based organizations.

Its mission is to empower its clients by reducing social and health disparities in Newark. NJCRI's premiere LGBTQ youth program, Project WOW (web outreach works), utilizes online outlets and social media to cultivate peer-to-peer relationships amongst LGBTQ youth ages 14–24. Project WOW creates a safe and affirming space where LGBTQ youth can socialize, build community, develop leadership skills, and access relevant sexual health, mental health, and substance abuse services and education. Project WOW believes that every LGBTQ person has a voice that should be heard and recognized as fierce and fabulous change agents in our communities.

A key element of Project WOW's engagement strategy is hosting KiKi Ballroom events, house meetings, practices, and classes. These activities bring out a large and diverse group of young people who immerse themselves in the freedom, openness, and creativity of Ballroom. As it was once explained to me, young, gay, transgender, and gender-expansive people who were not quite ready to compete in the main Ballroom scene cut their teeth and sharpened their skills in the KiKi scene, the Ballroom scene's younger sibling.

In my apartment, the sounds of Newark's ballroom scene traveled through the walls just as freely as the rodents. However, its presence was much more welcomed. From my front-row seat, I listened to the soundtrack of Ballroom. This soundtrack included laughter, fighting, revelry, triumphant, sadness, all against a background of uniquely remixed popular songs, original beats, and tongue-twisting commentators narrating every move. For months I listened and watched a beautiful cast of characters find their way to the first-floor apartment. It was only a glimpse, but it was a priceless introduction to the power Ballroom has.

By 2012 I had co-produced two pride festivals with NEPC [Newark-Essex Pride Coalition], hosted one of the city's most popular weekly nightclub parties for lesbians, and returned to the nonprofit sector after working at an NYC boutique PR agency and freelancing. I had grown with a dynamic LGBTQ community in Newark and, through my work, was charged with helping it thrive. One of my most impactful jobs at that time was at Project WOW. I was no longer living at my South 16th Street apartment with my ancillary view of Newark's Ballroom scene. Instead, I was working directly with some of the scene's standout young people and newcomers. I had landed a gig at Project WOW.

I managed the drop-in center and was a counselor providing one-on-one sessions to 60–100 youth and young adults in that role. With much of the work grant-funded and having strict deliverables about how many young people the program needed to serve, we latched onto the Ballroom scene. We leveraged it as critical recruitment and engagement strategy. If a house wanted to use one of NJCRI's rooms to practice for a ball, instead of charging them a rental fee, we'd require the members to complete their counseling sessions first. If the youth leadership, often comprised of Icons and Legends in the Kiki scene, wanted to host a ball at Project WOW, we'd require everyone in attendance to complete an intake session. I remember 80–100 young people crammed into the space, voguing, battling, and every few minutes being whisked away for a few minutes by another staffer or me.

The KiKi scene had brought people together, being a sanctuary and family for Black and Latinx youth and young adults. Many LGBTQ youth-serving organizations have a similar aim, so it is no surprise those organizations, NJCRI/Project WOW, looked to the Kiki/Ballroom to ensure the success of their programs. Providing space and opportunity for the KiKi scene members to compete, showcase & hone their skills, and assemble gave organizations such as Project WOW and Hetrick-Martin Institute access to this otherwise guarded community.

The results of which were mostly positive. Young people received supportive health and wellness treatment and resources, gained leadership skills, increased their connection to the community, and built strong relationships with organizations, leaders, and decision-makers. I was lucky. I got to bear witness to the creative genius of so many young people.

Today, many of the youth we served have pursued their dreams. Some are working in entertainment, fashion design, interior design, all kinds of fields. I think what's most telling is that many of the young people who started as clients in the programs have become staff members. They are now serving a new generation of young, Black/Brown LGBTQ young people. It's not an overstatement that Newark's Ballroom/KiKi scene is the unsung hero of its LGBTQ youth empowerment and HIV/AIDS prevention work. I saw firsthand how the Ballroom scene has been a lifesaving experience. The houses, the families, the mothers, and the opportunity to be seen and celebrated were, for many involved, transformational, including me.

Notes

1. Karen McCarthy Brown, "Mimesis in the Face of Fear: Femme Queens, Butch Queens, and Gender Play in the Houses of Greater Newark," in *Passing: Identity and Interpretation in Sexuality, Race, and Religion*, ed. Maria Carla Sanchez and Linda S. Schlossberg (New York: New York University Press, 2001), 208–227, here 209, 222.

2. Marlon M. Bailey, *Butch Queens Up in Pumps: Gender, Performance, and Ballroom Culture in Detroit* (Ann Arbor: University of Michigan Press, 2013), 29–30.

3. Unless otherwise cited, all interview material in this chapter comes from the Queer Newark Oral History Project and thus carries no further citations. Full audio recordings and transcripts of the interviews can be accessed at https://queer.newark.rutgers.edu/interviews. Quotations are verbatim except for minor grammatical edits, though for the sake of easier reading, not all elisions are marked.

4. Barbara J. Kukla, *Swing City: Newark Nightlife, 1925–50* (New Brunswick, NJ: Rutgers University Press, 2002), 76, 114–115.

5. "In the Matter of Disciplinary Proceedings against Polka Club, Inc.," Alcoholic Beverage Control Bulletin 1045, No. 6, December 27, 1954, available at https://dspace.njstatelib.org/xmlui/handle/10929/53142.

6. Jewel Box Revue ad, *Star-Ledger*, February 25, 1968.

7. Timothy Stewart-Winter and Whitney Strub, interview with Peter Savastano, June 23, 2015, Queer Newark Oral History Project (QNOHP), 19, https://queer.newark.rutgers.edu/sites/default/files/transcript/2015-06-23%20Peter%20Savastano%201-edited%20and%20final.pdf.

8. Whitney Strub and Craig Blunt, interview with Pucci Revlon, April 12, 2017, QNOHP, 6, 4–5, https://queer.newark.rutgers.edu/sites/default/files/transcript/2017-04-12%20Pucci%20Revlon%201.pdf.

9. Whitney Strub and Craig Blunt, interview with Pucci Revlon, May 12, 2017, QNOHP, 18–19, 20, https://queer.newark.rutgers.edu/sites/default/files/transcript/2017-05-12%20Pucci%20Revlon%20pt.%202.pdf.

10. "Transvestites Have Two Balls," *Female Impersonator News*, no. 10 (n.d., ca. 1976–1978).

11. Naomi Extra, interview with Aaron Frazier, March 23, 2016, QNOHP, 35–37, https://queer.newark.rutgers.edu/sites/default/files/transcript/2016-03-23%20Aaron%20Frazier%20interview%20by%20Naomi%20Extra_0.pdf.

12. Whitney Strub, interview with Aaron Frazier, June 7, 2017, QNOHP, 8, https://queer.newark.rutgers.edu/sites/default/files/transcript/2017-06-07%20Aaron%20Frazier%20part%202_1.pdf.

13. Carrie Stetler and Cynthia Parker, "The Gay Clique of Newark Is Finding Its Voice," *Star-Ledger*, December 27, 2007; Amy Kuperinski, "How N.J.'s Mj Rodriguez Became 'Pose' Royalty, and Why She Deserves All the Flowers," NJ.com, May 2, 2021, https://www.nj.com/entertainment/2021/05/how-njs-mj-rodriguez-became-pose-royalty-and-why-she-deserves-all-the-flowers.html.

14. Esperanza Santos, interview with Bernard McAllister, October 10, 2019, QNOHP

15. Naomi Extra, interview with Tracy "Africa" Norman, October 31, 2016, QNOHP, 36–39, https://queer.newark.rutgers.edu/sites/default/files/transcript/2016-10-31%20Tracey%20Africa%20Norman%20interviewed%20by%20Naomi%20Extra.pdf.

16. Candace Bradsher, interview with James Credle, February 15, 2015, QNOHP, 37–38, https://queer.newark.rutgers.edu/sites/default/files/transcript/James CredleQNOHP.pdf.

17. Naomi Extra, interview with Douglas Says, May 31, 2016, QNOHP, 35, https://queer.newark.rutgers.edu/sites/default/files/transcript/2016-05-31%20Douglas%20Says%20interviewed%20by%20Naomi%20Extra.pdf.

18. Naomi Extra, interview with Kyshief DeGraffenreid, March 9, 2016, QNOHP, 1, 2, 3–4, https://queer.newark.rutgers.edu/sites/default/files/transcript/2016-03-09_DeGraffenreid-Kysheif_Session-01_Transcript.pdf.

19. Naomi Extra, interview with Rejean "Tornado" Veal, December 11, 2015, QNOHP, 13, 15, 18–19, https://queer.newark.rutgers.edu/sites/default/files/transcript/2015-12-11RejeanTornadoVealinterviewedbyNaomiExtra.pdf.

20. Esperanza Santos, interview with Tyra Gardner, February 20, 2020, QNOHP.

21. Esperanza Santos, interview with Kiyan Williams, October 11, 2019, QNOHP, 22, https://queer.newark.rutgers.edu/sites/default/files/transcript/Kiyan%20Williams%20ES%20Edits.pdf.

CHAPTER 7

At Home in the Hood

Black Queer Women Resisting Narratives of Violence and Plotting Life at the G Corner

LEILANI DOWELL

> Many activists take Newark as their political ground, imagining it as a home that is worth staying and fighting for. Construing Newark as an intimate political space that can be re-appropriated and reclaimed, these Black women activists envision and enact the politics of "home-making," the collective production of an oppositional space that nurtures the life-chances of young African-Americans.
>
> —Zenzele Isoke

> "Oppression" and "resistance" may not be opposites at all, but rather two energies necessarily entangled in a crisis of change.
>
> —Gayle R. Baldwin

In *Out in the Night*, the 2014 documentary chronicling the case of the New Jersey Seven, Renata Hill describes her hometown of Newark as the "hood" in relation to the homophobia of its residents. This description comes by way of a brief debate, after her friend, Terrain Dandridge, suggests that they are not from the hood. Hill responds: "We from the hood. . . . You know what I'm saying, we can't go to downtown Newark with our dildos on, you know what I'm sayin? And you see the print through our pants without somebody, like, 'Oh, you seeing that, yo, you seeing that?' Or, 'You effing dyke,' blah blah blah. Being gay, actually, in none of our families is an issue, but in Newark, people aren't really cool with it." In her response, Hill uses a key concept that has organized the perception of Newark by outsiders: the "ghetto."

In this chapter I examine the ways in which Newark is variously read as geographically in/habitable in relation to the concentration of Black lives and its residents are viewed as un/lamentable. Since so much of that conceptualization revolves around the city's purported status as one of the most violent places in the United States, we must explore the narratives surrounding violence to ask who is victimized, and how, within those narratives. Like many places shaped by Western capitalist epistemologies of sex and gender, Newark faces the issue of homophobia; yet, it is not paid attention to in the same way that other forms of violence are.[1] In this chapter, however, I am less interested in why the homophobic violence that occurs in Newark goes unremarked upon as a function of ghetto violence. Rather, I am asking that we return to questions about several levels and structures of violence that occur in the Black ghetto in particular. The image of Newark as a site of recursive violence allows the denial of structural homophobia, racism, and their intersections at the levels of discourse, resource allocation, and dispossession. We must then question if the activist-driven focus on homophobic violence—in which queerness is also read as a form of innocence—creates its own limitations in relation to our understanding of structural conditions of oppression. An understanding of the maneuvers of racial capitalism is diverted through the continued focus on Black criminality—also a response to these crises—in these same spaces.

This chapter highlights the primacy in Newark of Black queer women—a diverse group of people who have fought to build a safe community there—as both authorities and agents in the city's contested histories. It also marks the ways that erasure does not negate the existence and propulsion of life for Black queer women, in Newark or elsewhere. To get a fuller picture of Newark, I argue, we must hear from the Black queer diaspora there in response to the overwhelming narration of Newark as both ghetto and rehabilitated city.[2] Such narratives evade the complexities of a non-monolithic Black community. They also leave unquestioned both the notion of extreme Black homophobia (a creation of white racist structures), and, simultaneously, the homophobia that *does* exist in the Black community (a result of many factors, including the influence of capitalist patriarchy and Black nationalism's emphasis on challenging the depiction of "abnormal" Black gender roles by a turn to the extreme reverse).

One organization that has been key in raising the voices and narratives of queer people in Newark is that of the Rutgers University–based Queer Newark Oral History Project (QNOHP), which since 2011 has recorded oral histories of queer Newark residents, many of them people of color and many of them women and gender-nonconforming people. This chapter mines the QNOHP archives to help uplift the perspectives of Black queer women in Newark in particular, in order to ascertain how their understanding of Newark political and social life correlates to the characterizations that have fueled both the carcerality and the assumed "revitalization" of Newark. As this chapter reveals, Black queer women theorize, live, and build despite their erasure as a major component of the city's life and politics. In doing so, they create lives and communities that negate various forms of containment—including invisibility, enclosure, and imposed identities. While the Black ghetto is almost always presented as a hopeless place that is almost impossible to leave, many of us learn to wage our collective struggles of liberation there. I encourage us to think about the creativity that arises in the ghetto, and about how the tension of violence there is neither unique nor spectacular.

Newark in the Public Imaginary

In modern times, the uninhabitability of Newark has often been related as a sense of the mostly Black city possessing a heightened level of violence. Much has been made of Newark—the entire city, not just certain neighborhoods—as a menacing ghetto; for instance, *CNN Money* ranked Newark as one of the ten "most dangerous U.S. cities" for two years in a row in 2013 and 2014, marking the city as a place for tourists and capital to avoid, as well an example of the ways Blackness is coterminous with violence.[3] A description for the 2009 Sundance Channel documentary series *Brick City*, in which "Newark's citizens and its Mayor, Cory Booker, fight to raise the city out of a half century of violence, poverty and corruption," features a definition of the city from urbandictionary.com: "Newark: the hardest, most ghetto city in America, possibly the world. If you think your city is ghetto, come here and prepare to be blown away."[4] This last quote locates Newark, a city whose government has been run by cisgender Black men ever since a 1967 rebellion there, as not just a ghetto but the *quintessential* ghetto. This characterization has, until recent years, prevented outside resources from flowing into the city, while positioning those coming from Newark as dangerous and threatening.

Jewish sociologist Louis Wirth theorized the ghetto in 1927 as "a form of accommodation through which a minority has effectually been subordinated to a dominant group," making it "an instrument of control."[5] That control is discursive as much as it is carried out through heightened policing and reduced infrastructure; "ghetto" has become a metonym for a mindset of laziness, violence, and backwardness, conjuring images of the "welfare queen" and the hyperviolent Black man, alone or in a gang.

Like many low-income Black communities throughout the United States, Newark is a city rendered as ghetto/uninhabitable, which explains away the effects of what David Harvey calls "spatio-temporal fixes."[6] In response to cyclical crises of overaccumulation, which involve surpluses of both labor and capital, a strategy of temporal displacement is used to defer the circulation of excess capital, while spatial displacement moves the surpluses through the creation of new markets and production capacities in another location. In Newark, once a thriving industrial port city—in 1939 a Works Progress Administration guide called the city "the picture of a huge industrial beehive" and noted that the intersection of Broad and Market Streets, then known as Four Corners, "has been called the third busiest traffic center in the United States"—manufacturers fled the city for lower-wage regions beginning in the Great Depression, and then again as taxes were raised by the city's first African American mayor, Ken Gibson.[7] Meanwhile, an investment in highways, meant to build up the infrastructure to support capitalist development, resulted in the continuing pattern of labor in the city: workers who commute to Newark to work, but do not stay to invest in the city itself. Coupled with these conditions, an increasing property tax structure and the suburbanization of nearby areas encouraged flight away from the city for those who could afford it, both before and after the 1967 Newark rebellion. Violence has been an important discursive conduit for deflecting attention away from the effects of capital on the city's residents.

However, there is a selectivity to the violence that is focused on in these narratives, and the occurrence of homophobic violence in the city is ignored as part of that spectacularization. Newark, the largest city in the state of New Jersey, was home to the New Jersey Seven, a group of young Black lesbians and gender-nonconforming people, mostly from Newark, who were met with grotesque, lengthy criminal charges after defending themselves against a street harasser in

New York's Greenwich Village, and to Sakia Gunn, a Black lesbian who was stabbed to death in 2003. That same year Shani Baraka, a Black lesbian, Newark resident, daughter of Black Arts luminaries Amina and Amiri Baraka, and sister of Newark's current mayor, Ras Baraka, was murdered along with her partner, Rayshon Holmes, in Piscataway, New Jersey. These murders, along with the case of the New Jersey Seven, reveal not only the violence Black queer women face, but also the existence of a Black queer community in Newark. We should note that violence against queer people of color is routinely ignored by local and national media outlets across the country; what makes this phenomenon remarkable in relation to Newark is its stark juxtaposition to the sensationalization of other forms of violence there. Shani Baraka's murder gained attention only because of the notoriety of her parents; meanwhile, it took the active organizing of women of color to make Gunn's death a focus.

The conceptualizations of homophobia in Newark can be found in sociological and anthropological accounts of the city; for example, in 2001, anthropologist Karen McCarthy Brown, writing on Newark's ball scene, stated that "the intense, creative, and convoluted mimesis of Newark's Ballroom Scene makes sense against a ground of homophobic and racist violence, extraordinary and quotidian, personal and systemic." She noted that "according to members of the Houses," Newark was "especially homophobic," involving both gay-baiting and bashings as a "disturbingly common occurrence." This quantification of homophobia begs the question of what rubric is being used to make comparisons—what counts as an "average" of homophobia, and who makes those assessments? The use of this relational term may reflect a general sense of danger felt by members of the Houses; it may also reflect the biases of the researcher. Might there be other reasons for the ballroom scene's existence than the violence Brown cites?[8]

An interesting snapshot of the intersectional homophobia that Black women face in Newark is Ana Y. Ramos-Zayas's research on "Race, Affect, and Neoliberal Personhood in Latino Newark." A whole chapter of her book *Street Therapists*, published in 2012, is dedicated to what she describes as a Latino perception, in Newark, of Black women's sexuality, and of Black lesbians in particular, as violently aggressive. She cites "numerous references" in her hundreds of pages of research to "lesbian gangs," "aggressive Black lesbians," or "Black female gangs"—language startingly familiar to the depiction of the New Jersey Seven by mainstream media outlets, which depicted them as a "lesbian wolf pack" and a "gang of angry lesbians" who attacked an "innocent" man.[9] (Likewise, less than a year after Sakia Gunn's murder, West Side High School in Newark would ban the donning of apparel with the Pride rainbow flag on it, claiming that it was "gang paraphernalia").[10] What is particularly intriguing about this study is the fact that some of Ramos-Zayas's main informants about purported Black lesbian violence and aggressiveness were Latina lesbians. Their depictions turn on tropes of Black female hypermasculinity that negate claims to solidarity.

A final aspect of violence that goes unmentioned in the sensational narratives about it in Newark is that of police harassment and brutality. Patreese Johnson, whose brother was killed by a former police officer, describes how "the police was just—we watched them rob the drug dealers, and it was like that day they [the dealers] wasn't even selling drugs. . . . So they aren't really doing real policing, they're just aggravating the situation. I feel like that's why Newark [is] the way it is now, because of all of that aggravation. You didn't make it any better. You didn't make your community trust the police."[11] That this police violence was inflicted with particular severity upon queer communities is clear from both LGBTQ Newarkers' testimony and a 2016 U.S. Department of Justice consent decree with the city that singled out police "bias against lesbian, gay, bisexual, and transgender persons," as Danielle Shields and Carse Ramos discuss further in chapter 10.

Nonetheless, despite this evidence calling attention to an LGBTQ presence, African American Mayor Sharpe James actually suggested at one point that gay people did not exist in Newark; June Dowell-Burton, founder of Newark Gay Pride, reports that "Sharpe told me this personally and . . . when I'm talking to him about issues, he's like, 'there are no gay people in Newark.' He was like, 'Show me the votes.'"[12] James was able to successfully campaign against Cory Booker in 2002 by, among other tactics, calling him the antigay slur "faggot" while on the record with journalists.[13] Although Booker would win the following election and serve as Mayor of Newark from 2006 to 2013, his undeclared sexuality remained the subject of rumor and conjecture in the city, at least until he publicly came out as heterosexual while gearing up for his unsuccessful run for the 2020 Democratic Party presidential primary. These violent erasures can help create an antigay sensibility—and yet, our oral histories also tell a divergent story of queer visibility in the city. In contrast, Venice Brown, one of the New Jersey Seven, remarked in an interview that "growing up all of my friends were gay . . . so it was never like, I never needed an ally or I never needed anybody to talk to, like I never needed that kind of stuff, because everybody I hang around was already lesbian or gay or bisexual, whatever." Likewise, Patreese Johnson asserts that "a lot of my generation is gay. Um, yeah, most of us—most of everybody I grew up with in church is gay."[14]

Living Freely in Enclosure

When asked what places in Newark she associated with LGBTQ people, Renata Hill, former Newark resident and one of the New Jersey Seven, mentioned what was colloquially known as the "G corner": "The G corner was on Broad and Market and that's where you would go and see like, especially after school hours, all gay people would be down there. It would just be like flooded, like you would think it's a march going on or something. Like everybody gravitate towards that corner and just be out there talking to each other, chilling, hanging out whatever."[15]

Walk ten minutes east from the intersection of Market and Broad Streets, the location of the G corner, in downtown Newark, and you will have arrived at Newark's Penn Station, a major transportation hub for the city that includes bus service and twenty-minute trains to Manhattan. Young queers of color who have lived in Newark for decades use these transportation circuits to travel between their neighborhoods and New York's Greenwich Village. In 2006, Hill, along with friends Venice Brown, Khamysha Coates, Terrain Dandridge, Lania Daniels, Patreese Johnson, and Chenese Loyal, would take the train from Newark to Greenwich Village on a weekend like any other. There they would face the kind of violent physical attack that is discursively associated with the sexist and homophobic Black "ghetto." Convicted on gang assault charges, Brown, Dandridge, Hill, and Johnson (thereafter better known as the New Jersey Four) would receive three-and-a-half to eleven years in prison for insisting on their right to self-defense against a Black man who threatened to rape one of the seven, ripped hair off the head of another, and choked a third. In its sensationalization of the attack and the trial that ensued, local media outlets in New York would remind their readers that all but one of the seven were bridge-and-tunnel invaders from Newark, New Jersey.[16]

Hill's locating of the G corner as a space resembling a march and also a space where queers "chill"—in the heart of the ghetto—speaks to the ways resistance takes many forms. A "march," in relation to working-class communities and communities of color, is an act of defiance, often in protest of status quo, quotidian forms of state repression and discrimination. It is a form of visibility that demands, first and foremost, the right of the subjects to exist. "Chilling" is a slang term expressing relaxation, ease, the letting down of one's guard in a safe space—here, safety in the company of others. In this instance and many others, the very act of queer sociality is one of defiance—to capitalist impulses to constantly produce; to racist loitering laws; to the homophobia that sometimes keeps queers at home; and to the depiction of the Black community as more homophobic than others.

Hill's enthusiastic description of the G corner denies the ways Greenwich Village has been figured as a place of fugitive escape from the homophobic Black ghetto of Newark. She describes it as a site of resistance that makes the plantation "a location that might also open up a discussion of Black *life*" as opposed to solely emphasizing a necropolitical focus on Black dispossession in that geographic space. For theorist Katherine McKittrick, the plantation is both a figurative device for analyzing Black geographies and also a very literal extension of lived Black histories. Deciphering the logic of the plantation involves identifying the ways the plantation serves to normalize both Black repression and land exploitation; paying attention to our "collective participation and rhetorical commitment" to reproducing the plantation system as normal and natural; and imagining the plantation, in conjunction with the plot, as a new analytic to reject such normalization and envision a new future.[17] I argue that the voices of Black queer women, hidden by the standard narrative of the ghetto as a hyper-heterosexual space (the same narrative, as Jason Chernesky shows in chapter 5, that obscured gay struggles with AIDS in Newark),[18] can help challenge our common-sense assumptions about abject Blackness, violence, and living under carceral conditions. These perspectives describe violence as present but not all-consuming and express a sense of a complicated yet tight-knit community and family that is largely absent from tales of Black ghetto depravity.

Reminiscent of the plot, the space provided enslaved people that they then used as a space *to* plot, the G corner represents a site of fugitivity *within* enclosure. As an informal outdoor space that reflects a lack of recreational spaces and resources for young queer people in Newark, the G corner also represents the ways that queer people in Newark have navigated the city they claim as their own, taking up space in highly visible ways with a sense of agency and mobility. Venice Brown confirms the size and prominence of the G corner in the lives of young queer people in Newark: "It used to be hundreds of young Black, white,

Spanish, like it didn't matter—if you were gay, you used to be on the corner after school every single day like clockwork, Monday through Friday. *That same corner that Sakia got killed on.* Across from there."[19]

Returning from another excursion to Greenwich Village on a night in 2003—three years before the New Jersey Seven's fateful evening there—a fifteen-year-old Black lesbian named Sakia Gunn was waiting for the #1 New Jersey Transit bus at Broad and Market when two Black men propositioned her and her friends. After they rejected the men and told them that they were lesbians, one of them, Richard McCullough, stabbed Gunn in the chest. She would die at nearby University Hospital.

That Gunn's death—the catalyst for an organizing effort never before seen among Black queer people in Newark—would take place precisely at the G corner also speaks to the negotiations Black queer people in Newark make between life and death and sociality. However, following the lead of the subjects of this chapter, I wish to emphasize life, and sociality, in the face of continued attempts at erasure—and the possibility of creating life that is *produced through* carceral conditions. This is not to suggest that the constant imposition of necropolitical life onto Black subjects is exaggerated by the various forces that attempt to intervene. However, I argue that the elision of the life that continues, of the triumphs of life despite these conditions, constitutes another form of anti-Black violence that we would do well to attend to. Patreese Johnson asserts that "it was just, like, it was crazy how the youth claimed that spot as the G corner. . . . *If any teen lived freely, it was the LGBT community in Newark.*"[20] Johnson's statement asks us to reconsider notions of freedom as they exist simultaneously with discursively unbearable conditions.

In addition to the outdoor sociality of the G corner, Hill discusses going to The Globe, "this little party where you didn't need no ID to get in" in Newark, as part of her identity formation:

> I was new to being in the life, you know, so I didn't understand what it meant to even be an aggressive or a dyke or a stud. So it was like, you know, going to The Globe, seeing all these different people, different personalities, different appearances, and I'm just like trying to figure out, okay, now where do I fit in at? So then I found myself sagging my pants and wearing my hat backwards with a do rag, and you know [my] voice getting deeper when I was around everybody, and stuff like that, and hand in my pants. And I mean I guess the Globe is where you can just do

> whatever. . . . This is a place you could go to try to figure out how you want to be and nobody looks at you any different.[21]

The assertion that "nobody looks at you any different" is made verbatim by Hill in the documentary *Out in the Night,* but instead of a Newark club, Hill is referencing Greenwich Village. We are thus presented with a proliferation of spaces for exploration of self and identity. Kara Keeling looks at "Black lesbian butch-femme sociality" as an attempt to survive amid the insurmountable odds of anti-Black capitalism and in relation to anti-capitalist Black Liberation movements with approaches that are limited in their responses to the needs and desires of queer people and women, and the "Black femme function" as "that which might offer alternatives to the organization of sociality that capital currently sanctions."[22] The Black women whose stories I explore in this chapter do not all identify as femme—in fact, a greater sense of fluidity seems to be embraced by Black queer women in Newark, who pointedly use the term "lesbian" rather than what they perceive as the more rigid classificatory terms such as "butch" and "femme." Nonetheless, these women, as both living, breathing beings with agency and as symbols, provide such alternatives through the narratives they create of the city they live in, love in, and love.

Hill notes that the same spaces that community members utilize as safe spaces are also, ironically, spaces in which they are the most vulnerable: the on-the-street visibility of the G corner, the very spot where Sakia Gunn was murdered; and The Globe, a space that could be easily policed for violating underage drinking laws, and its customers criminalized. Johnson says that the Globe itself was "just so ghetto." Nonetheless, the existence of this space of exploration and fun can be seen as pivotal to the shaping of the New Jersey Seven and others into the kinds of queers who resist. Hill also noted "how dangerous it is in Newark for us," stating that she had personally been harassed "plenty of times," while also discussing the perils of living amid drug dealing and use in the community, describing her first Newark neighborhood, on South Walnut Street, as "just really gangsta." This is an important intervention to narratives that would separate quotidian violence from "homophobic" violence.

That is, concerns with homophobic violence often are made in a vacuum that ignores other types of violence queers, and particularly queers of color, must struggle against. Rather than a laundry list of violent interactions, we can view violence from a broad and interconnected angle—capitalist frameworks, which impose conditions of unemployment and underemployment due to the movement of capital, yield the kinds of alternative economies that foster violence. At the same time the imagining of Black sexualities as pathological, *in relation to* capitalist (re)production and labor, can produce responses that shun homosexuality within the Black community.

Robert Curvin, a former civil rights leader in New Jersey, suggests that despite the terrible living conditions in Newark's Third Ward, the section of the city where Blacks were displaced to after vast slum clearance programs in the Central Ward, "an extensive network . . . made physical discomfort secondary for many who enjoyed the kinship of living among their own people and institutions."[23] This complex assertion parallels the various readings on violent Black homophobia among Black queer women living in Newark. In 2011, in seemingly direct contrast to the idea of the Black ghetto as exceedingly homophobic—that is, homophobic without recourse—Black trans woman and Newark resident Eyricka Morgan stated "nobody messed with us because the majority of us, like, we lived like in a hood. . . . We created our own safe space for transwomen."[24] Two years later, Morgan was tragically murdered in a boarding house in New Brunswick, New Jersey, a college town that Wikitravel cites as "generally safe for visitors and students."[25] When asked if she was "extra nervous being gay" while growing up in Newark, Venice Brown, one of the New Jersey Seven, cited the familiarity of community as a source of safety: "It never mattered, because . . . I literally grew up with the people. . . . Like you know how, we're not cousins by blood, but your mom is my aunt because we've known each other forever and I'm spending the night at your house and things like that. So I didn't have those issues. Nobody ever had those issues."[26]

For both Morgan and Brown, living in the hood means the kind of community and space-making that mitigates the kinds of harm inflicted by homophobia and transphobia. Ramos-Zayas also cites a "general perception that gays and lesbians were accepted and more visible in Newark than in other cities," which may mean that despite the dissolution of the G corner, and despite the violence that may have led, in part, to its demise, queer people in Newark continue to remain visible in various ways.[27]

An examination of these narratives highlights the ways that the *life* exuded by the Black queer diaspora, while always parleying with fatality, throws a bit of shade on the continual Afro-pessimist portrayal of Black life as death, social and otherwise. Katherine McKittrick's *Demonic Grounds* thinks geography through an "imperative perspective of Black struggle [that] is undermined by the social processes and material three dimensionalities that contribute to the workings of the geographies of slavery," arguing that the reification of space as fixed and unchanging in traditional geographies denies that space is socially and continually produced. Acknowledging that space is a social production, in contrast, allows us to understand that the boundaries—including differentiation along lines of race and sex—that seem put in place through, in part, the physicality of geographic locations such as the slave ship are in fact malleable, open to "differential and contextual histories." This is apparent in Newark, where a nationally reproduced narrative of the city as "ghetto" collapses a city teeming with varied perspectives and understandings that counter a picture of abject suffering. Focusing on Black women's geographies as "demonic grounds," McKittrick writes, "I am suggesting that the relationship between Black women and geography opens up a conceptual arena through which more humanly workable geographies can be and are enacted."[28] The local is of fundamental importance; if we laud the New Jersey Seven for fighting back, we must also understand that they *learned to do so* in Newark. Can we hold the tension between the ghetto as violently policed, as a primary site of the "state-sanctioned or extralegal production and exploitation of group-differentiated vulnerability to premature death" *and* as a space of safety and comfort?[29] The danger in not holding that tension is to allow the discursive production of space that, in being marked unhabitable, can be then be *claimed* for others.

(Re)making Life

Standing at the G corner today, one doesn't find the throngs of gay people that Hill described. Black and other people of all ages, genders and, assumedly, sexualities, pass through the bustling corner; there is a sense of urgency in their movements, even in the movements of those posted there asking for money, and a sense of expansiveness due to the sheer size of the downtown corner itself. The area still retains the feel of a working-class shopping district, with a very busy 7-Eleven convenience store, bus stops for various lines on each corner, fast food chains, and independent and franchise stores selling everything from clothing for the entire family (one storefront sign advertises "juniors—plus—accessories—lingerie—shoes") to eyewear, video games, and cellphones. A seven-minute walk north on Broad, however, will take you to Newark's first Whole Foods market, which

FIGURE 7.1. The G corner—at the intersection of Broad and Market Streets—in the age of gentrification (2017). Photo by Erin Santana, courtesy Queer Newark Oral History Project.

opened in 2017 and was considered a major accomplishment of Mayor Cory Booker's administration in terms of getting the upscale grocery store to agree to set up shop in the area. As in Harlem, the arrival of Whole Foods is seen by some as a marker of community rehabilitation, and by others as a sign of encroaching gentrification. Yet if one were to assume that the G corner no longer exists because an influx of resources for queer youth of color, as part of the city's rehabilitation, rendered the outdoor social space unnecessary, they would be mistaken.

Nonetheless, this is also the story of the purported revitalization of Newark, a city that has struggled with striking levels of poverty and economic inequity both before and since a 1967 rebellion against police brutality that resulted in massive white flight. Mayor Sharpe James announced that Newark was undergoing a "renaissance" in the 1990s, a conceptualization of the city that has been hotly debated in the decades since. In recent years, a new narrative of rehabilitation has revolved around neoliberal gentrification—the push for "market solutions" to crises that, rather than actually preventing the problems they claim to solve, primarily serve the movement of capital into previously redlined areas and the movement of people out. Newark was once the city with the most public housing complexes in the country. But the demolition of these structures, supported by federal programs that advocate for the replacement of public housing with mixed-use communities, had led to more housing insecurity for low-income Newarkers—all under the veneer that things are improving for the residents of these communities. A March 2015 *Politico* article, "Is Newark the Next Brooklyn?" was part of a series in which the magazine "featured innovative ideas from cities across the United States at a time of unprecedented urban reinvention."[30] The report announced early on that "the story of Newark's revitalization is all about buildings," noting the creation of a mixed-use complex, Teachers Village, in the downtown area and plans for a district dubbed SoMa—south of Market—by the lead developer of the project. A response article published a month later denied the analogy between Brooklyn and Newark and raised the question of what a "revitalization" meant—that is, who it was directed at—when it had done little in the way of creating desperately needed jobs. Meanwhile, in April of 2018 Mayor Ras Baraka announced the launch of "Citizen Virtual Patrol," a panopticon-like apparatus that allows Newark residents to participate in the surveillance of fellow city dwellers. By full implementation, the administration planned to have 125 live-monitored cameras installed on streets throughout the city.[31]

The term "revitalization" suggests a renewal of life, a kind of spring-like emergence after a winter of retreat. To suggest that Newark is undergoing/has undergone a revitalization is to suggest that life in the populous city had somehow gone underground or into hibernation before the intervention of presumably straight, Black male politicians. However, any emergence of queer life during this period is related more to the self-organization of queer people, particularly in response to violence (including the violence of anti-LGBTQ religious views). That is to say, to capture a fuller picture of what revitalization is in Newark, one must in fact turn to the lives and stories of Black queer women who have helped shape what that revitalization actually looks like.

Despite the rhetoric that things have taken a turn for the better, some Black queer women lament the changes that have occurred. Jerri Mitchell-Lee states that in the "early days," "People were more connected. . . . Communities were more connected. There weren't a whole lot of grants for programs and things like that, but because the community was more connected, you had things for the kids to do." She also expresses concern with the city's continuing wealth imbalance and the impact of gentrification in the downtown area—"They say they're building affordable housing, but affordable for who? So I think that is driving away the minorities."[32] These dichotomies—between community connectedness and state resource allocation, between "affordable" housing and more urban removal—suggest what Gayle R. Baldwin identifies as the dialectic struggle between oppression and resistance.[33] Mitchell-Lee notes that people comment on the neighborhood surrounding the LGBTQ Community Center, saying that "it reminds them of the Village in New York," and we are reminded of the conditions that precipitated the criminalization of four of the New Jersey Seven, even as the resemblance to the Village is puzzling—a lesbian-owned shop and the Center, a small storefront edifice, are surrounded by permanently closed businesses; while business closure does happen in the Village as rent prices rise, the turnover is generally more rapid there than in Newark, where empty storefronts often sit stagnant for longer periods. Patreese Johnson, the member of the New Jersey Seven who served the longest prison sentence, describes a childhood of safety in Newark in contrast to a "revitalized" Newark in 2015, the year of her interview: "We played a lot in my childhood, wasn't scared to walk outside as today, you know, kids definitely gotta be in before the light, the streetlights come on. . . . The community has got worse as far as violence, drugs infesting the community, not no real support or direction for the youth that's coming up today."[34]

However, though conditions of oppression continue, so too do strategies of support and resistance; Johnson notes that "the community is still the same as far as like elders watching out for the little ones. . . . Everybody still as today look out for each other whether they know you or not." Meanwhile, longtime activist Alicia Heath-Toby expresses concern about the gentrification of Newark: "Yes, the projects are not the best place to live, but they had a place. They tore those down, and moved in. Where did those people go? They go to the streets, and they go to the shelters, and they go to the prisons. It's just a vicious cycle." Heath-Toby also points out that despite the revitalization, there are no social spaces, outside of the church and Diamondz N Da Ruff, a café and lounge, for the LGBT community.[35]

Sarah Jane Cevernak cites the liberatory potential of Black feminist wandering, paying attention to the plot of land that an enslaved Harriet Jacobs wandered on as a space that preconditioned her successful bid for freedom.[36] The notion that LGBTQ teenagers on the G corner were free lends itself to this kind of wandering, in which freedom is a state that exists on the same plane as danger but exists nonetheless, in which one can explore one's identity, build connections and community, and enjoy life regardless of the ever-present circumstances. If this sociality, the G corner, had the attention of media-makers, would it be criminalized? It is unclear whether the G corner was a site that was heavily policed as such, although the lack of mention of a police presence at the G corner by the interviewees suggests that it wasn't. In contrast, the New Jersey Seven were profiled and criminalized in Greenwich Village. These separate instances reveal that both the so-called Black ghetto *and* the so-called gay ghetto are simultaneously sites of violence and liberation for Black queers.

However, the continual back-and-forth between New York and New Jersey suggests a different approach than that of escape; it marks the space of complicated identities and complicated communities, and the attempt to police the boundaries and borders of geography, sexuality, and gender that ends in both state and quotidian violence. Venice Brown notes that while she and her friends spent their weekdays on the G corner, weekends involved a trip across the Hudson River to Greenwich Village: "Mind you, it was like, the Village. Like everybody, we go every weekend."[37] Likewise, Curvin notes that Black people residing outside the city regularly patronized Black churches in Newark.

If the revitalization pursued by Newark's mayors and other politicians is one of neoliberal gentrification, then we can also speak of the creation, by Black queer women, of what Ruth Wilson Gilmore terms "abolition geographies," in which people "destroy the geography of slavery by mixing their labor with the external world to change the world and thereby themselves—as it were, habitation as nature—even if geometrically speaking they hadn't moved far at all. . . . Ordinary people, in changing diversity, figure out how to stretch or diminish social and spatial forms to create room for their lives."[38]

Rather than a relatively new restructuring in relation to the flow of capital, rhetoricized as one of Black uplift in the urban city, these women have been creating Newark as an abolitionist space against homophobia, the AIDS crisis, and poverty. Many cite the activism that emerged after the 2003 murder of Sakia Gunn as the catalyst for the increased visibility of the Black queer community in Newark, and particularly that of Black lesbians—what Mitchell-Lee describes as "a whole Pandora's Box as far as being more out and more open with it."

Unlike other sites of gentrification that hail their neighborhoods as gay-friendly, Newark has displayed some hesitancy toward, or at least only pays lip service to, promoting queer rights. When I began this project, I was perplexed by the fact that the mostly Black organizers who created the city's struggling LGBT Center had renamed the office space that houses the center from Liberation in Truth to the LGBT Center—which, to my ignorant eyes, and knowing the history of Black Power and Black Arts in the city, seemed like a retreat from the more militant term "liberation." However, interviews with the founders of the center reveal that the renaming occurred out of the recognition by community members that unless they created one themselves, there would be no Center—that is, all requests to the city government to build and support an LGBT Center had gone unheeded. Alicia Heath-Toby explains:

> It came out of a discussion around Newark needs an LGBT Center. It needs to be very clear that it's a space for LGBT folks. A group of leaders who had been part of our family for years said, "Why don't we just rename this place the LGBT Center?" We said, quite frankly, "Why not?" . . .
>
> Now, when Sakia Gunn was killed, at the time Sharpe James was mayor. He made promises that there would be support to have a Newark LGBT Center and those promises never came to fruition. Then Cory Booker said the same thing and it didn't happen under his leadership. The community said, "Let's just do this."[39]

That Center—a small building located in the middle of Halsey Street that struggled for funding, received none from the city, and employed an all-volunteer staff—was displaced by the encroaching gentrification of the downtown area when a developer evacuated the site to make way for new rental and retail units. While Burley Tuggle, a Black lesbian who has lived in Newark since 2006, lauds the existence of more LGBT dining and drinking venues, Alicia Heath-Toby, former board president of the Newark LGBTQ Community Center Board of Directors, stated in a 2016 interview that

> I think the community is doing great work, but I think it's just still no support. I'm disappointed in the administration just as I was disappointed when Sakia was killed. I think that there is, there's a lot of platitudes that are made. I think that there's not a real commitment to community in ways that it can be. There's certainly no funding that is provided to people doing work, LGBT organizations. . . . We've been doing this work forever without, I would say . . . very little to none. There is no support and I think that's egregious.[40]

Meanwhile, the complications of attending to race, gender, and sexuality simultaneously are exemplified in the naming of a center for women in 2017. Laquetta Nelson, a cofounder of Newark Pride Alliance in 2003, was concerned with the ways that mainstream LGBTQ organizations focused almost exclusively on Gunn's sexuality, disregarding other aspects of her identity that contributed to the circumstances of her death.[41] As such, the organizing that emerged after Gunn's death uplifted a focus on violence against Black women, without separating "women" from "lesbians" as discrete categories. This effort was reflected in the opening of the Shani Baraka Women's Resource Center in 2017, when Mayor Baraka specifically raised the names of Sakia Gunn and Rayshawn Holmes during the inauguration—but not their sexual identities.

Rod Ferguson argues that "culture produces houses peopled by queers of color, subjects who have been expelled from home. These subjects in turn 'collectively remember home as a site of contradictory demands and conditions.'"[42] In Newark, those contradictory demands and conditions include safety and violence, a lack of state resources and a plethora of community support, and structures of queer inclusion and denial. Resistance includes joy, acts of deviance, and disavowal of the characteristics set upon the ghetto and the individuals who reside in it. Black queer women in the Newark "ghetto" defy the strictures of punishment and invisibility through community-building, resistance, and mobility.

Notes

1. Zenzele Isoke, *Urban Black Women and the Politics of Resistance* (New York: Palgrave Macmillan, 2013), 10; Gayle R. Baldwin, "Whose Black Church? Voices of Oppression and Resistance in Response to the Murder of a 'Gay' Black Teenager," in *Churches, Blackness, and Contested Multiculturalism: Europe, Africa, and North America*, ed. R. Few Smith, William Ackah, and Anthony G. Reddie (New York: Palgrave Macmillan, 2014), 235–249, here 237. In recent decades, a shift toward limited acceptance of certain LGBTQ peoples—that is, those who fit into a racialized neoliberal rubric of personal responsibility and privacy—has led to the promotion of homonationalist critiques of other countries. The conflation of this limited acceptance with both a national tolerance for queerness and an acceptance of *all* queers gives added weight to claims that urban "ghettos" like Newark are homophobic *in contrast* to the nation as a whole. See Lisa Duggan, *The Twilight of Equality?: Neoliberalism, Cultural Politics, and the Attack on Democracy* (Boston: Beacon Press, 2003); Jasbir Puar, *Terrorist Assemblages: Homonationalism in Queer Times* (Durham, NC: Duke University Press, 2007).

2. My work follows Rinaldo Walcott's theorization on Black queer diasporas as a geographical and theoretical space that opens up epistemologies of Blackness, challenging the standard definition of Blackness both within and without the Black community. Walcott argues for the Black queer diaspora as a counterweight to forces, both white and Black, that position Black queer sexuality as either nonexistent or in need of spokespeople on its behalf. In this way, then, the Black queer diaspora functions simultaneously as an internal critique of Black homophobia and a critique of white racism. Rinaldo Walcott, "Homopoetics: Queer Space and the Black Queer Diaspora," in *Black Geographies and the Politics of Place*, ed. Katherine McKittrick and Clyde Adrian Woods (Cambridge, MA: South End Press, 2007), 233–246.

3. Les Christie, "Most Dangerous Cities," *CNN Money*, February 3, 2014, money.cnn.com/gallery/real_estate/2014/02/03/dangerous-cities/; Christie, "Most Dangerous U.S. Cities," January 23, 2013, money.cnn.com/gallery/real_estate/2013/01/23/dangerous-cities/.

4. *Brick City*, firstrunfeatures.com/brickcitydvd.html. Accessed December 10, 2018.

5. Louis Wirth, "The Ghetto," *American Journal of Sociology* 33, no. 1 (1927): 57–71, here 58.

6. David Harvey, "The 'New' Imperialism: Accumulation by Dispossession," *Socialist Register*, vol. 40, March 19, 2009, 63–87.

7. Federal Writers' Project, *The WPA Guide to New Jersey: The Garden State* (San Antonio, TX: Trinity University Press, 2014), 313.

8. Karen McCarthy Brown, "Mimesis in the Face of Fear: Femme Queens, Butch Queens, and Gender Play in the Houses of Greater Newark," in *Passing: Identity and Interpretation in Sexuality, Race, and Religion*, ed. Maria C. Sanchez and Linda Schlossberg (New York: New York University Press, 2001), 208–227, here 224. However, Alicia Heath-Toby, who served as assistant pastor in Newark's Liberation in Truth Unity Fellowship Church, asserts that "we always will have to deal with as a community, LGBT, color, otherwise, with homophobia, but in communities of color, homophobia is steeped in religiosity," suggesting a different ideological lineage for homophobia in the Black community—the church—than the "thug" mentality generally associated with the hood. Kristyn Scorsone, interview with Heath-Toby, January 27, 2017, Queer Newark Oral History Project (QNOHP), 7, https://queer.newark.rutgers.edu/sites/default/files/transcript/2017-01-27%20C.%20Alicia%20Heath-Toby%20interviewed%20by%20Kristyn%20Scorsone.pdf.

9. Ana Ramos-Zayas, "Of 'Black Lesbians,' Hate Crimes, and Crime Talk: The Sexuality of 'Aggression' in the City," in *Street Therapists: Race, Affect, and Neoliberal Personhood in Latino Newark* (Chicago: University of Chicago Press, 2012), 246–281.

10. Isoke, *Urban Black Women*, 113.

11. Whitney Strub, interview with Patreese Johnson, October 12, 2015, QNOHP, 40, https://queer.newark.rutgers.edu/sites/default/files/transcript/2015-10-12%20Patreese%20Johnson%20final.pdf.

12. The quote continues, "and I was just like, 'I don't think there's a LGBT line for, like, to say what party you're going to vote for. I'd show you the votes, what, you need a hundred LGBT people to [vote] for you, is that going to get something done?' That was my frustration, and nothing against the Sharpe administration, let's just be clear here, I'm just going by what he said. And me being a young transplant from Newark who was eager to do something, I didn't expect the mayor of the freaking city to say something so insensitive." Whitney Strub, interview with June Dowell-Burton, December 1, 2015, QNOHP, 37, https://queer.newark.rutgers.edu/sites/default/files/transcript/2015-12-01JuneDowell-BurtoninterviewbyWhitneyStrub.pdf.

13. "Street Fight," *POV*, season 18, directed by Marshall Curry, aired July 5, 2005, on PBS, season 18.

14. Kristyn Scorsone, interview with Venice Brown, October 12, 2015, QNOHP, 5, https://queer.newark.rutgers.edu/sites/default/files/transcript/2015-10-12VeniceBrowninterviewbyKristynScorsone.pdf; Strub, interview with Johnson, 19.

15. Tim Stewart-Winter, interview with Renata Hill, October 12, 2015, QNOHP, 27, https://queer.newark.rutgers.edu/sites/default/files/transcript/2015-10-12RenataHillinterviewbyTimothyStewart-Winter-Approved_0.pdf.

16. For a more in-depth study of the so-called New Jersey Seven, see LeiLani Dowell, "Wolf Packs: U.S. Carceral Logics and the Case of the New Jersey Four" (PhD diss., City University of New York, 2019).

17. Katherine McKittrick, *Demonic Grounds: Black Women and the Cartographies of Struggle* (Minneapolis: University of Minnesota Press, 2006), 5, 11. "Necropolitics" is most comprehensively theorized by Achille Mbembe in his book *Necropolitics* (Durham, NC: Duke University Press, 2019), and in its broadest formation refers to the ways racist and colonial states administer not only life to their desired subjects but also "deathworlds" to their subjugated ones.

18. But not hyper-heteronormative; in fact, the portrayed sexuality of the ghetto is one of rampant and violent heterosexual pathology.

19. Scorsone, interview with Brown, 11 (emphasis mine).

20. Strub, interview with Johnson, 30, 35 (emphasis mine).

21. Stewart-Winter, interview with Hill, 22.

22. Kara Keeling, *The Witch's Flight: The Cinematic, the Black Femme, and the Image of Common Sense* (Durham, NC: Duke University Press), 9.

23. Robert Curvin, *Inside Newark: Decline, Rebellion, and the Search for Transformation* (New Brunswick, NJ: Rutgers University Press, 2014), 37.

24. Eyricka Morgan testimony, November 12, 2011, QNOHP, 3-4, https://queer.newark.rutgers.edu/sites/default/files/transcript/2011-11-12%20Eyricka%20Morgan_0.pdf

25. "New Brunswick (New Jersey)," WikiTravel, https://wikitravel.org/en/New_Brunswick_(New_Jersey).

26. Scorsone, interview with Brown, 3.

27. Ramos-Zayas, *Street Therapists*, 267.

28. McKittrick, *Demonic Grounds*, 145.

29. Ruth Wilson Gilmore, *Golden Gulag: Prisons, Surplus, Crisis, and Opposition in Globalizing California* (Berkeley: University of California Press, 2007), 28.

30. Jason Nark, "Is Newark the Next Brooklyn?" *Politico Magazine*, March 19, 2015, politico.com/magazine/story/2015/03/newark-new-jersey-development-what-works- 116234.html.

31. "Newark Launches 'Virtual Patrol' Program to Help Deter Crime," *The Associated Press*, April 26, 2018, apnews.com/a5c5cf4117ba4e989966 1ea1c793016c.

32. Anna Alves, interview with Jerri Mitchell-Lee, March 9, 2016, QNOHP, 22, 29, https://queer.newark.rutgers.edu/sites/default/files/transcript/2016-03-09%20Jerri%20Mitchell%20Lee%20interviewed%20by%20Anna%20Alves%20.pdf.

33. Baldwin, "Whose Black Church?"

34. Strub, interview with Johnson, 1, 2.

35. Scorsone, interview with Heath-Toby, 15.

36. Sarah Jane Cervenak, *Wandering: Philosophical Performances of Racial and Sexual Freedom* (Durham, NC: Duke University Press, 2014).

37. Scorsone, interview with Brown, 18.

38. Ruth Wilson Gilmore, "Abolition Geography and the Problem of Innocence," in *Futures of Black Radicalism*, ed. Gaye Theresa Johnson and Alex Lubin (New York: Verso, 2017), 225–240, here 231.

39. Naomi Extra, interview with Heath-Toby, May 23, 2016, QNOHP, 7, https://queer.newark.rutgers.edu/sites/default/files/transcript/2016-05-23%20Alicia%20Heath-Toby%20%28Part%202%29%20by%20Naomi%20Extra%20Final.pdf.

40. Extra, interview with Heath-Toby, 21.

41. Isoke, *Urban Black Women*, 108.

42. Roderick A. Ferguson, *Aberrations in Black: Toward a Queer of Color Critique* (Minneapolis: University of Minnesota Press, 2004), 3.

Oral History Excerpt #4

June Dowell-Burton

On Zanzibar, one of Newark's most iconic clubs:

ZANZIBAR, WOW. Okay. So first of all you had to be dressed to impress at Zanzibar. Melvin was at the front door. He was the gatekeeper. Always—whatever the fashion was he was in it or he was creating his own. So there was this velvet rope and you had to stand in line and unless you knew somebody, you know, you were standing in that line. So most of the time I got in around the rope just simply because [of] who I was with. Thank God, because some of those people standing in the line, I mean it's like Newark's only Studio 54, like that's really what it was. The bottom floor is where you would have the house dancers that would sprinkle the powder on the floor and twirl and slide. They would play the old-school house music and then upstairs that's the larger space with the strobe lights and the ball and stage. I think I performed with—because Wink and Errol they also did choreography, so you know I'd end up dancing. I can't remember the artist but yeah, we ended up performing for somebody. I mean the space was huge. It was just huge. I remember these old velvet red couches for some reason. It was just something for everybody and anybody in there just dancing. Performers would come on a regular and they would not close until literally like 3:00 or 4:00 in the morning.

I met my first girlfriend actually at Club Zanzibar bar and it was during that crazy time period and that was just when—that was Pandora's Box right there and it was done. She was dancing to "Was That All It Was" by Jean Carn. And I'll never forget like she was up—she was just dancing with herself in the mirror and the room was smoky blue and it seemed like we were only two people in the entire space, but I knew there had to be more people there but that's how I remember it. She turned around and that was the end of that. We didn't start off like in a relationship. I mean we definitely started out as friends and then my sexual encounter happened. I think one night after the club we went to her house and then we were watching what was it on—*Malcolm X*. It was a bootleg VCR cassette tape. But the tape was so lousy, it was just fuzzy, and I'm just like I'm looking at her, I'm like this is fuzzy, and the next thing you know like we're kissing and then that was the end of that. So no more bootleg or *Malcolm X*.

And then when Zanzibar closed it was just kind of like everybody just started going to Murphy's. And then it was either Murphy's or the city. Then once Murphy's was gone it was just like, oh God what happened.

Lightly edited for cohesiveness. Listen to or read the whole oral history at https://queer.newark.rutgers.edu/interviews/june-dowell-burton.

CHAPTER 8

Let's Talk about Sex, Baby!

Queer and Trans Black Women and the Politics of Sex Talk in the Archive

DOMINIQUE ROCKER

Queer Newark and the Language of Sex

In 2011, the Queer Newark Oral History Project (QNOHP) was founded in response to the invisibility of a rich culture in New Jersey's largest city. Newarkers felt an urgent call to document and preserve their LGBTQ history by way of community research in collaboration with the city's Rutgers University campus. In the decade since, QNOHP has collected and archived hundreds of interviews with queer community members from broad and differing backgrounds for public use and preservation. Coming out of a Black majority, working-class city, Queer Newark's narrators discuss a range of topics, often at the intersection of their queer identities but not always.[1]

Yet whether for work or for pleasure, even within discussions of sexuality, the topic of sex itself is not always forthrightly addressed by either narrators or interviewers, especially in formal or otherwise public spaces. Both the public and academic nature of oral history collection and its archiving may make it difficult to delve deep into such a personal and taboo topic, especially for underrepresented and multiply marginalized narrators. Thus, discussions of sex (outside of its potential harms) have largely remained elusive in oral history, particularly (and perhaps predictably) Black women's oral history.[2]

It is important to be cautious when discussing the topic of sex in oral history interviews. Interviewers should consider the audience of the archive as well as the comfort level of individual narrators when considering the subject. Sexuality is not reducible to sexual behavior or sex acts, but an open dialogue with queer narrators about queer sexual cultures can help destigmatize queerness and queer sex in public memory and preservation. Sex is a central aspect of the human experience and discussing it more deeply can offer a lot of insight into the events of a person's life and the broader sexual politics under which they lived. In the introduction of their queer oral history anthology, *Bodies of Evidence*, Nan Alamilla Boyd and Horacio N. Roque Ramírez remind us that "queer oral history cannot afford to ask questions solely about the past and its narration but also about how public memories in the present continue to have a politically implicated life in the future."[3] Documenting the cultural norms of language and sex for those whose voices have been silenced or ignored can shift both the content of cultural discussions about sex and how those conversations occur. It can offer listeners searching for themselves—and their desires—in the public archive the hope of recognition. It also reasserts the importance of sex to queer (as well as straight) Newark history.

Collectively, the interviews in the QNOHP archive portray a large array of LGBTQ histories and articulations of sex and sexuality. Regardless of race or ethnicity, men appear more comfortable discussing sex in formative or impactful experiences. Gay men might bring up sex when recounting memories of gay sexual culture at the height of the HIV/AIDS crisis in 1980s. James Credle, for example, talks candidly about his first sexual experiences on the way to Vietnam and, later, about his activism in safe-sex education for gay men at the time.[4] Darnell Moore also speaks openly about his formative sexual experiences.[5] John Calendo is unabashed when speaking about his experiences in the mid-2000s viewing adult films and engaging in sexual activity "behind the seats" of Newark's Cameo theatre and Little Theatre.[6] Both theaters have since closed—Cameo shuttered in 2010, the Little Theatre in 2018, just before the rise of the COVID-19 pandemic—but in their prime, they were culturally significant landmarks for gay sexual encounters.[7]

One other narrator, a white man who simply used his first name, John, was particularly candid on the topic of sex throughout his interviews. John, born in 1938, shared vivid memories of cruising spots around Newark in his teen years and was descriptive when describing the types of sex one could expect in certain places. Penn Station was a hot spot for sex in the men's room, as was Central Station, and the Globe Theater was a favorite for sex in the corridors and in the seats while the movies played all night.[8] Bickford's Cafeteria served as "one of the places where Blacks and whites could make contact" before retiring to Military Park to engage in sex, and it's where John notes that he met the first Black man he had sex with.[9] John also named Washington Park and the "Road to Ruin" between Penn Station and the Public Service bus terminal as two favorite cruising spots.[10]

John located an island at the north end of Branch Brook Park between Bloomfield Avenue and Ballantine Parkway as the "most sensational" cruising spot of his youth.[11] When asked by one of the interviewers to discuss what people did on the island, John described the sex that predominately white gay men of all ages engaged in there as "mostly oral," though he followed up the assertion, saying, "Well, they were probably doing other things, as well. I don't know. I didn't engage in anal sex out of doors. That's something I didn't do."[12] John's description may have been guided by the interviewer's own candidness in the suggestion that he be "as graphically or clinically" detailed as he was "willing to go" in his response, but it is also clear throughout his interviews that John was comfortable discussing his own dating and sexual experiences, practices, boundaries, and pleasures.[13] His frankness in describing the early 1950s cruising scene in Newark is invaluable to our overall understanding of gay life and culture in Newark at midcentury.

In John's interview, the interviewers display a balance between approaching the topic of sex without hesitation and leaving room for the narrator to speak within the bounds of their own comfort. This nuance in approach is important when discussing sex in oral history interviews given the personal nature of the topic. Sex and sexuality can be sources of joy and pleasant memories, but they can also be a space of pain and trauma in a world that has historically and presently been violent to queer people. Black queer and trans women in the QNOHP archive speak of the sexual and gender-based harms they have experienced and the struggles they have faced. Miss Pucci Revlon and Tracey "Africa" Norman touch on the more difficult topics of survival sex work and childhood trauma when they talk about sex, though neither one goes into detail and the interviewer does not press the narrators to speak beyond their comfort zone. Three of the New Jersey Four were also interviewed for QNOHP and each discussed, in varying degrees and capacities, the gendered, racialized, and sexualized violence they experienced the night of a life-changing assault and in its legal aftermath.[14]

Still, there are positive representations of sex and sexuality in the QNOHP archive as well. Patreese Johnson and Venice Brown of the New Jersey Four (discussed more in chapter 7) recount pleasant memories of being gay in Newark in addition to the trauma they experienced. Angela Raine mentions sex briefly and positively in her interview, but the topic appears in a greater variety of ways in her magazine, *La'Raine*. By founding the magazine in 2006, Angela became the first Black trans woman in Newark and in New Jersey to publish a magazine.[15] From erotic stories to survival tips for "The Stroll," *La'Raine* unabashedly talks sex with its readers. Though it is a lifestyle magazine that is not explicit in nature, *La'Raine* often features erotic literature, HIV/AIDS and other health and safety resources, and relationship and sex advice. The January–March 2010 issue is typical of the magazine and includes a sexually graphic short story titled "Between Lovers." The story, written by Angela's husband T. T. Wardell, explicitly follows the queer sexual escapades of its main characters.[16] The fifteenth issue also includes "La'Femme-Queen Newsletter: Transgender Dating: An Interview with a Tranny Lover," a short piece that reframes dating for trans women outside of sexual fetishization.[17] Peppered among the writings are advertisements and information about HIV/AIDS testing, Medicaid, and a mini op-ed on the importance of vaccines.[18] *La'Raine*'s inclusion of explicitly erotic literature and frank discussions of sex and health for the queer community removes what Boyd refers to as "the veil of normativity" and dares to address the impermissible.[19]

La'Raine magazine offers a glimpse into the potential for sex talk in the print archive, and Black queer and trans women who provided testimony for QNOHP did not entirely shy from explicit sex talk, though they were rarely as explicit as a narrator like John. Yet as some of the most vocal Black women on the subject, Patreese, Venice, and Angela provide a glimpse into the way that Black queer and trans women talk about sex—or don't—in public history.

Black Queer and Trans Women "Talking Sex"

Jezebel. Sapphire. Brown Sugar. Hottentot Venus. *Saartje "Sara" Baartman.* "I am a marked woman, but not everybody knows my name."[20] When Hortense J. Spillers opened her seminal 1987 "American Grammar Book" with these words, she laid bare a cyclical crisis rooted in the transatlantic slave trade that continues to render the American Black woman simultaneously named and unnamed, at once hyper-visible and unseen. The racial and highly sexualized stereotypes associated with Black women have endured for centuries beyond their origins, morphing into new iterations but never abandoning their general meanings or

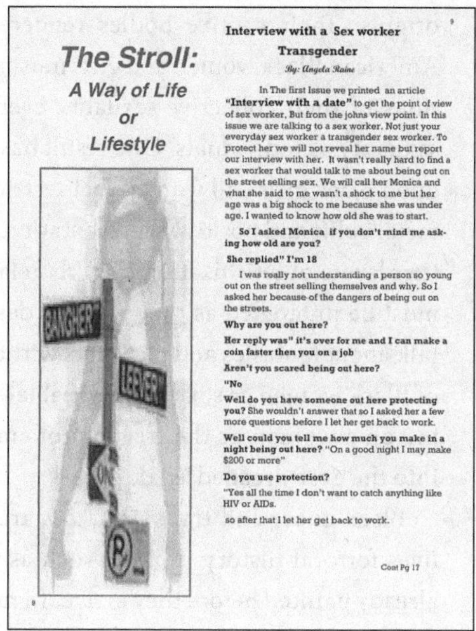

9

Interview with a Sex worker

Transgender

By: Angela Raine

In The first Issue we printed an article **"Interview with a date"** to get the point of view of sex worker, But from the johns view point. In this issue we are talking to a sex worker. Not just your everyday sex worker a transgender sex worker. To protect her we will not reveal her name but report our interview with her. It wasn't really hard to find a sex worker that would talk to me about being out on the street selling sex. We will call her Monica and what she said to me wasn't a shock to me but her age was a big shock to me because she was under age. I wanted to know how old she was to start.

So I asked Monica if you don't mind me asking how old are you?

She replied" I'm 18

I was really not understanding a person so young out on the street selling themselves and why. So I asked her because of the dangers of being out on the streets.

Why are you out here?

Her reply was" it's over for me and I can make a coin faster then you on a job

Aren't you scared being out here?

"No

Well do you have someone out here protecting you? She wouldn't answer that so I asked her a few more questions before I let her get back to work.

Well could you tell me how much you make in a night being out here? "On a good night I may make $200 or more"

Do you use protection?

"Yes all the time I don't want to catch anything like HIV or AIDs.

so after that I let her get back to work.

Cont Pg 17

FIGURES 8.1. *La'Raine* magazine, with cover model Angela Raine, publisher. Courtesy Angela Raine.

FIGURES 8.2 AND 8.3. Documenting the lives of transgender sex workers in *La'Raine* magazine. Courtesy Angela Raine.

origins. Their captive bodies rendered both overly sexual and undesirable, American Black women and girls must navigate these deep historical representations of their collective sexuality even before they begin to understand their sexuality as individuals. One result has been a "politics of respectability" thrust upon Black girls and women that restricts their sexual expression in the name of racial uplift and positive representation.[21] For queer and trans Black women, further layers of fetishization directly related to their gender and sexual identities must be untangled as they work to describe their sex practices. How does one talk about fantasies and pleasures without appearing to reinforce the stereotype of Black women as sexually insatiable? How does one talk about the joys of loving on a woman or the freedom of embracing one's sexuality without feeding into the ever-dreaded "male gaze"?

Black queer and trans narrators are interviewed about the fullness of their lives for oral history projects such as QNOHP with this American backdrop already painted before they arrive. In many ways, they are aware of the potential public audience their stories may reach and the educational implications of this representation. It may not be much of a surprise, then, that for a variety of potentially overlapping reasons, Black queer and trans women don't appear to talk about sex as readily in their interviews as do gay male narrators. Where they do, their stories can be weighted with abuse and violence, both at the individual and state levels. For the narrators and interviewers who share stories of their lives under advanced capitalism in the twentieth and twenty-first centuries in the United States, leisure and pleasure can often be an afterthought to the struggles of working and surviving. This can be especially true for those embodying multiple marginalized identities.

For queer Black women, there can be dual anxieties over their representation of two contested identities that individually and collectively have been hypersexualized in public memory. As a result, narrators might shy from talking about sex in interviews in anticipation of future educational audiences. Boyd points to "a self-conscious production of a particular kind of representation—a representation fit for public consumption" as the reason for this omission.[22] Queer narrators can be unintentionally self-conscious because they know that their narratives are for public consumption, and thus they might edit or avoid discussion of queer sexual culture and activities that have already been pathologized in public memory. Further, Boyd notes that there is a "veil of normativity [that] allows certain speech acts and not others" and renders "nonnormal" (queer sexual cultures) "impermissible."[23] For queer people, as for Black women, this understanding of public representation is always imbued with the politics and power relations that situate their experiences in a particular time and place.

Perhaps in response to these social factors, in addition to an array of personal choices, queer and trans Black women may not be as quick to bring up sexual practices themselves. Jason Ruiz notes that the lesbian-identified women he interviewed were more likely to be superficial and "more reticent" than men in their discussions of sex, mainly detailing the emergence of their sexual *identities* and avoiding discussions of their sexual *practices*.[24] This process of talking *around* sex to describe relationships can be heard in a few of the interviews of Black women, both queer and straight. Angela Raine, for example, who self-identifies as a heterosexual woman, never mentions sex outright, but instead uses a euphemism, "slept together," to describe why she selected a particular date as her wedding date. Her discussion is interspersed with laughter, possibly indicating that she experiences some discomfort when recounting the story.

ANGELA RAINE: A year from the first time we slept together, we got married. I'm talkin' really slept—

[Laughter]

ANGELA RAINE: Cuz he couldn't understand why I picked this particular day for us. I told him, "This is the first time that we—" He was like, "Ew, you remember that?"

[Laughter]

ANGELA RAINE: I'm like, "Yeah."

[Laughter][25]

The reader can infer the significance of the date as the first time Angela and her future husband had sex based on what was both said and left unsaid. Further, based on her husband's reaction, one can still infer a general hesitation to talk about sex, even as it clearly holds meaning for Angela and ultimately influences her life narrative.

Angela also extensively traces the different labels that have been used throughout her lifetime to describe her trans identity. She notes the terms that fit for her and the ones that don't, negotiating the terms in relation to her self-conception in real time. In detailing the variety of labels, Angela is negotiating a cycle of naming, renaming, and reclamation. The language she uses to describe this negotiation suggests a struggle with how dominant labeling seeks to categorize sexuality and gender in ways that don't always align with the personal experiences and connections felt by individuals. Angela ultimately settles on the identity of heterosexual woman as feeling most true for her, which she leads with before detailing her journey grappling with the labels that came before.

In a similar vein, Venice Brown's interview illuminates the ways that lesbian women describe themselves and their sexual preferences in real time and how those labels may be racialized, classed, and situated within a particular time and place. Brown describes a gay aunt as a "stud," and when the interviewer asks for clarification, she explains that "stud" is southern slang for an "aggressive female," or what Newark lesbians would call an "AG," short for aggressive. Here, Brown gives us a greater understanding of regional differences in lesbian slang. When asked if she prefers "other femmes or other butches," Brown refers to herself as a femme, or feminine lesbian, and explains that she prefers femmes or stud women, who are still somewhat feminine and less "butch."[26]

In Boyd's conversation with Cheryl Gonzales and Rikki Streicher, this terminology is discussed in ways that illuminate a class structure within lesbian sex, at least in their experiences in the 1940s and 1950s. These narrators reveal a gender dynamic attached to the terms as well; for example, Gonzalez describes femme women as "possessions" who definitely "had to stay in her place."[27] Streicher later mentions that a dyke—a term neither Johnson nor Brown use—"was low class."[28] This is elaborated on in a more explicit discussion of oral versus digital sex, where Streicher describes "the industrial set" as working-class lesbian women who "emulated men" both in gender performance and sexual practice, which she implied was largely digital and penetrative.[29] Interestingly, in revealing lesbian sexual practices as having a classed and gendered dynamic that emulated men even in the bedroom, Streicher also inadvertently reveals the gendered dynamic of heterosexual sex by implying that performing reciprocal oral sex was itself a more "feminine" practice perhaps not taken up by straight men.

Brown does not speak about this class dynamic or about the specifics of her sexual encounters, and perhaps if she had been asked more explicitly about sexual practices she would have provided additional insight into whether the digital versus oral debate transcended race and time, or if her understandings would have been different than those expressed by Streicher. Yet it is important to note that roughly fifty years later, Brown still employs similar terms but does not seem to connect as rigidly gendered or classed understandings to them. This reveals the fluidity of language, the particular importance of understanding meanings specific to time and place, and the urgency of talking sex in oral history.

Patreese Johnson is a rare female narrator who speaks freely about sexual practices and how they can be rooted in social politics. In her discussion of threesomes, she uses humor to turn a common stereotype into a positive rather than negative representation of lesbian and queer sexual cultures, such as non-monogamy. Johnson mentions the difference she sees in what appears to be an intentionally humorous tone, when she claims that societal expectations for sex within heterosexual couples are more strict ("No, you're not supposed to have threesomes") than those for gay couples ("Lesbians, we like, let's have orgies! *[Laughs]* Let's just go all—let's have fun"). Johnson furthers her argument by claiming it is the very openness and "out-of-pocket" rebelliousness of gay sex that makes heterosexual couples "jealous," and thus they feel compelled to pathologize it.[30]

Adding another layer of analysis, Johnson articulates the difference in social acceptance based on gender. Where it might be acceptable for two women and one man to engage in sex together, a woman who dreams of sex with two men might "never know if it can happen," because society has deemed it nonnormative and impermissible.[31] In her own less-explicit way, Johnson comes to a conclusion similar to Boyd's when she interviewed two older, presumably white, lesbians: that sex and sexuality "function as vectors of political economy," meaning that "conversations about sex are never unmediated by the power relations that situate them in time and place."[32] Patreese never mentions political economy or power relations specifically, but her theorizing on the policing of queer sexual practices speaks directly to those themes.

Conclusion: Let's Talk about Sex, Baby!

Though the focus of this chapter has been primarily narrator engagement, the onus for talking about sex in oral histories should not be solely placed on them. While interviewers can and should be cognizant of potential social forces that encourage Black queer and trans women to shy away from openly discussing sex topics in oral histories, they should also consider the rich cultures that stand to be uncovered if only someone dares to ask. When historians consider oral history work as a shared authority with the community, they can offer queer narrators the space to speak in their own terms about taboo but nonetheless integral life topics such as sex and sexuality, thus producing powerful narratives that provide a deeper understanding of queer America. Documenting the language and cultural sexual norms of those whose voices have been silenced or ignored can shift the content of cultural discussions and how those conversations occur. It can offer listeners searching for themselves—and their desires—in the public archive the hope of recognition.

Primarily using the QNOHP interviews of Patreese Johnson, Venice Brown, and Angela Raine as guides, this chapter examined the hesitations potentially present for interviewers and Black queer narrators, particularly those who also identify as women. It also analyzed the historical imperatives for talking about sex in public oral history. A brief examination of "sex talk" in each of the interviews offers us an understanding of how these narrators use the language of sex and how they talk about themselves and their sex lives in relation to their sexualities. While Patreese, Venice, and Angela are not the only people in the QNOHP archive to touch on the subject of sex explicitly, they are some of the most open Black women on the topic and the only narrators who weigh in on some of the pleasures of sex for queer and trans Black women. Each narrator digs into the language of sex in relation to their individual identities and experiences, and each struggle over sexual language is an opportunity for interviewers to learn about the sexual cultures of Black queer and trans women in Newark. Though these women have experienced violence related to their gender identities and sexualities, they have also found power in reclaiming and renaming their sexual selves in different ways, and this merits preservation in oral history.

Notes

1. Darnell L. Moore, Beryl Satter, Timothy Stewart-Winter, and Whitney Strub, "A Community's Response to the Problem of Invisibility: The Queer Newark Oral History Project," *QED: A Journal in GLBTQ Worldmaking* 1, no. 2 (Summer 2014): 1–14.

2. Tricia Rose's 2003 project, *Longing to Tell: Black Women Talk about Sexuality and Intimacy*, is the most extensive oral history of Black women candidly discussing their intimate and sexual lives. Though both queer and straight women are subjects of the project, Rose is intentional in not flagging specific identity markers so as not to immediately categorize the narratives and to allow for more fluid understandings of sexuality and intimacy. Though the aims of *Queer Newark* are certainly different, *Longing to Tell* is a good model for the kinds of sex talk that could benefit

the archive more broadly. Tricia Rose, *Longing to Tell: Black Women Talk About Sexuality and Intimacy* (New York: Farrar, Straus and Giroux, 2003).

3. Nan Alamilla Boyd and Horacio N. Roque Ramírez, "Introduction: Close Encounters," in *Bodies of Evidence: The Practice of Queer Oral History*, ed. Boyd and Roque Ramirez (Oxford: Oxford University Press, 2012), 1–20, here 13.

4. Candice Bradsher, interview with James Credle, February 15, 2015, Queer Newark Oral History Project (QNOHP), 12, https://queer.newark.rutgers.edu/sites/default/files/transcript/JamesCredleQNOHP.pdf.

5. Timothy Stewart-Winter, interview with Darnell Moore, March 15, 2016, QNOHP, 4, https://queer.newark.rutgers.edu/sites/default/files/transcript/2016-03-15DarnellMooreinterviewedbyTimStewart-Winter-FINALAPPROVED.docx_.pdf.

6. Whitney Strub, interview with John Calendo, November 27, 2020, QNOHP, 2–8, https://queer.newark.rutgers.edu/sites/default/files/transcript/John%20Calendo%20Interview%20-%20KS%20vetted%20031722.pdf.

7. Whitney Strub, "This little porn movie house learned to survive for decades–until last week," *NJ.com*, July 3, 2018, https://www.nj.com/opinion/2018/07/this_little_jersey_porn_movie_house_learned_to_sur.html.

8. Whitney Strub and Kristyn Scorsone, interview with John, August 3, 2016, QNOHP, 11–12, https://queer.newark.rutgers.edu/sites/default/files/transcript/2016-08-03%20John%20final%20version%20to%20post.pdf.

9. Strub and Scorsone, interview with John, 15, 17.

10. Strub and Scorsone, interview with John, 16.

11. Strub and Scorsone, interview with John, 9–10.

12. Strub and Scorsone, interview with John, 10.

13. Strub and Scorsone, interview with John, 9.

14. In the late summer of 2006, the group of lesbian-identified Black women were out in Greenwich Village in New York City when they were harassed by a straight Black man on the street. When the women refused his sexual advances and told him they were gay, he grew more derogatory and intense. In the ensuing physical altercation, the aggressor suffered a stab wound and claimed the attack was a "hate crime against a straight man" by the group of lesbian women, who would later be described in the media as a "gang," as "killer/bloodthirsty lesbians," and as "a seething sapphic septet," rhetoric used to signal their race, gender, and sexuality as destructive and threatening. Four of the seven women in the group were tried and convicted for the assault, with each woman serving time ranging from two to seven-and-a-half years. See Cara Buckley and Kate Hammer, "Man Is Stabbed in Attack after Admiring a Stranger," *New York Times*, August 19, 2006; Anemona Hartocollis, "Woman in Gang Assault Trial Says Man Started the Fight," *New York Times*, April 14, 2007; Laura Italiano, "Attack of the Killer Lesbians," *New York Post*, April 12, 2007; "Four Women Sentenced over Attack on Man," NBC News, June 15, 2007, https://www.nbcnews.com/id/wbna19233888.

15. Anna Alves, interview with Angela Raine, October 20, 2016, QNOHP, 19, https://queer.newark.rutgers.edu/sites/default/files/transcript/2016-10-20%20Angela%20Raine%20interviewed%20Anna%20Alves%20with%20Lorna%20Ebner_0.pdf.

16. T. T. Wardell, "Between Lovers," *La'Raine*, no. 15 (January–March 2010): 4–8, 20–23.

17. Anastasia Willis, "La'Femme-Queen Newsletter: Transgender Dating: An Interview with a Tranny Lover," *La'Raine*, no. 15 (January–March 2010): 11.

18. "Vaccines Are Important," *La'Raine*, no. 15 (January—March 2010): 17. Viewing this magazine a little over eleven years later during the COVID pandemic is a reminder that history can sometimes appear ironic and resonate in profoundly unexpected ways.

19. Nan Alamilla Boyd, "Talking about Sex: Cheryl Gonzales and Rikki Streicher Tell Their Stories," in *Bodies of Evidence: The Practice of Queer Oral History*, ed. Nan Alamilla Boyd and Horacio N. Roque Ramirez (Oxford: Oxford University Press, 2012), 95–112, here 110.

20. Hortense J. Spillers, "Mama's Baby, Papa's Maybe: An American Grammar Book," *Diacritics* 17, no. 2 (1987): 65–81. Saartje Baartman, also known as Sara or Sarah, and most famously as the Hottentot Venus, was a South African Khoikhoi woman whose name and story have been distorted and misplaced throughout history. What is most well known about her is the time she spent "on display" in Europe from 1810 to her death in her mid-twenties in 1815. Her brain, skeleton, and sex organs (her large buttocks being the reason for the original exhibition) remained on display until 1974, and a cast of her body resurfaced again for display in the 1980s. Baartman's body was not fully put to rest until 2002. There is now a wealth of scholarship on Baartman, her life, and the cultural meaning of the Hottentot as it relates to Black women and sexuality. For a comprehensive look at Baartman's life, see Clifton Crais and Pamela Scully, *Sara Baartman and the Hottentot Venus: A Ghost Story and a Biography* (Princeton, NJ: Princeton University Press, 2009).

21. For more on the making of Black female sexuality and its representations, see Spillers, "Mama's Baby, Papa's Maybe"; Darlene Clark Hine, "Rape and the Inner Lives of Black Women in the Middle West," *Signs* 14, no. 4 (Summer 1989): 912–920; Mireille Miller-Young, "Putting Hypersexuality to Work: Black Women and Illicit Eroticism in Pornography," *Sexualities* 13, no. 2 (2010); Ariane Cruz, "Beyond Black and Blue: BDSM, Internet Pornography, and Black Female Sexuality," *Feminist Studies* 41, no. 2 (2015): 409–436.

22. Boyd, "Talking about Sex," 110.

23. Boyd, "Talking about Sex," 110–111.

24. Jason Ruiz, "Private Lives and Public History: On Excavating the Sexual Past in Queer Oral History Practice," in *Bodies of Evidence: The Practice of Queer*

Oral History, ed. Nan Alamilla Boyd and Horacio N. Roque Ramirez (Oxford: Oxford University Press, 2012), 113–129, here 119.

25. Alves, interview with Raine, 10.

26. Kristyn Scorsone, interview with Venice Brown, October 12, 2015, QNOHP, 5–6, https://queer.newark.rutgers.edu/sites/default/files/transcript/2015-10-12VeniceBrowninterviewbyKristynScorsone.pdf.

27. Boyd, "Talking about Sex," 100.

28. Boyd, "Talking about Sex," 107.

29. Boyd, "Talking about Sex," 107–108.

30. Whitney Strub, interview with Patreese Johnson, October 12, 2015, QNOHP, 33, https://queer.newark.rutgers.edu/sites/default/files/transcript/2015-10-12%20Patreese%20Johnson%20final.pdf.

31. Strub, interview with Johnson, 32–33.

32. Boyd, "Talking about Sex," 111.

CHAPTER 9

"Temos Muitas Coisas Pra Fazer"

Market Identities and Queer Community-Building in the Brazilian Ironbound and Greater Queer Newark

YAMIL AVIVI

"I DON'T THINK it's changed much," Bairon[1] tells me about Newark's Ironbound in the summer of 2019. I am revisiting my ethnographic interview project with queer Brazilians living there, which began in 2007 and concluded in 2009. "But [yet] it did change. You definitely see more gays around," he quickly adds. During summer 2019, I reinterviewed several interlocutors whom I had written about in two essays on queer Brazilian life in the city's historically white-ethnic immigrant neighborhood.[2] The Ironbound, once dominated by the Portuguese, "began to shift, as more Latin American migrants, especially from Brazil and other parts of South America, began to arrive in the area in the late 1980s" and has been principally recognized as a Portuguese and Brazilian neighborhood since the early 2000s.[3] Over ten years after my fieldwork ended, I wanted to understand what had changed and what had stayed the same. This time around, I had the opportunity to sit with new interlocutors, including Bairon, a middle-aged, masculine, cis-male Brazilian banker who was originally from São Paulo and had been living in the Ironbound while working in New York City since the late 1990s. I briefly met Bairon around the time I did my first round of interviews in 2007, but it was only now that I had the chance to sit and talk with him.

As we both eat seafood in a highly regarded Spanish restaurant—the kind marketed to moneyed tourists and downtown corporate workers who pay for fine dining and European food in Newark—situated on the far west side of the Ironbound, not far from McCarter Highway and downtown Newark near the

Prudential arena, I ask Bairon, "How has the Ironbound changed or not in terms of gay people living there [since the mid-to-late 2000s]?" Bairon says that even while you see "more gays around" than in the mid-to-late 2000s, the dominant culture remains heteronormative. I say, "Describe that. What do you mean?" He responds, "You can see gays holding hands. Like a couple of months ago, they had the Portuguese festival, I see two girls holding hands and I saw two guys holding hands. In 2009, I don't think we saw that." Bairon explains that there is now more visibility and openness as far as same-sex queer identity in public, not only in the annual Portuguese festival but also within ethnic festivals such as Brazilian Day and the everyday consumer and work culture in the Brazilian-owned stores my interlocutors frequent and in which they work. I examined these immigrant nationalist and heteronormative contexts in my previous essays.[4] Bairon's attendance at the Portuguese festival demonstrates how Brazilians and Portuguese comingle at different Lusophone (Portuguese-speaking) public events in the Ironbound and how queer identity is shared and experienced in them too. While my work focuses primarily on cisgender gay men, I have engaged with Brazilian transgender individuals and Brazilian and Central American lesbians living and/or socializing within the neighborhood, including going to St. Stephan's Lutheran Church and frequenting the nightlife there. In a previous publication, I documented the story of the late Daniel, who was transgender.

I proceed to ask Bairon, "Why do you think this visibility and openness is happening?" He responds, "[The] LGBTQ community is now more . . . I think they're opening more and more. . . . It's helping everyone [to be open]. The new generation has a totally different mentality. It's like who cares what they are?"

Overall, my ethnographic interviewing and fieldwork in the summer of 2019 suggests—as Bairon has explained—that the Ironbound neighborhood has grown more queer-friendly and that Lusophone and Hispanophone queer immigrants who live and consume in the neighborhood and market have grown more visible. First, as Bairon explains, a later generation of queers, either newly arrived immigrants or young adults who came of age in the Ironbound, are louder and more confident ("who cares what they are?") than the earlier queers I interviewed when their ways of being in public were more subtle or "tacit": not "coming out [which] may sometimes be redundant . . . is already understood or assumed . . . [and] neither secret nor silent."[5] Even queer folks like Joilson, whom I interviewed in 2007–2008 and will soon introduce, have become less tacit and more open, while Nelson, another interviewee from that period, has remained tacit since I first met him. The Ironbound is a densely populated neighborhood that makes visibility imminent. Some of my interviewees, particularly Joilson and Danilo, have lived and worked within the neighborhood market and have achieved status and belonging within a heteronormative immigrant majority despite their sexual and gender difference. For example, when I was walking on Ferry and Wilson Streets with Joilson and his work colleague, Fernando, several men and women, either queer or straight, waved hello to us on the street with a smile or came over to us and initiated a conversation. These men were not marginal or reserved but highly familiar and respected by those who engaged us on the street.

While these are hopeful signs of a more tolerant sexual diversity within the Ironbound neighborhood, particularly from the viewpoint of Brazilians there, this chapter points to the limits of this tolerance. Specifically, I examine how the Ironbound's established market success, beginning with retail, tourism, dining, and entertainment in Newark's "neoliberal" economy of the 1980s and up to the present—a local economy that depends on the individual success and sufficiency of privately owned small and big businesses—impacts the individual and communal LGBTQ life of its service workers, small entrepreneurs, and patrons. This historically distinguished immigrant market, long assumed to be part of a heteronormative neighborhood in Newark, sidelined LGBTQ residents and workers. That is, the Ironbound's commercialization and long-established neoliberal success has shaped, or rather disciplined, the neighborhood's "sexual diversity" through standing ideologies of good ethnicity[6] and individual worth[7] established through hard work and self-sufficiency directed toward Ironbound's historically consistent ethnic market success.

The Ironbound has long been regarded as contributing to the area's economic vitality, sustained tourism, and stable political economy despite Newark's long-term problems with urban decay and violence. For example, the Portuguese of the neighborhood and their "good ethnicity" were revered for their immigrant industriousness, which generated a market and consumer culture that brought tourists into their neighborhood for shopping and dining when Newark overall was in decline. As Kimberly Da Costa-Holton explains, former Newark mayor Sharpe James lauded the Portuguese Ironbound section of the city in a 2002 keynote speech for "its active participation in the Newark renaissance . . . [and] low crime rates, carefully maintained residential buildings, and a booming commercial district replete with ethnic restaurants and shops [of] Ironbound's Little Portugal."[8] In that vein, later-arriving immigrant groups, particularly Brazilians, have assumed this same market and consumer culture—as evident, for example, in their business leadership on Ferry Street and Wilson Avenues since the mid-1990s—to achieve and be recognized for the same level of industry, if not more.

How does this market and consumer culture impact the way queer Brazilians assume their communal lives, when it appears that their individual worth and local market success is more valuable than prioritizing their queer communal identity that vocalizes their needs and demands as a social group in the city? Ramos-Zayas writes, "The neoliberal policies of the 1980s and 1990s implicitly required that a normative style of emotional management—in which characterizations of the city as aggressive or angry were concealed or redressed—be instituted if attractive real estate . . . and the promotion of tourism [and nightlife] were to be successful."[9] In effect, Ramos-Zayas's discussion of "emotional management" also reflects depoliticized soft skills and attitudes of LGBTQ service workers and self-employed entrepreneurs, who "conceal or redress . . . [individual and collective] angers [or] aggressions," including politicized awakenings, over their actual marginality, disparities, or lived inequality. Specifically, I examine how my interviewees' overvaluing of individual worth (their distinction as self-entrepreneurs and model workers in the market economy) and overall individual self-sufficiency and progress limits urgent forms of anti-heteronormative and anti-homonormative queer community-building within the Ironbound and greater Newark. For these queer immigrants, individual progress is what Ulla D. Berg refers to as "a cultural and class aspiration, and a demand for citizenship status and belonging."[10] I argue that in the past fifteen years, even while queer Brazilians living in the Ironbound have gained a more openly queer positioning and have become less tacit, they are contained within certain parameters like market success and a strong work ethic that shapes their individual life and worth. In effect, the queers I (re)interviewed reify state ideals of good ethnicity ("good Brazilianness"), aspirational whiteness, individual progress, and self-sufficiency that limit politicized interracial and interethnic collaboration with other neighboring racial and ethnic groups in Newark.

This chapter presents a longitudinal ethnographic study of queer Brazilian immigrants who have either continued living in the Ironbound neighborhood or who have moved on. I conducted four interviews of former interviewees and four with new informants. These were either recorded or conducted via Zoom during 2019 and 2020. Several of these interviews were held at my interlocutors' homes, workplaces, and either Brazilian or Portuguese restaurants of the neighborhood. Using critical ethnography, I examine through these more recent interviews how my interlocutors situate themselves between American state values of individualism, "good immigrant" ideology, self-sufficiency, and anti-state relationships/solidarity-building among other Brazilians and other racial and ethnic groups in Newark. Using multi-sited ethnography, I analyze my interlocutors in different contexts or situations to observe how they assume state and anti-state values of race, diversity, community-building, and sexuality.

This chapter is divided into three sections. In the first, I provide four new interviews with Joilson, Carlos, Nelson, and Danilo (pseudonyms), whom I initially interviewed in 2007–2009. I offer an update on their recent lives and reexamine how their place in the Ironbound (or their relationship with it) has changed or stayed the same. In the second, I share how each interviewee demonstrates a contained queer identity through their individual market success, a strong work ethic, or a narrative of progress that ultimately debilitates queer community-building. I examine perspectives many of them raise about not having time for community organizing because of their commitment to their individual self-entrepreneurship or work ethic that diverts them from community involvement. In the last section, I examine queer nightlife at Guitar Bar and Twister, venues that Brazilians, non-Brazilian Latinxs, and African Americans frequented and where the Newark Pride Center attempted to build partnerships with them. To do this, I conducted several more interviews in 2020 with Karmyn and other frequenters, including Ricardo. Ultimately, my ethnographic interviews point to the fact that the owners, promoters, and staff of these establishments sustained distance and separatism between queer ethnics despite efforts from the Newark Pride Center and a Black promoter to bring everyone into the fold. Ultimately, queer Ironbound's nightlife, based on the perspectives I have gathered, is contained in consumer culture and fails to enhance any kind of genuine familiarity as "one queer Newark" among racial and ethnic groups. This suggests that these venues are establishments for consumption only, and at best a depoliticized racial diversity, in the name of economic vitality within the Ironbound, not a way to create true solidarity, partnerships, and a coalescence of ethnic and racial groups between the Ironbound and Newark at large.

Catching Up with the Interviewees

THE FAMILY BAKERY'S MODEL WORKER: JOILSON AT BOM PÃO

Joilson is now in his early fifties. He is of Afro-Brazilian and Portuguese descent, born in the department of Minas Gerais, Brazil. When I met him in 2008, he was working at Bom Pão,[11] where he still worked in 2019. In 2008, Joilson was undocumented and had no means of applying for legalization. Today, Joilson remains undocumented but is in the process of applying for his permanent residency with a VAWA self-petition[12] from his unsuccessful marriage with his African American husband, Richard. During the time I reinterviewed him, Immigration Equality, a nonprofit immigration firm in New York City, accepted his case. When I first interviewed Joilson in 2008, I found that he was reticent to talk about his identity as an Afro-Brazilian or his engagement with other African Americans in Newark or elsewhere in the United States. Yet, in my recent engagements with him, he was evidently more open and forthright about his personal connections with African Americans and his own identity as Black than in previous interviews. Before, Joilson's Brazilian identity superseded his racial identity within a "colorblind" Brazilian market of mostly lighter-skinned Brazilians. For example, this time around, he described to me one very positive memory while he was married to his husband and was meeting his family. Joilson felt drawn to his husband's family, and they reminded him of his Afro-Brazilian family in Brazil. In effect, this is a moment in which Joilson related with U.S. Blackness and moved away from the aspirational whiteness of the Ironbound market and neighborhood.

Joilson has grown more outspoken and confident and less tacit about his sexual identity and effeminate gender performance since I first met him. Joilson recounts that in Brazil, he was the target of constant ridicule and harassment at school and work because of his effeminate disposition. He found it very difficult to maintain his professional job as an educator because of the deep homophobia he encountered. After arriving in the Ironbound and finding employment at Bom Pão, he explains, "I continue working at Bom Pão because of the comfort. It is a place that accepts me as a human being, that accepts me for having homosexual friends and to also have the ability to express my points of view with my colleagues at work, my boss, and [with] the community." Here, Joilson reflects, like he did in 2009, about the high level of "comfort" he has at Bom Pão to be "just as he is" without facing discrimination or bullying by his boss or coworkers. In fact, during a tour of the bakery, one of the older cooks came up to see what we were doing in the back office. As we headed back to the bakery, Joilson began twerking at him. The assumedly straight and reserved cook laughed it off, but it surprised me to see a comfortably bold version of Joilson I had never seen before, especially at his job at a busy establishment where there is no time for play. In effect, the boss has created a tolerant work environment for Joilson and others over the years even though people with different religious views also work there. Joilson says that the work atmosphere, "não é um Paraiso, existe as diferencias" (it's not a paradise; there are differences) because some of the other workers are fervent evangelicals. Yet, overall, there are several queer employees at the bakery, and thus it is not surprising that they also would find the work environment affirming and "comfortable" despite evident religious differences among those who tolerate homosexuality and those who do not.

However, even though Bom Pão is a favorable place to work because of its queer-friendly environment, Joilson describes the downside to working there. He admits, "Financially, I think I'm not satisfied with working at Bom Pão." He has been working there for nearly fifteen years and the wages continue to be insufficient to raise his quality of life or allow him to consider future plans for savings or retirement. Joilson continues to live in cramped rooming houses or basement apartments. The one I visited this time is in a basement without any windows. Despite these downsides, he says, "There are [other] reasons why I have stayed there, like a sense of feeling so dependable and loyal the boss feels in me." In other words, he has stayed there because of his strong sense of market worth, instilled by his boss, who has successfully run a small local business with Joilson's exemplary model-worker dependability. Many in the community have known Joilson working for years at the bakery, and because of this he has gained a public status as an efficient, hard worker, despite any prejudices about his effeminacy and sexual orientation. As an efficient worker, Joilson remains a safe and known public figure who is not threatening to anyone in the community nor planning on demanding any rights (more on this in the next section) but remains complicit with the everyday life and work in the Ironbound market.

MARRIED AND A HOUSEOWNER IN FLORIDA: CARLOS'S NOSTALGIA FOR THE IRONBOUND

When I met Carlos in 2006, he was an undocumented early-twenty-something living in the Ironbound. When he arrived in the neighborhood, he started working in the construction business to pay off his $9,000 coyote fee for entering the United States undocumented. In the local male heterosexist labor force that is construction, Carlos stayed just long enough to pay off his debt. He then moved into independent domestic cleaning in New York City, which he would do for the rest of his time in New Jersey until he moved with his husband Kevin to Florida in 2017.

Carlos and Kevin met at a gay club called Feather's in River Edge, New Jersey. Kevin is a masculine-acting and introverted Italian American who was born and raised in Pennsylvania. He is a monolingual English speaker. As they grew more serious, they lived together in the Ironbound while Carlos was undocumented. Even though they had different statuses, this did not affect their plans to build a household together. At first, they lived in a basement apartment, and they eventually rented an apartment in a two-family house for several years before they made the decision to move out of the Ironbound. They would buy their first home in Rahway, New Jersey, and their second in Plainfield, New Jersey.

Around 2009, Carlos applied for political asylum based on sexual orientation persecution in Brazil. But after gay marriage was legalized, Carlos and Kevin eventually decided that they should marry and discontinue the asylum process because it was taking too long. It was also likely that Carlos's asylum case would not be approved. Eventually, Carlos became a U.S. resident through gay marriage.

At the time of my first interview with Carlos in 2008, he was already disillusioned with life in the Ironbound due to its density and the rise in crime. More importantly, he wanted to move out of the Ironbound, away from Brazilians, and experience living in the American mainstream. It is evident that his goal in moving out of the Ironbound was to gain a sense of personal success, progress, and mobility. In our recent talks in Florida—in the couple's self-designed and newly built massive five-bedroom, four-bathroom home there—he expresses his critical view of his long-time queer friends (some of whom are in committed relationships) who continue paying rent in the Ironbound without any motivation to pursue home ownership and wealth. In effect, Carlos sees these friends as limiting their progress or not working hard enough in U.S. society by remaining in the Ironbound. Over the years since Carlos and Kevin have moved out of the Ironbound, they have had less and less interaction with their queer friends there.

Yet, Carlos was the central figure of sociability among his queer friends when he lived in the Ironbound. This slowly changed after he left the Ironbound for suburban New Jersey and became nonexistent when he moved to Florida. When I first approached the topic of returning to visit the Ironbound and rekindling his friendships with those who still live there, Carlos was disinterested and not optimistic. He commented that his friends were full of drama, envious of his mobility, and basically still up to the same things (over-partying, overspending, hooking up) he was doing ten years ago. Carlos's and Kevin's communication with this group of friends occurs mostly through social media and very infrequently over the phone. But the more time we spent remembering the Ironbound, the more Carlos seemed to grow nostalgic about the good times with his friends at local eateries, karaoke nights, and home parties he threw, including visits to Asbury Park, for example. When he realized that I was going back for a second time this past summer and we reminisced about these memories, he wanted to go back even though he at first seemed adamantly disinterested in returning to visit. In effect, Carlos and Kevin have moved away from communal life among queer friends and built an individualized family as mobilized and aspiring homonormative queers. By "homonormative," I mean that these queers aspire to be like heteronormative citizens in their ability to assume a whitened positioning that is self-sufficient, depoliticized, and of middle-class standing with family values that reify American values of individualism, meritocracy, and assimilation.[13] Eithne Luibhéid illustrates that this type of coupling between a "good homosexual" (Kevin) and his/her/their immigrant partner (Carlos) "seeks inclusion within the existing system rather than challenging structures of domination."[14]

BUSINESS IS GOOD, WHY LEAVE? NELSON DECIDES TO STAY

Nelson, who was fifty-nine years old in 2019, is the eldest of my interviewees. I met Nelson at St. Stephan's Grace Community Lutheran Church, where I met several Brazilian queers, including Carlos. Carlos and Nelson also met at church, became good friends, and worked together in domestic housecleaning in New York City. In 2008, Nelson was undocumented, and it was not until around 2012 that he arranged a marriage agreement with a Brazilian woman to become legalized. Nelson, a Brazilian of European descent who was born and raised in Southern Brazil, passes as a white, assumedly straight male. Because he can perform a heterosexual masculinity, Nelson likely convinced immigration authorities that his marriage to this woman was truthful. Nelson gained legal permanent residency.

Nelson is now in a relationship with Louis, a Jewish American private attorney, whose practice is based in New York City. Nelson met Louis on a dating site online, and after some time they began seeing each other. Louis hired Nelson for his cleaning services. Louis saw how meticulous Nelson is as a domestic cleaner and even helped him to think about marketing himself more professionally (i.e., using aromatherapy with his cleaning services, which would be attractive to the corporate class living in the city). However, Nelson remained informal and did not follow Louis's business-savvy advice.

Even while Nelson remains informal with his domestic cleaning services, he has been very successful, working three to four cleaning jobs in one day and up to six days a week. Over the holidays, Nelson receives bonuses from his clients, which he saves. In all, he has been able to accumulate significant life savings while sending generous monthly remittances and building a comfortable home for his three sisters in Brazil. (Both his parents had died by 2008 and he could not visit them beforehand because he was undocumented). A lot of his ability to save stems from being frugal and cutting costs. For example, he has been renting a room in the same four-bedroom apartment since I met him in 2006. By 2009, the landlord put him in charge of all the subleases in the apartment, and as a result he was able to free himself from paying rent while charging the other subleasers higher rent for their rooms to cover his. Also, Nelson has never had a car while living in the United States and does not intend to because he is in the Ironbound, a transportation hub for metro New York/New Jersey and a quick Lyft ride away from his partner.

Despite Nelson's financial success and business integrity, Louis has found him, according to Nelson, to be much below his league. For example, Nelson explains that Louis has behaved in ways that demonstrate he is embarrassed to be Nelson's boyfriend because of his "modest" work and the fact that he was an undocumented immigrant. It has taken Louis a long time to introduce Nelson to his friends and parents and it was left unestablished that they were together. Even so, Nelson has proven to be financially dependable for Louis; in one instance some years back, when Louis needed $15,000 because he was between checks, Nelson was able to easily withdraw that $15,000 from his savings account to lend to Louis.

In the last year, Nelson has started a new business selling fantasy jewelry from Brazil to mostly women and queers in the hair salons throughout Newark, Kearny, and Harrison. On some days, he can make up to $1,000. This has allowed him to work four days a week at cleaning and the rest of the week selling jewelry directly from Brazil to his established clientele in the Ironbound and nearby Harrison and Kearny. Nelson mentions that the women and queer men in the salons have asked him, "Are you married? Are you gay?" But he is discreet and straight-acting compared to the eccentric men in the hair salons. On occasion, these men say racy things; for example, a man who was trying to fit a ring that Nelson was selling said, "This does not fit my finger but it fits my clitoris." Nelson tells me this with laughter and disgust and insists on staying reserved about his own sexuality with them. While he does laugh with these men over rather crude comments like that, which assures them that he is in fact queer, Nelson maintains a boundary between him and them through his professional profile rather than building more genuine familiarity with them.

DANILO: A PROMOTER AND KARAOKE HOST "FOR ALL"

Danilo has lived in the Ironbound since the early 2000s. Hanging out with Brazilians in the local scene early on, he caught a break from one friend who decided to move back to Brazil. She hosted a karaoke night that Danilo frequented. Seeing great potential in him to host, she told him, "Danilo, I'm leaving back to Brazil for good, but I'm going to pretend I'm coming back, and in the meantime, you could host and take over the karaoke night." This friend left him with her karaoke equipment, which he would use for many years. Since that moment, Danilo has remained an entertainer, host, and promoter for different establishments in the neighborhood for over fifteen years. Danilo explains how his public stature as a host and entertainer grew over time. He says, "My main job is still karaoke. That's where I started. So doing karaoke and people seeing the singing and then the energy, they started inviting me to do shows, openings, festivals, Brazilian festivals (when we celebrate Brazilian Independence Day over here)."

Bairon, a new interviewee who arrived in the Ironbound in 1998, offers his view about Danilo's legacy of hosting parties in the Ironbound. He comments, "Danilo has done so much because you know he goes bar to bar with his karaoke thing and he would gather all kinds of people together. He does that. He brings people together." In effect, Bairon's view is that Danilo "has done so much" to ease tensions and hostilities and create familiarity among the ethnic diversity of those in the Ironbound as residents and consumers. Joilson adds that Danilo "is involved with the gay community because [when] he does events the gay community joins him where he goes. He's super personable, right? With the gay community. [For example] if he has an event in Casa Nova, the gay community will also join because he is super personable with the gay community." In this discussion, I ask him if the party is straight, gay, or mixed. He explains that it is "uma mistura" or a mixture "because he is super personable with *all*, and so the gay community joins him." In effect, Joilson establishes Danilo's ability to create events of peaceful sexual diversity. But even more, Joilson explains "ele é uma pessoa formadora de opinão" (he is an opinion-maker) as a publicly, openly gay man whose opinions and perspectives are valued because he is a public community figure within the Ironbound. In other words, his ability to build mixed parties with sexual diversity has helped create a peaceful cohabitation in the dense neighborhood of the Ironbound.

In line with Bairon's view, Danilo offers his view about what being a host, entertainer, and promoter in the Ironbound means to him that resonates with his ability to bring people together. He has created gay nights at several establishments, including Brasilia Grill, Guitar Bar, and Rosie's Bar, and says, "[My] work is bringing a variety of happy moments to people that come from Brazil or come from other countries.... This is a Brazilian [neighborhood] and everyone comes—the Brazilians, the Hispanics, and the Americans. And that's my main goal, is working the nightlife bringing in a little bit of happiness." By "little bit of happiness," Danilo is suggesting that this diverse mixing of people brings a temporary happiness in the consumer context of the Ironbound market and nightlife. It's a temporary happiness that is not about tackling larger social issues of racism, homophobia, and transphobia by forging a genuine familiarity. When he says "Americans," I'm left wondering if Danilo is referring to both Black and white Americans. By not specifying who he serves as a host and entertainer among "Americans" in a Black-majority city, his narration is tellingly colorblind in a way that avoids the racial dynamics of queer Newark. The scene that Danilo describes is contrary to what Jill Dolan writes about how an event becomes a utopian performative for an audience—in this case for the crowd at a nightlife establishment—or "a moment of utopia [that] gestures toward a potentially better future," evoking a more hopeful tomorrow together.[15] It is similar to what Fiona Buckland describes as the "queer worldmaking" of togetherness on dance floors at nightlife venues among a diversity of local ethnic and racial groups.[16] These venues encourage a mingling of diverse bodies and a centering of their energies of nonheteronormative desire and relationality through a potpourri of music segments with mingled dancing and even messages of a brighter, fairer tomorrow together. I think about what the implications of Danilo's colorblind approach are for our discussion of diversity and about who he means by "everyone" in a Black-majority city. Danilo's colorblind view helps to situate Joilson's and Bairon's earlier discussion of who "everyone" is at Danilo's parties, which essentially feature the ethnic mixing and familiarity of Brazilians and Spanish-speaking Latinx foremost and where African American Blacks remain outliers, as this chapter will further explore.

Individual Market Identity versus Queer Community Identity

"TEMOS MUITAS (OUTRAS) COISAS PRA FAZER" (ALÉM DA QUESTÃO DA COMUNIDADE): THE COMPROMISE BETWEEN INDIVIDUAL MARKET IDENTITIES, THE NARRATIVE OF INDIVIDUAL PROGRESS, AND QUEER COMMUNITY-BUILDING[17]

In one way or another, my interlocuters have suggested how their market identities are important in terms of how they either relate with other queers in the neighborhood or gain status in their roles in the market or in their (long-term) association with a particular business in the Ironbound. In the cases of Joilson, Danilo, and Nelson, whether they are dedicated long-term service workers (Joilson) or self-entrepreneurs of informal businesses (Nelson) or nightlife (Danilo), their market identities sustain a depoliticized consumer culture and relationship that limits or discourages politicized queer community organizing.

Unlike the previous interviewees, Carlos (with his husband Kevin) moved out of the Ironbound to move forward in his American life by achieving homeownership and moving away from everything. In his recent interview, Carlos explains that his friends—still in the Ironbound—have fallen behind and continue being renters who haven't grown out of the party circuit in Newark. Yet, during his interview, Carlos begins to grow nostalgic over those pastimes in the neighborhood given that he himself was the center of organizing house parties there with his queer friends. Suddenly, as we sit together in his Florida kitchen nook hearing our voices bounced from the many walls of his grandiose house in conservative, majority-white Port St. Lucie, where only Carlos and Kevin live with their three dogs, his facial expression becomes a blank stare. He asks me when I will visit the neighborhood again. The blank stare, in my view, represents the contrast between the stillness and individual life he now lives amid isolated suburban houses far apart from each other and the density of his old neighborhood and sense of strong community he had in the Ironbound, which I wrote about previously.[18] Carlos was someone who could have easily been a community organizer or dedicated leader for LGBTQ issues in the neighborhood. While it's perfectly fine to move on with your life, such as by seeking homeownership in New Jersey or elsewhere, I take issue with how Carlos views still living in the Ironbound as a sign of immobility instead of the potential to sustain the supportive community he had while living there and to continue developing it. Rather, it's the place where he's at now in life—in conservative white suburban Florida as a homeowner—that matters to him.

In contrast to Carlos, Nelson is committed to staying put in the neighborhood. While his partner Louis and his friend Carlos have suggested he move out of the Ironbound because he is able to do so, Nelson is content living in the neighborhood and will not easily leave because it is where he's lived since coming to the United States and where he's achieved financial stability, where his Brazilian culture and ties are concentrated, and where he enjoys eating at Brazilian restaurants daily. Nelson does not show much interest in displaying to others that he has achieved financial success through markers of progress that indicate that he has moved up, such as a high-end car or an exclusive place to live outside of the Ironbound where his partner would want him to move or where Carlos would think is dignified. Yet, despite Nelson's commitment to staying in the Ironbound, he has not been invested in building relationships among queers there. Instead, Nelson goes about his individual life and engages with others mostly through his own self-entrepreneurship.

Aside from self-entrepreneurship that queers like Nelson have developed for themselves to get ahead within the Ironbound, Danilo shares in his interview the visibility and openness of queer Brazilian service workers within the context of a local popular Brazilian restaurant, Delicias De Minas. Danilo explains that at least "70 percent of the employees are queer." Very much like Joilson at Bom Pão, who claims the work environment is overall favorable to queers despite the presence of "fervent evangelicals," Danilo describes a very comfortable work environment for these gay workers and clients. For example, "They [the queer workers] do funny things, the waiters and bartenders they have this funk Brazilian music that have steps . . . they all come to the front and they dance. The guys come, they dance and they do the twerking thing, Brazilian twerk, and are living their best lives." In effect, these queer workers "go shamelessly to the front" and openly flaunt in the safe space of a gay-tolerant restaurant business amid a heterosexual majority clientele. This sense of openness within a heteronormative market space shows how these workers work under circumstances of tolerance for sexual diversity; yet, they could use this gain to further explore politicized queer community-building instead of being contained by their market identity as queer service workers.

Joilson offers a historical understanding of why queer community-building within the queer Brazilian Ironbound has not sufficiently progressed. He explains, "Listen, unfortunately, what queers attempted to do . . . [now over] ten years ago unfortunately was not realized or forged. The community stopped [moving in that direction]. [Right now] there isn't a social political organization for the gay community in the Ironbound." Joilson is recalling when ABGINUSA (Asociaçao Brasileira Gay Ironbound Newark USA) was formed within the space of St. Stephan's Grace Community Church, a persistently gay-affirming church on the corner of Ferry Street and Wilson Avenue that continues hanging an LGBTQ flag over its main entrance, where it is impossible to miss from both street corners. In 2008, several meetings were held with interested residents to discuss forming a group with social activities and shared topics of interest, including queer immigration rights.[19] We invited an attorney from the American Friends Service Committee to give a talk on political asylum based on sexual orientation. Not only was the launch of ABGINUSA about creating social and recreational activities among queer immigrants and their allies, it was also about building a deeper familiarity with each other by discussing such topics as quality of life, working conditions, safety concerns, and issues with prejudice or homophobia and transphobia.

Joilson continues by saying, "And there's so much to do to work with the gay community [in the Ironbound] on various issues in the areas of [HIV, STD, and PrEP] education, health, recreation, and culture.[20]" Here, he recognizes the urgency ("there's so much to do") of queer community-building in light of the issues he points out. He adds, "In Newark-at-large's LGBTQ community, I know that it has done more, but specifically in the Ironbound there isn't anyone to bring the community who lives here together."[21] In effect, Joilson makes comparisons between Newark-at-large and the Ironbound and acknowledges the progress the latter has made to bring the LGBTQ community together.

Bairon either lacks information about the Newark Pride Center and LGBTQ Community Center or demonstrates a distance between the Ironbound queer community and the greater-Newark LBGTQ community. When we met in July 2019, he had tried to go to the gay pride parade in downtown Newark, but due to back problems he was not able to go. A Brazilian friend was interested in going with him. In our conversation, it became evident that Bairon did not know that the Newark gay pride parade had formed years ago. I asked him, "Do you think that there could be a way to bring, say, African American gays at Newark Pride and Brazilian Ironbound gays together?" He answered, "Yes, that can be done," but explained that the gay pride wasn't "around here, it [is] a little far." Yet, Joilson, in his previous discussion, did not necessarily make the connection with Newark-at-large and the Ironbound coming together for this kind of work. Ultimately, both consider the geographic divisions between Newark-at-large and the Ironbound. Joilson also hints at a distinction between the Ironbound queer immigrant culture and the majority–Black American queer culture of greater Newark by essentially saying that someone from within the community "who lives here [in the Ironbound] and understands our immigrant queer culture should assume leadership." Similarly, Danilo suggests the need to build a strong queer Brazilian social network (like a Facebook group), which already exists among Ironbound Lusophones, to share information, resources, and opportunities.

Danilo's suggestion is anchored in designing a noncommittal social network that, as described below by the interviewees, appears most realistic. Joilson adds that time is a priority for many in the community: "They refuse to take a half hour off to engage in discussions to improve gay community." Joilson is pointing out that queers are "too busy" ("vidas tão corridas") in their individually driven lives—starting with their long workdays—to devote time to communal initiatives among queers. Bairon, on the other hand, reasons that "There's no interest in the political. . . . They don't care. They're still partying." In other words, like Carlos, Bairon views most queers as working and playing hard without any interest in organizing. After we discuss the potential for organizing a local Ironbound LGBTQ organization, Danilo explains, "I don't see no one organizing it at this moment right now." Similarly, Joilson says, "I think a person is missing [with the values and motivation] to organize." In effect, Danilo and Joilson arrive at the fact that someone needs a strong vision outside the individualized neoliberal context of the Ironbound to forge a communal vision among queers. Additionally, both Joilson and Danilo admit that they are unavailable for this kind of communal initiatives, but for different reasons. Even while Danilo would be a strong candidate for this organizer position, given his public stature and because he has proven his ability to relate well with others and bring different people together, he says, "I don't think I would be the best person to do it." Specifically, he explains that he does not have the time for "organizing . . . being responsible for the organization" because of his other commitments, like his nightlife gigs as an entertainer and promoter. Yet, he ends by saying, "But I would love to be part of something like that. And I think it's needed." In contrast, Spanish-speaking Latinx immigrants in the Ironbound have long organized around issues of labor, immigration, empowerment, and community solidarity. More recently, New Labor, a statewide grassroots organization, which has an office in Newark and a partnership with St. Stephan's Grace Community Church, has a queer Mexican community organizer, Rafael Chavez, who has stimulated organizing and solidarity among Mexican and Central and South American queers. It's evident from the organizing going on that there has not been a substantial mixing of Hispanophone and Lusophone immigrants within New Labor.[22] This is an example of the lack of politicized community solidarities between Luso- and Hispanophone queers and non-queers in the neighborhood, which suggests sustained social boundaries and ethnic differentiation. However, these boundaries and differentiation could recede for New Labor in the future through Chavez's (and other leaders's) continued commitment to local queer diversity and visibility, collective action and change.

Joilson expresses fear that he cannot lead because of his current undocumented status: "I'm going to be very exposed given my immigration and HIV status and that may burden my immigration process." Joilson believes that his intent to organize may be perceived as a threat or as "starting trouble," or what would be contrary to good citizenship and being a docile model worker at Bom Pão. As an Afro-Brazilian, "starting trouble" in his view may also mean that Joilson's Blackness and queerness may be negatively racialized[23] or viewed, as Ana Ramos-Zayas suggests, as "angry,"[24] in contrast to his everyday performance as a diligent, manageable, and loyal service worker. In this interview, Joilson is vocal about these issues, unlike ten years ago. After the previous interview, I wrote, "Joilson's queer and effeminate Black sexuality is the epitome of non-heteronormativity and subversion, and can become a threat to the nationalist . . . space if he performs" them in a way that accentuates a politicized Blackness.[25]

Missed Opportunities for Community Organizing

BETWEEN NEWARK-AT-LARGE'S LGBTQ COMMUNITY AND THE IRONBOUND'S LGBTQ COMMUNITY: A VIEW FROM GUITAR BAR AND TWISTER

In my discussion with Danilo about several parties he has thrown throughout the Ironbound, we discussed particular moments when he was connected with Newark's Pride Center, which he referred to as the "Pride people." He recounts that early on there was engagement among the owners, workers, and himself at Guitar Bar—a nightlife venue that blossomed with the (re)development in the area and was frequented by different crowds for specialized music parties, including "Lounge, House, Dance, Trance, Techno, Reggaeton, Salsa, Merengue, Bachata, Hip Hop."[26] The bar was located at the fringes of the Ironbound until 2011[27] and just across the street from one of the rail lines parallel to McCarter Highway, which marks a racial boundary between the largely immigrant (white) neighborhood and the majority (Black and Brown) African American and Puerto Rican and growing South and Central American immigrant neighborhood:

> I'm not sure how they connected. But when we used to do Guitar Bar, we actually had an event with them. So they might have heard about the place or went there, or I don't know if [x person] was the manager there and contacted them for the Pride month. I think that what [people from the Pride Center] wanted to do [was] something different every Wednesday, happy hour. They might have looked for a gay place to do that. This happened during the last year at Guitar Bar, 2010 or 2011.

In this comment, Danilo remembers an event held by the Pride Center for Pride Month. While Danilo treats this more as a business incentive between Guitar Bar and Newark's Pride Center, these Pride events are indications of the Pride Center bridging proximity and relationality to the Ironbound community. Danilo's posturing here suggests that, when the Pride Center reached out to the Guitar Bar to host an event, they were not trying to build stronger ties between the Ironbound and larger Newark queer communities. Several different parties were thrown by Brazilian, Latinx, and African American promoters and DJs for their specific crowds, as Ricardo and Karmyn relay in interviews that appear later in this essay. The Guitar Bar is significant to African Americans because it is close to downtown African American and Latinx/Puerto Rican LGBTQ historic sites of a Black and Brown nightlife and ballroom culture of the late 1960s through early 1990s that fought for safety, local rights, and dignity.[28]

Our conversation shifts from then to now when we discuss Twister, a new "full-time gay bar" that opened in 2019 at the end of Ferry Street, far in East Ironbound and directly opposite where the Guitar Bar was located. Danilo recalls the recent Pride events held at Twister:

> On the Pride month, [the owners at Twister] started doing a happy hour with the Pride people that organize Pride here at Newark. They are having this whole different crowd come in. It's more Black people and some Latinos, but it's more the Black crowd. So now we have this mix. It was Brazilians before that . . . [they] still come. So like yesterday I worked . . . the karaoke [and there was] a good amount of Black people, a good amount of Brazilians, and a good amount of Latin[x] people. It's a mixed crowd, all singing their styles [with] karaoke.

From his description, we see that Danilo was more engaged ("I worked . . . the karaoke") with "this whole different crowd" coming in that is not from the Ironbound and that included members of Newark's Pride Center. He emphasizes that "It's more Black people and some Latinos" that changes the ethnic and racial composition of this event from what Danilo seems accustomed to. Instead of it being mostly Brazilians and Spanish-speaking Latinxs, it becomes a "different, culturally unfamiliar crowd" of African Americans and Spanish-speaking Latinxs in the space of the Twister. Danilo then notes that before, "It was [just] the Brazilians," and that even with the arrival of a Black crowd, "Brazilians . . . still come," which suggests that the presence of African Americans from outside the Ironbound could turn off the Brazilians in the neighborhood.

In line with this, Ricardo, a second-generation Brazilian American who lives near the Rutgers campus and whose roommate is a queer African American, explained that he enjoyed going to Twister because of "the Brazilian representation of the bar." To Ricardo, the bar is a Brazilian gay bar foremost rather than one that is invested in equally representing all LGBTQ gay music and groups in Newark. For Ricardo, the presence of non-Brazilians is fine so long as Brazilian music and culture outweighs all the other musical and cultural elements when he visits the venue. Twister's location in the extreme east side of the Ironbound, which is heavily populated by Brazilians and Spanish-speaking Latinxs, suggests that the culture of this gay bar is more that of a queer immigrant clientele drawn to Latin and Brazilian musical styles that do not necessarily appeal to U.S.-born Latinxs

FIGURE 9.1. Twister Bar in 2019, photograph by the author.

and African Americans, who are deeply invested in 90s golden-era hip hop, present day hip hop, ball culture and voguing, and New York City, Newark native, and Chicago-style deep house.

Karmyn (she/they), an African American lesbian, promoter, and member of the Newark Pride Alliance whom I interviewed in 2020, offers a dismal story about their attempted partnership with Twister. Karmyn explained to me that they did

FIGURE 9.2. Twister Bar ad, September 28, 2019, from Twister Lounge Facebook account. Twister's now-defunct social media page is a rich and rare archive of queer Latinx Newark history.

not like or identify at all with the music that the DJs spun and wanted to bring DJs who spun the kind of music styles they and their crowd enjoyed. Karmyn did see potential in Twister as a space of future dance nights with their African American majority crowd, but with the music they enjoyed, which was non-Latin/Brazilian and not what the resident DJ played. Perhaps the need to create separate parties for different music tastes is highly important, as was done at Guitar Bar (see next section) while also attempting to create genuine familiarity among different racial and ethnic groups from the Ironbound and from greater Newark.

The Black presence at Twister, therefore, is what is different, or what Bairon witnessed as a stark separatism between African American and Brazilian clubgoers at Twister when only Brazilian music was being played. At Twister he heard songs by Pabllo Vittar, a cis-male Brazilian drag queen who became famous overnight, mixed by resident Brazilian DJs on several nights. Pabllo Vittar's songs include successful collaborations with Latinx reggaeton and hip-hop/pop artists (like Lali and Karol G) that build cultural proximity between Lusophone and Hispanophone queers in the context of Ironbound nightlife. This may further explain and support why Ricardo insisted on referring to himself as "Latinx" first, not "Brazilian," because of the growing relatability between Lusophone Brazilian and Hispanophone queer music and culture among Latin(x) immigrant and U.S.-born clubgoers. For example, Danilo explained that Hispanophone Latinx music like reggaeton and bachata are frequently played at his parties. At the Guitar Bar, he said,

> Most of the people coming were Hispanic. . . . One of our DJs, we have Marcos Carnival. He is a house music DJ only. He doesn't even play Brazilian songs like Brazilian funk . . . they want to hear their reggaeton, bachata. And he would do some sets, he would play those kinds of songs, but he would stick more to his style [house music]. But we worked together for a long time—and people actually love him.

Danilo suggests here that Brazilians also relate to Hispanophone Latinx popular music like "reggaeton and bachata," so much so that they will show up to a Hispanic-majority party. The relationality Danilo expresses here is strictly between Lusophone and Hispanophone queers who see African American musical styles and culture as different.

KARMYN: BLACK LESBIAN PROMOTER AT TWISTER

Karmyn was in her mid-thirties and had moved to Newark about seven years ago, or roughly in 2013. Karmyn uses the pronouns "she/they" (she/her in lesbian homosocial spaces and in professional, heteronormative settings; they/them in mixed queer spaces). They are from Asbury Park, a redeveloped beach town and gayborhood an hour and ten minutes south of Newark in Ocean County, New Jersey. Asbury Park redeveloped into a gay-friendly beach town with nightlife and rainbow-branded hotels and businesses. One of Karmyn's reasons for moving to Newark, however, was the vibrant gay and Black—specifically Black lesbian—scene in Newark, which was harder to come by in Asbury Park. Before she moved to Newark, Karmyn frequented Guitar Bar on Thursdays, where Ms. Theresa organized a Black lesbian night. Guitar Bar managed to hold specific nights catered to specific social groups. By their retelling, "Only Black lesbians went on that night." Karmyn's account of Black lesbian Thursdays suggests that Guitar Bar's management allowed specific social groups to have their own space and dominion over the venue on given nights. Well-attended Lusophone- and Hispanophone-dominated nights were reserved for the weekend. Karmyn is a poet and band singer who has developed activities for Newark Pride members and poetry readings and band performances throughout Newark's local venues. They have gained a following, given their artistry and queer civic activities. Overall, however, Karmyn's outlook on nightlife in the Ironbound, particularly in the present, was not positive.

Karmyn professed feeling limited in the Ironbound, suggesting that the neighborhood and its nightlife was not really a place for Black queer visibility, incorporation, or empowerment. This resonates with other Black queer accounts, such as a Queer Newark Oral History Project interview in which Don Ransom recalled his friends being called both racist and homophobic slurs there; he concluded, "the Ironbound is like, they don't think they are a part of Newark."[29] From the beginning, Karmyn said of their attempts to organize parties at Twister, "I experienced anti-Blackness." When I began interviewing Karmyn, they asked me, "Why would you choose to study gay nightlife in the Ironbound? It is so underdeveloped because New Yorkers or gays from Jersey City won't come to Newark for gay nightlife." In general, they explained that New York City or Jersey City, a 30- to 45-minute train ride away, was where most Newarkers flocked for gay nightlife anyway.

Yet, Karmyn has worked to build a queer nightlife in different parts of Newark, including at Twister. The owner and manager who Karmyn worked with to develop two parties in 2019 seemed genuinely interested in building their relationship with the Pride Center and marketing themselves to a potential Newark gay/queer clientele and establishing themselves as a gay Newark club, not just a gay Ironbound club. But according to Karmyn, neither the owner nor the manager did enough to create a space of tolerance and healthy mixing among racial groups. Karmyn organized a voguing house night for their Black ball followers in June 2019 and a Halloween party on November 1, 2019. They saw that the owner and manager were hesitant to post the Halloween flyer on Instagram to inform Brazilian clubgoers. When Karmyn pushed to intermix with the Brazilian majority of Twister's nightclub, the manager pushed back. The manager was also reluctant to allow Karmyn's DJs to play at Twister because hip-hop, ball culture, and Black-inspired house music was avoided. At the parties, Karmyn's crowd, according to their clubgoers' feedback, was met with rude staff and bartenders, and overall the club had a "bad energy" of anti-Blackness from the Brazilians who went on that night. Even while Karmyn's pool of African American–majority nightlife goers could walk into the club, they were met with resistance to Blackness and to allowing a queer Black music and cultural scene to assume the space of Twister's club.

In conclusion, these ethnographic interviews have offered us an understanding that Brazilian queer life has grown more visible and louder between generations of immigrants and youth born in the Ironbound. Even more, many establishments in the market and nightlife scenes practice tolerance of sexual diversity, when years ago queer LGBTQ folks only practiced a firm tacit disposition. Now, as Bairon explained in the opening of this essay, there is more room to be who you are. Despite these steps forward, this essay reveals that the queer Brazilians I interviewed live highly individualistic lives of "good ethnicity" and a strong work ethic intimately tied to the market culture and economic vitality of the neighborhood, a slavish and historicized narrative embedded in the neighborhood's immigrant labor culture. These LGBTQ folks also fiercely contribute to the aspirational model minority myth of "hard-working Brazilians" by being an asset to Newark's economy and the burgeoning market of the Ironbound. The centering of these ideologies among my interviewees in their individual lives leads them to fail to truly devote time (in their already busy working lives) to building a queer community life within and outside the Ironbound that explores issues that impact them as LBGTQ immigrants. Ultimately, my interviewees reflect that no one is taking the lead within the queer Brazilian Ironbound to launch this much needed leadership "because no one has the time," despite this population's contributions to the retail, service, and entertainment industries of the neighborhood.

Aside from the community organizing needed among Lusophones and Spanish-speaking Latinx within the Ironbound, I examined how queer Ironbound nightlife has been fortunate to be frequented by the Newark Pride Alliance and LGBTQ folks outside of the Ironbound seeking to support these businesses. In fact, it is in the nightlife that the potential for building familiarity with African American queers could happen. As Anna Lvovsky and Kristyn Scorsone note in chapters 2 and 4, respectively, bars and clubs have long served as crucial foundations of queer Newark community. They can be venues that engender familiarity and a better future among people. Creating music segments where different types of music are played among different audiences dignifies the different social groups attending; it's a start. Having the DJ express positive words of togetherness, as in "ONE NEWARK," is also a start. Unfortunately, based on the experiences I examined, African American queers were met with resistance, as if they were not welcome. Ultimately, the Ironbound queer Brazilian community needs to enact a community leadership that begins to help queers think of pertinent questions outside their individual lives within and outside of the Ironbound. Brazilian queer immigrants need to view themselves as not only Ironbound Newarkers but Newarkers in general, as a part of one queer Newark that fights for their queer rights and finds genuine ways, through dialogue, of building trust with other racial and ethnic groups of the city, particularly African Americans. Guitar Bar closed in 2011 and Twister in 2020, the latter due to the economic decline caused by COVID-19. Hopefully, if Twister reopens, it will keep in mind creative ways to bring everyone into the fold as One Queer Newark.

Notes

1. Chapter title's translation from Portuguese to English: "We Have Many Things To Do." The actual names of the interviewees have been changed to protect their identities.

2. Yamil Avivi, "Queering Political Economy in Neoliberal Ironbound Newark: Subjectivity and Spacemaking among Brazilian Queer Immigrant Men," *Diálogo: An Interdisciplinary Journal* 18, no. 2 (2015): 105–118; Avivi, "Betina Botox and Lobixomen 'Tão Engraçados!' Queer Brazilian Televisual Representations Shaping Spatial (Im)possibilities in Newark," *The Bilingual Review/La Revista Bilingüe* 33, no. 4, (2017): 45–59.

3. Ana Ramos-Zayas, *Street Therapists: Race, Affect, and Neoliberal Personhood in Latino Newark* (Chicago: University of Chicago Press, 2012), 145.

4. Avivi, "Queering Political Economy," 106.

5. Carlos Decena, "Tacit Subjects," *GLQ: A Journal of Lesbian and Gay Studies* 14, no. 2–3 (2008): 339–359, here 340.

6. By "good ethnicity," I am referring to the acknowledgement of an ethnic community's hard work, discipline, profitability, and sufficiency that contributes to the social and economic success of a given context. As a group, good ethnics are often docile, governable, and complicit with government values, often without demands. See how the Portuguese and Brazilians are regarded as "good ethnics" in contrast to Newark's Puerto Ricans and African Americans. Ana Ramos-Zayas meticulously explores the socioeconomic and historical positioning of these four ethnic groups in Newark in *Street Therapists*. See also Avivi, "Betina Botox and Lobixomen," 48.

7. By "individual worth," I am referring to the value of an individual person (in this specific case LGBTQ Brazilian immigrants) who contributes to the success of a given context's neoliberal economy (in this case Newark's) through hard work, discipline, and self-sufficiency even while facing a disparity in basic needs and social marginalization that could be vocalized through politicized organizing. Good individual worth is met by valuing the person who forges the service or market industry and sacrifices basic rights or demands by putting their head down, fending for themself, or getting ahead through hard work while staying complacent to government values without any desire to organize against government interests or demand rights, benefits, or equality. Individual worth goes hand in hand with good ethnicity. The person who matters or is worthwhile is the one who contributes to the success of the local market with their everyday individual hard work, discipline, and self-sufficiency.

8. Kimberly Da Costa-Holton, *Performing Folklore: Ranchos Folclóricos from Lisbon to Newark* (Bloomington: University of Indiana Press, 2005), 178.

9. Ramos-Zayas, *Street Therapists*, 46.

10. Ulla D. Berg, *Mobile Selves: Race, Migration, and Belonging in Peru and the U.S.* (New York: New York University Press, 2015), 5.

11. "Bom Pão" is not the actual name of the bakery where Joilson works. The name has been changed to protect my interviewees' identity.

12. Under the Violence Against Women Act (VAWA), male and female immigrants who face domestic violence from his/her/their spouses can divorce or separate from their batterers and proceed to apply for residency. In order to proceed, it is strongly encouraged to first get legal advice from an immigration attorney to review the details and merits of the case.

13. Avivi, "Betina Botox and Lobixomen," 48.

14. Eithne Luibhéid, "Sexuality, Migration, and the Shifting Line between Legal and Illegal Status," *GLQ: A Journal of Lesbian and Gay Studies* 14, no. 2–3 (2008): 289–315, here 307.

15. Jill Dolan, *Utopia in Performance: Finding Hope at the Theater* (Ann Arbor: University of Michigan Press, 2005), 8.

16. Fiona Buckland, *Impossible Dance: Club Culture and Queer World-Making* (Middletown, CT: Wesleyan University Press, 2002).

17. Translation from Portuguese to English: "We Have Many (Other) Things To Do" (Besides the Question of Community).

18. Avivi, "Queering Political Economy," 113–115.

19. Avivi, "Queering Political Economy," 113.

20. Taken from the CDC website, "Pre-exposure prophylaxis (or PrEP) is medicine taken to prevent getting HIV. PrEP is highly effective for preventing HIV when taken as prescribed." For more information, visit: https://www.cdc.gov/hiv/risk/prep/index.html. See also: https://hivinfo.nih.gov/understanding-hiv/fact-sheets/pre-exposure-prophylaxis-prep.

21. For more information on Newark's main LGBTQ organizations, see the web pages of the Pride Center, https://www.facebook.com/pridecenter.nwk/ and the Newark LGBTQ Community Center, https://www.newarklgbtqcenter.org/. Both organizations are based downtown.

22. Author interview with Brazilian American Pastor Moacir Weirich of St. Stephan's Grace Community Lutheran Church, who partners with New Labor, November 17, 2021.

23. Roderick A. Ferguson, *Aberrations in Black: Toward a Queer of Color Critique* (Minneapolis: University of Minnesota, 2004); Jafari S. Allen, "Blackness, Sexuality, and Transnational Desire: Initial Notes toward a New Research Agenda," in *Black Sexualities: Probing Powers, Passions, Practices, and Policies*, ed. Juan Battle and Sandra L. Barnes (New Brunswick: Rutgers University Press, 2009), 82–96.

24. Refer to endnote 9.

25. Avivi, "Queering Political Economy," 113.

26. See the description of the Guitar Bar here: https://411newyork.org/clubs/events/2010/04/02/guitar-bar-18/.

27. See https://www.loopnet.com/Listing/17241493/179-181-New-Jersey-Railroad-Ave-Newark-NJ/. This link shows a picture of the bar and map of its place within Newark.

28. Timothy Stewart-Winter and Whitney Strub, "How NJ's LGBT-Friendly Clubs Have Long Strived for Safety," *Star-Ledger*, June 20, 2016.

29. Don Ransom, quoted in Whitney Strub's interview with Aaron Frazier on November 17, 2017, Queer Newark Oral History Project, 31, https://queer.newark.rutgers.edu/sites/default/files/transcript/2017-11-21%20Aaron%20Frazier%203_1.pdf.

Oral History Excerpt #5

Alicia Heath-Toby

In this excerpt, Heath-Toby discusses joining the landmark New Jersey lawsuit Lewis v. Harris *with her wife Saundra "Honei" as the only Black litigants among six other couples fighting for legal recognition of same-sex marriage. The case was successful in 2006, resulting in the creation of civil unions for same-sex couples in New Jersey; full marriage equality required another court battle, won in 2013.*

We were at an event in New York, me and my wife, and a friend of mine was with us. At this event, Lambda Legal was tabling and they were asking for couples to sign up if they were interested in being plaintiffs for the *Harris v. Lewis* case that they were building. My friend submitted our name. We didn't even do it. We didn't do it. We got a call from David Buckle, who no longer is with Lambda Legal, awesome man. He came and he interviewed us. We were then invited to be part of the lawsuit with six other couples. We were the only African American lesbian couple. There was an interracial lesbian couple. There were two white lesbian couples and a white gay couple. Initially I didn't wanna do it. I didn't wanna do it because I was doing a lot. I was doing a lot. I was in ministry. We were doing prevention, HIV prevention. We had the Social Justice Center. Life was going on and I didn't wanna do it. My wife said, "That's not an option. We have to do this." I said okay. It was five years and it was rewarding, but yet it was very—there were times where we felt very unsupported. There were some threats made. Overall it was a wonderful experience. The other difficulty was that we were the Black couple.

There was an expectation. We had our own expectation of what that meant. We were clear about two things; one is that we were asked because we were African American. We were clear about that. That was very clear. Two, we had a responsibility to see this thing through and to be the face of what it meant for our community to engage, at least, in the conversation of marriage, of same-sex marriage, and have the opportunity to do so. It was a lot of pressure. Everywhere we were invited to go, we went. Wherever we were asked to speak, we went. There were times when we would look out into the room and as usual—you know, it's one of those things, like you know when you're growing up and you're the only Black or one of three in the space, that that feeling never goes away no matter how old you are. For me, it was difficult looking out into the audience and not seeing many of us. At some point, [I was] really resenting that here we are fighting for the people, and where are the people? Where are our people? That was hard.

What kept me grounded was the bigger picture, which was the opportunity to marry your same-sex partner and it not be a big deal. That we could do that. That that was an option for us. While we're in it, again we're traveling a lot, which was wonderful. It was wonderful. Meeting amazing people. It also, because it was us, we also—then there was the movement, right? The movement was excited that we were part of it because the movement had had its reservations about same-sex marriage and what it meant. We really brought a face to what it was. That was very powerful. It was a journey that I'm glad that I took. It was important.

Lightly edited for cohesiveness. Listen to or read the whole oral history at https://queer.newark.rutgers.edu/interviews/alicia-heath-toby.

CHAPTER 10

"Newark Police Don't Do Nothing for Me; They Don't Protect and Serve"

Policing LGBTQ+ Communities

DANIELLE M. SHIELDS AND CARSE RAMOS

SINCE ITS INCEPTION IN 1857, the Newark Police Department (NPD) has amassed significant and ongoing controversy due to its legacy of problematic policies, practices, and behaviors, particularly toward communities of color and LGBTQ+ communities. A long history of civil rights complaints from outraged residents and local advocacy groups finally reached a fever pitch in 2011, when the Department of Justice (DOJ) formally began an investigation of the Newark Police Department. Following its investigation, in 2016, the City of Newark entered into a consent decree; this agreement formally installed an independent monitor to ensure the NPD meets benchmarks related to training and improving police/community interactions.[1] Much of the DOJ's investigation focused on the disparate racial impact of the NPD's approach to policing via an overreliance on invasive contacts, unreasonable use of force, and violations of various civil rights. In concluding its fifty-page report, the DOJ noted "discriminatory policing practices based on sexual orientation or gender identity" by the NPD, including the "harassment of female transgender persons" due to NPD officers regularly—and erroneously—assuming these women were engaged in sex work. The DOJ also described "a lack of cultural competence and insensitivity by NPD officers" toward LGBTQ+ people, but labeled these accounts "anecdotal evidence" rather than a verifiable pattern. Though the DOJ's report did call for improvements related to policing Newark's LGBTQ+ communities, these calls were not legally binding, and it is unclear whether they have generated meaningful change.[2]

Thus, there are several important reasons to study interactions between LGBTQ+ people—particularly LGBTQ+ people of color (POC)—and the police in Newark. First, national trends have indicated LGBTQ+ people are more likely to identify as POC.[3] Consistent with both national data and Newark's demographics (most of its residents are people of color), due to overrepresentation of people of color throughout the criminal legal system, understanding compounding marginalization stemming from status as *both* an LGBTQ+ person *and* a POC, as well as their influence upon key criminal legal processes, is pressing. Due to their already amplified marginalization throughout American society and its structures, like trends related to POC more broadly versus whites, LGBTQ+ people are also more likely to accumulate police contacts throughout their lives relative to their heterosexual peers, leading to overrepresentation in the American correctional system.[4] Once incarcerated, LGBTQ+ prisoners—particularly transgender and gender-nonconforming (TGNC) people—are subjected to particularly punitive mistreatment (e.g., failure to provide proper medical accommodations for TGNC people and heightened victimization from both staff and inmates).[5] Taken together, justice-related policies have had important ramifications for LGBTQ+ people throughout the United States (for example, mandatory arrest policies result in more frequent "dual" arrests for same-sex couples), with some scholars asserting these patterns constitute the "hyper-incarceration" of LGBTQ+ communities.[6]

Notably, LGBTQ+ communities are particularly susceptible to generalized forms of victimization compared to their heterosexual and/or cisgender counterparts, including stigma-laden and underreported crimes more prevalent among LGBTQ+ communities (e.g., intimate partner violence [IPV], anti-LGBTQ+ bias crimes, and sexual assaults).[7] As a result, there is a critical need for the police to competently respond to LGBTQ+ crime victims in order to apprehend the perpetrator(s). However, promoting increased reporting and cooperation with the police hinges upon an improved relationship between police departments and communities who, despite their vulnerability, are still incredibly skeptical of the police's ability to effectively assist them. Thus, it appears the police would do well to address broader, socially shared perceptions of police legitimacy among residents.

Like other under-resourced institutions throughout Newark, systemic gaps related to the behavior of the police have impacted the operations of Newark's police force; this is troubling, as perceived inefficiencies in policing are consistent with a reduced sense of procedural justice, or the belief that the police generally behave in fair, equitable, and respectful ways when interacting with citizens. Unfortunately, as an emergent body of empirical work has demonstrated, LGBTQ+ people routinely opt out of reporting crimes enacted against them.[8] Perhaps even more problematically, when the police are summoned, LGBTQ+ people experience adversity in multiple ways during routine interactions with police, which operate in distinct ways (e.g., police responses to IPV).[9] Further, involuntary police interactions (i.e., those in which the police are not summoned) involving LGBTQ+ people also appear to generally produce poor outcomes; this is of critical importance, as involuntary interactions appear to be particularly salient in perception formation toward the police.[10] These trends are concerning, as they have, both individually and collectively, suppressed a sense of legitimacy and procedural justice among LGBTQ+ people concerning the police. This phenomenon has also been observed in research that has considered these dynamics within environments where POC tend to reside, which tend to be urban, overpoliced, and often crime prone.[11]

In sum, because of multiple negative encounters with the police, both individually and among LGBTQ+ communities more broadly, victimized LGBTQ+ people may avoid interacting with them despite an elevated need for their help. Further, a deleterious relationship between LGBTQ+ communities and the police detracts from their overarching goal of promoting public safety via effective crime control; however, the police cannot effectively perform their duties if local residents do not feel comfortable interacting with them and assisting them in solving crimes. Thus, it is of great importance to better understand the nature of interactions between police and LGBTQ+ people to determine the scope and nature of deficiencies and to correct these ongoing problems.

By relying on narratives provided by Newarkers, we specifically considered how the multiple forms of marginalization (e.g., race, ethnicity, and LGBTQ+ status) operated for LGBTQ+ people of color in the Newark, New Jersey, metropolitan area via a qualitative analysis. The first author and her research team conducted 12 focus groups (N = 98) with LGBTQ+ people of color that touched on a range of topics; these included the tone and content of participants' encounters with the NPD and their disposition toward the NPD.[12] These narratives provide a unique opportunity to examine intersectionality, which assumes that interlocking, complex, and layered forms of marginalization can emerge due to the totality of one's identity; in essence, if a person is a member of multiple traditionally marginalized groups simultaneously (e.g., being an LGBTQ+ person who is also a person of color), they are at increased risk of attracting various forms of social bias and discrimination.[13] Though undoubtedly POC encounter varying degrees of societal stigma and oppression, so too do LGBTQ+ people; thus, if a person's identity is simultaneously comprised of both statuses, theoretically intersectionality assumes they will accumulate more punitive, retributive outcomes compared to more privileged groups (e.g., people who are heterosexual, cisgender, and/or white). Thus, our analysis also encapsulated the juxtaposition of race, ethnicity, and sexual orientation/gender identity status in steering these interactions and shaping participants' regard for the NPD.

This chapter covers several topics to frame the complex, pressing, and timely issue of how LGBTQ+ people—particularly if they are also people of color—interact with and view the police. We begin with a brief review of the available empirical research related to interactions between the police and LGBTQ+ people and factors that may intensify these interactions, such as being a POC or being transgender and gender-nonconforming. Next, we consider historical context related to policing in an attempt to contextualize LGBTQ+ participants' narratives by (1) discussing some key events critical to understanding the dynamics that later emerged concerning Newark's LGBTQ+ communities and the way they have been—and are still being—policed; (2) discussing broader philosophical movements in policing that have long posed problems for marginalized communities, including broken windows policing, due to their particular relevance for Newark and its populace; and (3) describing historical aspects of both the New York Police Department (NYPD) and the NPD, with a particular focus on lingering controversies that have embroiled the NPD for decades, culminating in a 2011 investigation of its alleged misconduct by the Department of Justice (DOJ).

Further, in line with a person-centered approach, we introduce and foreground trends revealed in the focus group discussions by first presenting excerpts from notable life narratives collected via the Queer Newark Oral History Project (QNOHP). We then conclude with a brief discussion of these findings and potential future directions, including developing applied policies responsive to Newark's history and present trends.

A Brief Review of the Current Literature Concerning Policing LGBTQ+ Communities

Unfortunately, despite an increasing—albeit uneven and still burgeoning—awareness around and support for LGBTQ+ people among the American public, the police have continued to take a heavy-handed and quasi-militarized approach to policing LGBTQ+ communities.[14] Not only do LGBTQ+ people interact more frequently with the police compared to heterosexual and/or cisgender people, they are routinely marginalized by the police. Indeed, the emerging literature in this area reflects widespread and commonplace accounts of verbal, physical, and/or sexual abuse and violence enacted by police officers during encounters—both voluntary and involuntary—with LGBTQ+-identified people; an anemic and seemingly uncaring response from officers, including officers who do not formally record complaints linked to LGBTQ+ crime victims; and an endemic, disproportionate targeting of LGBTQ+ communities by the police—particularly Black and Latinx transgender women—in public spaces. Existing research indicates LGBTQ+ people who perform targeted outreach work to serve their communities are interrupted by police, who assume they are engaged in sex work. In sum, there are widespread administrative and pragmatic deficiencies throughout core criminal legal processes that uniquely and disproportionately impact LGBTQ+ people accused of crimes.[15]

Thus, taken as a whole, available research appears to indicate that homophobic and/or transphobic notions—which are surprisingly commonplace among individual officers, in addition to being embedded in policing occupationally and organizationally—continue to be a defining feature of policing culture. Problematically, however, policing's historic ties to hypermasculinity and its tendency to promote a traditionally defined gender binary in which men are perceived as being especially effective crimefighters is philosophically and pragmatically antithetical to developing more culturally competent responses toward LGBTQ+ people.

Beyond historically informed difficulties for LGBTQ+ people who interact with the police, it appears that in contemporary policing, LGBTQ+ POC, in particular, experience difficulties well above and beyond those encountered by white LGBTQ+ people; this has operated, generally, through more frequent exposure to various forms of police misconduct and operates alongside a particularly low regard for the police, especially for transgender women of color.[16] In addition to theoretical concerns raised by intersectional perspectives and analyses, the police have tended to use problematic approaches—namely aggressive order maintenance or zero-tolerance policing—to over-police POC who reside in environments like Newark, which may further compound problems already regularly directed toward LGBTQ+ people during police encounters.

Broken Windows Theory and Policing in Newark during the 1990s and Beyond

Despite high-profile examples of recorded police misconduct, harassment, and brutality toward LGBTQ+ people—such as the events surrounding the Stonewall Inn riots in New York City in 1969—anti-LGBTQ+ policing behaviors have continued to persist nationally. Indeed, analogous to the increasingly covert and structurally entrenched impacts of institutional racism deeply lodged within and throughout the criminal justice system, anti-LGBTQ+ maltreatment enacted by the police has continued through renewed iterations that may feature comparatively greater subtlety but are still incredibly harmful and, at their core, are inherently alienating (e.g., verbal discourtesy, an officer's refusal to document an LGBTQ+ victim's complaint).

Traditionally, the policing of LGBTQ+ people has also been impacted by approaches aligned with broken windows policing strategies based upon the seminal, but controversial, work of Rutgers University-Newark criminologist George Kelling and Harvard government professor James Q. Wilson; indeed, this line of scholarship has had an unforeseen and significant impact upon the field of policing despite its tenuous empirical support.[17] Under the auspices of broken windows theory, specific policing tactics (i.e., order maintenance and zero-tolerance policing) allowed officers to aggressively stamp out crimes indicative of disorder termed "quality of life offenses" (e.g., visible sex work, panhandling, public drug use and/or intoxication). Authors like Wilson and Kelling assumed "quality of life" offenses converged with environmental factors (e.g., litter and garbage; dilapidated, unkempt buildings), which signaled areas were disordered and thus presented a signal to prospective criminals that crimes in these spaces are permissible and tolerated; this process is a compounding one, eventually descending into what Kelling and Wilson termed a "criminal invasion."[18]

The flawed policing strategies descended from broken windows theory can also be understood as another artifact of the "Tough on Crime" and "Law and

Order" movements that emerged during the crime wave of the 1970s to the mid-1990s. These approaches were heavily espoused by Mayor Rudy Giuliani and Police Commissioner William Bratton of New York City in the 1990s before proliferating throughout the United States, despite their problematic impact upon already marginalized communities; this can be observed via the continued misapplication of policies such as stop, question, and frisk (SQF), which have disparately and punitively impacted POC.[19] In spite of these consequences, politicians and policing practitioners have repeatedly advocated for the continued use of broken windows tactics such as SQF, erroneously claiming they triggered the unforeseen and unprecedented crime drop in New York; in reality, however, this crime drop was reproduced nationally (i.e., crime dropped at the same time in locales that did not engage in broken windows tactics).[20]

Due to their myriad consequences, however, these aggressive forms of policing have prompted calls for change from residents and, though rare, have triggered official investigations by the DOJ. In response, some communities, such as Newark, have attempted to adopt the philosophically and theoretically distinct guise of community policing but have, in practice, simply perpetuated the damage that broken windows philosophies have produced in general (e.g., a reduced sense of police legitimacy among POC) and specifically toward already over-policed communities. For instance, enduring legal debates surrounding the application of SQFs in New York City notwithstanding, like the NYPD, the NPD still routinely performs SQFs, as do other major metropolitan police departments; notably, these departments have also been marred by scandals and criticism due to their rumored misconduct, including the Philadelphia Police Department and the Chicago Police Department.[21]

The Influence of the NYPD and NYC upon Newark and the NPD

To effectively trace the antithetical dynamics between Newarkers and the NPD, it is necessary to describe key historical events in Newark that have disparately impacted POC and LGBTQ+ people, both separately and in conjunction, consistent with the theoretical perspective of intersectionality, which emphasizes the adversities produced by possessing multiply marginalized identities. However, the NPD and the New York Police Department are, without a doubt, historically linked; indeed, some of the same policies espoused by the NYPD, which have also long been criticized for their uneven application based upon race and ethnicity, have been adopted by and are still performed by the NPD. According to data publicly released by the NPD and compiled by the New Jersey chapter of the American Civil Liberties Union (ACLU), proportionately, the NPD may actually outpace the NYPD in its use of SQFs: "From July to December 2013, officers made 91 stops per 1,000 Newark residents—nearly one person stopped for every ten residents—exceeding the rate in New York City of eight stops per 1,000 residents over the same period."[22]

Due to the demographic composition of Newark, residents are especially likely to identify as LGBTQ+ and as a person of color simultaneously. As a result, anti-LGBTQ+ incidents and long-term policing responses to LGBTQ+ people in Newark are inextricably bound to and compounded by race and ethnicity. Indeed, racial tensions and allegations of racially disparate policing tactics have plagued the NPD for quite some time, which has served as a significant stumbling block in forging a better relationship with local residents.[23]

Unlike New York City, however, Newark did not have a specific historical flashpoint concerning its LGBTQ+ communities that operated in the same vein as the Stonewall Riots. Instead, starting in the 1950s and continuing well into the 1960s and beyond, Newark became well-known for its economic instability, triggered by the disappearance of its manufacturing prowess, resulting in the "white flight" of its formerly white-ethnic immigrant working-class populace. These core changes to Newark's economy and demography and preexisting racial tensions, underscored and intensified by the Civil Rights Movement, led to the NPD's use of heavy-handed tactics to quell widespread racial unrest. Now charged with policing a majority-minority population ripe with considerable resentment toward the police, the NPD unsurprisingly began to attract attention stemming from high-profile instances of race-based animus. For instance, in 1967, prompted by the NPD publicly brutalizing a cab driver in the aftermath of a traffic stop, explosive riots lasting multiple days—and causing significant property damage and the death of nearly thirty people—were unleashed by furious residents. The violence that unfolded appears to have been specifically aggravated by the actions of the police in response to rioters.[24]

Over time, these dynamics continued to escalate, and in 2011, after repeated requests, the NPD was formally investigated by the Department of Justice to determine if the allegations brought forth by citizens were warranted. After concluding its investigation in 2014, the DOJ released a rather damning report that, as described in the introduction, described the NPD as exhibiting an ongoing "pattern of practice" in which the police were systematically engaging in misconduct toward Newarkers in general and Black Newarkers in particular.[25]

The DOJ also investigated complaints of the NPD engaging in similar practices toward LGBTQ+-identified Newarkers. As noted at this chapter's outset, though the DOJ's report pointed to insufficient evidence the NPD targeted LGBTQ+ people in a demonstrable pattern, investigators still uncovered "anecdotal evidence" of NPD officers engaging in anti-LGBTQ+ misconduct. In addition to a general lack of cultural competency, the complaints outlined in the report ranged from a lack of police responsiveness to violence and harassment directed toward LGBTQ+ people, particularly during incidents involving TGNC people. Notably, despite their inability to prove these behaviors constituted a consistent pattern, the DOJ was still compelled to recommend the NPD "engage with the LGBT community around the concerns noted and develop training on policing related to sexual orientation and gender identity."[26]

Lived Experiences with the NPD: Examining the Queer Newark Oral History Project

To frame our discussion of the focus groups, we will first present several accounts collected by the Queer Newark Oral History Project (QNOHP). These illustrate themes and dynamics *also* documented by participants during their focus group discussions.

In describing her animus toward the police, Patreese Johnson, known for her involvement in a high-profile New York case against a group of lesbian women popularly called "The New Jersey Four," recounted how her experience fighting charges related to self-defense was made worse by uncaring legal actors. Patreese's frustration with the system speaks to larger empirical trends, which suggests the police can represent secondary victimization for communities of color seeking their assistance. In addition to trauma associated with the death of her brother during an incident with police, Patreese herself was subjected to a protracted legal battle after she fought back against street harassment while in public. As a result, she concludes the police are ultimately untrustworthy, citing her lived experiences:

> I didn't have a good rapport from the police growing up in Newark. The police was just . . . we watched them rob the drug dealers and it was like that day they

> wasn't even selling drugs . . . and you realize like the police is really scared of the drug dealers and the killers, you know what I'm saying. So they aren't really doing real policing, they're just aggravating the situation. I feel like that's why Newark [is] the way it is now, because of all of that aggravation. *You didn't make it any better. You didn't make your community trust the police.*[27]

Similarly, Aminah Washington, a transgender Black woman, disclosed her reticence to interact with the police, citing feelings of unsafety and uncertainty, directly informed, once more, by her direct experiences: "for me, I don't feel safe when the cops are around. That's from personal experiences. However, at the same time, I just feel as though when it comes to the trans community at large, completely—no matter where it is—cops are so, so, so misinformed. By them being misinformed, it creates that understanding of disrespect because they don't respect the gender pronouns and/or what's being presented to them."

Later in her interview, Aminah specifically attributed these perceptions to feeling disrespected by the police through behaviors such as misgendering her and feeling as if the police did not affirm her basic humanity. In doing so, she stated, "it's all about respect. If you could just accept and/or be willing to put the effort forth, you'll get that in return."[28]

Finally, in discussing a highly localized dynamic related to how LGBTQ+ Newarkers have come to view the Newark Police Department, Aaron Frazier, a well-known activist in Newark, described "The Stroll," or areas colloquially known to be linked to sex work and police harassment in Newark's various public parks, and to be an especially active area for local sex workers. In describing these spaces in Newark, Aaron related an incident concerning Dana Rone, an openly lesbian local councilwoman; she was publicly linked to "The Stroll" after her nephew was arrested for attempting to solicit sex. In describing the ubiquitous nature of police harassment relative to "The Stroll," Aaron stated: "Rutgers Police were very nasty to people on the stroll. . . . If they knew you on the regular, they would say, just like the cop, 'Ah, get up out of here, okay, I'm gonna let you go, you're gonna get, give you a warning now, but I catch you back out here, I'm lockin' you up.' Shit like that."[29]

These examples provide important background to understand ongoing tensions between vulnerable groups and the police in spaces such as Newark, where locals may need assistance but are acutely aware of the consequences summoning the police for help can unleash.

Using Focus Group Research to Examine Interactions with and Perceptions of the NPD

The remainder of this chapter will outline the findings of 12 focus groups with LGBTQ+ people living in the Newark metropolitan area (N = 98). Of note, nearly all participants identified as POC. Unsurprisingly, participants overwhelmingly indicated that troubled dynamics between the NPD and Newark residents continue, particularly vis-à-vis LGBTQ+ people and people of color. There is little trust among the LGBTQ+ communities in Newark toward police, based both on historical conflict and current experiences of queer Newarkers, for whom the NPD more often represents persecution than help.

Participants also expressed a general reluctance to engage with the police. Of those who indicated that they would engage with the police, nearly all said that they would only consider doing so in specific circumstances. Brandy, an eighteen-year-old transgender woman, called police "girlfriends." Although she specified that while she would use the police to press charges or file a restraining order, for example, she continued, "But to call the cops if you need help? No."

For Micah, a twenty-one-year-old gay man, his likelihood of calling the police was determined by the severity and physicality of the situation. "If it is more than one person harassing, then I should say go for the police, but if it's [just] that one person you can tell yourself you can ignore it until they decide to put their hands on you. That's where you draw the line."

This reluctance stems from a variety of causes, but distinct themes emerged through the discussions. One recurring issue raised was the unwillingness of police to intervene in useful ways and the length of time that they took to arrive. Lamar, a twenty-five-year-old gay man, indicated he often contacted the police, stating, "[I call] the cops for everything. If I feel some type of way, I'm still calling. If you look at me a certain type of way, I'm calling. If you cough a certain type of way, bitch, I'm calling." However, he continued: "[The police] would take their time. They would come. The operator would tell you that they'll be there within like, the next five to seven minutes, but in reality, depending on how deep in Newark or what ward you're in, it could range anywhere from, like, fifteen to forty-five minutes."

Vivan, a twenty-year-old lesbian woman, in conversation with Alexis, a nineteen-year-old gay man, shared an anecdote about the police taking an extraordinarily long time to arrive when her mother called for assistance.

VIVAN: My mom and her ex-boyfriend was fighting and it got to the point where somebody was bleeding really bad and, you know, we called the cops because the aggressor was, like, really like, beating, like, my mom up. So, we called the cops or whatever and it took them, like, at least forty minutes to get to the damn thing. By the time they were there, we done already, like, we beat the dude up, all of that. We did all of that. He left. Now y'all coming at the last minute.

ALEXIS: That's why I don't waste my time . . . even calling them. I just do what I got to do.

VIVAN: I always think . . . what if, what if the guy would've beat my mother to the point where it wasn't no coming back? . . . I have no faith in law enforcement.

These critiques are consistent with notable incidents of neglect on the part of the police, including the murder of Sakia Gunn in 2003 (discussed in several other chapters) and the unresolved 2020 death of Ashley Moore, a young transgender woman in Newark, which many LGBTQ+ Newarkers believe was under-investigated by the NPD.[30]

Several other participants voiced concerns about the competency of the NPD. Sierra, a twenty-one-year-old trans woman, recalled a time when she believed herself to be in danger during a domestic dispute and the police took over ninety minutes to arrive. She said that she "would rather die" than call them again.

Blake, a nineteen-year-old gay male, shared: "It was three incidents I would call the cops. One, these Mexicans were beating this boy with two-by-fours on Hill Street, across from the police station. I called the cops. They never came. *(Laughs)* Another got carjacked in front of my house with a shotgun. [The police] came a hour later. Then I called the cops because I was getting attacked and I got locked up. So, therefore, I just don't use no cops, they're useless. They don't get nothing done."

Jace, an eighteen-year-old lesbian woman, added, "I probably wouldn't even call them. Because what's the point? . . . They like, really don't help you." Khalilah summed this up, "I would contact my friends because I feel like the squad, like, could get, excuse my French, could get shit done better than the police could."

Another common theme discussed by participants was a feeling that the NPD did not take the complaints or well-being of LGBTQ+ people seriously. Many also expressed feeling disrespected by the police. Xander, a twenty-one-

FIGURE 10.1. Community vigil outside the downtown YMCA for Ashley Moore, a young transgender woman whose death went underinvestigated by the Newark police according to many in the local LGBTQ community (August 2020). Photo by Kevin Sedano Vazquez, courtesy Queer Newark Oral History Project.

year-old gay man, stated: "Newark cops, or cops in general, they have to deal with gay people, regular people, transgender people, they take it as a joke. They need to take it more seriously. Like, everything, like, I'll call the cops—I've seen gay people and the cops dealing with them, they take it as a joke, laughing at them, making fun of them. . . . [T]hey need to respect us."

Brayton agreed, noting that "a lot of people feel uncomfortable going to the police because they are gay" and believe they will not be treated "in a respectful manner." Lashawn, a lesbian woman in her twenties, expanded on this idea:

> If it's a gay situation they, when they get there they're going to crack jokes, they're going to have their own personal biases towards you and they're not even going to hide it. They're not going to wait until they get in the cop car to make these remarks. No, they're going to pull up to the scene, snicker when they see that, like, two men or two women who are romantically involved, they'll start snickering like, "We're here for this?" You can see, like, their whole body disposition just changes and their attitude towards helping you and asking you questions.

Lauren, an LGBTQ+ advocacy worker, also indicated an unwillingness to call the police because she believed that the NPD did not care about LGBTQ+ people. She went on to discuss incidents that had happened at their center, where "some of the kids have been attacked by people, by boys and stuff in our community that we could actually point out, but they choose not to say anything because we feel like the cops are not going to do anything. They'll probably be like, 'Oh, this is just a faggot. We don't care.'"

Similarly, Lashawn recalled an incident where two males who were romantically involved were: "Hav[ing] a little altercation and somebody else jumped in so they ended up, like, beating the other guy. So, then they called the cops. [W]hen [the police] saw that it was two gay guys who . . . beat this other guy up it was like, 'You let these two fags beat you up? We shouldn't even take this report.'"

Latasha concluded that

> Police officers don't take . . . certain things with the LGBTQ community seriously. Like when we argue or we fight they don't, they just look at it and be like, "Oh, well, y'all need to go separate." Like, there's a video on YouTube and it's like a brawl of lesbians fighting and all the police are looking and they think it's cute. It's just like, "Oh, get her! Get her! Get her!" and I'm like, but y'all just standing there watching them fight. They shirts coming off, that's why they liking it. "Oh, her shirts coming off! And, oh snap, oh snap!"

In some cases, participants indicated that this lack of respect toward LGBTQ+ people led police to feel at liberty to be physically violent. Kobe, a twenty-four-year-old gay man, stated, "I just personally think that [the cops] too aggressive. I've been thrown around. I've been tossed around by the police. . . . I don't like to be touched like vigorously like that. I did have an issue with that when it occurred. It was nothing I could really do about it unfortunately, but . . . I feel like they are kind of invading my space in a way. It's kind of being . . . forceful." Tristan, another twenty-four-year-old gay male, agreed: "[the police] take their authority too seriously."

A related theme raised by many participants was their belief that the NPD would not take them or their claims seriously due to their gender expression, particularly in situations of violence. Jace, an eighteen-year-old lesbian woman, discussed some of the complications she had experienced when calling the police in that "they hear that I'm a female but when they come I'm dressed like a guy . . . everything changes. Like, 'Oh, well she's a guy.' 'We think she's a man so why does she call me.'" Similarly, Octavia, a fifty-six-year-old lesbian woman, shared an experience in which a police officer looked at her directly, then at her driver's license, and still misgendered her, calling her *sir.* "I'm like, 'You have my driver's license in your hand. You don't know I'm a woman? Did you look at it?'" To her visible exasperation, however, the officer then looked at her license again and continued to call her sir during the remainder of their interaction.

Dana, an eighteen-year-old lesbian woman, recalled an incident the year prior when she had been put in jail. The police were observing her through a clear wall, and one said, "Yo, this girl look just like a boy . . . She's going to make all the girls go crazy in here." Bernice, a thirty-year-old lesbian woman, described a domestic violence situation with a former partner in which the police assumed that she was at fault because she was the more masculine of the two:

> I was with a feminine female but I was being abused by her. I called the police, for my safety, and at this point I had, like, a black eye or two and, like, a missing tooth and everything. And when the police came, they actually just went straight to me and I ended up going to jail without [them] even having asked questions at all and, like, the questions weren't even asked until, like, I was already in a holding cell, until like that Monday when I spoke to a judge. Like, it was just, I mean, even though I was the person that was carrying the bruises and everything like that, I was the person that went to jail because, first of all, they automatically thought that I was a man so the, the officers that were there, they were male officers that searched me for everything and that, um, patted me down and that actually arrested me. But then even once they realized I was not a male, I was still the person that went to jail. And I was the first line to the cops.

Alexis, a nineteen-year-old gay man, recalled a time when he "was up in drags" and the police pulled him over. "[T]hey tried to force me to give them a boy name when I kept giving them girl information. And . . . I forgot how they found out I was a boy, but . . . I would just never give them my boy name for information. I would just keep giving them girl information." As Alexis was leaving, an officer said to him, "You know, if you was a girl, we would have sex."

Wanda, a twenty-year-old lesbian, recounted her interactions with the NPD while they were searching her:

> They, like, still, "Get on the wall." Last time I checked, y'all can't check me. He's like, "Oh, why can't we check you?" I have breasts and a vagina. Just because I have on baggy clothes that don't mean that I'm a guy, but they still checked me and they

didn't care. . . . I was trying to be funny. I was like, "I'm on my period, so be careful." So, he was like, "Oh, you're going to get blood on me or something?" And then he really thought I was playing that I was a female until I . . . took my zipper down and everything because they was like, "Take everything off, like, your, your coat or whatever." And I'm like, "I'm a female. Like, I don't have to lie to you."

Another theme discussed was the mistreatment of TGNC people by the NPD. Latasha recalled a time when Ayana, a transgender woman and fellow focus group participant, was repeatedly called a "faggot" by police officers. Ayana also reported that the police barred her from using the women's restroom in a public space after telling her, "Well, you're a guy." The following exchange between three transgender women, Ingrid (twenty-two), Shakia (twenty-three), and Charlene (fifty-five), highlights another example:

INGRID: So if I get in a altercation with a biological female, she feel like, she want to do something, I'm not gonna do that. I'm calling the cops. . . . Because if I touch her, then I know when the cops come—

SHAKIA: They gonna break it up—

CHARLENE: When [the police] do come . . . if it was a fight between me and a biological female, I don't care if I had double D's, they gonna say "You are a man," and they gonna lock me up.

Similarly, Shakia, Charlene, and Erica (who also identified as a transgender woman) discussed the propensity of police officers to fixate on their gender identity and presentation rather than the issues at hand.

SHAKIA: You could've been the one calling them and they'll make it about you—

CHARLENE: You, mmhmm.

ERICA: Mmhmm.

SHAKIA:—and your transition. What does that have to do with me calling you? I called you to help me.

The following excerpt from Harmony, a transgender woman, illustrates many of the issues discussed by other participants and highlights how they can converge in extremely troubling ways.

I've had so many run-ins with [the NPD] to the point where it's not funny anymore. . . . [T]he situation happened, like, maybe about two years ago. I was . . . in the process of switching areas . . . but the cop that pulled me over, [and] it was like, well, "Why are you out here? You need to be in the house. You know, um, only people that's out is your kind." I'm like, "Well, what do you mean *my* kind? Like, specify that." So, he's like, "Well, you know what I mean. Y'all he-she's," quote unquote. So, me being the outspoken person that I am, I let him know I'm not a he-she. Respect me as a woman. So, they'll be like, "Oh, well if you still got a penis between your legs, you're a man." "No. I'm a transgender *woman*. Respect me how I live my life and then I'll give you respect." "Oh, well, you want, you want to talk bad, well how about this? Give me your purse. I'll take you to the station. Fingerprint you, you know, see if got warrants." "For what? What y'all trying to prove? I don't have nothing on me. I'm not out here doing nothing. Y'all didn't see me stop cars. Y'all didn't see me wave anybody down. You didn't catch me in the act doing anything. So, what are y'all charging me with?" "Oh, we're just going to charge you with solicitation." Solicitation? Like, I'm not soliciting nobody. . . .

[T]hey're very disrespectful. Once . . . they see . . . somebody from the LGBTQ community come in it's like, "Oh, we got one of them things here. Oh lord. Here come the he-shes." . . . And I think that, you know, something really needs to be done as far as them respecting the LGBTQ community and respecting others because if they don't know how to respect others . . . what can I say? That's why people lash out at them, because they don't know how to talk to people, and then when we get out of control they want to mace us, kick us, do all this other stuff and that's not called for. . . . [T]he past six years . . . I've been getting harassed by the police for absolutely nothing.

Conclusion and Discussion

Overall, in their discussions of crime reporting and the police, and in line with the excerpts included from the QNOHP presented above, focus group participants did not see the NPD in a particularly positive light. Instead, most expressed that they would hesitate to reach out to the police, citing issues such as slow response times and sentiments that the police were uncaring or did not take them seriously. Others feared officers would behave in homophobic ways, with some participants recounting such experiences. Their concerns appear warranted, as when participants interacted with the police, their interactions were overwhelmingly (84%) negative. Further, when asked who they would contact if they were the victim of an anti-LGBTQ+ crime, most participants said they would reach out to their informal social networks first rather than the police, reflecting their distrust of the police to appropriately handle these incidents. This is compounded by the limited bias crime training officers receive because—if it is given at all—it is often limited and simplistic, and may facilitate adverse interactions with already hesitant victims.[31] As a result, it seems likely that the same underlying dynamics for which the NYPD was castigated in the years that followed the Stonewall riots also very likely existed and continue to persist in Newark and other large metropolitan areas with ecological similarities to New York City. For instance, as of 2017 and 2013, respectively, both Baltimore and New Orleans—which are, in terms of both their overall demography and their collective crime rates, extremely similar to Newark—were formally disciplined for their documented maltreatment of LGBTQ+ people and have entered into consent decrees enforced by the Department of Justice. Thus, from this perspective, Newark represents a modern-day, slow-motion, long-standing perpetration of the same bigotry, homophobia, and transphobia that precipitated and ultimately unleashed the fury of the rioters present at the Stonewall Inn.

Notes

1. U.S. Department of Justice, *Investigation of the Newark Police Department* (2014), https://www.justice.gov/sites/default/files/crt/legacy/2014/07/22/newark_findings_7-22-14.pdf; Department of Justice, *An Interactive Guide to the Civil Rights Division's Police Reforms* (2017), https://www.justice.gov/crt/page/file/922456/download.

2. DOJ, *Investigation of the Newark Police Department*, 48.

3. David Deschamps and Bennett Singer, *LGBTQ Stats: Lesbian, Gay, Bisexual, Transgender, and Queer People by the Numbers* (New York: New Press, 2017).

4. Winston Luhur, Ilan H. Meyer, and Bianca D. M. Wilson, *Policing LGBQ People* (2021), UCLA School of Law Williams Institute, https://williamsinstitute.law.ucla.edu/wp-content/uploads/Policing-LGBQ-People-May-2021.pdf.

5. See, for instance, Patricia Elane Trimble, "Ignored LGBTQ Prisoners: Discrimination, Rehabilitation, and Mental Health Services during Incarceration," *LGBTQ Policy Journal* 9 (2019): 31–38.

6. Brandon Robinson, "The Lavender Scare in Homonormative Times: Policing, Hyper-Incarceration, and LGBTQ Youth Homelessness," *Gender & Society* 34, no. 2 (2020): 210–232.

7. Emily Rothman, Deinera Exner, and Allyson L. Baughman, "The Prevalence of Sexual Assault against People Who Identify as Gay, Lesbian, or Bisexual in the United States: A Systematic Review," *Trauma, Violence, and Abuse* 12, no. 2 (2011): 55–66; Edward Dunbar, "Race, Gender, and Sexual Orientation in Hate Crime

Victimization: Identity Politics or Identity Risk?" *Violence and Victims* 21, no. 3 (2006): 323–337.

8. Kristen Kuehnle and Anne Sullivan, "Gay and Lesbian Victimization: Reporting Factors in Domestic Violence and Bias Incidents," *Criminal Justice and Behavior* 30, no. 1 (2003): 85–96.

9. For a detailed review, see Danielle M. Shields, "Stonewalling in the Brick City: Perceptions of and Experiences with Seeking Police Assistance among LGBTQ Citizens," *Social Sciences* 10, no. 1 (2021): 1–27.

10. Jessica Hodge and Lori Sexton, "Examining the Blue Line in the Rainbow: The Interactions and Perceptions of Law Enforcement among Lesbian, Gay, Bisexual, Transgender and Queer Communities," *Police Practice and Research* 21, no. 3 (2020): 246–263.

11. Rod Brunson "Police Don't Like Black People": African-American Young Men's Accumulated Police Experiences," *Criminology & Public Policy* 6, no. 1 (2007): 71–102.

12. For a detailed description of the methodology employed during the collection and analysis of the data presented here, see Shields, "Stonewalling in the Brick City." All but two participants for whom demographic information was available self-identified as people of color.

13. Though intersectionality has generated an enormous body of literature, for the classic iteration of this perspective, see Kimberlé Crenshaw, "Mapping the Margins: Intersectionality, Identity Politics, and Violence against Women of Color," *Stanford Law Review* 43, no. 6 (1991): 1241–1299.

14. Various scholars have offered their critiques of the legal system as it relates to LGBTQ people; for examples, see Ann Cammett, "Queer Lockdown: Coming to Terms with the Ongoing Criminalization of LGBTQ Communities," *The Scholar and Feminist Online* 7, no. 3 (2009); Noami G. Goldberg, Christy Mallory, Amira Hasenbush, Lara Stemple, and Ilan H. Meyer, "Police and the Criminalization of LGBT People," in *The Cambridge Handbook of Policing in the United States*, ed. Tamara Rice Lave and Eric J. Miller (Cambridge, UK: Cambridge University Press, 2019), 374–391; Kelly Strader and Lindsey Hay, "Lewd Stings: Extending *Lawrence v. Texas* to Discriminatory Enforcement," *American Criminal Law Review* 56, no. 2 (2019): 465–509.

15. See Shields, "Stonewalling in the Brick City," for a detailed review. Other notable works on this topic include, but are not limited to, Lambda Legal, "Protected and Served? A Community Survey of LGBTQ+ People and People Living with HIV" (2015), www.lambdalegal.org/protected-and-served; Kristina Wolff and Carrie Cokely, "'To Protect and to Serve?': An Exploration of Police Conduct in Relation to the Gay, Lesbian, Bisexual, and Transgender Community," *Sexuality and Culture* 11, no. 2 (2007): 1–23; Leonore F. Carpenter and R. Barrett Marshall, "Walking While Trans: Profiling of Transgender Women by Law Enforcement, and

the Problem of Proof," *William and Mary Journal of Women and Law* 24, no. 1 (2017): 5–38.

16. Sandy E. James, Jody L. Herman, Susan Rankin, Mara Keisling, Lisa Mottet, and Ma'ayan Anafi, *The Report of the 2015 U.S. Transgender Survey* (Washington, DC: National Center for Transgender Equality, 2016).

17. See James Q. Wilson and George L. Kelling, "Broken Windows: The Police and Neighborhood Safety," *Atlantic Monthly*, March 1982, 29–38; Kelling and Catherine M. Coles, *Fixing Broken Windows: Restoring Order and Reducing Crime in Our Communities* (New York: Simon & Schuster, 1997). For a critique of Broken Windows, see Cory Haberman and Nathan W. Link, "Broken Windows, Hot Spots, and Focused Deterrence: The State and Impact of the 'Big Three' in Policing Innovations," in *Criminal Justice Theory: Explanations and Effects* (vol. 26), ed. Cecilia Chouhy, Joshua C. Cochran, and Cheryl Lero Jonson (New York: Routledge, 2020), 221–252.

18. Kelling and Wilson, "Broken Windows," 33.

19. Andrew Gelman, Jeffrey Fagan, and Alex Kiss, "An Analysis of the New York City Police Department's 'Stop-and-Frisk' Policy in the Context of Claims of Racial Bias," *Journal of the American Statistical Association* 102, no. 479 (2007): 813–823.

20. Franklin Zimring, *The City that Became Safe: New York's Lessons for Urban Crime and Its Control* (New York: Oxford University Press, 2011).

21. For a recent expression of this policy, see Newark Public Safety, "What to Do when Stopped by the Police" (2021), Newark Police Department, https://npd.newarkpublicsafety.org/stoppedbypolice.

22. American Civil Liberties Union of New Jersey, "ACLU-NJ Report Reveals Troubling Use of Stop-and-Frisk in Newark," February 25, 2014, https://www.aclu.org/press-releases/aclu-nj-report-reveals-troubling-use-stop-and-frisk-newark.

23. Kevin Mumford, *Newark: A History of Race, Rights, and Riots in America* (New York: New York University Press, 2007).

24. Albert Bergesen, "Race Riots of 1967: An Analysis of Police Violence in Detroit and Newark," *Journal of Black Studies* 12, no. 3 (1982): 261–274.

25. DOJ, *Investigation of the Newark Police Department*.

26. DOJ, *Investigation of the Newark Police Department*, 48.

27. Whitney Strub, interview with Patreese Johnson, October 12, 2015, Queer Newark Oral History Project (QNOHP), 40, https://queer.newark.rutgers.edu/sites/default/files/transcript/2015-10-12%20Patreese%20Johnson%20final.pdf (emphasis added).

28. Jason Boehm, interview with Aminah Washington, April 24, 2017, QNOHP, 23, 40, https://queer.newark.rutgers.edu/sites/default/files/transcript/2017-04-28%20Aminah%20Washington_0.pdf.

29. Whitney Strub, interview with Aaron Frazier, November 21, 2017, QNOHP, 21, https://queer.newark.rutgers.edu/sites/default/files/transcript/2017-11-21%20Aaron%20Frazier%203_1.pdf.

30. "Family of Dead Transgender Woman Accuse Police of Not Taking Investigation Seriously," *News12 New Jersey*, November 19, 2020, https://newjersey.news12.com/family-of-dead-transgender-woman-accuse-police-of-not-taking-investigation-seriously.

31. A. C. Thompson, Rohan Naik, and Ken Schwencke, "Hate Crime Training for Police Is Often Inadequate, Sometimes Nonexistent," *ProPublica*, November 29, 2017, https://www.propublica.org/article/hate-crime-training-for-police-is-often-inadequate-sometimes-nonexistent.

CHAPTER 11

Walk This Way

Reframing Queer History through a Walking Tour

MARY RIZZO AND CHRISTINA STRASBURGER

Starting Point: Military Park

We gather in downtown Newark's Military Park and raise our rainbow flags to signal that those looking for the Queer Newark Walking Tour are in the right place.[1] Developing the walking tour gave us an opportunity to shape the stories we've gathered from the oral histories into a format accessible to the public in new ways.[2] But like all partnerships, it comes with constraints. We must begin in Military Park because the tour is part of a series called Downtown Tours offered by the Newark Public Library, each of which starts in the same location. While the park is a central gathering spot it does not have deep meaning to our interviewees. This requirement also shapes the tour's possibilities. A walking tour can only cover so much ground. Since we cannot expect attendees to walk for hours or at a fast pace, we timed our tour to run approximately one hour and forty-five minutes, including short breaks. Being community-driven means that we accept and create opportunities to share our work, and that we adjust our vision to meet the needs of our partner institutions and the people in the community for whom we do this work.

Walking tours are popular ways to share historical information with the public. Many appeal to tourists by regaling them with stories of scandal, sex, and horror.[3] We position ourselves within a different genealogy of walking tours that intend to make visible the stories of marginalized people from their own perspectives as a way to show urban space as "a perpetual object of social production and contestation."[4] Such tours can also reveal how powerful interests such as the police and criminal justice system shape space.[5] More than simply a series of anecdotes about geographical locations, a good walking tour is focused around a theme, engages the attendees, and encourages new ways of looking at cities. It calls attention to what is often ignored or hidden.

Since the founding of QNOHP in 2011, our team, which includes faculty, staff, and students representing a variety of racial, ethnic, gender, and socioeconomic backgrounds, has remained committed to our core principle of "fostering local intergenerational queer historical knowledge." Although the project is based at Rutgers University-Newark and we have been fortunate to have strong institutional support, it is the community listening process that has shaped our direction and approach. Recognizing that white voices are often privileged in queer spaces, it was crucial for us to prioritize the perspectives of Black queer Newarkers, whose rich lives and contributions equally deserve to be highlighted and preserved.

The intensive work of building and sustaining this project has been rewarding, but also not without challenges. Our team is largely volunteer based (including our directorship), though some graduate students have been paid to work on the project. A central issue has been administrative capacity. Our small team has created the walking tour, a traveling exhibit (created by a graduate class in 2017), a podcast, lesson plans, and held numerous public events, alongside conducting interviews and maintaining the website. To create more accessible forms of history than those produced for professional academic audiences, we have had to address a variety of issues, including financial (paying for interview transcription and hosting archival material), legal (how to protect our narrators' rights while allowing the most access to their words and insights), and technical (how to tag and preserve digital material).

As with our founding conference, the walking tour began with a listening process. The creative team, which included graduate and undergraduate students Kristyn Scorsone, Anna Alves, Lorna Ebner, and Ames Clark, reviewed hundreds of hours of interview audio. Through team conversations, including with the authors of this essay, we decided to focus on how LGBTQ Newarkers have created community since the 1920s. Although Newark is not known as a queer city in the way that San Francisco or New York are, LGBTQ people have made their lives here, as shown in our interviews. We wanted to explore the process of community-building. While not every walking tour attendee would be queer, most would be members of several different communities. This hook would allow us to draw connections between their lives and the stories we wanted to tell. While we often talk about communities in static terms, we know from our own experiences that communities form and change. They are created through the efforts of individuals and made visible in businesses, leisure spaces, and community institutions, all stories we could include on our tour. While we wanted to emphasize the resiliency and creativity of the LGBTQ community in Newark, we also wanted to acknowledge how racism, poverty, homophobia, sexism, and transphobia have affected it—both from external and internal sources. Rather than leave attendees with a simplistic celebratory narrative, we hoped to get them to participate in a deeper conversation. Our goal was for attendees to leave knowing that LGBTQ people have lived and made community in Newark for generations in the face of extraordinary challenges that continue today.

In this chapter, we will take you on a textual version of the tour, showing why we organized it the way we did and how we incorporated the disparate stories in our interviews. Much of the scholarship in the field of queer oral history focuses on the interview process.[6] How does the relationship between the narrator and interviewer affect the interview? How do race, class, religion, and language change the possibilities of what information is revealed? While this scholarly work is critical, there are a growing number of public history projects that use queer oral histories to tell public stories about the queer past.[7] Yet there is comparatively little published scholarship on how to process the raw oral history, to use Michael Frisch's evocative language, into the cooked public history project.[8]

As our experience with the walking tour reveals, doing so requires attention to three issues. First, how do we create a narrative out of multiple voices, which may disagree with each other, without distorting them? How do we honor the complexity of individual stories while also thinking about them as part of the larger historical record? Oral histories are not simply factual records about the past. They are the stories that people tell us about their experience of the past. We recognized this by combining archival and other research with the interviews. While the walking tour script focused on specific locations and themes, we did not ignore stories that contradicted each other. Instead, we incorporated these contradictions into the tour by, for example, acknowledging transphobia and racism within the LGBTQ community.

Secondly, how do we ethically discuss traumatic events in the past without simply turning queer people into victims? This issue was particularly important

FIGURE 11.1. Queer Newark Walking Tour in downtown Newark, 2021. Courtesy Queer Newark Oral History Project.

in telling the story of Sakia Gunn, a young Black lesbian who was murdered on the streets of downtown Newark in 2003. Her murder catalyzed the contemporary wave of LGBTQ activism that resulted in the creation of several community organizations still operating today. While this story of activism in the face of violence is important, we were wary of simply using Gunn's story in this way. We also did not want the tour to emphasize violence, which plays into stereotypes of Newark as dangerous and in need of more policing. We felt the need to be sensitive to the fact that Gunn's family, friends, and acquaintances may still live in the city. The project has worked hard to develop strong relationships of mutual trust with the LGBTQ community. Our telling of Gunn's story in this public format needed to feel respectful to all parties and help strengthen our community relationships, not strain them.

Finally, we faced the challenge of walking people through a city where most of the LGBTQ community landmarks mentioned in our interviews are gone. Newark, like other legacy cities with long histories of urban renewal, redevelopment, and gentrification, has seen its built environment change dramatically, and this process is ongoing. Between 2017 and 2021, when this essay was being drafted, we had to revise the walking tour script because of gentrification, which has led to the closure of several queer businesses and the move of the LGBTQ Community Center to two new locations. We chose to interpret these absences in the tour to examine the impact of uneven development on queer POC communities. We showed that gentrification is a queer issue—albeit one that is more complicated than it might seem.

First Stop: Murphy's Tavern

We lead the group into Newark's noisy downtown.

Pay attention to the sights and sounds of this vibrant place.

Bootleg DVDs on a table. Incense perfuming the air. Mothers and grandmothers pushing strollers. Kids messing around. Someone asks for change.

The historic home of Black Newarkers, the downtown is predominantly a space for people of color. We continue through its heart, the intersection of Broad and Market Streets. Another long block, and we pause to let the group gather for our first stop. We stand in front of a giant silver statue of an ice hockey player adorning the plaza leading to the Prudential Center arena, which opened in 2007 as the home arena for the New Jersey Devils hockey team. The juxtaposition is jarring. What does ice hockey mean to the Black and Brown residents of this city? What does any of this have to do with LGBTQ history?

Urban renewal efforts have dramatically remade large swaths of downtown Newark. On the site now occupied by the Prudential Center and its plaza once stood blocks of businesses and homes (and, before that, Newark's Chinatown).[9] Among these businesses was Murphy's Tavern, an unpretentious bar repeatedly mentioned by narrators in their interviews as one of the most important gay bars in the city. As scholars have demonstrated, gay bars and nightclubs have been critically important in developing gay communities and participating in the fight for gay rights.[10] We have seen throughout this book the crucial role they played in Newark, from the midcentury bars chronicled by Anna Lvovsky in chapter 2 through the Black queer cultural renaissance of the 1970s centered around Halsey Street, discussed by Kristyn Scorsone in chapter 4. Murphy's was the only bar to cut through both of these eras and survive into the twenty-first century. Not only did Murphy's welcome members of the LGBTQ community through its doors, it was one of three New Jersey bars that fought back against homophobic discrimination after its liquor license was revoked by the state Division of Alcoholic Beverage Control (ABC). Its crime? Allowing gay people to be themselves, flirting, dancing, and touching just as straight people in a bar might. In 1967, the New Jersey Supreme Court ruled that the state Alcoholic Beverage Control could no longer target bars serving queer people.

Yet no historic marker or sign commemorates Murphy's' role in the battle for gay civil rights. The Stonewall Inn in New York City, the site of an antipolice riot by queer and trans people of color in 1969, was the first LGBTQ site in the country to be listed on the National Register of Historic Places (1999) and named a National Historic Landmark (2000). It was named a city landmark in 2015, a State Historic Site in 2016, and part of the Stonewall National Monument in 2016. In Newark, however, the forces of development and gentrification erased the city's history of LGBTQ community-building and battles for civil rights. Against the neoliberal backdrop of the Prudential Center, we tell the story of Murphy's as a semi-safe space for LGBTQ Newarkers, a forgotten chapter in the fight for gay rights in New Jersey before Stonewall, and an example of how the forces of development wipe away the history of marginalized groups. We ask attendees how they would define a landmark, to get them thinking about the process by which we deem a site important enough to our collective story to be recognized physically and politically.

Murphy's Tavern was already a place where gay people congregated in the 1950s. By the 1960s, it was one of a handful of bars in Newark where gay people could spend time openly, though it did not exclusively serve gay people. Given the closing of many gay bars in cities around the country over the last decade, there's a danger of waxing nostalgic about their history as we mourn this loss. In reality, who felt safe at a gay bar was determined by race, gender, and gender presentation. While Murphy's served an important community function, it may be most accurate to describe it as a semi-safe space for queer people. Time of day and gender presentation determined who felt comfortable at Murphy's.

According to Queer Newark narrators, Murphy's served both straight and gay people, but at different times. Straight people tended to come during the day. According to Aaron Frazier, "[Y]ou could get a good lunch there. That was the whole thing. I'm talkin' about an affordable, decent lunch," which drew employees from local offices and nearby government agencies.[11] At night, however, the bar shifted to a gay community space. June Dowell-Burton remembers "two sexy bartenders, male, of course, with no shirts on" who worked at night. House music, especially popular in New Jersey, "unified everybody in the gay community."[12] Gay couples could freely touch and dance at Murphy's. Yvonne Hernandez, a Puerto Rican lesbian, "felt safe there."[13] Darryl Rochester remembered both gay men and lesbian women patronizing Murphy's but "not too many trans people."[14] Angela Raine, who is a trans woman, remembers Murphy's as unfriendly to transgender women. "He [the owner] just wasn't crazy about trans women being there. The only way that you actually were able to come in is if you really knew somebody that was close to the owner, and the owner knew you, or if they had a drag show. If they had a drag show, they didn't want you seen. They wanted you in the back or you had to leave after the show."[15] While Murphy's became a central spot for LGBTQ Newarkers, and was increasingly patronized by queer people of color over time, our narrators report that trans people, especially trans women, were not as welcome there.

While Murphy's staff surveilled trans women, the state surveilled Murphy's and other gay gathering places. When undercover agents working for the ABC reported men exhibiting "feminine actions and mannerisms," and, even among the male clientele, "the odor of perfume on the premises," it was cause enough to suspend Murphy's liquor license for sixty days in 1961.[16] Murphy's joined with two other New Jersey gay bars that had their licenses suspended to fight back. In November 1967, the New Jersey Supreme Court ruled that the ABC could not "impair the rights of well-behaved apparent homosexuals to patronize and meet in licensed premises," establishing the right of gay people to congregate in public.[17]

Having weathered repressive state sanctions, Murphy's continued to serve queer people in Newark for several more decades. By the early 2000s, another threat loomed: urban redevelopment. This time, Murphy's could not withstand the pressure exerted by local, state, and corporate entities who sought to reimagine downtown Newark for upwardly mobile residents and tourists. A "dark, seedy stomping ground" like Murphy's was not part of these neoliberal plans.[18]

Large-scale redevelopment was nothing new in downtown Newark. In the 1960s, the Gateway complex demolished several blocks to build office towers connected to Newark Penn Station through skywalks that allowed suburbanites to commute to Newark without setting foot on the city streets.[19] Office space was soon accompanied by investments in leisure activities. Cities struggling with rising drug use and crime and diminishing life prospects for many of their citizens competed with each other for tourists by offering them cultural amenities.

Baltimore opened Oriole Park at Camden Yards baseball stadium in 1992, while Cleveland opened its baseball stadium in 1994. In 1997, Newark became home to the New Jersey Performing Arts Center, a venue for live theater and concerts.[20] Although plans for sports arenas had been suggested in Newark over the decades, the vision did not coalesce until the end of the twentieth century.[21]

The intersection of Mulberry and Market Streets was chosen as the location for the development due to its proximity to Newark Penn Station, a regional transit hub. That people owned homes and businesses there mattered little. The "40-acre area of obsolete industrial buildings, parking lots and scattered homes," was simply less valuable to the city, state, and developers than the complex, which would supposedly increase tax revenue for the city and spur future development.[22] As Mayor Sharpe James, who would leave office under a cloud of corruption before being convicted of federal fraud charges, argued, the arena would make Newark a "destination," catalyzing economic activity.[23] The area was demolished, including Murphy's Tavern, with groundbreaking for the arena taking place in October 2005.

Murphy's was not the only queer-friendly establishment erased by development. Club Zanzibar, a nightclub and center of the New Jersey house music scene, was attached to the Lincoln Motel (about a mile north on Broad Street, too far to get to on foot during the walking tour). Described by a local real estate developer as a "blemished, rat-infested drug-haven eyesore," the motel and Zanzibar were torn down in 2007.[24] Cory Booker, who was mayor at the time, courted private funders and developed close relationships with conservative think tanks, and even jumped into the cab of an excavator to gleefully tear into the building's facade. Just down the street from Zanzibar, Newark's two adult movie theaters, the Cameo and the Little Theatre, held on for a few years longer, but also closed in 2011 and 2018 as the influx of developer capital continued rolling into the area, leaving little space for such illicit cruising grounds.[25] As of this writing in late 2023, none of these spots have yet been built over, but their collective destruction makes the area along Broad Street more investor friendly.

For queer Newark residents, Zanzibar and Murphy's were not eyesores, but historic places that had nurtured their community when other doors were closed to them. During the 2014 "Out in Newark! Queer Club Spaces as Sanctuary" panel, Bernard McAllister, a Newark icon and house mother, recalled Zanzibar as a safe space, one where "gay people had status," where straight people "looked to gay people for fashion, for style . . . we was their conduit for them to have any

FIGURE 11.2. Prudential Center arena in downtown Newark, 2022. Along the adjacent brick wall is the site of Murphy's Tavern, currently without a historical marker, reflecting the absences experienced in the Queer Newark Walking Tour. Photo by Mary Rizzo.

type of anything and when they came to us they were in our sanctuary."[26] Fashion designer Douglas Says saw the closing of Murphy's as a huge loss to Newark's gay community. He said, "we have no place to go. There's no gay spots. None, absolutely none. Once Murphy's left, that was the last of it . . . It's like we've been shunned, kicked—it's like we've been pushed back in the closet."[27] Says's words complicate media narratives about LGBTQ communities, which often describe gay people as experiencing more freedom over time. While Murphy's was only a semi-safe space for queer people in Newark and a leader in the 1960s in the fight for gay rights, the twinned forces of capitalism and urban redevelopment destroyed a location that many gay people in Newark would have called a landmark. As Says notes, destroying the spaces where gay communities exist can force people back into a kind of closet as other public spaces are inaccessible to them by virtue of cost or interest. While gay Newarkers can and do attend events at the Prudential Center, it does not function in the same way as a small bar like Murphy's. By telling the story of Murphy's as the first stop on the walking tour, we try to create a framework for the rest of the tour, emphasizing how community spaces are not immune to economic and political forces.

Second Stop: The G Corner

We stand silently, heads bowed, at the intersection of Broad and Market Streets. Sometimes called the "G corner," it is referenced in several of our interviews as a place where gay young people in Newark hung out, finding community among the bustling crowds and, as LeiLani Dowell shows in chapter 7, resisting stifling narratives of Newark public space. Patreese Johnson described the G corner as "the one spot and one place where freshmen and sophomores would come together and be comfortable. Nobody would bother us. Not one person . . . that was the community right there of youth that was LGBT and we ain't have really nowhere else to go at that time. That was it. And it was fine. It was awesome."[28]

But not always. In 2003, a fifteen-year-old Black lesbian named Sakia Gunn was stabbed to death by a stranger when she rejected his advances near this corner. Although there is no plaque to make note of this senseless murder, as writer, theologian, and former chair of the Newark LGBT Concerns Advisory Commission, Darnell Moore, lamented, the "blood of this child of Newark forever stains the sidewalk."[29] Gunn's death is roundly recounted by local activists as shocking the gay community into a new level of organizing. As Moore said, "the ghost of her death" shaped "the more recent development of activism."[30]

As public historians, we knew we had to tell the story of Gunn's murder because of its importance to our theme of community-building. Out of her death several organizations sprang, committed to fighting against homophobic and sexist violence and safeguarding the lives and futures of gay youth. We struggled, however, about how to tell this story respectfully. As scholar Zenzele Isoke (whose epilogue follows this chapter) has shown, the complexity of Gunn's identity was reduced to her sexuality by national LGBTQ organizations. Their discourses ignored how race, class, age, and gender presentation affected her life and death.[31] Beyond ignoring the intersectionality of her identity, these organizations dehumanized Gunn by presenting her as simply another victim of homophobic violence in a city known for violence. While antigay violence is a critical issue for queer Newarkers, we were also painfully aware how easily a story like Gunn's fits into racist narratives that paint Newark as a violent hellhole in need of rescue by increased policing.

We tell Gunn's story in an alleyway between the Prudential Center and the corner of Broad and Market Streets. The space is quieter, ensuring that everyone can hear us and each other and that we can pass around photos of Gunn. Gunn was waiting for a bus with friends on May 11, 2003, after coming back to Newark from New York City. Two men in a car pulled up and propositioned them. The women rebuffed the men's advances by explaining that they were gay and uninterested. The men attacked them. In trying to protect her friends, Gunn was fighting back when she was stabbed in the chest by Richard McCullough. In part because a local police kiosk was unstaffed, she died on the way to the hospital. Gunn's death, as we explain, was simultaneously an antigay hate crime, an instance of violent misogyny, and an example of the random street violence made possible through racism and structural neglect.[32]

The outcry sparked by Gunn's murder was deeply shaped by issues of race, class, and gender presentation. First, the media covered this story much less frequently than similar ones. As journalism professor Kim Pearson showed, in the 8 months following Gunn's death, 21 stories about it appeared in the news database LexisNexis. However, 8 months after the murder of Matthew Shepard, a white gay man in Wyoming who was killed five years earlier, there were 683 stories.[33] News outlets may have treated the death of a young Black woman as normal because it happened in Newark, a city known for high rates of crime. Looked at through this perspective, Gunn's death was not an unusual enough occurrence to warrant media attention, unlike Shepard's death in Wyoming, nor did her presentation as a Black, gender-nonconforming "aggressive" bestow upon her the forms of sentimentalized and saintly martyrdom through which Shepard's death was narrated in the media.[34] By making this point in the walking tour, we explore how racism shaped media coverage. What do we ignore if we interpret her death solely as an example of homophobia? What anti-Black racism is revealed when we see that the media treats a young Black girl's death in Newark as uneventful and not worth covering? We also use this stop to tell the story of the New Jersey Four (NJ4), covered in more detail by Dowell in chapter 7.

For activists, though, Gunn's death allowed them to petition the city for greater resources. Newark's Mayor, Sharpe James, had ignored earlier calls by activists for municipal support for gay youth. With Gunn's death as a rallying cry, Laquetta Nelson and James Credle cofounded the Newark Pride Alliance to address the high rates of hate crimes, murders, and suicides of queer people in Newark. This was followed by the creation of the Newark Mayor's Advisory

Commission on LGBTQ Concerns in 2009 and the Newark LGBTQ Community Center in 2013. While many gay rights organizations were fighting for marriage equality, activists in Newark understood that marriage was not the utmost concern for LGBTQ people in the city. As Credle asserted, "it's not about marriage equality . . . our agenda is about survival of our youth."[35]

But did that survival require police? Police play a contradictory role in the Newark LGBTQ community's efforts to safeguard young people. On one hand, our narrators tell stories of siblings and friends killed by the police, and Danielle M. Shields and Carse Ramos show how deep this distrust runs in chapter 10. Queer people of color also suffered violence at the hands of police. DeFarra Gaymon, a Black man visiting family in the area, was shot and killed by an Essex County Sheriff's officer in Branch Brook Park. Police officers regularly conducted undercover stings targeting men cruising for sex in the park.[36] According to a 2014 report by the Department of Justice, the Newark police harassed trans women and others with a gender-nonconforming appearance, assuming that they were "prostitutes."[37]

However, community members also see under-policing as an example of the inequities that working-class queer people of color live with. They feel that their lives are valued less than those of other people who are protected by the police. QNOHP narrators tell stories of homophobic and transphobic violence that occurred on the street. Renata Hill's earliest memory of Newark is of being attacked by a man who shouted slurs at her about her masculine gender presentation. While strangers helped her and stopped the fight, Gunn's murder made her reflect on this incident: "I just realized how dangerous it is in Newark for us."[38] What is the police's role in stopping antigay violence? Gunn's peers blamed lax policing, in part, for her death. A police kiosk was less than 100 feet from where the attack took place, but it was unmanned at the time. At Gunn's funeral, members of the queer-friendly Liberation in Truth Church were asked by the police to serve as mediators between enraged young people and police who were working as security at the funeral.[39] For the LGBTQ community, police both cause violence and have ignored their duty to protect and serve people who are targets for violence because of their gender presentation and sexuality.

After telling Gunn's story and listening to any questions or comments from participants, we walk to the corner where she was murdered. Having prepared the group at the last stop, they know that we will not be talking at the corner.

Instead, we bow our heads in a moment of silence together, reflecting on Gunn's life and death. By doing so, we honor Sakia's humanity. Her death is a tragedy, not just a tool by which national LGBTQ organizations influence public policy on hate crimes. By explaining how local activists leveraged the community's anger after Gunn's murder to create new spaces to support queer youth, we emphasize the resilience of this community. Our moment of silence is conspicuous, given the bustle of this corner, but this makes it more meaningful. Through our bodies standing together in silence, we create a momentary marker to her memory. (As this book goes to press, Academy Street in downtown Newark has been renamed Sakia Gunn Way, a testament to the ongoing memory-work of LGBTQ Newarkers.)

Last Stop: Halsey Street

For our last stop, we walk to Halsey Street, near the campus of Rutgers University-Newark. If Newark has a gay street, it's Halsey, a block of rowhouses with street-level storefronts selling everything from fabric to upscale espresso drinks to Indian-spiced hamburgers. We end the tour here to highlight the many businesses owned by queer entrepreneurs and to take attendees inside the Newark LGBTQ Community Center, which offers services for queer community members. Queer community-building takes place on Halsey in both commercial and nonprofit spaces. But, like Murphy's Tavern, Halsey Street has been affected by development. In the 1970s and early 1980s, clubs like Le Joc, the Dollhouse and SRO dotted Halsey, but all have long since closed. One factor is the location of Rutgers University-Newark's campus. According to Aaron Frazier, part of "the Stroll," the perimeter where gay men could cruise for sex, was policed out of existence to become a more "college town" when Rutgers-Newark expanded.[40] Even since our first tour in 2017, gentrification has remade Halsey and, by extension, our tour.

How does the process of urban redevelopment called gentrification affect queer communities of color? While the demolishing of Murphy's and other queer bars and clubs suggests only negative impacts, our interviews complicate the story. Revealed in interviews with Tamara Fleming, Peggie Miller, Jae Quinlan, and Burley Tuggle, among others, is a strong community of Black queer entrepreneurs in Newark, particularly among Black lesbians. As Kristyn Scorsone suggests, their relationship to gentrification is complex. On one hand, these women, whose businesses tend to be in the arts and culture, benefit from people with higher incomes moving into the city, as well as, at times, from municipal support for women-owned businesses. They are also aware, however, that their individual success does not help the majority of LGBTQ people in the city, many of whom are at risk of displacement due to rising rents.

These lesbian entrepreneurs are not only concerned with profits. They also use their position to support the LGBTQ community. As Scorsone explains, "in Newark these women are not only finding labor autonomy, they are also using their work to elevate others who are marginalized in their community" by making their businesses into queer community spaces.[41] Married couple Lynette Lashawn and Anita Dickens own the clothing stores Off the Hanger and ANĒ Clothier (formerly known as A Girl and Guy Thing). They sell feminine clothing as well as gender-neutral and masculine-style clothes for women. Dickens designs these clothes to fill the gap she experienced as a woman who has a masculine gender presentation and wore clothes designed for men. After having uncomfortable experiences when she used the women's dressing room in other stores, she created ANĒ as a place "where people, women like me, are comfortable to shop and you don't have to worry about whether the dressing room says men or women. It's open. It's for us."[42] These entrepreneurs also plan events for the LGBTQ community and help support each other through networking. Tamara Fleming and Kimberlee Williams, also a Black lesbian, started the New Jersey Pride Chamber of Commerce as an affiliate of the national LGBT Chamber of Commerce. The organization connects queer business owners around the state for the purpose of increasing the economic strength of LGBTQ businesses overall. As Scorsone shows us, Black lesbian entrepreneurs are community builders, even if they also profit from processes that may be detrimental to some Black working-class Newarkers.

Not all queer businesses and nonprofits can weather the changes caused by gentrification in the neighborhood. While in the earliest versions of the tour we could point out several Black queer-owned businesses on Halsey Street, in more recent years this celebration has been tempered as businesses like the Artisan Collective, a space where the four Black lesbian owners sold their handmade wares, have closed. Rising rents have shuttered the doors of many businesses on this street. Queer businesses are not the only ones affected. Artists who found relatively inexpensive studio space in the area in the 1990s were displaced in 2019 after helping to fix a building that the owners were letting deteriorate—at the same time that Newark's Mayor, Ras Baraka, was touting the city as an arts destination.[43] But when gentrification forced the LGBTQ Community Center to move, it became clear that the queer community was, in many ways, most vulnerable to gentrification's effects.

Following massive community organizing after Gunn's murder, Rev. Janyce Jackson Jones and Alicia Heath-Toby opened the Newark LGBTQ Community Center in 2013 at 11 Halsey Street in a storefront that faced the street. The landlord gave them a discount on rent, allowing them access to a space in downtown Newark. Jackson Jones, who served as the Center's first executive director, said that "being in this spot is just . . . perfect," because it was an area with a high level of foot traffic due to the nearby stores and Washington Park. Community feedback also emphasized the need for a downtown location, seen as more accessible and more safely anonymous for those who were not out at home. With such a central location, the Center "attract[s] all kinds of people," including, as she described, a man who stopped by to ask what the Q in LGBTQ stood for, leading to a conversation and the man attending a screening of *Dreams Deferred: The Sakia Gunn Film Project.*[44] The Center offers programs, services, and events that address many concerns of LGBTQ individuals and communities—including homelessness, economic empowerment, health and wellness, and social injustice. The location on Halsey symbolized the ideal of the Center as a community space—welcoming and allowing for these kinds of encounters.

In 2017, the Community Center received a notice from L+M Development Partners, a real estate development firm, that 11 Halsey would be demolished in late 2018. L+M was well known in downtown Newark for the restoration and redevelopment of the Hahne building, a department store that sat empty from 1987 to 2017.[45] That year it was reopened as a mixed-use residential and retail space that includes Whole Foods; a Marcus Samuelsson restaurant; apartments; Rutgers classrooms and office space; and Express Newark, a Rutgers initiative that incubates arts projects in the city.[46] While some saw the Whole Foods as indicating impending gentrification, this project did bring new life to an abandoned building located in the downtown area.[47] L+M's interest in 11 Halsey Street, however, was different, since the building already housed the community center as well as artists' studios. Because the Center was getting a discount on rent and prices in the vicinity were rising due to increased development, it couldn't find a new space that it could afford, including any space in other buildings owned by L+M. The developer, meanwhile, sent a representative to meet with the Center's board, promising assistance; "I don't even like to use the word 'displace,'" he explained, going on to offer little help as his firm did precisely that.[48]

While Center leaders engaged in conversations with Rutgers-Newark about space, Jeffrey Trzeciak, director of the Newark Public Library, offered the Center space in the main branch of the library. The Center moved into the library in 2019. Located around the corner from 11 Halsey Street and across from Washington Park, and the location for many of Newark's gay pride celebrations, the library was, in many ways, an excellent space for the center. Trzeciak, who is gay, noted that when he was growing up his local library was "the place where I discovered myself and my community—our community."[49] Given the challenges of finding affordable space, the library was a godsend to the Community Center, though at the cost of direct street-level access and reduced hours after city budget cuts. In early 2023, the Center moved into a coworking space in downtown Newark.

As of 2021, we ended our walking tour by taking groups into the library to see the Community Center and pull the threads of our story of community building in the face of Gunn's murder together. However, we refuse to end our tour as if queer Newarkers have solved their problems because the Center exists. We return to the issue of gentrification and urban development, encouraging attendees to think about the topic in the complicated ways suggested by our narrators as well as by the Center's history, and to show that the struggle continues.[50]

Takeaway: Keep Walking with Us

As Darnell Moore noted at the founding conference of the Queer Newark Oral History Project, "History is made through the living and the telling of our lives. It is made when we lift up our individual and collective lives."[51] By emphasizing how LGBTQ Newarkers have created a home in Newark, we show the longevity and resilience of this community. We do so, however, without eliding conflicts within the queer community in telling these stories. By acknowledging intracommunity conflicts, we tell a more honest story about this past that, we hope, strengthens the relationships we have with our many community partners. Although there are absences in the built environment, our tour, as an extension of the larger project, intervenes to make sure those absences do not extend to our collective memories and that our history is preserved for generations to come.

Notes

1. The first Queer Newark tour was led in 2017. It has been repeated many times since, often at the request of other community organizations including Newark Pride and Bloomfield Pride, and faculty teaching related courses.

2. Other examples include a podcast, a traveling exhibit, virtual walking tours, and curated audio clips available at the Queer Newark Oral History Project (QNOHP) website, queer.newark.rutgers.edu.

3. See Tiya Miles, *Tales from the Haunted South: Dark Tourism and Memories of Slavery from the Civil War Era* (Chapel Hill: University of North Carolina Press, 2017).

4. Andrew Hurley, *Beyond Preservation: Using Public History to Revitalize Inner Cities* (Philadelphia: Temple University Press, 2010), 40. While the People's History Tour of Baltimore is a bus rather than a walking tour, it remains an innovative public history project whose work is captured in Elizabeth Fee, Linda Shopes, and Linda Zeidman, *The Baltimore Book: New Views of Local History* (Philadelphia, PA: Temple University Press, 1991).

5. Rebecca Amato and Jeffrey T. Manuel, "Using Radical Public History Tours to Reframe Urban Crime," *Radical History Review*, no. 113 (April 1, 2012): 212–224.

6. Nan Alamilla Boyd and Horacio N. Roque Ramírez, eds., *Bodies of Evidence: The Practice of Queer Oral History* (New York: Oxford University Press, 2012).

7. For example, see the LGBT Center Central PA History Project, https://www.centralpalgbthistory.org; OutHistory, https://outhistory.org; Not Another Second: LGBT+ Seniors Share Their Stories, https://www.notanothersecond.com/; and Midwest Queer Spaces, https://www.midwestqueerspaces.com.

8. Michael Frisch, "From a Shared Authority to the Digital Kitchen, and Back," in *Letting Go?: Sharing Historical Authority in a User-Generated World*, ed. Bill Adair, Benjamine Filene, and Laura Koloski (Philadelphia: Pew Center for Arts & Heritage, 2011), 126–137.

9. Yoland Skeete-Laessig, *When Newark Had a Chinatown: My Personal Journey* (Pittsburgh: Dorrance Publishing, 2016).

10. Elizabeth Lapovsky Kennedy and Madeline Davis, *Boots of Leather, Slippers of Gold: The History of a Lesbian Community* (New York: Routledge, 1993).

11. Whitney Strub, interview with Aaron Frazier, November 21, 2017, Queer Newark Oral History Project (QNOHP), 20–22, https://queer.newark.rutgers.edu/sites/default/files/transcript/2017-11-21%20Aaron%20Frazier%203_1.pdf.

12. Whitney Strub, interview with June Dowell-Burton, December 1, 2015, QNOHP, 24, https://queer.newark.rutgers.edu/sites/default/files/transcript/2015-12-01JuneDowell-BurtoninterviewbyWhitneyStrub.pdf.

13. Beryl Satter, interview with Yvonne Hernandez, May 29, 2014, QNOHP, 40, https://queer.newark.rutgers.edu/sites/default/files/transcript/2014-05-29Yvonne HernandezinterviewedbyBerylSatter_0.pdf.

14. Timothy Stewart-Winter and Esperanza Santos, interview with Darryl Rochester, September 19, 2019, QNOHP, 47, https://queer.newark.rutgers.edu/sites/default/files/transcript/Darryl%20Rochester_REDACTED%20Transcript.pdf.

15. Whitney Strub, interview with Angela Raine, February 6, 2018, QNOHP, 12, https://queer.newark.rutgers.edu/sites/default/files/transcript/2018-02-06%20 Angela%20Raine.pdf.

16. Whitney Strub and Timothy Stewart-Winter, "Remembering *One Eleven Wines*, a Pre-Stonewall Win against Homophobic State Surveillance," *Slate*, November 30, 2017, https://slate.com/human-interest/2017/11/remembering-one-eleven-wines-liquors-a-pre-stonewall-win-against-homophobic-state-surveillance.html.

17. "*One Eleven Wines & Liquors, Inc. v. Div. Alcoholic Bev.*, Cont.," 50 N.J. 329, 235 A.2d 12 (1967), Justia Law, accessed September 28, 2021, https://law.justia.com/cases/new-jersey/supreme-court/1967/50-n-j-329-0.html.

18. Stewart-Winter and Santos, interview with Rochester, 46.

19. Trevor Boddy, "Underground and Overhead: Building the Analogous City," in *Variations on a Theme Park: The New American City and the End of Public Space*, ed. Michael Sorkin (New York: Hill and Wang, 1992), 123–153.

20. Elizabeth Strom, "Let's Put On a Show! Performing Arts and Urban Revitalization in Newark, New Jersey," *Journal of Urban Affairs* 21, no. 4 (1999): 423–435.

21. Laura Troiano, "Give Me a 'Ball Park Figure': Civic Narratives through Stadium Building in Newark, New Jersey" (PhD diss., Rutgers University-Newark, 2017).

22. Ronald Smothers, "2 Alternatives Proposed for Newark Sports Arena," *New York Times*, January 11, 2000.

23. Alan Drew Cander, "The Law and Practice of Municipal Land Assembly: Fifty Years of Urban Redevelopment and Community Opposition in Newark, New Jersey" (PhD diss., Rutgers University, 2011).

24. Andrew Jacobs, "Newark Loses Unwanted Landmark as Lincoln Motel Goes," *New York Times*, October 8, 2007.

25. Whitney Strub, "No Sex in Newark: Postindustrial Erotics at the Intersection of Urban and Adult Film History," *JCMS: Journal of Cinema and Media Studies* 58, no. 1 (2018): 175–182.

26. "Out in Newark! Queer Club Spaces as Sanctuary (Part 4)," Queer Newark, YouTube, December 4, 2014, https://youtu.be/_CFQ_zhiOqQ.

27. Naomi Extra, interview with Douglas Says, May 31, 2016, QNOHP, 36–37, https://queer.newark.rutgers.edu/sites/default/files/transcript/2016-05-31%20 Douglas%20Says%20interviewed%20by%20Naomi%20Extra.pdf.

28. Whitney Strub, interview with Patreese Johnson, October 12, 2015, QNOHP, 35, https://queer.newark.rutgers.edu/sites/default/files/transcript/2015-10-12%20Patreese%20Johnson%20final.pdf.

29. Darnell L. Moore, *No Ashes in the Fire: Coming of Age Black and Free in America* (New York: Nation Books, 2018), 216.

30. Timothy Stewart-Winter, interview with Darnell Moore, March 15, 2016, QNOHP, 38, https://queer.newark.rutgers.edu/sites/default/files/transcript/2016-03-15DarnellMooreinterviewedbyTimStewart-Winter-FINALAPPROVED.docx_.pdf.

31. Zenzele Isoke, *Urban Black Women and the Politics of Resistance* (New York: Palgrave Macmillan, 2013), 115–117.

32. Mark Anthony Neal, "Baby-Girl Drama: Remembering Sakia," *PopMatters*, January 27, 2004, https://web.archive.org/web/20040401215737/http://www.popmatters.com/features/040127-sakiagunn.shtml.

33. Kim Pearson, "On Being a Drum Major," *Kim Pearson Blog*, January 19, 2004, https://kimpearson.net/on-being-a-drum-major.

34. Zenzele Isoke explains "aggressive" as a particular Black, urban, lesbian identity expressed through "androgynous, often marked masculine, self-presentations rooted in African-American vernacular culture." *Urban Black Women and the Politics of Resistance*, 179

35. Candace Bradsher, interview with James Credle, February 15, 2015, QNOHP, 33, https://queer.newark.rutgers.edu/sites/default/files/transcript/JamesCredle QNOHP.pdf.

36. Michael Wilson and Serge F. Kovaleski, "No Charges for Officer in Death in Newark Park," *New York Times*, June 28, 2011.

37. U.S. Department of Justice, *Investigation of the Newark Police Department* (2014), https://www.justice.gov/sites/default/files/crt/legacy/2014/07/22/newark_findings_7-22-14.pdf.

38. Timothy Stewart-Winter, interview with Renata Hill, October 12, 2015, QNOHP, 32, https://queer.newark.rutgers.edu/sites/default/files/transcript/2015-10-12RenataHillinterviewbyTimothyStewart-Winter-Approved_0.pdf.

39. Christina Strasburger, interview with Kevin Taylor, December 9, 2017, QNOHP, 30, https://queer.newark.rutgers.edu/sites/default/files/transcript/2017-12-9%20Kevin%20Taylor%20interviewed%20by%20Christina%20Strasburger.pdf.

40. Strub, interview with Frazier, 20–22. "The stroll for the MSMs, for the men who have sex with men, was Halsey Street."

41. Kristyn Scorsone, "Invisible Pathways: Public History by Queer Black Women in Newark," *The Public Historian* 41, no. 2 (2019): 190–217, here 198.

42. Kristyn Scorsone, interview with Anita Dickens, December 8, 2016, QNOHP, 21, https://queer.newark.rutgers.edu/sites/default/files/transcript/2016-12-08%20Anita%20Dickens%20interviewed%20by%20Kristyn%20Scorsone%20EDITS%20COMPLETE%20-%20FINAL.pdf.

43. Colleen G. O'Neal, "Looking a Gift Horse in the Mouth: Artists, a Sick Building, and Gentrification in Newark," *Environmental Justice History in America Blog*, https://ejhistory.com/looking-a-gift-horse-in-the-mouth/.

44. Anna Alves, interview with Janyce Jackson Jones, May 13, 2016, QNOHP, 14, 15, https://queer.newark.rutgers.edu/sites/default/files/transcript/2016-05-13%20 Rev.%20Janyce%20Jackson%20Jones%20interviewed%20by%20Anna%20 Alves%2C%20Part%202%20-%20Final.pdf.

45. Chris Sheldon, "Transformation of Historic Newark Building Complete as Korean BBQ Joint Inks Lease," NJ.com, June 14, 2020, https://www.nj.com/essex /2020/06/transformation-of-historic-newark-building-complete-as-korean-bbq -joint-inks-lease.html.

46. Andaiye Taylor, "With Opening of Hahne and Co. Building, a Chance to Bring Life to a Long-Blighted Block," *Brick City Live*, January 24, 2017, http:// brickcitylive.com/news/andaiye/with-opening-of-hahne-and-co-building-a -chance-to-bring-a-life-to-a-long-blighted-block/.

47. Steve Strunsky, "Hahne's Building Opening Seen as Sign of City's Rebirth," NJ.com, January 24, 2017, https://www.nj.com/essex/2017/01/hahnes_ribbon _cutting_in_newark_1.html.

48. Quote from then board member Whitney Strub, personal communication, September 24, 2021.

49. Rebecca Panico, "Newark LGBTQ Center Finds New Home at Newark Public Library," *Tap Into Newark*, May 9, 2019, https://www.tapinto.net/towns /newark/sections/development/articles/newark-lgbtq-center-finds-new-home-at -newark-public-library.

50. Jacquetta Farrar, "Newark vs 'Nork' . . . Whose Block Is It Anyway?" *Ark Republic*, October 3, 2019, https://www.arkrepublic.com/2019/10/03/newark-vs -nork-whose-block-is-it-anyway.

51. "Queer Newark: Our Voices, Our Histories (Part 1)," Queer Newark, YouTube, November 12, 2011, https://youtu.be/95C7O6GdLhQ.

Epilogue

Remembering Sakia, Remembering Ourselves

ZENZELE ISOKE

SAKIA GUNN WAS BEAUTIFUL. Young, gifted, Black, and queer, she defied anyone's expectations of gender. She just wanted to be herself. She was gentle-hearted and mild-mannered, and she loved to play basketball.

Sakia became an ancestor at the age of fifteen. May 11, 2023, marks the twentieth anniversary of her death. She is mostly remembered for the ugly act of violence that ended her life. But I remember her warm and generous smile.

Sakia might have been quickly forgotten had it not been for the efforts of Black lesbians like Laquetta Nelson, SuSu Stewart, Janyce Jackson Jones, and an entire community of Black queer folks who rallied together in the thousands to honor her at her homegoing service. Some members of the community would have disremembered Sakia, relegating her to the status of sad statistic in a city that has too often been marked by intra-racial violence. Others would misremember Sakia, using her death to highlight homophobia and anti-LGBTQIA bigotry in the United States. But, as I argued in 2013 when I first wrote about Sakia in my dissertation, which later turned into my first book, Sakia was so much more than the act that ended her life. Her life and death exceeded the weighty chains of discourse that eventually brought her into our hearts and minds. Although her death never garnered the national attention of other hate crime victims like Matthew Shephard or James Byrd Jr., she was beloved and is fiercely remembered in Newark.

I can't help but wonder who Sakia might have been had she not been killed on that dark spring morning. What if Richard McCullough, her killer, and his co-conspirators had not harassed Sakia, Valencia Bailey, and their friends while they were on their way home from the club? What if McCullough had not responded in a killing rage when Sakia and her friends rejected his vapid insults from a car? What if he had not called her a "dyke"? What if there had been a police officer on duty in the empty security kiosk across the street from where she was stabbed? Would she have made it to the hospital on time and not bled to death waiting on a bus to take her to a hospital less than two miles away?

Who might Sakia have been? What would she have done had she survived? Perhaps she would have played women's basketball for the Scarlet Knights at Rutgers University, where she might have enrolled in a gender studies class taught by a Black professor who saw and valued her for all of who she was. Maybe she would have studied the poetry and essays of Audre Lorde, "The Uses of the Erotic" specifically, and decided to become an artist. Maybe she would have learned about the incomparably transformative intellectual legacy of Black lesbian feminism and used her studies to lift up others like her in her own way—as an educator, historian, or Black lesbian therapist. Maybe she would have been part of a national cohort of scholar-activist creatives like Alexis Pauline Gumbs and adrienne maree brown, helping to redefine the meaning and practice of Black feminism for up-and-coming generations of Black trans* educators like Qui Alexander and Matt Richardson. Maybe she would have traveled to Minneapolis to support CeCe McDonald during her trial there. Or maybe she would have just smiled a huge smile while she sang along to "Tightrope" by Janelle Monáe and breathed deeply, happy to be alive, happy to just be. Like a flower in full bloom in early June.

The possibilities of what her life could have been are endless. That is what makes this epilogue so difficult to write.

Today, there is more social space for Black queer people to identify and fulfill their highest aspirations, but not nearly enough. Still too many lesbian, gay, and trans young people have to withstand repeated traumatic experiences born of the contempt and ignorance of family members, schoolmates, teachers, and preachers who bully them, misgender them, alienate them, and abandon them—leaving them without the emotional and social support that they need to truly thrive. Black gender-variant teenagers and young adults are still pushed into the margins—criminalized, othered, and misunderstood. Even today, if they are lucky enough to have the support of their families and communities, they must still contend with social indignities from trans-exclusionary feminists who remain steadfastly loyal to hopelessly outdated understandings of gender and womanhood, allowing gender norms that have origins in white supremacist ways of inhabiting and practicing power and identity politics to override any sense of compassion and shared humanity.

At the same time, young people are pushing back. In schools, communities, and workplaces young people are refusing to conform, refusing to apologize for their queer aesthetics and existences and choosing to embrace their gender variance by claiming it a source of power and aliveness. In this way, Black queer youth have eviscerated the margins by creating new centers of Black queer expressivity. We see this in the incredible work of Black queer folks who have risen to national and international acclaim, including Chicago mayor Lori Lightfoot, Minnesota Lynx superstar Seimone Augustus, screenwriter and producer Lena Waithe, healing justice somatic practitioner Prentis Hemphill, and so many others.

Things have changed. Today a large and loud critical mass of the Black students I teach in gender studies identify as gender fluid, nonbinary, and/or trans*. Today trans*ness is not defined by whether or not a person had a surgery, but how one understands, relates to, and defies the regulatory power of gender and culture. Blackness, queerness, and trans*ness are now paradigms to see and critique politics—not just the politics of social movements, but the politics of relationality and everyday life. There are now notable and highly influential Black queer communities across the humanities, wherein we write our own histories and locate and create our own written and virtual repositories of cultural knowledge and Black resistance, redefining notions of family and kinship to rethink and retheorize the meaning and practice of Black life. The scholarship of Omise'eke Tinsley, Matt Richardson, C. Riley Snorton, and Savannah Shange have been central to this beautiful and important effort. At Pride 2022, Mayor Ras Baracak even flew the Pride flag high, bright, and glorious at Newark City Hall in an important and inspiring display of Black solidarity with the Black lesbian and gay communities. And after a long and arduous struggle, the Human Rights Campaign has finally named a Black queer woman as its Executive Director.

But public names of acclaim are not enough. Short-lived moments of recognition and affirmation are not enough.

The struggle for Black queer life continues—it is multifrontal and lethal. The backlash to increased visibility and recognition of Black queer and trans folks, regardless of their racial identity, has been ferocious and persistent. Before the fall of 2022, there were over thirty unsolved murders of trans women of color in our cities, including Regina "Mya" Allen (Milwaukee), Hayden Davis and Dede Ricks (Detroit), Kandii Redd (Kansas City), and Keshia Chanel Geter (Augusta), and more. (We miss you, we remember you. We feel your absence and your presence.) Community organizations and local formations like SHEBA (Sisters Helping Each Other Battle Adversity), BTAC (Black Trans Advocacy Coalition), The Okra Project, Southern Fried Queer Pride, and the hard-won Newark LGBTQ Community Center founded by Liberation in Truth, Unity Fellowship Church following the outcry of Sakia's murder keep our hearts tender and our wills strong.

The backlash to Black queer and transgender visibility has been enormous. In the past two years, more than a hundred bills across thirty-three states have introduced laws to erode the rights of transgender people. Conservatives have introduced and passed bills to ban transgender athletes from participating in women's sports. They have made it illegal to teach about gender and gender nonconformity in public schools by attempting to ban critical race theory and gender studies, and they are seeking to outlaw gender-affirming medical care for minors. Under the horridly transphobic leadership of Governor Glenn Youngkin, the State of Virginia passed a flurry of anti-trans legislation reversing the protections of transgender students, including requiring students to file legal documents if they want to go by a pronoun different than the one listed on their birth certificate, requiring teachers to inform parents if students request the use of a different pronoun or otherwise defy gender norms, and disallowing trans students to use facilities of the gender they most identify with. Florida governor Ron DeSantis and other Republicans also capitalize on trans-bashing and anti-queer policies for political gain, and as this book goes to press, three school districts in New Jersey's Monmouth County are attempting to defy state law to mandate the outing of trans and nonbinary students. In short, the goal of too many politicians in America is trying to make it illegal to educate the masses about racial and gender justice paradigms that make it possible to understand and embrace young people like Sakia Gunn as fully human. They are trying to force gender-dissident kids back into a deadly closet. One step forward, five steps back. And yet here we are.

Here we are.

From time to time over the years, Sakia has whispered to me in my dreams, quietly yet insistently urging me to nestle her memory sweetly within the warm and complex web of social relationships that comprise Blackness and Black queer personhood. She is one of us. And she will never be forgotten.

May all of the advocacy and organizing, storytelling and artmaking, struggles and victories, losses and cries of the long and beautiful legacy of Black lesbian, queer, and trans culture and resistance pay homage to Sakia and young people like her, and those who are so much more than we can ever imagine them to be.

Rest in freedom, Sakia.

ACKNOWLEDGMENTS

THE QUEER NEWARK ORAL HISTORY PROJECT was founded by Beryl Satter, Darnell Moore, and Christina Strasburger in 2011. Timothy Stewart-Winter and I joined when it began, and Mary Rizzo rounded out the core team a few years later. You couldn't ask for better, more brilliant colleagues, and my thanks as editor begins with them (Christina in particular, as the project could never have survived without her commitment, intellect, and unstinting generosity)—and from here, the thanks also comes *from* them, since this book was a joint effort in every way.

At Rutgers University-Newark, we have always been supported, and among so many others, thanks are due to Nancy Cantor, Sherri-Ann Butterfield, Jacqueline Mattis, Alison Lefkovitz (on the NJIT side), Karen Caplan, Gary Farney, Mark Krasovic, John Keene, Maren Greathouse, Mel McCuin, Yoleidy Rosario, Gary Santos Mendoza, Cat Fitzpatrick, Jody Miller, Vanessa Panfil, Corey Clawson, and Marta Esquilin. Jyl Josephson has long supported this work and helped shape this book. James Credle and Louie Crew Clay were pioneering out, gay, and proud leaders on campus, and the dearly missed Jan Ellen Lewis, Clement Alexander Price, and Krista White contributed greatly to our work too.

So many undergraduate and graduate students, as well as community volunteers, have shaped this project. Thanks to Mi Hyun Yoon, Esperanza Santos, Erica Fugger, Andy Lester, Anna Alves, Keishla Rivera-Lopez, Dominique Rocker, Brennan Sutter, Naomi Extra, Isabella Sangaline, Jamisha/Jay Montague, Brendan Fox, Lorna Ebner, Adam Varoqua, Daniela Valdes, Molly Stevens, Kiyan Williams, Kenneth Morrissey, Mel Mott, Emily Posyton, Whitney

Fields, Alex Rosado-Torres, Brandon Morrissey, Kennedy Didier, Monica Liu, Vanessa Castaldo, Laura Hoge, Moira Armstrong, Paige Trapnell, and especially Kristyn Scorsone.

The Newark LGBTQ Community Center has long been a central community partner, and a crucial site for sustaining queer life in Newark. Rev. Janyce Jackson Jones and Alicia Heath-Toby deserve particular gratitude for building the center, as do Beatrice Simpkins and Denise Hinds for keeping it alive and thriving. Thanks too for the hard work of Joya Thompson, Steve Malick, Jeffrey Trzeciak, Jerri Mitchell-Lee, Jim Cramer, Dean Dafis, Albert Mrozik, Atiya Jaha Rashidi, Jewell Palmer, Julio Roman, Julie Schwartzberg, Thomas Steele, and so many others.

Newark has a research brain trust that could give any city a run for its money. So much of the research for this book relies on the tips, knowledge, and labor of Gail Malmgreen and the Newark Archives Project; Tom Ankner and everyone at Newark Public Library; Natalie Borisovets and the whole team at Rutgers University Libraries's Dana Library; Peter Savastano; and Gary Jardim.

There are *so* many members of the Newark LGBTQ community who deserve gratitude—if only there were enough space to list everyone! But we especially owe thanks to June Dowell-Burton, Noelle Lorraine Williams, Sharon Davis, Tamara Fleming, Dinean Robinson, Peggie Miller, Pastor Kevin Taylor, Gary Paul Wright and everyone at the African American Office of Gay Concerns, Ingrid Betancourt, Marc Sir Dane, Coleen Barr, Ms. Theresa Randolph, Dani Cooper, Sharronda Wheeler and Newark Pride, Inc., Emma Wilcox, Evonne M. Davis . . . and hundreds of others. It's an honor to work with this diverse, powerful, inspiring community.

Finally, every person who has generously offered their time, memories, and wisdom to the Queer Newark Oral History Project has shaped this book. The archive is too extensive to list all fully, but it can be browsed at https://queer.newark.rutgers.edu/interviews. We must single out Rodney Gilbert and Darryl Wayne Rochester, both now gone and remembered with loving gratitude; Angela Raine for supporting this project for years; Jae Quinlan for so much, including carrying archival materials to the QNOHP office; Bernard McAllister for his years of activism and deep community connections; and Aaron Frazier for his endless commitment to LGBTQ life and history, as well as for his permission to reprint his poem "I am not dead yet" as the epigraph to this volume. Eyricka Morgan, who spoke at the inaugural "Queer Newark: Our Voices, Our Stories" conference in 2011, was murdered in 2013; we grieve for her and so many others lost to physical and/or social violence, and we hope that our historical work honors their memory.

Readers who wish to support LGBTQ Newark organizing are encouraged to donate and volunteer with the Newark LGBTQ Community Center and the African American Office of Gay Concerns. All editorial royalties will be split between those wonderful organizations and the Queer Newark Oral History Project.

NOTES ON CONTRIBUTORS

YAMIL AVIVI received his PhD in American Culture from the University of Michigan in 2016. Avivi is currently a 2023–2024 Research Postdoctoral Scholar in History and Latina/o/x Studies at Penn State University. He has published articles on subjectivity and spacemaking among Brazilian queers in Newark and Colombian queer asylum seekers in South Florida. Avivi is working on his first book manuscript, *Young and Brown in Jersey: Latinx Subcultures in Elizabeth, NJ, 1980s-1990s,* which examines Latinx youth subcultures—such as house, gay ball, skate, and goth—to amplify Latinx youth subjectivity, subject making, and cultural citizenship.

JASON M. CHERNESKY is the CLIR Opioid Industry Research postdoctoral fellow at the Johns Hopkins University School of Medicine. He received his PhD in the history and sociology of science from the University of Pennsylvania. His dissertation, and current book project, focuses on how the HIV/AIDS pandemic affected American children and their families. Jason is a historian of twentieth-century medicine, healthcare, children's health, public health, and environments in the United States, with an emphasis on race-based health disparities among American children and their families in the context of the built environments in which they live. His research interests include the histories of epidemic disease, drug use, biomedical technologies, and nursing.

LEILANI DOWELL is a longtime activist and a 2018–2019 American Association of University Women fellow who earned her PhD in English from the City

University of New York Graduate Center. Her dissertation project investigated the media, activist, and court rhetorics surrounding the case of the New Jersey Four, a group of lesbian and gender-nonconforming people imprisoned for defending themselves against an attack in New York's Greenwich Village in 2006. Dowell currently serves as an associate director of Southern Vision Alliance.

ZENZELE ISOKE is a Black feminist theorist, urban ethnographer, and political storyteller. Drawing from the ideas of Black decolonial thinkers, Isoke writes the contemporary history of cities through the political struggles of self-identified Black/queer women of the African diaspora. Writing across the fields of geography, political science, and urban anthropology, her scholarship spans several cities in the United States, Middle-East, and the Caribbean. Her new book project, *Unheard Voices at the Bottom of Empire,* develops a set of "counterpoetic" writing practices to theorize and explore Black feminist politics through the mediums of collaborative artmaking, breath and meditation, and conventional grassroots organizing in racially segregated urban spaces. She is author of *Urban Black Women and the Politics of Resistance.* Her writing has been featured in several peer-reviewed journals and anthologies including *Souls: A Critical Journal of Black Politics, Culture and Society, Transforming Anthropology,* and *Gender, Place and Culture,* among others. She is also the mother of two teenage Black girls, one a (slowly) rising poet and one an organizer in her own right.

ANNA LVOVSKY is a professor of law at Harvard Law School, where she writes on the history of policing and gay life, the legal and cultural dimensions of law enforcement, and the role of expertise in court. Her first book, *Vice Patrol: Cops, Courts, and the Struggle over Urban Gay Life before Stonewall,* received the 2022 Lambda Literary Award in LGBTQ studies. Her articles have appeared in the *Harvard Law Review,* the *Yale Law Journal,* the *University of Pennsylvania Law Review,* and the *Journal of Urban History,* and she has cowritten historical amicus briefs in LGBTQ-related cases before the Supreme Court and the U.S. court of appeals. She received her JD from Harvard Law School and her PhD in the history of American civilization from Harvard University.

CARSE RAMOS (she/they) is an assistant professor of sociology and justice studies at Rhode Island College, where she also teaches in the International Nongovernmental Organization Studies program. She also serves as a periodic research consultant with the Cardozo Law Institute in Holocaust and Human Rights on its Confronting Structural Violence project, which focuses on developing materials to introduce atrocity prevention frameworks into legal curricula. Dr. Ramos has a background in advocacy, having worked and volunteered with such organizations as the European Roma Rights Centre in Budapest, Land and Equity Movement in Uganda in Kampala, Amnesty International, and the Northeast New Jersey Legal Services. Her research is located at the nexus between atrocity prevention, legal spaces, transitional justice, access, and social memory, with a particular lens on victimhood designation processes.

MARY RIZZO is associate professor of history at Rutgers University-Newark. She has served as a faculty advisor for the Queer Newark Oral History Project since 2015 and led the curation process for the traveling exhibit *At Home in Newark: Stories from the Queer Newark Oral History Project.* In 2022, she received the Oral History Association's Article Award for "Who Speaks for Baltimore?: The Invisibility of Whiteness and the Ethics of Oral History Theater," published in the *Oral History Review.* She is the author of *Come and Be Shocked: Baltimore beyond John Waters and The Wire* and *Class Acts: Young Men and the Rise of Lifestyle* and is a cofounder of the Chicory Revitalization Project, which uses vernacular poetry for intergenerational civic dialogue.

DOMINIQUE ROCKER, MA, was born and raised in Southern California. She is currently a PhD student in American studies at Rutgers University-Newark, where her research focuses on digital and cultural expressions of Black femme sexuality.

PETER SAVASTANO is associate professor of anthropology and religious studies at Seton Hall University. He specializes in the intersection/clash of religion with sexuality, gender, and race. He is a native of Newark, New Jersey, where he came of age in the 1960s. Dr. Savastano is one of the charter members of the Organization for Gay Awareness (OGA), which originated in Newark around 1974 but is no longer in existence. He is also a former administrator and program developer for the Newark Project, a program focused on field-based, experiential learning that was awarded a Ford Foundation Grant and conducted at Drew University Theological Graduate School and Seminary from 1994 to 2002. The Newark Project studied every aspect of religious/spiritual life in Newark, including the LGBTQ+ community, with Dr. Savastano's focus being primarily on the houses of the Ballroom community.

KRISTYN SCORSONE (they/them) is a PhD candidate in the American studies program at Rutgers University-Newark and longtime member of the Queer Newark Oral History Project. Their forthcoming dissertation, *A Way Out of No Way: The Labor and Activism of Black Queer and Transgender Women in Newark, New Jersey,* examines Black queer and transgender women's labor and related activism in Newark from the 1970s to the present. In addition to cocurating the 2017 traveling exhibit *At Home in Newark: Stories from the Queer Newark Oral History Project* and producing and hosting the Queer Newark podcast, they have been published in *The Public Historian, NJ.com, History@Work, Notches, Out History, Out in New Jersey,* and *Los Angeles Music Blog.*

DANIELLE M. SHIELDS (she/hers) is pursuing her PhD in criminal justice at Rutgers University-Newark. Her research primarily centers upon understanding LGBTQ (lesbian, gay, bisexual, transgender, and queer) and/or questioning people and their interactions with the police. As a scholar-activist, Danielle is also intensely interested in other historically and contemporarily marginalized groups and criminal justice contexts, including people of color and women. She has authored publications in several areas, including LGBTQ criminology, police–citizen interactions, gangs, and juvenile justice.

TIMOTHY STEWART-WINTER is associate professor of history at Rutgers University-Newark, where he has been involved with the Queer Newark Oral History Project since its inception. His first book, *Queer Clout: Chicago and the Rise of Gay Politics,* examined the sexual and racial politics of policing in urban America since the 1950s and was awarded the John Boswell Prize by the Committee on LGBT History. Stewart-Winter is now working on a book about the scandal surrounding Walter Jenkins, a longtime aide to Lyndon B. Johnson who resigned from the White House staff in 1964 after being arrested on disorderly conduct charges. He has written regularly about LGBTQ politics and activism and his scholarship has appeared in the *Journal of American History,* the *Journal of Urban History, Gender & History,* and several edited volumes.

CHRISTINA STRASBURGER is an administrative and academic professional with over two decades of experience in higher education. As department administrator for history and Africana studies at Rutgers University-Newark, she provides a range of education, information, and advocacy services for students, faculty, staff, and community members. She is cofounder of the award-winning Queer Newark Oral History Project, a community-directed initiative dedicated to recording and preserving the history of LGBTQ+ people in and of Newark, New Jersey.

WHITNEY STRUB is associate professor of history at Rutgers University-Newark, where he codirects the Queer Newark Oral History Project. He is the author of *Perversion for Profit: The Politics of Pornography and the Rise of the New Right* and *Obscenity Rules:* Roth v. United States *and the Long Struggle over Sexual Expression,* and coeditor of *Porno Chic and the Sex Wars: American Sexual Representation in the 1970s* and *ReFocus: The Films of Roberta Findlay.* A former board member of the Newark LGBTQ Community Center, he lives in the Newark Ironbound.

INDEX

Page numbers in *italics* refer to figures.